D0153585

Southeast Asian History

SOUTHEAST ASIAN HISTORY

Essential Readings

Edited by

D. R. SarDesai

University of California
at Los Angeles

Westview Press
A Member of the Perseus Books Group

Copyright © 2006 by Westview Press
Published by Westview Press,
A Member of the Perseus Books Group

All rights reserved. Printed in the United States of America. No part of this book may be reproduced in any manner whatsoever without written permission except in the case of brief quotations embodied in critical articles and reviews. For information, address Westview Press, 5500 Central Avenue, Boulder, Colorado 80301-2877. Find us on the World Wide Web at www.westviewpress.com.

Westview Press books are available at special discounts for bulk purchases in the United States by corporations, institutions, and other organizations. For more information, please contact the Special Markets Department at the Perseus Books Group, 11 Cambridge Center, Cambridge MA 02142, or call (617) 252–5298 or (800) 255–1514, or e-mail special.markets@perseusbooks.com.

Library of Congress Cataloging-in-Publication Data
Southeast Asian history : essential readings / D. R. SarDesai [editor].
    p.   cm.
  Includes bibliographical references and index.
  ISBN-13: 978-0-8133-4337-2 (alk. paper)
  ISBN-10: 8-8133-4337-2 (alk. paper)
  1. Southeast Asia—History—1945– .   I. SarDesai, D. R.
DS526.7.S6865   2005
959.05—dc22

                                                                2005025943

Contents

PART IV: FRUITS OF FREEDOM

Acknowledgments

I want to thank the following publishers, institutions, and individuals for permissions to reprint:

Ian W. Mabbett, "The 'Indianization' of Southeast Asia: Reflections on the Pre-historic Sources," *Journal of Southeast Asian Studies*, 8, (March 1977) pp. 1–14, reprinted with the kind permission of the Journal.

Robert Heine-Geldern, "Conceptions of State and Kingship in Southeast Asia," *Far Eastern Quarterly*, 2 (1942), pp. 15–30, reprinted with the kind permission of the Association for Asian Studies.

C. C. Brown, trans., "Sejarah Malayu (The Malay Annals)," *Journal Malaya Branch Royal Asiatic Society*, 25, 2–3 (1952), pp. 52–59, reprinted with the kind permission of the Society.

John Leddy Phelan, *The Hispanization of the Philippines*, Madison, WS: University of Wisconsin Press, 1959, pp. 53–71, reprinted with the kind permission of the publisher.

Kartini, Raden Adjeng, *Letters of a Javanese Princess*, Lanham, MD: University Press of America, 1985, pp. 55–64, reprinted with the kind permission of the publisher.

Jose Rizal, "Mi Ultimos Adios," in *Rizal's Poems*, III, 1, Manila: National Historical Commission, 1972, pp. 160–62, reprinted with the kind permission of the National Historical Institute, Manila.

Norodom Sihanouk, "Cambodia Neutral: The Dictate of Necessity," *Foreign Affairs*, 36 (July 1958), pp. 582–86, reprinted with the kind permission of the quarterly magazine.

Clark Clifford, "A Vietnam Reappraisal," *Foreign Affairs*, 47, 4 (July 1969), pp. 609–622, is reprinted with the kind permission of the quarterly magazine.

Larry Berman, "The Tet Offensive," in Marc J. Gilbert and William Head, eds., *The Tet Offensive*, Westport, CT: Praeger, 1996, pp. 17–44, reprinted with the permission of the Greenwood Publishing.

Ben Kiernan, *The Pol Pot Regime: Race, Power and Genocide in Cambodia, 1975–1979*, New Haven, CT: Yale University Press, 1996, pp. 9–27, reprinted with the permission of the publisher.

Greg Fealy, "Islam in Southeast Asia: Domestic Pietism, Diplomacy and Security," in Mark Beeson, ed., *Contemporary Southeast Asia: Regional Dynamics, National Differences*, Hampshire, UK: Palgrave Macmillan, Houndmills, 2004, pp. 136–155, reprinted with the kind permission of the publisher.

Preface

This volume of readings on Southeast Asia had been due for quite some time. Over the years since *Southeast Asia: Past and Present* (Westview Press) first appeared, my colleagues teaching courses in the diverse aspects of Southeast Asia—history, politics, anthropology, arts—have been urging me to create a companion volume of documents and articles that would provide a background and context for the events and ideas presented in the classroom. In the absence of such a book, many instructors, including myself, have had to resort to photocopying documents, extracts from literature, and significant journal articles for classroom use. Often these have tended to reflect our particular discipline or geographical subregion of specialization. A more comprehensive volume, which would be interdisciplinary and cover the entire region, was the expressed need. This volume purports to be an answer to that pedagogical problem.

Several decades ago, the Columbia University Press published its admirable series of readings, or as they called them, "Sources of Tradition," focused on various world regions. The series encompassed India, China, and Japan, but no volume existed for Southeast Asia, perhaps because of the very few colleges and universities offering courses in Southeast Asian studies at that time. The situation has changed dramatically, particularly in the wake of the Vietnam conflict and the increasing global interest—economic, political, and strategic—in the ASEAN region. Not only have academic course offerings proliferated, but increased trade and investment in the region as well as media attention have grown exponentially and led to renewed interest. All this has created the need for a better understanding of the region's cultural and political history.

I have arranged the volume in four chronological sections not just to conform to the sections in *Southeast Asia, Past and Present* but also because I feel that this framework is likely to suit the needs of course instructors. The volume is organized around four themes: Cultural Heritage (from ancient times to the fifteenth century); the Colonial Interlude (from the sixteenth to the nineteenth century); the Nationalist Response (from the late nineteenth century to the era of decolonization following World War II); and Fruits of Freedom (from the middle of the twentieth century to the present). I have also provided an updated bibliography for further reference.

No text covering the entire region of Southeast Asia can be expected to please all specialists. Constraints of space have limited the choice of what is "essential." This volume is truly a balancing act of pre-modern and modern, the relative importance of various historical events, and the availability of materials. In choosing documents that reflect the roles of notable nationalist leaders and crucial decision-makers in the West, I have included scholarly works that I regard as crucial for understanding the cultural and political history of the region. The choice is indeed subjective, and I am aware that it cannot be perfect. I feel confident, however, that students will benefit from the diversity and depth provided herein.

I am deeply grateful to the generations of students of Southeast Asian history at the University of California–Los Angeles, who have provided me a testing ground for ideas and materials. Among the many individuals who have assisted me in this project are the head of the UCLA History Department's Computer and Technical Division, Shijuka Suzuki, and her efficient staff. At the publishing level, I appreciate the cooperation and warmth at all times from Westview Press Senior Editor Steve Catalano. And, as always, I am grateful to the members of my family for tolerating the long stretches of time spent away from them when I was working on this project.

D. R. SarDesai
Los Angeles, August 2005

PART I

CULTURAL HERITAGE

1

The "Indianization" of Southeast Asia

IAN W. MABBETT*

Most scholars of Southeast Asia before 1950—British, Dutch, French, and Indian—held that with the exception of Vietnam, the culture of Southeast Asian countries was a superstructure built on foundations borrowed overwhelmingly from India. In their view, the cultural dissemination did not come through political conquest but through Brahmans and traders from India, who were responsible for the spread in Southeast Asia of Indian religions, script and literature, art and architecture. Only Vietnam, which was directly under Chinese rule from 111 BC to AD 939 and from AD 1407 to 1428 and indirectly up to 1885 through China's tributary system, was considered to be in the Chinese sphere of cultural influence.

This neat division discounted the existence of an advanced culture in many parts of Southeast Asia prior to the advent of Indian culture and the possibility that Southeast Asian monarchs initiated the selective importation of particular aspects of Indian culture. A new genre of writings goes even further in the opposite direction and lauds the Southeast Asians as "cultural pioneers" from whom both China and India benefited. In 1977, Ian Mabbett wrote two important journal articles examining the phenomenon of the "Indianization" of Southeast Asia, one focusing on prehistoric sources and the other on historic sources. In the article focusing on prehistoric sources, reproduced here, Mabbett demonstrates that India and Southeast Asia were not two separate "organic cultural units" but were

---

*Ian W. Mabbett, "The 'Indianization' of Southeast Asia, Reflections on the Pre-historic Sources," *Journal of Southeast Asian Studies* 8 (March 1977): 1–14.

linked by "a complex pattern of cultural interaction" spreading across Asia. He also draws a distinction between processes that occurred in two separate time periods: the rise of principalities or city-states with Indian culture in the first two or three centuries after Christ and the later "growth of peasant societies supporting civil, priestly and military elites."

~

How did Indian influence spread in Southeast Asia during the opening centuries of our era? The following quotations give some idea of the extent to which authorities are agreed:

> It seems almost to be a universal law, that when an inferior civilization comes into contact with a superior one, it gradually tends to be merged into the latter, the rate and extent of this process being determined solely by the capacity of the one to assimilate, and of the other to absorb. When the Hindus first settled in Suvarnabhumi and came into close association with her peoples, this process immediately set in, and produced the inevitable result.[1]

> It is well known that a group cannot adopt an important development from another group if it is not, approximately, on the same technological and social level.[2]

> There were, then, no 'Hindu colonization' in which 'colonial states' arose from intermittent trading voyages followed by permanent trading settlements; no 'Hindu colonies' from which the primitive indigenous population and first of all its headmen took over the superior civilization from the west; and no learned Hindus in the midst of Indian colonists as 'advisers' to their countrymen.[3]

> One is therefore led to characterize the eastward expansion of Hindu civilization at the beginning of the Christian era as the result—at least to a great extent—of a continuous influx of navigators from within a 'sea-merchant' milieu.[4]

> Until a decade or so ago it was believed that this important development [the emergence of kingdoms with ideas of royalty based on Hindu or Buddhist cults] was brought about by Indian traders themselves, who were conceived as proselytizing colonists, but we now know that this was not so.[5]

These propositions, presented here out of context, are not necessarily as mutually inconsistent as they are thus made to appear. Indeed, it would be possible to agree with most of the authorities who have written on the 'Indianization' of Southeast Asia—to a greater extent, perhaps, than some of them agree with each other. But there can be no doubt that the character of Indian influences in the lands across the Bay of Bengal is a complex matter of dubiety and debate. A survey of the evidence and of modern opinions about it, even a superficial one which is all that can be achieved in a narrow compass, is obviously desirable. It is all the more desirable because there is reason to think that recent developments in the prehistory of Southeast Asia have made it possible to view the 'Indianization' process in a perspective which historians have been slow to use; it is this perspective which will be the subject of the present article.

The new interpretations are far from an established orthodoxy; indeed, many of them are tenuous and speculative, and many are contested. Final judgment must wait on the consensus of prehistorians and on the passage of time, which brings new discoveries constantly. But it should be stressed that, for the purposes of the present discussion, it is not actually necessary to accept the view that most of the attributes of civilization except for stratified societies and political centralization were pioneered in Southeast Asia long before China or India had them. On the contrary, the product of recent research most important to the following analysis is one of the less controversial—the new recognition that people in Southeast Asia need not have turned decisively at a particular point in time from 'folk' hunting and gathering to 'peasant' agriculture: for a long period they may have followed an eclectic subsistence pattern, with agriculture constituting often only a minor segment. With such a pattern, communities could have been highly self-sufficient, and thus when we turn to the beginnings of the historical record, it begins to seem likely that the early stages of 'Indianization' could take place with extremely few repercussions among the indigenous societies, and that therefore the development of stratified peasant societies such as in Sailendra Java or Angkorian Cambodia must be thought of as a later process distinct from the introduction of Indian culture in the early 'kingdoms' such as 'Funan.'

Traditional Theories

Pre-eminent among an older generation of scholars is R. von Heine-Geldern, whose theories, though not achieving the status of orthodoxy, have been widely influential. For him, the relatively sophisticated cultures of the societies that became subject to Indian influence belonged to the Austronesians, who were distinguished by their use of adzes of quadrangular section. In his view their ancestors, possibly related to the bearers of the

North Chinese Yangshao culture, migrated to the Southeast Asian archipelago between about 2000 and 1500 BC.[6] Perhaps associated with them were the 'Austro-Asiatics' represented by mainland groups such as the Mons and Khmers. The coming of these people ushered in the neolithic period. Following this line of thought, descendants of the displaced mesolithic peoples, whose cultures are familiar to archaeology under the heading 'Hoabinhian,' are to be sought chiefly in hill tribes. Throughout these arguments, the idea of discrete cultures and waves of population is explicit.[7]

For von Heine-Geldern, the bronze age of the Dongson culture (named after its northern Vietnamese type-site) was introduced, not by a new migration, but by the importation of a cultural package from the north. Arguing from the similarity of artistic motifs, he traced Dongson culture to a European origin, in the Black Sea area, and postulated its diffusion to parallel destinations in China and Indochina, and ultimately to Oceania, through migrations from the west from the eighth or ninth century BC.[8]

One other important item in the established inventory of prehistory sometimes seen as evidence of migrations is the megalithic culture of Southeast Asia, represented by slabs, menhirs and massive funerary jars in many parts of the region—for example, the funerary monoliths and jars in Tran Ninh province, Laos, or the menhirs in the Hua Pan province.[9] Megaliths, which cannot be associated with dated strata in the ground, are difficult to date and megalithic chronology is problematic.[10] It is probably erroneous to regard the 'megalithic' as in any sense a homogeneous culture. Megaliths pertain to disparate cultures without natural unity. As for jar burials, W. G. Solheim II considers that they represent an isolated practice which spread independently among different peoples; the differences between burials in different parts of East and Southeast Asia are too great to be the product of the passage of time, and there is thus no real evidence that they represent migrations.[11]

If we were to regard 'Indianization' as the experience or activity of distinct neolithic racial groups with an imported bronze culture, there would be no need to dig back further to the so-called middle stone age in order to examine the context in which Indian influences appeared. But traditional periodizations and migration theories have been challenged; terms such as 'neolithic' are of limited value outside Europe. It is necessary to recognize that those who adopted Sanskrit names and Indian religion are likely to have been descended fairly directly from some of the possessors of the mesolithic cultures known as Hoabinhian; further, their way of life may not have been in all respects radically different. It is therefore necessary to take some account of the archaeological evidence even from early times, and it is desirable to start with the 'Hoabinhian' culture or cultures which were in existence for most of the last ten millennia BC.

The Archaeological Record

The identification of the Hoabinhian (named, like Dongson, after a type-site in Vietnam) was largely the work of M. Colani in the 1930s; it connotes a cluster of traits found in various parts of the region.[12] These traits, particularly the use of stones worked on one side, place their cultures in the middle stone age or mesolithic period, but the utility of terms such as 'mesolithic' or 'palaeolithic' sometimes has been contested as an arbitrary periodization. J. M. Treistman has defended the idea as representing a cultural if not a chronological reality, indicating populations that were 'anchored' to particular localities where they could intensify plant collection and river exploitation.[13] The term 'Hoabinhian' has itself been described as a 'technocomplex,' a grouping of cultures sharing certain techniques, rather than as a single culture.[14] As such, it spans a large area and a long period.[15] The earlier sites are riverine, chiefly upland but also in coastal areas which were by the sea even when the sea level was lower. Conceivably, there were lowland sites since obliterated by rising seas, but C. Gorman thinks it likely that only late in the life of the Hoabinhian cultures did the appearance of agriculture cause populations to shift from mountain valleys to the hilly edges of the plains. (No lowland agricultural sites have been found dating from before the development of iron and irrigation technology.) By the end of the period, he suggests 'Hoabinhian' included edge-ground tools, cord-marked ceramics, and possibly early plant domestication (discussed further below).[16]

There are debated interpretations behind some of the conclusions mentioned above. But scholars have recognized for some time that Southeast Asia is *a priori* a likely scene for the early emergence of plant domestication. N. Vavilov noted in 1949 that the occurrence of many wild species (including various roots and fruits, and rice) made the area a likely hearth of cultivation.[17] Other writers have pointed to the presence of the humid tropical conditions which made it possible for populations originally dependent on other forms of subsistence, especially 'progressive fishermen,' to experiment with cultivation without risking their sustenance.[18] K. C. Chang has suggested a second link between fishing and plant cultivation: the fisherman's use of fibres for his nets and oakum for caulking.[19]

Rice is likely to have been first cultivated in a zone including parts of India and Southeast Asia. According to A. G. Haudricourt and L. Hédin, rice cultivation may have originated in the Ganges delta but in any case spread to Indonesia and Indochina.[20] In a recent study, R. D. Hill, appealing to Vavilov's principle that cultivation of a plant is most likely to have begun where the largest number of wild species is to be found, identifies a zone covering Orissa, Bihar, Bengal, Burma and perhaps Indochina as the area of origin.[21] Following Haudricourt,[22] he emphasizes that it is a mistake to suppose that dry rice cultivation came first, irrigated later; rice has some of the physiological characteristics of a marsh plant,[23] and could well have been first used by men in large swampy areas of grassy vegetation (ecologically, plagio-climaxes).[24] On general grounds the first form of cultivation is likely to have been of root crops, with short-term clearing of land for taro or yams, in ecological marginal zones by coasts, rivers or at savanna edges according to D. R. Harris,[25] and rice could have cropped up originally as a weed in fields of tubers[26] in such areas. In these circumstances, it is important to notice, rice would not have precipitated a socio-demographic revolution—it would at first, perhaps for long, have been an unimportant sideline. R. D. Hill in his study identifies a series of likely typological levels in the history of rice. The first is the 'ancestral Southeast Asian type' involving semi-permanent cultivation of land, permanent settlement, slash-and-burn techniques with perhaps two or three years of cropping followed by two or three years of fallow, and rice being only one crop among many.[27]

Such speculations underline the importance of the 'broad spectrum' characterization of subsistence patterns which combine different sources. J. Treistman, for whom the mesolithic stage was one in which populations were established in areas where wild collection could be intensified, suggests that early steps towards domestication may have involved clearing away other vegetation from the desired plants, and perhaps simple water diversion.[28] C. Gorman sees the late Hoabinhians as turning to agriculture within the compass of their original culture, continuing varied patterns alongside early domestication.[29] The culture represented by excavations at Ban-kao in central western Thailand, which may reflect either diffusion from China or late forms of basically Hoabinhian patterns,[30] was that of 'semi-agriculturalists,' who engaged in much hunting and fishing.[31] The development of lowland agricultural communities, then, with its potential for the centralization and urbanization associated with 'Indianization,' occurred before the Indians came; it may have occurred a long time before. It is even possible, if certain new hypotheses become established, that Southeast Asia will turn out to have been a pioneer in many of the elements of civilization.

Recent Finds

The question of the chronology of the appearance of plant domestication, rice culture, and other technical advances introduces a set of recent claims advanced especially by Wilhelm G. Solheim II and his colleagues, claims which uncompromisingly assert the primacy of Southeast Asians in all major Asian technical innovations and thus deny the region's dependence upon diffusion from China, India, the Far West or anywhere else. On the contrary, many things are held to have been transmitted to parts of China, Japan, and the coasts of the Indian Ocean by Southeast Asian sailors and traders. In a sense, W. G. Solheim is the van Leur of prehistory.[32]

The claims rest quite largely on excavations at two sites: Spirit Cave, in northern Thailand, and Non Nok Tha, in northeastern Thailand, both undertaken as part of a recovery program under Solheim's direction.

The earliest significant finds are of plants in Spirit Cave. These, from around 7200 BC, indicate the exploitation of wild or tended nuts, pepper, cucumber and beans among other things. According to C. F. Gorman, the large size of the seeds found suggests actual domestication.[33] Solheim has used such finds to suggest a date of 10,000 BC or even much earlier for the beginnings of plant domestication,[34] but this is offered speculatively. The first rice cultivation is another thing claimed for Southeast Asia. Excavations at Non Nok Tha yielded rice chaff at a level dated about 3000 or 3500 BC or earlier; according to D. T. Bayard, who was in charge of the excavation, rice agriculture may have begun by 5000 BC.[35] He suggests that multiple postholes on the site imply superimposed structures, suggesting migration and re-use of the site, a pattern consistent with swidden cultivation. If the dating is correct, rice appears to have been cultivated in Thailand well before it was in India or China.[36] In India, long thought to be the site of the first cultivation, rice has been dated to about 2000 BC but a similar or not much later date has been found for impressions of rice stalks in plastered walls belonging to the Ch'ü-chia-ling culture in the middle Yangtze.[37] This could represent diffusion through Eastern India and Szechwan.[38] It appears, however, that certain aspects of the chronology of rice in Asia are now back in the melting-pot, and the situation described here is liable to radical change.[39]

Moreover, the metal tools industry, necessary for sophisticated sedentary agriculture, is thought by some to have been pioneered in Southeast Asia. At Non Nok Tha, at a low level possibly representing the fourth millennium BC was found a partly copper socketed axe, probably one that was beaten rather than cast.[40] Its tin content was later shown to qualify it as bronze, thus pushing back the date of the bronze age.[41] This find, an isolated case, could be an importation, but in higher levels were found piece-moulds for bronze casting of local sandstone, crucibles and bronze nodules which could be spillage from casting, as well as bronze artifacts.[42] Bayard considers these finds to represent a well-developed tradition of bronze casting with double moulds well before 2300 BC, and suggests that the beginning of metal working in the area dates back to at least 2700 BC.[43] With these finds may be compared those of E. Saurin at Hang Gon near Saigon: bronze and double moulds dated to about the end of the third millennium BC, a chronology which was quite unexpected.[44] Early bronze of uncertain provenance has also been found by a Thai expedition at Ban Chiang.[45] If metal industry developed in Southeast Asia as early as is claimed, it is likely to have been independent. The appearance of bronze in China is associated with the Shang period in the second millennium BC, which it [sic] is considered to be an autonomous development.[46] According to Bayard, Chinese bronze is technically quite dissimilar to that found in Thailand.[47] In India, bronze appears in the Indus Valley civilization about 2300 BC,[48] rather later than the Thai industry, to which it also is dissimilar. Accordingly, Solheim is disposed to see the Dongson bronze culture, conventionally dated to varying periods in the first millennium BC, not as a late importation from southern China, but as a development within an indigenous tradition.[49] He also dates a Southeast Asian iron industry to the second millennium BC, well before Indian cultural influence.[50]

The thesis that Southeast Asians were cultural pioneers has found support in findings in other fields. In the sphere of language, proponents of the new chronology find corroboration in P. Benedict's suggestion that Thai should be grouped with an original Southeast Asian 'Austro-Thai' language family in whose debt Chinese stood for a part of its vocabulary; he considers that some borrowings represent the acquisition of a relatively advanced culture along with the words, while others correspond to words and cultural traits already possessed by the Chinese, who however preferred to use terms from the more developed and ceremonial 'Austro-Thai' complex.[51] According to P. Benedict's line of thought, writing itself was a borrowing by the Chinese (the term for 'ideograph' itself coming from Austro-Thai).[52]

As for trade and navigation, there is evidence of early links between the archipelago and distant coasts of the Indian Ocean. The Malagasy language is linked with the Ma'anyan Dayak speech of Borneo, which led O. Dahl to the conclusion that there was a migration from Borneo about AD 400.[53] This dating was influenced by, inter alia, the Sanskrit elements in Malagasy, requiring that the migration should not predate the beginnings of Indian influence in Borneo; but others have attributed nautical primacy to Southeast Asians in prehistoric times. G. Hornell, followed by W. G. Solheim, thinks that the outrigger canoe was invented on the Indochinese coast and that significant features of marine technology were pioneered by Southeast Asian seamen.[54] W. G. Solheim suggests that after the invention of the outrigger which by 400 BC Southeast Asian culture traveled by sea, and that traders from the region were important in the Indian Ocean by 2500 BC.[55] He claims for the Hoabinhians the invention of pottery by the tenth millennium BC[56] and the domestication of cattle probably by 4000 BC.[57] The domesticated cattle turn out to be not *Bos indicus* but a variety ancestral to the present-day cattle of Northeast Thailand, and evidence of water buffalo has been found at the earliest level of Non Nok Tha.[58] One other very important area in which primacy has been claimed for Southeast Asia is iron technology; various Thai sites yield iron from different times in the second millennium BC, and it has been claimed that the use of iron was probably diffused through central Thailand by about 1000 BC.[59]

So far we have noticed the dates and interpretations favored by the proponents of Southeast Asian primacy in the various spheres. But it is important to note that question marks hang over most of them, question marks which the authorities concerned do not conceal. For one thing, the new glottochronology for 'Austro-Thai' and its relations with Chinese is not clearly established. For another, the inference that plants were cultivated around the Spirit Cave site is not made inevitable by the fact that the leguminous plant seeds found were large. This fact could represent domestication; but equally it could also represent natural selection (sturdier plants from large seeds surviving at the expense of others), or elimination of less sturdy plants by men who, for whatever reason, weeded them out. This could be the sort of 'encouragement' envisaged by J. M. Treistman as noted above; it is not the same thing as domestication.[60] For a third, the chronology of the all-important bronze and moulds at Non Nok Tha rests upon interpretation of conflicting laboratory reports on carbon-14 dating. This technique measures radioactive decay of samples of organic material associated with appropriate levels of excavation. There are possibilities of contamination of the material from which samples are taken, both between excavation and laboratory and in the earth itself, where something from one level may contaminate another. At Non Nok Tha, there were problems with the small size of charcoal samples obtained, and possible contamination from rootlets and carbonized roots.[61] The presence of postholes and of many graves naturally adds to the dangers.[62] In the event, samples were obtained which were considered fairly secure, but reports from different laboratories were inconsistent and it was necessary to adopt the most plausible explanation of the inconsistencies.[63]

To these cautions can be added the general point that the mere occurrence of an innovation does not necessarily entail rapid change in the pattern of the society in which it occurs. Fishermen and gatherers may clear away the growth around some favored plants; they may tend them, they may even start growing them, without forsaking their earlier way of life. W. G. Solheim and his colleagues have indeed emphasized the role of 'broad spectrum' subsistence patterns in which several sources are combined. Bronze may be manufactured for ritual use, or for use by an elite few, or on certain occasions, while stone is still used by most of the people most of the time. Rice may first appear as a weed in a vegetable garden, and be cultivated as a sideline, while its consumers remain essentially vegetable horticulturalists. Thus the periodization of social change need not coincide with that of inventions.

It is clear all the same that prehistoric chronology has been thrown open. It is now difficult to chart the patterns of autonomy and diffusion in Asia. There is a risk in identifying any region as a self-contained zone which either exercised autonomy or interacted with other zones as a unit, but for many purposes it is possible to think of Southeast Asia as a zone; if we do this, we must recognize that it was less a cul-de-sac than a highway, or possibly a hub of traffic.

The Beginnings of History

The populations among whom appeared the principalities of 'P'an-p'an,' 'Tun Sun,' 'Funan' and the rest may therefore have possessed cultures that were of considerable antiquity and in some ways well advanced.

Modern frontiers are irrelevant to prehistory. Sparse populations dotted along coasts and rivers could communicate more easily by sea than across jungles and mountains, and 'India' and 'Southeast Asia' were not two organic cultural units separated by the Bay of Bengal. On the contrary, whatever the links may have been, communities in both areas were linked in a complex pattern of cultural interaction spreading across Asia, and had long been so, and it is necessary to consider that Indians visiting Southeast Asia were not so much foreign Aryans bringing a totally alien way of life—the Aryans had long been domesticated—as familiar neighbors visiting with new luggage.

Yet this is not to minimize the changes that occurred. Indigenous society may have developed much of its own technology independently, and even exported some of it, but there is still a big difference between small communities lacking well-developed cities, standing armies, alphabets, elaborate social stratification, or political centralization, and the relatively centralized states of historical times with armies and regular bureaucracies. What could be the mechanism of the change?

It is tempting to answer that the changes flowed from the importation by the Indians of irrigated rice cultivation. For example, it could be suggested that Indian traders first introduced paddy to their settlements;[64] wet rice encourages and supports dense population, so the settlements expanded and became major centers; within these societies the maintenance of irrigation and the increasing commercial traffic entailed ever greater interdependence and centralization; rice surpluses fed priests, full-time soldiers and royal servants; chieftains of petty clans or kampongs were so constantly brought into conflicts of interest that they could not co-exist, and supreme rulers emerged. Further, agriculturalists are more vulnerable to the demands of a state than are horticulturalists. They are tied to their fields, unable to migrate with their subsistence to remote forest clearings; they are thus exposed to the activity of royal officials, bandits and marauding aliens; and their subsistence mode is more likely to yield a surplus which makes taxation or looting a worth-while activity. These circumstances combine to make society more complex and the support of a warrior class or standing army acceptable and natural. Thus, we may be tempted to surmise, was the centralized urban-based state born.

The paradigm is appealing, and it probably finds at least some application to Southeast Asia. We are not entitled, however, to close the enquiry at this point. The reason for this is that the introduction of intensively cultivated wet rice cannot be neatly dated to coincide with the beginnings of Indian-style kingdoms. In fact it cannot be precisely dated at all.

Various earlier authorities, still sometimes cited, list wet rice as a possession of Southeast Asian communities before the Indians came,[65] but (except that rice tending probably originated with wild swamp rice, which is another matter) there is no certain evidence of this. Not only that, but there is no certain evidence of wet rice until well after the Indians came.

Possibly prehistoric canals and terraces have sometimes been seen as indicators of irrigated rice fields *(sawah)*. The Gio-linh terrace system of Quang-tri province, Vietnam, should be mentioned here, an integrated system involving stones, terraces and tanks.[66] It may be of Cham origin. Its purpose has been seen as ritual by some, and various authorities have incorporated it into postulated prehistoric culture complexes.[67] P. Wheatley, however, suggests it belongs to the fourth century, possibly the work of primitive Khmers from the neighborhood of Champa.[68] Indigenous field systems thought by some to represent tidal irrigation, which would involve complex works, have been seen by E. Gaspardone as merely reclaimed land.[69] P. Wheatley concluded in 1965 that whatever is known of agriculture in the Tong-king delta gives no support to the idea of an advanced technology.[70] The recent trend of archaeology in the Indochinese region, however, has encouraged some authorities to the belief that irrigated agriculture has a venerable past; Nguyen Khac Vien, for example, refers to 'submerged fields' in neolithic times.[71] It can only be said that the assumption that *sawah* is of pre-Indian origin is so far speculative, contrary to the widely held belief.

When we turn to proto-history, the evidence is no more decisive. In the Mekong Delta area, where 'Funan' appears to have been, the archaeological researches of L. Malleret have brought to light blackened rice grains from

Oc Eo, the site of a major port, and canals from about the fifth and sixth centuries AD.[72] These, however, could arguably have been for drainage of an area susceptible to flood, not irrigation.[73] The Ch'in History, in an interesting passage discussed by R. D. Hill,[74] says that people in Funan would plant *(chung)* one year and harvest for three; this probably refers either to *ratoon* crops (successive cropping of fresh shoots grown from stalks of previously harvested grain, a practice still observed in Johore), or to the clearing of land for three years' swidden cultivation.[75]

In the archipelago, the history of wet rice similarly does not seem to go back to the beginnings. T. Harrisson considers that rice came comparatively late to Indonesia, preceded by a long earlier stage of tuber cultivation.[76] The first epigraphic reference to the construction of a possible irrigation canal, Pumavarman's seven-mile canal alleged to have been made in twenty-one days, occurs about AD 400, but the reference is ambiguous.[77] The Changgal inscription associated with Borobudur, AD 732, mentions *yava*, a generic term for grain which could refer to millet.[78] Rice is certainly known to have been grown in Malayan early kingdoms from 'Tan-tan' onwards, but it may be questioned whether there is real evidence of irrigated rice fields *(sawah)*.[79]

It therefore appears increasingly likely that too much importance has been in the past attached to the role of irrigated rice in the initial stages of Indian influence. The crop yields of wet rice are on average substantially greater than of dry rice, but not in all places and conditions; there is an area of overlap.[80] The people of Southeast Asia could thrive without *sawah*.

Irrigated rice cultivation was indeed important as the basis of the grand empires of later times with their proud rulers, ubiquitous priesthoods, huge armies, and organized levies of state laborers thousands strong. It is probably also true, however, that the power and the centralization of these regimes have been exaggerated, but, with several harvests annually from a complex reservoir-fed system supporting a dense population over a wide area,[81] it is clear that a polity like that of Angkor commanded organization different in kind from that of any cluster of trading or fishing hamlets on a delta or any confederacy of clans in riverine clearings. The point to stress is that these rice-based empires, beginning perhaps with Angkorian Cambodia, came later; 'Indianization' at least began before them and is at least in part a distinct phenomenon.

'Broad Spectrum' Economics

It was suggested above that the people among whom Indian-style kingdoms first appeared were following eclectic subsistence patterns, using

combinations of sources with root crops rather than rice as a staple. If we
accept that some sort of 'Indianization' may have occurred before *sawah*
became the basis of the economy, it becomes pertinent to examine this
'broad spectrum' economy further. We have noticed that in prehistoric
times these communities appear to have been well adapted to their environment with various subsistence patterns available to them. In certain circumstances they may have been better off with vegetables, shifting cultivation,
hunting or gathering.[82] Field work by R. D. Hill in Kelantan and Trengganu
has shown that shifting dry cultivation, with a much smaller requirement of
labor than pioneer *sawah,* can produce fair yields from dibbled or broadcast seeding even in dry or very wet weather.[83] In another place he points
out that rice is not necessary for civilization: tubers supply more calories
from a given area, and require less labour.[84] They do not keep so well once
harvested, but before, stored in the soil, they allow their cultivators greater
freedom to move about following the needs of other subsistence modes. If
W. G. Solheim is right in postulating an extended 'lignic' period of Southeast Asian technology, each group had direct access to the basis of its technology—timber—and did not depend on other groups for trade in
materials (as was the case with the quite different Middle Eastern evolution
of civilization).[85] These 'broad spectrum' patterns support sparse populations moving slowly about over large areas, not competing with each other
for land as in areas of intensive cultivation and dense populations where access to land needs to be socially organized. Hence they lived (as many
groups still live) in small self-sufficient units with minimal organization.[86]

Some degree of incipient urbanization has been seen in southern China
and mainland Southeast Asia in prehistoric times, but it is equivocal and
amounts to very little.[87] It is perhaps not surprising, in the light of the considerations noted above, that even when 'Indianization' was well under way
there should be no social upheaval among the bulk of the population. The
great social readjustment was to come later, drop by drop, mounting by in-
sensible gradations, with the dissemination of new agricultural techniques
and increasing density of population that turned communities from 'folk'
into 'peasants.'[88]

Indianization

It is probable that when we speak of 'Indianization' we are referring to two
distinct processes that took place at different times. The first was the appearance of principalities or city states with Indian culture in the first two
or three centuries after Christ; the second was the growth of peasant societies supporting civil, priestly and military elites in the latter half, largely

perhaps in the last quarter, of the first millennium, and then only in relatively few places. The inelegant terms 'Indianization I' and 'Indianization II' may serve to identify these two processes.

Thus, when 'P'an-p'an,' 'Tun-Sun,' 'Funan' and other political or geographical entities known to protohistory were flourishing, the greater part of the population of the region continued its ways of life with little change. Some groups engaged in combinations of hunting, gathering, fishing, plant tending and root horticulture. Many, by this time, were more settled groups practicing grain agriculture with domesticated animals in the lowlands; these were to be the first to be drawn into the ambit of metropolitan culture, but even they were not organized and stratified communities permanently attached to particular fields. Rather, they were sparse and autonomous, and it is easy to imagine centuries passing before they came to aspire to the alien religion, letters and polity of the cities.

The relationship between cities and hinterland during 'Indianization I' must not be misunderstood; it is not one that falls neatly into a familiar category. It is necessary to imagine a contrast between these indigenous scattered communities and cosmopolitan trading centers thronged with expatriates and with local people who, by virtue of living there, had in large measure cut themselves off from their own society. They were there as coolies perhaps, slaves, adventurers, parvenus, outcastes, relatives of nearby headmen installed to represent some sort of political authority, unwanted daughters sold or attracted into an atomized society of woman-less and rootless fortune-seekers.

This is not like the relationship between Australian settlements and the aborigines, for in Southeast Asia the indigenous people had, for example, a developed metal industry, some agriculture, and long-established contacts with the outside world. But, on the other hand, it is also not like the relationship between the European trading factories around the Indian coast and the local kingdoms, for these kingdoms controlled dense agrarian populations fairly closely knit by a web of political and commercial interdependence, a web into which the newcomers were easily drawn, and through which new institutions were readily transmitted. The relationship between the Straits Settlements and the Malay sultanates of the interior is a closer fit, but in this case the advanced technology and communications of the westerners, and their high degree of political organization which made commercial competition a matter of state rivalry, were powerful factors condensing almost to a lifetime a process of assimilation which could have otherwise lasted centuries.

Nor is the relationship we seek to characterize exactly that between great tradition and little tradition, for these are the psychologically necessary 'high' and 'low' within a single society with an essentially homogeneous culture, where powerful myths work to unify discrepant traditions. We are dealing, instead, with distinct societies living side by side. Here, surely, to whatever extent there may be an at least nominal political authority incorporating both sorts (representatives in a city of a local headman), is an extreme case of a plural society.[89] It is misleading to say that Indian influences are superficial; they may be thoroughgoing in one sort of society and completely absent in the other, for they are separate orders. It is perhaps significant that some of the most recent research on the earliest 'Indianized' kingdoms, those which appeared in the Malayan peninsula and round the Indochinese coast, tends to minimize the impact of foreign influence outside the trading cities during the earlier centuries.[90]

It is missing the point to ask what must be the relative position on a notional ladder of progress or superiority of Indian and receiving culture. If one is to influence the other, this need not be because one is superior and is automatically preferred, or because the other is on a similar level of culture and therefore equipped to absorb the first. It will be because the two interact more than incidentally, the possessors of the second participating in a network of interdependence. 'Indianization II,' the process by which tribesmen become peasants, brings about the network of interdependence. Increasingly complex irrigation works require centralized organization; a 'state,' in the anthropological sense, appears; larger agricultural surpluses, warrior chieftains with liveries, full-time priests, dense populations, craft villages and other interacting consequences create a new relationship with the cities, each side now looking to the other for manpower, markets, supplies and legitimacy.

These speculations may clarify some of the issues confounded in the question of Indian influence, but they do not answer it. It remains open whether, in 'Indianization I,' the cities were created by Indian warriors, Indian traders, local chiefs, or some combination of these, and whether, in 'Indianization II,' Indian influence is deep, patchy or shallow.

NOTES

1. R. C. Majumdar, *Hindu Colonies in the Far East* (Calcutta, 1944/1963), p. 23.

2. B. P. Groslier, "Our Knowledge of Khmer Civilization: A Re-appraisal," *Journal of the Siam Society*, XLVIII, 1 (1960), 10.

3. J. C. van Leur, "On Early Asian Trade," *Indonesian Trade and Society* (The Hague/Bandung, 1955), p. 98.

4. G. Coedès, *Les Etats Hindouises d'Indochine et d'Indonesie* (Paris, rev ed. 1964), pp. 48f. 'On est ainsi amene a se representer l'expansion de la civilization hindoue vers l'est au debut de l'ere chretienne comme resultant, au moins pour une grande part, d'entreprises commerciales, d'un afflux continu de navigateurs, recrutes a l'origine dans ce milieu des marchands de mer.'

5. P. Wheatley, *The Golden Chersonese* (Kuala Lumpur, 1961), p. 185.

6. R. von Heine-Geldern, "Urheimat und Früheste Wanderung der Austronesier," *Anthropos*, XXVII (1932), 543–613.

7. See also *idem*, "The Archaeology and Art of Sumatra", *Sumatra: Its History and People,* ed. E. M. Loeb (Kuala Lumpur, 1972).

8. Idem, "Das Tochareproblem und die Pontische Wanderung", *Saeculum*, II, 2 (1951), 225—255, and "L'art prébouddhique de la Chine et de l'asie du Sud-est et son influence en Océanie," *Revue des Arts Asiatiques* XI, 4 (1937), 177–206. For a dating of Dongson to about 300 BC, see B. Karlgren, "The Date of the Early Dongson Culture," *Bulletin of the Museum of Far Eastern Antiquities*, XIV (1942), 1–29. See also L. Bezacier, *Le Vietnam,* Part I (Paris, 1972), pp. 79–253.

9. M. Colani, *Megalithes du Haut-Laos*, Publications de l'E.F.E.O., 25–26 (Paris, 1935. 2 vols.). See also H. H. E. Loofs, *Südost Asiens Fundamente* (Berlin, 1964).

10. M. Colani, *ibid.*, attributes the funerary jars of Tran Ninh to about the first century AD and links them with similar, older phenomena in Assam.

11. Wilhelm G. Solheim II, "Jar burial in the Babuyan and Batanes islands and in central Philippines, and its relationship to jar burial elsewhere in the Far East," *Philippine Journal of Science*, LXXXIV, 1 (1960), 115–148.

12. Such as one-faced tools, core tools, frequent use of flakes, a distinctive pattern of food remains, use of rock shelters, and towards the end, perhaps intrusive edge-ground tools and cord-marked ceramics. See C. F. Gorman, "Hoabinhian: A Pebble-tool Complex with Early Plant Associations in Southeast Asia," *Science*, CLXIII, 3863 (1969), 671–673, and "Excavations at Spirit Cave, North Thailand: Some Interim Interpretations," *Asian Perspectives*, XIII (1970), 79–107. For a recent description of North Vietnamese finds, see Nguyen Khac Vien, *Traditional Vietnam: Some Historical Stages* (Hanoi, n.d.), pp. 10f. Cf. L. Bezacier, *op. cit.*, pp. 25–53.

13. J. M. Treistman, "Problems in Contemporary Asian Archaeology," *J.A.S.*, XXIX (1970), 366.

14. C. F. Gorman, "Excavations at Spirit Cave," *op.cit.*

15. C. F. Gorman, *ibid.*, 82, dates the Hoabinhian 'technocomplex' to a period from the late Pleistocene to about 6500–5000 BC. W. G. Solheim, "Northern Thailand, Southeast Asia, and World Prehistory," *Asian Perspectives,* XIII (1970), 145–162, suggests that the Late Hoabinhian, attested by extant dated sites, emerged around 13000–8000 BC (while the Middle Hoabinhian, attested by edge-ground tools, may date from very much earlier). With the Late Hoabinhian he associates cord-marked pottery and animal or plant domestication. The passage from Pleistocene to Recent, about 8000 BC or so, may not have been significant in the tropics and need not represent a cultural watershed.

16. See C. F. Gorman, "Hoabinhian: A Pebble-tool Complex with Early Plant Associations in Southeast Asia," *loc. op. cit.*, and "Modelès a priori et préhistoire de la Thailande," *Etudes Rurales*, LIII–LVI (1974), 63f.

17. N. I. Vavilov, "The Origin, Variation, Immunity and Breeding of Cultivated Plants," *Chronica Botanica,* XIII, 1–6 (1949–1950) (trans. K. S. Chester).

18. See J. Barrau, "Gardeners of Oceania," *Discovery,* I (1965), 12–19, and "Witnesses of the Past: Notes on some food plants of Oceania," *Ethnology,* IV (1965), 282–294; C. O. Sauer, *Agricultural Origins and Dispersals* (New York, 1952).

19. K. C. Chang, "Prehistoric Archaeology of Taiwan," *Asian Perspectives,* XIII (1970), 63ff.

20. A. G. Haudricourt and L. Hédin, *L'Homme et les Plantes Cultivées* (Paris, 1943), p. 141.

21. R. D. Hill, "Rice in Malaya: A study in historical geography," unpublished Ph.D. thesis (Singapore University, 1973), 21; also Kuala Lumpur (OUP), in press; Cp. M. F. Chandraratna, *Genetics and Breeding of Rice* (London, 1964).

22. A. G. Haudricourt, "Domestication des Animaux, Culture des Plantes et Traitement d'Autrui," *L'Homme,* 11 (1962), 41.

23. E. B. Copeland, *Rice* (London, 1924), p. 21.

24. R. D. Hill, *op. cit.,* 34ff.

25. C. R. Harris, "Agricultural Systems, Ecosystems and the Origins of Agriculture," in *The Domestication and Exploitation of Plants and Animals,* eds. P. J. Ucko and G. W. Dimbleby (London, 1969), p. 12.

26. A. G. Haudricourt and L. Hédin, *op. cit.,* p. 153; A. G. Haudricourt, *op. cit.,* 41n.

27. R. D. Hill, *op. cit.,* 383.

28. J. M. Treistman, "Problems in Contemporary Asian Archaeology," *J.A.S.,* XXIX (1970), 363–371.

29. C. F. Gorman, "The Hoabinhian and After: Subsistence Patterns in Southeast Asia," *World Archaeology,* II, 3 (1971), 300–320, sees the exploitation, known from archaeology, of bovids, fish, seafood, pigs, deer and goat-antelopes as a good "pre-adaptation" to the introduction of cereals.

30. See P. Srensen, *Archaelogical Excavations in Thailand, II, Ban-kao* (Copenhagen, 1967), pp. 137ff; and D. T. Bayard, "Excavation at Non Nok Tha, North-eastern Thailand, 1968," *Asian Perspectives* XIII (1970), 109–143 at 140.

31. P. Srensen, *loc. cit.*

32. Several important articles discussing the implications of recent finds are listed by Wilhelm G. Solheim II, "Communication," *Southeast Asia,* 1, 4 (1971), 410–411. The author is much indebted to Professor Solheim for invaluable information and references.

33. C. F. Gorman, "Excavation at Spirit Cave," *op. cit.,* 102.

34. Wilhelm G. Solheim II, "New Light on a Forgotten Past," *National Geographic,* CXXXIX, XL 3 (1971), 330–339.

35. D. T. Bayard, "Excavation at Non Nok Tha," *op. cit.,* 135. W.

36. A very considerable variety of strains of wild rice, and many also of wild millet, have since been found in a valley near Spirit Cave. Wilhelm G. Solheim II, personal communication.

37. See J. M. Treistman, "Ch'ü-chia-ling and the Early Cultures of the Hanshui Valley, China," *Asian Perspectives*, XI (1968), 69–90; and K. C. Chang, "The Beginnings of Agriculture in the Far East," *Antiquity*, XLIV (1970), 175–185.

38. See J. M. Treistman, "China at l000 BC: A Cultural Mosaic", *Science*, CLX, 3830 (1968), 55; H. D. Sankalia, *Indian Archaeology Today* (New York, 1962). J. M. Treistman, "Ch'ü-chia-ling," *op. cit.*, contests the association of this culture with Lungshan.

39. See K. C. Chang, "The Beginnings of Agriculture in the Far East," *Antiquity*, XLIV (1970), 175–185; on the debated relation between Yangshao and Hoabinhian, see idem, "Radiocarbon dates from China: Some initial interpretations," *Current Anthropology*, XIV, 5 (Dec. 1973), 525–528; and Wilhelm G. Solheim II, "Northern Thailand, Southeast Asia, and World Prehistory," *Asian Perspectives*, XIII (1970), 145–162.

40. D. T. Bayard, "Excavation at Non Nok Tha," *op. cit.*, 123.

41. Idem, "Early Thai Bronze: Analysis and New Dates," *Science*, CLXXVI (1972), 141f.

42. Idem, "Excavation at Non Nok Tha," *op. cit.*, 136.

43. *Ibid.,* 131, 139.

44. E. Saurin, "Nouvelles Observations Préhistoriques à l'est de Saigon," *B.S.E.I.*, n.s. XLIII (1968), 1–17. Recent finds indicate that there was a well-established bronze culture in Vietnam in the second millennium BC along with relatively advanced political organization. W. G. Solheim, personal communication.

45. Cited by D. T. Bayard, "Excavation at Non Nok Tha," *op. cit.*, 134.

46. N. Barnard, "Bronze Casting and Bronze Alloys in Ancient China," *Monumenta Serica,* 1961.

47. D. T. Bayard, "An Early Indigenous Bronze Technology in North-East Thailand," *International Congress of Orientalists*, Seminar E (Canberra, 1971).

48. D. P. Agrawal, "Harappan Chronology: A Re-Examination of the Evidence," *Studies in Prehistory*, ed. Sen and Ghosh (Calcutta, 1966), pp. 139–148.

49. W. G. Solheim, "Research Report: Early Bronze in Northeastern Thailand," *Current Anthropology*, IX, 1 (1968), 59–62; "Reworking Southeast Asian Prehistory," *Paideuma, Mitteilungen zur Kulturkunde*, XV (1969), 125–139. See also Nguyen Khac Vien, *op cit.*, pp. 14–17.

50. Dates for the beginning of iron around l600–l200 BC have been advanced. See Wilhelm G. Solheim II, "Early Man in Southeast Asia," *Expedition*, XIV, 3 (1972), 29.

51. P. K. Benedict, "Austro-Thai Studies: 3 Austro-Thai and Chinese," *Behaviour Science Notes*, 11 (1967), 275–336.

52. Wilhelm G. Solheim II, personal communication.

53. O. C. Dahl, *Malgache et Maanjan: Une comparaison linguistique* (Oslo, 1951), pp. 370–372.

54. W. G. Solheim, "New Light on a Forgotten Past," *op. cit.*; and I. H. Burkili, "The Rise and Decline of the Greater Yam in the Service of Man," *The Advancement of Science*, VII, 28 (1951), 445.

55. W. G. Solheim, *loc. cit.*, and "Southeast Asia and the West," *Science,* CLVII, 3791 (1967), 896–902.

56. Idem, "New Light on a Forgotten Past," *op. cit.*

57. Idem, "Northern Thailand, Southeast Asia, and World Prehistory," *op. cit.*

58. Wilhelm G. Solheim II, personal communication. For evidence of water buffalo at or just before the earliest period of Indian influence, see B. Bronson and G. F. Dales, "Excavations at Chansen, Thailand, 1968 and 1969: A Preliminary Report," *Asian Perspectives,* XV (1972), 15–46.

59. B. Bronson and M. Han, "A thermoluminescence series from Thailand," *Antiquity,* XLVI (1972), 322–326.

60. On this distinction see R. O. Whyte, "The gramineae, wild and cultivated, of monsoonal and equatorial Asia. I. Southeast Asia," *Asian Perspectives,* XV (1972), 126–151.

61. W. G. Solheim, "Research Report: Early Bronze in Northeastern Thailand," *op. cit.*, 160.

62. See P. Srensen, "Prehistoric Iron Implements from Thailand," *Asian Perspectives,* XVI, 2(1973), 141.

63. The bronze-yielding layer 20 was accorded one dating of 1315 BC but this was discarded in favor of datings of 2290 BC and 2325 BC from two different laboratories for layer 19 samples. Reports from Florida State University suggested bronze manufacture at the conventionally accepted date of about 600 BC, but other tests elsewhere suggested that all the Florida samples must have been contaminated. On the newly accepted interpretation, however, one secure sample still yielded a surprisingly late date. See W. G. Solheim, "Research Report," *op. cit.*, 60; and D. T. Bayard, "Excavation at Non Nok Tha," *op. cit.*, 133. Whether the uncertain bronze-yielding level 3 should be dated to the third or second millennium BC has been debated; K. C. Chang, using Chinese synchronisms, favored the later dating in one place, but thermoluminescence tests support the earlier. So, perhaps, does the back-dating of the bronze age suggested by the analysis of the early-period socketed tool mentioned above. See K. C. Chang, "Radiocarbon Dates from China: Some Initial Interpretations," *Current Anthropology,* XIV, 5 (Dec. 1973), 525–528; B. Bronson and M. Han, "A Thermoluminescence Series from Thailand," *Antiquity,* XLVI (1972), 322–326; D. T. Bayard, "Early Thai Bronze: Analysis and New Dates," *Science,* CLXXVI (1972), 1411f.

64. This is suggested by B. Groslier in "Our Knowledge of Khmer Civilization: A Re-Appraisal," *Journal of the Siam Society,* XLVIII, 1 (1960). Indians appear to have brought to the isthmus area their own breeds of bullocks and grass for fodder: see R. O. Whyte, "The gramineae," *op. cit.*, 137f.

65. As late as 1964, G. Coedès listed irrigated rice fields among the material attributes of pre-Indian culture. *Les Etats Hindouises, op. cit.*, p. 27.

66. M. Colani, *Emploi de la Pierre en des Temps Recules, Annam-Indonésie-Assam,* Publication des Amis du Vieux Hue (Hanoi, 1940). L. Bezacier, *Asie Sud-Est,* II, *Le*

Vietnam (Paris, 1972), pp. 252ff., refers to the possibility that such sites represent arboreal cults.

67. H. G. Q. Wales, "The Pre-Indian Basis of Khmer Culture," *Journal of the Royal Asiatic Society*, (1952), 117–123; idem, *The Mountain of God* (London, 1953), pp. 97–103; J. E. Spencer and G. A. Hale, "The Origin, Nature and Distribution of Agricultural Terracing," *Pacific Viewpoint*, II, 1(1961), 1–40; see also III, 1 (1962), 97–101, 101–105.

68. P. Wheatley, *Discursive Scholia on Recent Papers on Agricultural Terracing and on Related Matters Pertaining to Northern Indochina and Related Areas* (Berkeley, Center for Southeast Asia Studies, Institute of International Relations, University of California Reprint #196).

69. E. Gaspardone, "Champs lo et Champs hiong," *Journal Asiatique,* CCXLIII, (1955), 461–477.

70. P. Wheatley, *op. cit.,* p. 131.

71. Nguyen Khac Vien, *op. cit.,* pp. 12f.

72. L. Malleret, *L'Archéologie du Delta du Mekong,* 11 (1960), 88; 111 (1962), 324; IV (1963), 131.

73. L. Malleret, *op. cit.,* IV (1963), 132. R. D. Hill suspects that irrigation began, not in deltaic areas (until well into historical times), but in areas of substantial slope where terracing was already known (personal communication).

74. R. D. Hill, *Rice in Malaya, op. cit.,* 73ff. On this thesis, as well as on a personal communication from the author, the present discussion of wet rice is largely based. See also P. Wheatley in K. Sandhu, *Early Malaysia* (Singapore, 1973), p. 43.

75. R. D. Hill, *loc. cit.* It is suggested in this source that the Mons probably had irrigation (though the evidence is scanty), that the Thais were good at drainage but not irrigation, and that there is a possibly long history of shifting cultivation among the Khmers, 82ff.

76. T. Harrisson, "100,000 Years of Stone Age Culture in Borneo," *Journal of the Royal Society of Arts,* CXII (1963–1964), 174–191.

77. See B. H. M. Vlekke, *Nusantara* (The Hague, 1959), p. 22.

78. R. D. Hill, *op. cit.,* 89, considers that millet was the chief cereal in Java, following E. D. Merrill, "The Botany of Cook's Voyages," *Chron. Bot.,* XIV, 5–6 (1954), 161–384, who points to the fact that *setaria italica,* millet, is figured at the Borobudur while rice is not, and suggests a link between the word for millet, *daua,* found in Malaya and Philippines, and the Sanskrit, *yava,* grain.

79. R. D. Hill, *op. cit.,* 91ff.

80. R. D. Hill, personal communication.

81. B. P. Groslier, *Angkor et le Cambodge au XVI Siècle d'après Sources Portuguaises et Espagnoles* (Paris, 1958), pp. 107–121.

82. See E. R. Leach, "Some Economic Advantages of Shifting Cultivation," *Proceedings of the Seventh Pacific Science Congress,* 1957.

83. R. D. Hill, "Dry Rice Cultivation in Peninsular Malaya," *Oriental Geography*, X, 1 (1966), 10–14.

84. Idem, *Rice in Malaya*, op. cit., 44.

85. W. G. Solheim, "Northern Thailand, Southeast Asia and World Prehistory," *op. cit.*

86. The author is indebted to G. Benjamin for suggestions and references on this important point. See his "Prehistory and Ethnology in Southeast Asia: Some New Ideas," Working Paper 25, Sociology Department, University of Singapore (1974).

87. The Lake Tien sites, near North Vietnam in Yunnan, show similarities to Dongson culture, with no writing or "mature urbanization" but with socially stratified villages, according to K. C. Chang, *Archaeology of Ancient China* (New Haven, 1968), p. 436. See also M. von Dewall, "The Tien Culture of South-West China," *Antiquity*, XLI (1967), 8–21. W. G. Solheim refers to urbanization in northern Thailand during the first millennium BC in "Northern Thailand, Southeast Asia and World Prehistory," *op. cit.*, 158. On the bronze-age fortified site at Co Loa, dated to the third century BC, see L. Bezacier, *op. cit.*, pp. 247–249; and Nguyen Khac Vien, *op. cit.*, 21f. The fortified village site at Chansen in Thailand had an early, pre-Indian phase (c. 200 BC–AD 0) characterized by use of bronze, iron and weaving: B. Bronzen and G. F. Dales, "Excavations at Chansen, Thailand, 1968 and 1969: A Preliminary Report," *Asian Perspectives*, XV (1972), 15–46.

88. On this special usage of 'folk' and 'peasant,' see R. Redfield, *The Primitive World and Its Transformations* (Ithaca, N.Y., 1953), pp. 37–42, and *passim*; and K. C. Chang, "Some Aspects of Social Structure and Settlement Patterns in Southeast Asia," *Bulletin of the Institute of Ethnology*, Academia Sinica, Taipei, VI (1958), 67–78.

89. J. S. Furnivall, *Netherlands India* (Cambridge, 1939/1944).

90. This is a point which will be taken up in a later article.

2

Foreign Influences
and the Vietnamese
Cultural Core

JOHN K. WHITMORE*

Selection 1 in this volume dealt with the question of the "Indianization" of Southeast Asia, not including Vietnam, which historically has been influenced by China. Vietnam was officially a province of China for slightly more than a millennium (111 BC–AD 939) and later was a tributary state for most of the second millennium of the Common Era (up to 1885). How much "Sinicization" did Vietnam undergo during the long period of Chinese direct and indirect rule? Historians and anthropologists are divided on the issue of how much Vietnamese society was influenced by Confucius. The French, who brought Vietnam under their rule between 1862 and 1885, favored the position that the Vietnamese elite was almost completely Confucian and that Confucianism had percolated substantially down to the village level. John K. Whitmore is among the non-French and more recent scholars who vehemently differ. They assert that a Vietnamese culture existed prior to the Chinese conquest and that it was revived and persisted after direct Chinese rule ended in AD 939.

Whitmore analyzes the question with the help of the "onion" theory first propounded by the bureaucrat-scholar Richard O. Winstedt in regard to

*John K. Whitmore, "Foreign Influences and the Vietnamese Cultural Core: A Discussion of the Pre-Modern Period," in *Borrowings and Adaptations in Vietnamese Culture*, ed. Truong Buu Lam (Manoa: Univ. of Hawaii Southeast Asian Studies, 1987), pp. 1–21.

Malaya. Many "national" cultures, including that of Vietnam, have a "core" culture over which there are layers of external influences. Whitmore carefully peels the layers to unravel the essentials of the Vietnamese culture, which have provided a basis for Vietnamese opposition to China over the centuries, including the recent past. Whitmore suggests that the onion theory may be applied to other countries of Southeast Asia as well for a better understanding of their core cultures.

~

An examination of the manner in which the Vietnamese people received external influences helps us acquire a sense of the culture itself. The pattern of influence that foreign sources had on the Vietnamese reflects what Vietnamese culture itself consisted of, what was malleable in this culture and what integral to it.

One way of doing this is to follow Richard Winstedt's "onion" theory of Malay culture or, as mentioned at the conference, a "jeepney" model[1] and peel off the successive layers and accretions until we reach an irreducible minimum. Thus, for Malaya, off goes the Islam, then the Hindu-Buddhism, before we reach the indigenous nature of the Malay. This, however, assumes an unchanging process of cultural accretion, such that original cultural elements are untransformed as they move across the centuries. Instead, we need to consider, in a linguistic sense, constant change and transformation taking place as the culture develops, whether or not it is influenced from the outside. Yet, while this temporal change is taking place, a continuity still exists that allows us to recognize the culture as *that* culture, despite its changes. The question, then, is what kind of transformation has taken place and to what degree.

My approach to this topic is to try to determine what forms the Vietnamese "cultural core," not in the unchanging sense that Winstedt suggests but as a part of the Vietnamese cultural dynamics of the past two millennia and more. I rely on concepts of cultural change that help to distinguish that which is more integral to a culture, and which thus forms its "core," from that which is more susceptible to change and consequently more "peripheral." While change is going on to some degree at some place in all societies, there is a need to determine those areas in a culture that undergo major changes and those times when the culture is more susceptible to change.[2]

Here we are concerned with those changes related, directly or indirectly, to borrowing from foreign sources. Thus, we are not looking for patterns of origination within Vietnamese culture but for diffusion from the outside and the manner in which this diffusion has affected the mode of life of the

Vietnamese. Yet such borrowing is rarely automatic and complete. The introduction of a borrowed item or process requires a perceptual or motivational adjustment on the part of the members of the indigenous culture, and this in itself is innovation. Each culture tries to fit new items into its own context and its own understanding of itself. This situation will inevitably be imperfect and may lead to tension and stress within the society.

Centuries of Vietnamese Borrowing

In the last millennium BC, the people who were to become the Vietnamese stood in the middle of a wide network of foreign contacts. These contacts extended into the Yangtze Valley and the Yunnan Plateau on the north and west, and down the coast to various parts of the island world of Southeast Asia on the south. The Vietnamese archaeological site of Dong-son in the Thanh-hoa province, just south of the Red River Delta, became the namesake for what has been termed a "civilization" covering a good part of Southeast Asia.[3]

Putting aside such an approach, what the Dong-son site represents to us is an almost classic case of diffusion, both direct and stimulus, reaching from the shores of Vietnam along the trading routes of the coasts and islands to other developing cultures able to blend such technology and ideas into their own patterns.

The early Vietnamese, known as the Lac, thus formed part of a Southeast Asian world which about 2,500 years ago was reaching out to make contact with the world at large and to expand the repertoire of cultural elements at its disposal. In the process, Vietnam and other parts of Southeast Asia were establishing an eclectic but not indiscriminate pattern of borrowing foreign elements that were adaptable to their own cultures and that could enhance their own advancement. What was important in this borrowing was the aid given the indigenous social, economic, and political developments of the time and the furthering of the cultural, artistic, and religious changes already taking place.[4]

The final centuries BC saw these early Vietnamese not only form a part of the expanding Southeast Asian world but also receive direct contact from the north. Imperial China crossed the Yangtze and reached the southeast coast in the effort to tap into the flow of goods and wealth circulating along the sea routes.[5] The Chinese activity set off disturbances throughout the south; one consequence appears to have been the Shu/Thuc invasion of the Red River Delta in the third century BC. This conquest led to the kingship of An Duong and the establishment of Co-loa, the first major imposition of northern influence in historic times. An Duong was quickly followed by direct Chinese intervention, first that of the Ch'in dynasty and Chao T'o, then a century later Han Wu-ti. While these contacts with China opened more direct communications with the north, witness the Han in 185 BC attempting to cut off trade in iron and cattle with the south,[6] the local inhabitants of the Red River plain and further south retained their cultural and social patterns.

Chinese Domination

The first century AD brought major changes to Lac society. Initially, the influx of Chinese fleeing the Wang Mang disturbances of north China, then the uprising of the Lac aristocracy in AD 40 and Ma Yuan's crushing victory ended Lac leadership and imposed direct Chinese control over the area. From the beginning, the Chinese sought, at different times and in different ways, to bring their own civilizing influence to bear on local culture and society.[7] Nevertheless, the major purpose of the Chinese presence in the south remained the wealth of foreign trade, and this meant a continuing Vietnamese contact with the maritime world through the following centuries.

As Keith W. Taylor has so well described in his study *The Birth of Vietnam,* the main impact of the Chinese control took place in the area of the central Red River Delta. This was not only an administrative but also a social, cultural, and religious center for the Han establishment. Here were formed the powerful Sino-Vietnamese families that undoubtedly both held large stretches of land and took part in the thriving trade. Through these families came the major influences of the period: the writing, loanwords from both spoken and learned spheres, the introduction to the Chinese intellectual world, literary forms, and general patterns of the Sinic style of life.[8] Members of this elite world also played major roles in developing the Mahayana Buddhist community that began to thrive from the second century AD.

The Buddhist influence represented not only the contacts with the north but also and more particularly the flow of ideas as well as goods along the maritime routes. Vietnam at different times in the first millennium AD formed an integral part of the international Buddhist world, connecting northern India, the island world of Southeast Asia, and China. Sanskrit formed the lingua franca of this exchange. In the eighth century, the Chinese had established a thriving cosmopolitan port area in the northern delta. Chams, Chinese, Persians, Khmers and Arabs, monks and traders circulated through its markets and quarters. This trading center seems to have been the major Chinese link to the coastal trade of mainland Southeast Asia, connecting the Yangtze Valley with the Cham ports, Cambodia, Dvaravati, and the Kra Isthmus. In these centuries, the region north of present-day Hanoi had become a major Mahayana Buddhist center, with influences derived from the sea routes and the south as well as the land routes and the north. Indian and central Asian (Hu), Chinese (Han), and Cham thoughts and artifacts mixed freely.[9]

Eventually, in Taylor's description, Buddhism would form the necessary synthesizing element in the transformation of Vietnamese politics, culture, and society from regional diversity and competition to a unified monarchy. Both the sixth and the tenth centuries saw an attempt by the Sino-Vietnamese elite to set up an autonomous, if not fully independent, regime at times of weakness in China, only to be succeeded by an upsurge of leadership tied to ancestral cultural patterns. Each case, however, saw a lack of complete political success by the indigenous forces and the need for Buddhist leadership to participate in the final political form.[10]

This time of Chinese domination was a period of the ebb and flow of central Chinese power, the rise and fall of local attempts at regional political overlordship, and the gradual spread of the cultural patterns. The result was not a society attempting to duplicate China's, but one which was transforming itself in reaction to both northern and southern influences. China's presence helped as well as hindered this development, and the Vietnamese society that emerged at the end of a thousand years had changed considerably. Nevertheless, this society can only be understood if we put aside any idea of a "little China," a "smaller dragon" for this period and look at the Vietnamese as taking part in many of the same efforts as their Southeast Asian neighbors.

The Buddhist Period

By the late tenth and early eleventh centuries, Sung China had its own links to the maritime routes in the ports stretching from Hangchou to Kuangchou (Canton). It did not need the Vietnamese connection anymore, even if it had been able to re-conquer the distant south.[11] The state of Dai Viet was thus able to set itself up unchallenged by northern power until it gained sufficient strength to repel any such major intrusion (in the 1070s). A more persistent challenge came from its sister state to the south, Champa. One major point of contention between the Vietnamese and the Chams in the tenth and eleventh centuries appears to have been international trade, most particularly the eastern trade route to the flourishing Angkorean empire in Kampuchea. Thus, in its early centuries of independence, the new capital of Thang-long maintained its links with the south at the same time that it continued to borrow from the north. Dai Viet participated in the flow of an

international network of exchange that had as its two poles China to the
north and Java to the south.[12]

With independence, Chinese influence remained in the use of political titles and terminology (such as using the title *de,* "emperor," for the ruler).
This, joined to indigenous patterns (such as the blood oath of loyalty), afforded the Vietnamese a political structure overarching the local power centers. The Vietnamese had, however, put aside any thought of forming part
of the Chinese empire itself and had begun, for example, to develop their
own writing system *(nom)* based on the Chinese characters. More important to the Vietnamese state in the tenth and eleventh centuries was the international Buddhist community. Monks served the Vietnamese throne as
officials and clerks, handling the diplomatic correspondence, among other
activities. These monks were the residue of the earlier international contacts
when monks had congregated from both north and west, from India and
China.[13] They formed the major link between the Vietnamese court and
foreign cultures.

Northern Champa, just below the then southern border (Nam-gioi) of
Hoanh-son, was also a thriving Buddhist center and had contacts with the
Buddhist world of Java and the Malay Peninsula as well as with that of
China. The Vietnamese and Cham Buddhist communities were in contact
with each other and with the international scene. For example, one tenth-
century monk of Cham ancestry lived in a Vietnamese temple probably
north of the capital and traveled through the southern Vietnamese territory
of the time (Thanh-hoa and Nghe-an provinces). Vietnamese conquests of
the Cham capital in 982 and 1069 brought back first an Indian, then a Chinese monk to take important parts in royal Vietnamese Buddhism. Cham
masters seem to have played a significant role in the development of Vietnamese religious life.[14]

From 1010, the Vietnamese capital sat in the middle of the Buddhist community, at the site of the present Hanoi. From this location, the Vietnamese
ruler contended as much with the Chams, the Khmers, and the hill peoples
as with the Chinese. Within the Buddhist framework, the Vietnamese state
faced many of the same political problems faced by other contemporary
Southeast Asian states. In response to these problems, the Ly rulers built
up, surrounded themselves with, and took part in the Buddhist establishment. They sent to China for copies of the Tripitaka and had many temples
built. In the second reign (1028–1054), Avalokitesvara, of importance in
Champa and Cambodia, appeared as a cult object, and in the third reign
(1054–1072), it was Brahma (Phan Vuong) and Indra (De-thich).[15]

The art and music of the time well reflect the eclectic selection of the period. At the 140-foot-high Van-phuc Temple, built (or re-built) in 1057 in

the region north of the capital, we can see the blend of Vietnamese borrowing at the time. The Ly architects and artists followed a Chinese Buddhist
model, constructing the temple with basic Vietnamese methods, and employed sculptures that reflected both the T'ang Lung-men style of Central
Asia and patterns showing a definite Cham influence. Through their contact with the Chams, the Vietnamese would also have been exposed indirectly to Khmer and island architectural elements.[16]

At this temple has also been found a number of identical friezes in the
T'ang Central Asian style that show a range of musical instruments known
to the Vietnamese of the eleventh century. Eight of the ten sculpted figures
are carrying recognizable instruments, and only one or possibly two of
them can be said to be of purely Chinese origin. This, the eminent Tran Van
Khe notes, "makes us think of the joint influence of two types of music, Indian and Chinese, in Vietnamese music, with a certain dominance of Indian
music."[17] Like the transverse flute, this Indian influence undoubtedly arrived via the sea lanes and Champa. An instrument that came directly from
the Chams was the hourglass drum, known to have been used with rice
cakes smeared across its two surfaces. Later, in 1060 and 1202, the Vietnamese historical records note the playing of Cham tunes at the royal
court.[18] As Tran Van Khe demonstrated so beautifully at this conference,
the Vietnamese took the spirit of the foreign musical elements and adapted
them to their own tastes.

The important point here is that these centuries, down to the fifteenth,
formed a period of cultural influences from both north and south. The
Buddhist world, and the world of international trade with which it was
connected, served as the link in both directions. Tran Van Khe points out
that this period may indeed be called one of Sino-Indian cultural forms,
while for Jean Boisselier, in his study of Cham statuary, it was a time of mutual artistic exchange between Vietnam and Champa.[19] Cultural relativity
and the easy interaction among members of the Cham and Vietnamese aris-
tocracies continued through the twelfth century and into the thirteenth
during times of both peace and war. As the states on the eastern mainland of
Southeast Asia grew in power, they expanded and collided. From the 1120s
into 1210s, warfare and allegiances shifted back and forth among the capitals of Thanh-long, Vijaya, and Angkor. The cultural interaction thus continued both among the elite and through the channels of the Buddhist
world. This we can see in such instances as the Vietnamese prince who took
the Cham princess in marriage (1154) and the Vietnamese Buddhist monk
in the early twelfth century who practiced Indian asceticism.[20] The Vietnamese ate "Cham rice," and the Chams show Vietnamese influences in
their sculpture.[21] Buddhism continued to act as a common ground between

Vietnam and the states to the south. On two separate occasions in 1118, Khmer and Cham envoys were feted and received at celebrations marking the completion of Buddhist temples.[22]

Yet, while their Cham and Khmer competitors were borrowing Sanskrit names and titles, the Vietnamese continued to use Chinese for the same purpose. They also, at different times, chose to introduce specific elements of Chinese court ritual and procedure into their Mahayana Buddhist world. Ly Thai-tong in the 1030s and 1040s appears to have begun to mesh indigenous and Sinic ritual, personally plowing a field, honoring his father, and promulgating, we are told, a law code with mourning regulations. Thai-tong did not pretend to grasp the true significance of these actions and relied on the advice of his literati counselors, drawing praise from later historians.[23] The 1070s and 1080s are the years that have had the most impact on recent historians of the Vietnamese past. Following soon after the reforms of Wang An-shih in China, these years saw the introduction of the Temple of Literature, Confucian examinations, the National College, the Han-lin Academy, and the graded bureaucratic hierarchy from China.[24]

Nevertheless, however striking, these changes seem not to have been deep or profound. They merely provided a small group of scholars versed in the Chinese classics and in Confucian rites whom the royal court could call upon for aid in dealing with China and for enhancement of the royal position through their ritual observances. Indeed, the Confucian examinations were used sparingly through the twelfth century before they were merged with Buddhism and Taoism into one "Three Religion" (Tam-giáo) examination in 1195. The products of these examinations and holders of the foreign knowledge were posted only in the capital and would have formed a small fraction of the courtiers serving the royal clan.[25] As the selection of men in 1076 has indicated, those who were loyal, honest, and talented were promoted to run the state, while those who were literate (in classical Chinese) went into the National College.[26]

The Vietnamese court in the late eleventh century and into the twelfth was apparently interested in developing useful techniques, ritual and otherwise, to further the power of the state. At the same time that the Confucian activities were being established there, the Vietnamese ruler was seeking authorization from the Chinese throne to purchase books on the military arts, occult sciences, and other such practical subjects. Though the request was denied, the Vietnamese continued their quest. At about this time we have the first mention of the Vietnamese use of elephants in warfare.[27]

Through the twelfth century and into the thirteenth, Chinese innovations crept piecemeal into the Vietnamese cultural fabric. Only in the middle third of the thirteenth century did the Vietnamese begin to make use of the Chinese administrative model in order to centralize power. With the greater administrative control came a higher development of Chinese classical studies in Vietnam, as members of the elite took a greater interest in its intellectual advancement. The 1230s and 1240s saw a new kind of examination meant to produce more generalized administrators (thai-hoc-sinh). Those who passed began to take administrative positions in the central government and eventually to be posted to provincial offices as the Tran extended direct government control out from the capital region.[28] In 1253, the Tran established the National College, setting up statues of Confucius and other classical heroes (the Duke of Chou, Mencius, and the Seventy-two Sages) and ordering literati (nho-si) to expound on the Four Books and the Six Classics. A prince set up the first major school of Chinese classical studies, and in 1272 Le Van Huu presented his Sinic-style history of Vietnam, with appropriate commentary, to the throne. Literature in *nom* began to appear.[29]

The Mongol threat in the second half of the century both ended this experiment with Chinese-style administration and intertwined the fates of the Vietnamese and the Chams for over a century. Princes and their entourages took control of local and central government. Chams and Vietnamese jointly resisted the Mongol scourge. Thus, after the wars of the 1280s, literati appeared in the government as protégés of powerful figures,[30] while the Vietnamese aristocracy interacted with their peers to the south. Buddhism continued to form the major cultural link between Champa and Vietnam. Nhanh-tong, ruler of Vietnam during the Mongol wars, followed tradition thereafter by abdicating for his son and entering Buddhist life. Eight years later, in 1301, he [Nhanh-tong] journeyed south to Champa in order to visit its sacred Buddhist sites. While on his pilgrimage, he spent several months as a guest of the Cham royal court and felt so well received that he promised the hand of his daughter, sister of the ruling king, to his good host the Cham king. In return, the Vietnamese received Cham territory.[31]

The result of this match was decades of antagonism when the Cham king died, the Vietnamese seized the princess from the funeral pyre, and the Chams demanded their territory back.[32] In 1312 and 1318, the Vietnamese took the Cham capital of Vijaya, then began to lose interest in the Cham situation thereafter. The situation exploded in their faces after 1370 as the great Cham king Che-bong-nga not only retrieved his old northern provinces but proceeded to invade the Red River Delta at will and to take Thang-long several times. In these years of crisis for the Vietnamese, intellectual as well as political, a tale based on the *Ramayana* of India served to explain the nature and situation of the Chams.[33]

The Vietnamese aristocracy of the fourteenth century saw merit in foreign exchanges (in a number of different directions), but they did not see any reason to change their basic way of life. In the 1320s, Tran Minh-tong declared to literati who urged change,

> (Our) country has already established rules and regulations for itself. North (China) and South (Vietnam) are very different, (and) if (we) follow the schemes of pale scholars in seeking progress, then (it) will give birth to immediate Chaos.[34]

Almost half a century later (in 1370), a son of Minh-tong's, Nghe-tong, restated this philosophy in even stronger terms:

> (When) the earlier reigns established the country, (they) had their own system of law (and) did not follow the (Chinese) system of the Sung. (This) was because in the North (China) and the South (Vietnam) each ruler had his own country and had no need to follow the other. (In the 1360s), pale scholars were employed who did not understand (the depth of) the establishment of law (in our state) (and) who changed the old customs of our ancestors to follow the customs of the North entirely, as if (our customs) were clothes, music, (or) literature. We cannot select anything (of theirs.)[35]

The Chinese Model

Within a century of the last statement, Vietnam had adopted the Chinese model of government and philosophy, setting the ideal pattern that would rule the country until the French conquest. This hundred years saw Vietnam rise from a time of deep crisis in the late fourteenth century to reestablish itself as a powerful and prosperous land. The means to this end was taking the modern China of that age as the lodestone and putting aside the old pattern of eclectic borrowing from numerous directions.

The movement toward the Chinese model began in the intellectual crisis of the 1380s. Yao and Shun, mythic emperors of China, were called upon in the search for rule in place of anarchy. The powerful minister Ho Quy Ly drew on the original Confucian classics (not the more recent Neo-Confucian texts) and put some of them into *nom* so as to justify his position in the state, first as the Duke of Chou guiding a young king, then, when he seized the throne, as the Emperor Shun himself. Yet, in the first years of the fifteenth century, Confucian literati remained as intellectuals and did not serve as officials in the Ho government, Nguyen Trai and his father being the exemptions. Trai himself began to make significant contributions to

Vietnamese language and literature. Despite the political changes, the Ho state was structurally more similar to its predecessors than to the Chinese model that would follow. Ho Quy Ly did borrow certain useful practices directly from the founder of the Ming dynasty, practices such as controlling the Buddhist church, holding a census, and circulating paper money.[36]

A more difficult question than assessing the impact of the Ho on the Vietnamese is to estimate the significance of the Ming colonial period. The tangible aspects are easy to point out—the crushing military might, the tight bureaucratic structure, the spread of schools and their libraries (Confucian and otherwise) across the Red River Delta, and the imperial orthodoxy imposed upon China and its territories. Yet it is hard to say precisely how this affected the path the Vietnamese state would take later in the century. On the one hand, a number of Vietnamese sided with the Chinese and helped them run the colony; on the other, many young Vietnamese attended the schools. In later years, after the Ming defeat, the former were destroyed or driven underground, while the latter remained and seem to have played a very significant role in the future of the Vietnamese state.[37]

Certainly the Ming period gave the Vietnamese people a much closer experience with bureaucratic administration and modern Neo-Confucian orthodoxy than they had ever had before. While the regime established by Le Loi after his victory in 1428 was similar in structure to those of the Ho and the Tran before him, he did retain certain features of the Ming system, such as the schools, a greater sense of law and peasant landholdings, and the establishment of a firm coinage system. On his death, Le Loi's tomb was modeled on that of the Ming Yung-lo Emperor, built a decade earlier outside Peking. Yet, under the rather traditional and parochial rule of the first Le rulers, a clash grew in force between those literati (like Nguyen Trai) who wished to retain the traditional style of Confucian belief in Vietnam and those (the younger scholars) who wanted Vietnam to follow the modern tenets of Ming China. In the late 1430s, the two groups squared off on the matter of court ritual, with the Ming modernists victorious. These same years saw the Le ruler adopt the stance of the Chinese emperors in calling to heaven to acknowledge the errors that he, as ruler, had made, in using the Ming calendar for ritual events, and in replacing the earlier eel-like water creature of the Vietnamese with the Sinic-style dragon.[38]

From the 1430s and 1460s, the influence of the modernist literati grew, despite being buffeted by the political turmoil of the years. The examinations of 1442 and 1448 are considered the first of the orthodox Chinese-style examinations in Vietnamese history.[39] Finally, under the rule of the young Le Thanh-tong, the Ming administrative and philosophical systems became the official way in Vietnam. For the first time, the Vietnamese chose to follow the Chinese administrative system closely. The Ming model led Thanh-tong to do away with the counselors who stood between the throne and the administration and to take direct control of the administration through the Six Boards. The Vietnamese, however, adjusted the Ming structure to fit the realities of their smaller country. They staffed this administration with the successful scholars of the triennial examinations, which followed the Neo-Confucian orthodoxy and standard Chinese literary forms, thus bringing more Chinese terms into the language. The reorganization had almost immediate effect as Thanh-tong crushed an unrecalcitrant Champa in 1471. The Chinese model also meant a foreign policy that stressed morality over the earlier practice of cultural interaction. Later in the decade Thanh-tong would invade Laos for the first time. Ultimately, the major change made by Thanh-tong was to transform the Vietnamese concept of kingship from the earlier more personal ruler *(vua)* to the moral Confucian emperor *(hoang-de)* of China, at the same time as he implemented the Nam-giao, the Ming ritual of the Confucian sacrifice to heaven, in place of the blood oath of personal allegiance.[40]

Nevertheless, not all aspects of Le government took the form held by contemporary Ming China. Most important here is the law code. As Nguyen Ngoc Huy has recently argued,[41] the core of the Le Code (Le *Trieü Hinh Luat*) was put together in the 1430s and 1440s, undoubtedly following the pattern of the earlier Tang dynasty code rather than the contemporary Ming code. Even though Thanh-tong stressed the Ming pattern, he did not attempt to adopt its legal code, despite its obvious applicability to what he was attempting. This has yet to be fully explained, yet it is indicative of the fact that the Vietnamese did not borrow completely or indiscriminately in the fifteenth century.

From the 1460s into the middle of the following century appears to have been the period of the greatest Ming influence. During Thanh-tong's reign of thirty-seven years (1460–1496), he brought much of the ideological orthodoxy attached to Ming Neo-Confucianism into Vietnam. His regulations deal with the "proper" way of life as defined by this orthodoxy. As he noted in the 1460s, ritual and correct behavior were "what separated man from the beasts."[42] Thanh-tong particularly focused on the family, emphasizing mourning regulations among kin and correct marriage procedures. A good example of this concern for the family is that, at the beginning of his reign, he introduced the concept of *huong-hoa* land to support the ancestral sacrifices. One-twentieth of inherited land was reserved for this purpose and was to go to the eldest son (where possible). In this way, Thanh-tong sought to bring the concepts of patrilineal succession and primogeniture into Vietnamese social structure where they had not existed before.[43] Indeed, we have on record an indication that he might have been trying to go too far too fast. In 1485, a senior minister and former imperial tutor, Tran Phong, who had long been in and out of Thanh-tong's graces, was executed for complaining about the extent of Ming influence.[44]

The Le rulers of the first quarter of the sixteenth century continued this emphasis on Confucian morality and Sinic social organization when they could, in the midst of the political turmoil of the years. Despite our assumptions about Mac Dang Dung, this powerful general and his clan picked up the Neo-Confucian mantle of Le Thanh-tong's famed Hong-duc period (1470–1497) and, it would appear, continued the latter's efforts to bring Vietnamese society in line with that of Ming China. The Confucianism of the Mac family went back two centuries to the famed scholar Mac Dinh Chi as well as the Mac Thuy, prime Vietnamese supporter of the Chinese during the Ming occupation. Even though Mac Dang Dung himself rose to power as a military man, we should not ignore his family background in discussing his impact on sixteenth-century Vietnam.[45] If anything, the Mac family was too sinophile in orientation to fit the Vietnamese tradition. Its emphasis in this direction continued the development of the *huong-hoa* institution and undoubtedly helped to make it a part of Vietnamese social structure.[46]

The defeat of the Mac in 1592 and their flight into the northern mountains brought the Le restoration (itself a Chinese concept) and began to deflect the strong Ming emphasis that had existed for over a century. Warfare continued into the second half of the seventeenth century, now between the Trinh and the Nguyen, and the status of the Confucian literati, well maintained it would seem during the Mac dynasty, dropped drastically. Indigenous power relations came to the fore. Only in the 1660s, when the Trinh had put aside the attempt at military re-conquest of the Nguyen on the southern border, did they turn back to the Chinese model of administration, with its emphasis on bureaucracy and moral righteousness. In 1663, the Trinh, via the Le on the throne, promulgated an edict containing the moral dicta the Confucian elite expected the Vietnamese population to follow. This was very much an imposition of elite, Chinese-derived social patterns on indigenous social structure. Much of the activity involved setting up new procedures to insure correct handling of the reestablished Sinic ideals.[47] Yet it would appear that the elite backed away from the heavy Ming emphasis of Thanh-tong and the Mac.

The period from the 1660s to the 1760s saw the Trinh in the north and the Nguyen in the south continue to implement the Chinese model as it had been established earlier. In a time of demographic, social, and economic change, the government in the north tried desperately to maintain its hierarchy of power through the countryside. As fiscal problems mounted, it attempted to control the tax base and to keep land and population out of the hands of the large landholders. Part of this was the effort to restrict the movement of "vagabonds," those not tied to the village registers.[48] At the same time, the government was imposing a hierarchy on the spirit cults of the countryside, drawing them under the central power of the cult to heaven (Nam-giao) and driving less desirable elements underground.[49]

These decades saw a growth of both Confucian orthodoxy among the literary elite and popular religious belief. The latter included Mahayana Buddhist and Roman Catholic movements and is linked to some degree to the growth of foreign trade in the seventeenth and eighteenth centuries. One major contribution of future significance from abroad was the romanization of the Vietnamese language by Western Catholic missionaries, though initially it was used only for Catholic documents. The government attempted to counter the growth of heterodoxy by controlling the printing of books.[50]

All the countervailing forces of the times exploded in the rebellions of the eighteenth century, that of the Tay-son in particular. We need to know the extent of foreign contacts that the various Vietnamese factions had before we can discuss the degree of such influence. For example, can Chinese White Lotus elements be found in the movements of the period? A specific stance of foreign participation was Nguyen Anh's involvement with the Bishop d'Adran and his sending his eldest son, Prince Canh, to Paris to seek aid. The resulting "bizarre handful of French soldiers and priests," to borrow Alexander Woodside's phrase, served the Nguyen with other foreigners, Chinese, Khmers, Thais, and Malays. The French contributed military expertise and most particularly brought the architectural concepts of Vauban, which helped the construction of citadels (as at Hue) once success was achieved.[51]

Even under the Gia-long Emperor, the French did not gain great power, and when his son, the Minh-mang Emperor, reached the throne in 1819 there was little chance that European influences could be strong. As Woodside has shown so well, the 1820s and 1830s saw the full adoption of the Chinese model. Gia-long had already adopted the Ch'ing code of China almost in toto, and now Minh-mang set up the full bureaucratic array of offices and pushed central power to the outer reaches of the kingdom. He also implemented a Chinese-style tributary system as the pattern for his foreign relations. The Vietnamese ruler even went so far as to borrow what he *thought* existed in China, even though it did not. Yet, as Woodside points out, Minh-mang did not allow his strong adoption of the Chinese model to rule out any consideration of Western elements at all. He took European technical and military items of interest, accepting or rejecting them on what he considered their merits in the Vietnamese situation.[52]

Minh-mang's successors were as much if not more Confucian than he, and not nearly so flexible as he intellectually. The emperor was a scholar in the classical Chinese meaning of the word, reflecting a view of the world more in tune with Chinese philosophy than with Vietnamese reality.[53] The result appears to have been a dangerous gap between the Vietnamese people and the throne in Hue just at the time of the French invasion.

Ideas on the Vietnamese Cultural Core

As elsewhere in Southeast Asia, throughout Vietnamese history there exists a theme of borrowing from external sources. The close involvement with China over the past two millennia has meant much adopted from that direction. Yet we should not let this fact blind us to other foreign sources. Through many of these centuries, trade was important to the Vietnamese economy and culture, adding elements of value to the Vietnamese from along the sea routes.

As life changed through the centuries for the Vietnamese, what remained constant in this life? To use the anthropological terms noted at the beginning of the paper, what can we say belongs to the Vietnamese cultural core and what to the periphery? As was stated in the 1370 quotation noted above,

> ... pale scholars ... changed the old customs of our ancestors to follow the customs of the North entirely as if they were clothes, music or literature.[54]

This is a good distinction between what is considered integral to the culture and what is considered stylistic. Let us examine "the old customs of our ancestors" and make some suggestions for the Vietnamese cultural core.[55]

Social

The patterns underlying Vietnamese society may be seen from early Chinese references as having been bilateral in nature with flexibilities that the Chinese tried unsuccessfully to convert. Evidence from the Ly period suggests that even in the royal family there was neither primogeniture nor indeed any strict practice of succession.[56] The status of women has been consistently higher in Vietnamese society than in China, as women played significant political roles (witness the Trung sisters and Lady Trieu) and formed the transitional link between dynastic powers. Both Chinese and European sources have long noted the relative freedom of movement obtained by Vietnamese women, and this movement held in general for members of Vietnamese society, including children. Overall, the key point to be made for Vietnamese social organization has been its flexibility and the nature of choice so fundamental to it. Without a strict lineality and rigid clan organization, Vietnamese could choose the nature of their kin alignments and of the social organizations they joined.[57]

Cultural

The mythic pattern in Vietnamese culture goes back into the early centuries of its history. A strong continuity exists in these myths, despite the transformations of certain of their elements to accord with cultural changes that had taken place. It is through these myths that the Vietnamese people maintained their relationship with the past, not by means of the Chinese-style histories. In a sense, this is a timeless approach to the past, since by means of the myths significant figures and events of the past remained alive in the present. While retaining significance the myths do change with the times and thereby remain contemporary. A good example of such change was the turtle claw of King An-duong becoming a dragon claw in the story of the sixth-century Trieu Quang Phuc. Yet in the myth of Le Loi, the central figure was once again a turtle.[58] Despite the changes, the continuity is there in the form of the water creature and its political power. Of interest here, then, is the eel-like water creature (probably similar to that in the original of Dragon Lord Lac in the Vietnamese origin myth), which appears prominently as a motif in Vietnamese sculpture from the eleventh century into the fifteenth. It too would turn into a dragon.[59]

Another major element in Vietnamese culture is the language and the *nom* script derived from the Chinese for it.

Religious

Linked to the myths and forming a major part of Vietnamese life are the spirit cults. The range of spirits involved in the cults is large and goes from peculiar individuals who died violent deaths in strange ways to the great, heroic figures who performed memorable deeds in striving to defend the realm. Like the myths, of which they form a part, the cults too bring the past into the immediacy of the present and make it live. Not only are they of temporal significance but also spatial, as they help define the landscape of Vietnam. The cults have their own specific locales, and the range of the locales provides definition to Vietnam itself.[60]

Political

The power of the spirit cults reached into the political realm as well. Given the flexible nature of Vietnamese social organization discussed above, there was a major need for charismatic leadership that would draw the choice of significant individuals to follow. Leadership then depended greatly on the quality of the leader-follower relations, and a major task for any would-be ruler was to strengthen and broaden loyalty beyond the personal ties of kin and lieutenants.[61] A major way by which this was done was through the blood oath whereby courtiers and officials swore loyalty to the ruler before the spirit world and asked the spirits to punish them severely if such loyalty were not delivered.[62]

Economic

I would again argue that international trade, of however limited a scope, formed a major part of Vietnamese life through the centuries. In general, the Vietnamese have been more open to the sea routes than their northern neighbor and more open as well to cultural elements and *ideas* that moved along these routes. Vietnamese society generally seemed to allow greater participation by both sexes and all social classes in trade.[63]

A glance at the legal code of the Le dynasty (the Le *Trieü Hinh Luat*) will give us a hint of the relationship to the cultural core held by the items discussed above.[64] The purpose of the Le Code appears to have been to maintain the cultural core and at the same time to control it, thus both keeping in touch with the culture and reinforcing the introduction of Chinese elements, Confucian and bureaucratic. Within the borrowed framework of the code, the Vietnamese insured the continuity of key elements of their civilization.

Yu Insun has shown very well, in his doctoral dissertation "Law and Family in Seventeenth and Eighteenth Century Vietnam,"[65] the strength of indigenous bilateral social patterns through the eighteenth century. References to the oath (articles 103, 107) indicate the continued concern of the government for threats from traditional charismatic leaders, and numerous other articles show the worry over control of manpower by private (and public) individuals. The mythic and religious aspects were dealt with more administratively than legally, as the matter of the spirit cults reflects. The government sought to control "heterodoxy" in the code (see for example articles 215, 413) without actually detailing intrusion into cultic and spiritual practices. The extent of government control appears most strongly in the code as regards foreign trade. Articles 71–77 call for major restrictions in Vietnamese contacts with such merchants, yet we know from contemporary witnesses (viz. Samuel Baron) that the opposite was quite often the case.

In looking at the Vietnamese cultural core through time, I tend to see a series of transformations occurring, transformations that had differing impacts on the core itself. Buddhism seems to have had an additive effect, drawing indigenous elements under the broad umbrella of the Hindu-Buddhist view of the cosmos. Confucianism seems to have been much more revolutionary in the changes it expected of the core elements. During the Le dynasty, these changes were handled more sensitively and gradually than under the succeeding Nguyen, yet the Le changes were no less revolutionary for all their Vietnameseness.

The major issue now existing is: How Confucian did the Vietnamese become? And when? A large gap presently exists between pre-modern historians (like myself) who follow the historical development of an initially shallow Confucianism in Vietnam and students of the twentieth century, especially anthropologists, who have found a deep-set Confucianism in modern Vietnamese society.[66] Part of the answer lies in the as yet uninvestigated impact of Confucianism—how deeply into Vietnamese society did it go? Another part may well be a product of the Vietnamese ruling class under the immobilizing hand of French colonial rule. (See, for example, the emphasis placed on the family by the Franco-Annamite group in the 1920s and 1930s.)[67] We need to know much more about the modern transformation of the elite in Vietnam and of Vietnamese society in general before we can speculate further in this direction. It may be that the Viet Minh and the communists hewed closer to the cultural core of their people than their opponents, despite the former's foreign ideology. We need to ask now and in the future the contribution of Marxist ideology to Vietnamese culture in the same way that we ask it of Buddhism and Confucianism.

The Vietnamese cultural core would be a constant though shifting entity. What would count within it would be that which was considered essential and integtra1 to the culture at any given time. Foreign elements and ideologies would become grafted onto it, and the "core" of the twentieth century would differ greatly from that of two millennia before. The important fact is the Vietnamese ability to make any such "foreign-ness" Vietnamese.

NOTES

1. R. O. Winstedt, *The Malay Magician* (London, 1951); see Terry A. Rambo in Truong Buu Lam, ed., *Borrowings and Adaptations in Vietnamese Culture* (Manoa: Univ. of Hawaii Southeast Asian Studies, 1987).

2. For other statements on change in cultural systems, see Terry A. Rambo and Neil Jamieson in Truong Buu Lam, ed., *Borrowings and Adaptations*.

3. G. Coedès, *The Making of Southeast Asia,* trans. H. M. Wright (Berkeley, 1967), 17–19; K. W. Taylor, *The Birth of Vietnam* (Berkeley, 1983), 7–10, 312–313.

4. J. Kennedy, "From Stage to Development in Prehistoric Thailand," in K. Hutterer, ed., *Economic Exchange and Social Interaction in Southeast Asia* (Ann Arbor, 1977), 23–38; J. K. Whitmore, "The 'Opening' of Southeast Asia," in *ibid.,* 139–141.

5. Taylor, *Birth of Vietnam,* 14, 17–18, 29, 32, 78; Keith W. Taylor, "An Evaluation of the Chinese Period in Vietnamese History," *The Journal of Asiatic Studies* (Seoul) 23, 1 (1980): 142.

6. Taylor, *Birth of Vietnam,* 35.

7. *Ibid.,* 33–34, 36–41, 45–48; Taylor, "Evaluation of Chinese Period," 146–148.

8. Taylor, *Birth of Vietnam,* 48–57, 72–84; Taylor, "Evaluation of Chinese Period," 148–152.

9. K. R. Hall, "Eleventh Century Commercial Developments in Angkor and Champa," *JSEAS* 2 (1979):425–428; Taylor, "Evaluation of Chinese Period," 152; Wang Gungwu, "The Nan-hai Trade," *JMBRAS* 31, 2 (1958): 81–82, 84, 91, 93, 103, 104.

10. Taylor, *Birth of Vietnam,* 163–164, 264; Taylor, "Evaluation of Chinese Period," 153–154, 159.

11. O. W. Wolters, *The Fall of Srivijaya in Malay History* (Ithaca, N.Y., 1970), 34–35; F. Hirth and W. W. Rockhill, *Chau Ju-Kua* (New York, 1966 reprint), 45.

12. Hall, "Eleventh Century," 428–432; J. K. Whitmore, "Vietnam and the Monetary Flow of Eastern Asia, Thirteenth to Eighteenth Centuries," in J. F. Richards, ed., *Precious Metals in the Later Medieval and Early Modern Worlds* (Durham, N.C., 1983), 373–375; Peggy Chôy-Sutton, "The Rice Economy of Fourteenth Century Majapahit," in J. K. Whitmore, Chatthai Panananon, and K. R. Hall, eds., *Explorations in Early Southeast Asian History,* vol. 2 (forthcoming).

13. Tran Van Giap, "Le Bouddhisme en Annam," *BEFEO* 32 (1932): 220–227, 235–238, 243–245.

14. J. Boisselier, *La Statuaire du Champa* (Paris, 1963), 27, 77, 83–84, 88–89, 135–138, 143, 402; Giap, "Bouddhisme," 235, 253–254, 256, 261; K. W. Taylor, "The Rise of Dai Viet and the Establishment of Thang-long," in K. R. Hall and J. K. Whitmore, eds., *Explorations in Early Southeast Asian History,* vol. I (Ann Arbor, 1976), 179.

15. Taylor, "Rise of Dai Viet," 174–180.

16. L. Bezacier, *L'art vietnamien* (Paris, 1954), 17–18, 28, 34, 35, 53, 139–141, 181–186; Boisselier, *Statuaire,* 298–301.

17. Tran Van Khe, *La musique vietnamienne traditionelle* (Paris, 1962), 19.

18. *Ibid.,* 17–19, 21–22; A. B. Woodside, *Vietnam and the Chinese Model* (Cambridge, Mass., 1971), 23.

19. Khe, *Musique,* 16; Boisselier, *Statuaire,* 299, 303.

20. *Dai Viet Su Ky Toan Thu (TT)*, 4, 11a-b; trans., 1st ed. (Hanoi, 1967), I:286; Giap, "Bouddhisme," 250–252.

21. Ma Tuan-lin, *Ethnographie des peoples étrangers à la Chine*, trans. (Paris, 1883), II: 356; Boisselier, *Statuaire,* 299, 301.303.

22. *TT,* 3, 18b, 19a; (Hanoi), I:248–249; Giap, "Bouddhisme," 247, 261.

23. Taylor, "Rise of Dai Viet."

24. *Ibid.,* 180; TT, 3, 8a, 10a, llb, 12a; (Hanoi), I:236, 239–241.

25. Phan Huy Chu, *Lich Trieu Hien Chuong Loai Chi (HC),* trans. (Hanoi, 1961), II:6–7; III:6; R. B. Smith, "The Cycle of Confucianization in Vietnam," in W. F. Vella, ed., *Aspects of Vietnamese History* (Honolulu, 1973), 6–7.

26. *TT,* 3, 10a; (Hanoi), I:239; Chu, *HC,*II.69, 86.

27. Bezacier, *Art Vietnamien,* 117.

28. Chu, *HC,* II:69, 87; III:6–8; *TT,* 5, 11b, 17a, 20a; (Hanoi), II:16, 22, 25.

29. Chu, *HC,* II:115; IV:64; *TT,* 5, 15b; (Hanoi), II:20; Pham The Ngu, *Viet Nam Van Hoc Su* (Saigon, 1963), II:51–54; O. W. Wolters, "Le Van Huu's Treatment of Ly Than Ton's Reign (1127–1137)," in C. D. Cowan and O. W. Wolters, eds., *Southeast Asian History and Historiography* (Ithaca, N.Y., 1976), 203–226.

30. Chu, *HC,* II:69; Smith, "Cycle of Confucianization," 7–9.

31. *TT,* 6, 16b, 21a; (Hanoi), II:87, 92.

32. *TT,* 6, 22a–23b; (Hanoi), II:93–94.

33. Tran The Phap, *Linh Nam Chich Quai,* trans. (Saigon, 1960), 10, 98; Taylor, *Birth of Vietnam,* 356–357. Originally, this tale was placed second in the collection, behind only that of the original Vietnamese kings, but at the end of the fifteenth century, following the crushing defeat of the Chams in 1471, it was placed twenty-first.

34. *TT,* 7, 21a–b; (Hanoi), II:145.

35. *TT,* 7, 33a-b; (Hanoi), II:158–159; O. W. Wolters, "Assertions of Cultural Well-Being in Fourteenth Century Vietnam," *JSEAS,* 10, 2 (1979): 444, 447–448.

36. J. K. Whitmore, "Crisis, Reform, and Defeat: Vietnam and Ho Quy Ly, 1360–1407," ms., 1976; Nguyen Dinh-Hoa in Truong Buu Lam, ed., *Borrowings and Adaptations*; Smith, "Cycle of Confucianization," 9.

37. J. K. Whitmore, "Chiao-chih and Neo-Confucianism," *Ming Studies* 4 (1977):51–91.

38. J. K. Whitmore, *Transforming Dai Viet* (forthcoming), chap. 2; Khe, *Musique,* 29–32.

39. Whitmore, *Transforming Dai Viet,* chaps. 3–4.

40. *Ibid.,* chap. 5; Smith, "Cycle of Confucianization," 11–12. On the new Chinese terms coming into the Vietnamese language, see Nguyen Dinh-Hoa in Truong Buu Lam, ed., *Borrowings and Adaptations*; for the standard Chinese poetic forms, see Cong Huyen Ton Nu Nha Trang in Truong Buu Lam, ed., *Borrowings and Adaptations*; and for a statement on Confucian beliefs, see Nguyen Dang Liem in Truong Buu Lam, ed., *Borrowings and Adaptations.*

41. Nguyen Ngoc Huy, "Le Code des Le: *Quoc Trieu Hinh Luat ou* 'Lois Penales de la Dynastie Nationale'," *BEEEO* 67 (1980): 147–220; "On the Codification of the National Dynasty's Penal Laws (Quoc Trien Hinh Luat)," *The Vietnam Forum* 1 (1983): 34–57.

42. *TT,* 12, 52a; (Hanoi), III:226.

43. "Legal Section," *Thien Nam Du Ha Tap* (A.3334); R. Deloustal, "Du huong-hoa," *BEFEO* 11 (1911): 50–62.

44. S. B. Young, "The Law of Property and Elite Prerogatives during Vietnam's Le Dynasty: 1428–1788," *Journal of Asian History* 10, 1 (1976): 12–13.

45. J. K. Whitmore, "Mac Dang Dung," *Dictionary of Ming Biography* (New York, 1976), II:1029–1035; "The Five Hundredth Anniversary of Mac Dang Dung's Birth," *The Vietnam Forum* (forthcoming); Smith, "Cycle of Confucianization," 14–16.

46. J. K. Whitmore, "Social Organization and Confucian Thought in Vietnam," *JSEAS* (forthcoming); Deloustal, "*Huong-hoa,*" 58, n. 1; *Hong-duc Thien Chinh Thu* (A. 330), 1a, 4a–8a.

47. K. W. Taylor, "The Literati Revival in Seventeenth Century Vietnam," in Whitmore, Chatchai Panananon, and Hall, *Explorations in Early Southeast Asian History,* vol. 2; Smith, "Cycle of Confucianization," 15–18; R. Deloustal, "Code de Procedure," *BEFEO* 19, 4 (1919): 435–515.

48. Nguyen Than Nha, *Tableau économique du Vietnam aux XVIIe et XVIIIe Siècles* (Paris, 1970); Smith, "Cycle of Confucianization," 18.

49. J. K. Whitmore, "Bureaucratic Control of the Spirits," paper presented at the Association of Asian Studies meeting, Washington, D.C., 1980.

50. Woodside, *Chinese Model,* 262; Taylor, "Literati Revival"; Smith, "Cycle of Confucianization," 16–17, 19; John DeFrancis in Truong Buu Lam, ed., *Borrowings and Adaptations*; Whitmore, "Monetary Flow," 379–387.

51. Woodside, *Chinese Model,* 3, 16–18; Smith, "Cycle of Confucianization," 20–21.

52. Woodside, *Chinese Model;* Smith, "Cycle of Confucianization," 21–24.

53. See J. K. Whitmore, "Note: The Vietnamese Confucian Scholar's View of His Country's Early History," in Hall and Whitmore, *Explorations in Early Southeast Asian History,* vol. 1, 193–203; Taylor, *Birth of Vietnam,* 165.

54. *TT,* 7, 33a—b; (Hanoi), II:158–159.

55. Taylor, *Birth of Vietnam,* 13, 34, 36, 39, 75–78, 130.

56. Wolters, "Le Van Huu," 203–226.

57. Whitmore, "Social Organization."

58. Taylor, *Birth of Vietnam,* 1–7, 303–305, 316–319, 334–339, 353–357; J. K. Whitmore, "The Vietnamese Sense of the Past," *The Vietnam Forum* 1 (1983): 4–8.

59. Whitmore, *Transforming Dai Viet,* chap. 2.

60. Whitmore, "Bureaucratic Control of Spirits."

61. Whitmore, "Vietnamese Sense of the Past," 8–10.

62. J. K. Whitmore, "The Oath of Alliance in Southeast Asia," in Whitmore, Chatchai Panananon, and Hall, *Explorations in Early Southeast Asian History,* vol. 2.

63. Whitmore, "Monetary Flow," 363–393; "Social Organization."

64. Luong Than et al., trans., *Le Trieu Hinh Luat* (Saigon, 1956).

65. Yu Insun, "Law and Family in the Seventeenth and Eighteenth Century Vietnam," Ph.D. diss., 1978, University of Michigan.

66. See articles by Whitmore and Haines in *JSEAS* (forthcoming) and by Neil Jamieson in Truong Buu Lam, ed., *Borrowings and Adaptations.*

67. D. G. Marr, *Vietnamese Tradition on Trial, 1920–1945* (Berkeley, 1981), 110–112. For another example of such a statement, see the article by Pham Quynh's granddaughter, Phung Thi Hanh, "The Family in Vietnam and Its Social Life," in J. K. Whitmore, ed., *An Introduction to Indochinese History, Culture, Language, and Life* (Ann Arbor, 1979), 77–84.

3

State and Kingship in Southeast Asia

ROBERT HEINE-GELDERN*

Robert Heine-Geldern (1885–1968), an Austrian aristocrat who taught at the University of Vienna, was an eminent ethnologist, anthropologist, and art historian of the established but controversial diffusionist school of thought, which held that culture was transmitted through migration and trade. Beginning in 1923, when he "opened the field of Southeast Asian anthropology," he wrote extensively in German and English, principally on Southeast Asia, until his death in 1968 at the age of eighty-three. By the time he migrated to the United States during World War II, he had received the highest honors from Great Britain, France, the United States, and, indeed, Austria for his distinguished scholarship. While in the United States, he worked at New York's American Museum of Natural History. He was, with Margaret Mead, a co-founder in 1941 of the East Indies Institute of America (later known as the Southeast Asia Institute), which later was absorbed into the Association for Asian Studies. The *Far Eastern Quarterly* later became the *Journal of Asian Studies.*

Of all Heine-Geldern's writings, his essay "Conceptions of State and Kingship in Southeast Asia," published in 1942, has been rightly regarded a "classic." His ideas on the origins, rituals, and notions of obligation of monarchy in the diverse countries of Southeast Asia in the pre-modern period remain essentially valid, though the manner in which they were

---

*Robert Heine-Geldern, "Conceptions of State and Kingship in Southeast Asia," *Far Eastern Quarterly* 2 (1942): 15–30.

brought to the region—either by diffusion or by local initiative—is still controversial.

~

What were the religious and philosophical conceptions which underlay and shaped the states of Southeast Asia? Are they still living forces with which we have to count or are they dead and gone? . . . In view of the limited space, I shall confine myself to a discussion of some conceptions of state and kingship in those parts of Southeast Asia where Hindu-Buddhist civilization prevailed.

Macrocosmos and Microcosmos

The primary notion with which we shall have to deal is the belief in the parallelism between Macrocosmos and Microcosmos, between the universe and the world of men. According to this belief, humanity is constantly under the influence of forces emanating from the directions of the compass and from stars and planets. These forces may produce welfare and prosperity or work havoc, according to whether or not individuals and social groups, above all the state, succeed in bringing their lives and activities in harmony with the universe. Individuals may attain such harmony by following the indications offered by astrology, the lore of lucky and unlucky days and many other minor rules. Harmony between the empire and the universe is achieved by organizing the former as an image of the latter, as a universe on a smaller scale.

It is well known that this astrological or cosmo-magic principle, as we may call it, originated somewhere in the Near East. It was well established in Babylonia in the 3rd millennium BC and there are indications that it may go back there at least as far as the middle of the 4th millennium, and possibly farther. Again, we have indications that it existed in northwest India in the second half of the 3rd millennium. It influenced Europe in various ways and at various times, specially during the periods of Hellenism and of the Roman empire and in the Middle Ages. It is difficult to tell when it first reached China. Anyway it had developed there into a highly specialized system during the Chou and Han periods. It came to Southeast Asia by way of India as well as of China, and this double influence may account for its prominence there and for the strong hold it had on the minds of the peoples of Farther India and Indonesia. Its long life-span and its spread over vast regions with divergent cultures, and even more so the fact that it had to adapt itself to the locally dominant religions, to various forms of paganism as well as to Hinduism, Buddhism and Confucianism, and occasionally even to Christianity and to Islam, naturally resulted in the development of numerous variants with often widely differing traits. It is with the special aspect of the cosmo-magic principle as expressed in the organization of Hindu and Buddhist kingdoms in Southeast Asia (and to some extent in their Mohammedan successors in Malaya and Indonesia) that we are here concerned.

Relation Between State and Universe

Whereas speculation pertaining to the relation between state and universe formed an important subject of ancient Chinese literature, we would look in vain for a theoretical treatise on this topic in the various literatures of Southeast Asia.[1] Yet, there is overwhelming evidence of the cosmological basis of state and kingship in this area. This evidence is found in numerous passages in literature and inscriptions, in the titles of kings, queens and officials, in the "cosmic" numbers of queens, ministers, court priests, provinces, etc., in rites and customs, in works of art, in the lay-out and structure of capital cities, palaces and temples. One need only put these various items together to obtain a relatively clear picture. This picture will be more complete in continental Southeast Asia, where the old forms of Buddhist state and kingship survived into very recent times. It will be hazier in the archipelago as a result of Mohammedan and European influences.

According to Brahmanic doctrine, the world consists of a circular central continent, Jambudvipa, surrounded by seven annular oceans and seven annular continents. Beyond the last of the seven oceans the world is closed by an enormous mountain range. In the center of Jambudvipa, and thus in the center of the world, rises Mount Meru, the cosmic mountain around which sun, moon and stars revolve. On its summit lies the city of the gods surrounded by the abodes of the eight Lokapalas or guardian gods of the world.

In the Buddhist system, too, Mount Meru forms the center of the universe. It is surrounded by seven mountain ranges separated from each other by seven annular seas. Beyond the last of these mountain chains extends the ocean and in it lie four continents, one in each of the cardinal directions. The continent south of Mount Meru is Jambudvipa, the abode of men. Here, too, the universe is surrounded by an enormous wall of rocks, the Chakravala range. On the slopes of Mount Meru lies the lowest of the paradises, that of the four Great Kings or guardians of the world, on its summit the second paradise, that of the thirty-three gods with Sudarsana, the city of the gods, where Indra reigns as king. Above Mount Meru tower one above the other the rest of the heavenly abodes.[2]

It will be seen that the Brahman and the Buddhist systems, in spite of differences in detail, agree in fundamental traits: their circular form and the arrangement in concentric zones around Mount Meru. An abbreviated image of either of them thus has the same symbolic meaning for devotees of both faiths.

The Capital as the Magic Center of Empire

In Southeast Asia, even more than in Europe, the capital stood for the whole country. It was more than the nation's political and cultural center: it was the magic center of the empire. The circumambulation of the capital formed, and in Siam and Cambodia still forms [in 1942], one of the most essential parts of the coronation ritual. By this circumambulation the king takes possession not only of the capital city but of the whole empire. Whereas the cosmological structure of the country at large could be expressed only by the number and location of provinces and by the functions and emblems of their governors, the capital city could be shaped architecturally as a much more "realistic" image of the universe, a smaller microcosmos within that macrocosmos, the empire. The remains of some of the ancient cities clearly testify to the cosmological ideas which pervaded the whole system of government. Fortunately a number of inscriptions and some passages in native chronicles may help us in interpreting archaeological evidence.

As the Universe, according to Brahman and Buddhist ideas, centers around Mount Meru, so that smaller universe, the empire, was bound to have a Mount Meru in the center of its capital which would be if not in the country's geographical center, at least in its magic center. It seems that at an early period natural hillocks were by preference selected as representatives of the celestial mountain. This was still the case in Cambodia in the 9th century AD. Yasodharapura, the first city of Angkor, founded towards 900 AD, formed an enormous square of about two and a half miles on a side, with its sides facing the cardinal points and with the Phnom Bakheng, a small rocky hill, as center. An inscription tells us that this mountain in the center of the capital with the temple on its summit was "equal in beauty to the king of mountains," i.e., to Mount Meru.[3] The temple on Phnom Bakheng contained a Lingam, the phallic symbol of Siva, representing the Devaräja, the "God King," i.e., the divine essence of kingship which embodied itself in the actual king. More frequently the central mountain was purely artificial, being represented by a temple only. This was quite in accordance with prevailing ideas, practically every temple in Southeast Asia, whether Hindu or Buddhist, whether built of stone, brick or wood, being considered as the image of a mountain, usually, though not invariably, of Mount Meru. In ancient Cambodia a temple was quite ordinarily referred to as "giri," mountain, and the many-tiered temples of Bali are still called Meru. The Cambodian inscriptions are very explicit with regard to such identifications. Thus, to give an example, one of them says that King Udayadityavarman II (11th century) "seeing that the Jambudvipa had in its center a mountain of gold, provided for his capital city, too, to have a golden mountain in its interior. On the summit of this golden mountain, in a celestial palace resplendent with gold, he erected a Lingam of Siva."

The Lay-out of Angkor Thom

The actual ruins of Angkor Thom are the remains of the latest city on this site, built by King Jayavarman VII in the second half of the 12th century AD. As Jayavarman was an adherent of Mahayana Buddhism, the central "mountain" in this case was a temple not of Siva, but of the Bodhisatva Lokesvara, the "Lord of the World," whose four faces adorn its numerous towers. The city was surrounded with a wall and moat forming a square almost two miles on each side, its sides being directed towards the four cardinal points. There are gates in the middle of each side and a fifth one on the East leading to the entrance of the royal palace. The towers above the gates are crowned with the same four-fold faces of Lokesvara as those of the central temple. Thus, that smaller world, the city of Angkor and through its means the whole Khmer empire, were both put under the protection of the "Lord of the Universe." The cosmic meaning of the city was further emphasized by a curious device. The balustrades of the causeways leading over the moat to the city gates were formed by rows of giant stone figures, partly gods, and demons, when they used the serpent king Vasuki as a rope and Mount Meru as a churning stick.[4] This implies that the moat was meant to symbolize the ocean and the Bayon, the temple in the center of the city, on which the lines of churning gods and demons converged, Mount Meru itself.

The Capital of Burma [Myanmar]

Burmese chronicles say that Srikshetra (Old Prome) on the lower Irrawaddy, the capital city of the ancient kingdom of the Pyu, was built by the gods with Indra at their head, built as an image of Indra's city Sudarsana on the summit of Mount Meru, with thirty-two main gates and a golden palace in its center. The remains of the city show in fact a decided attempt at a circular lay-out though complete regularity has not been achieved. It seems to have been an old custom in Burma that each of the capital's gates corresponded to one of the empire's provinces or vassal states. Thirty-two vassals or heads of provinces with the king as thirty-third in the center would of course correspond to the thirty-three gods who reside on the summit of Meru and among whom Indra is king. Thus not only the capital city but the whole empire of the Pyu must have been organized as an image of the heavenly realm of Indra.

In later capitals of Burma the square form was substituted for the circular one though the cosmological principle as such was retained. It will suffice to say a few words about Mandalay, the last capital of independent Burma, built by King Mindon in 1857 AD. The inner city was surrounded by a wall and moat forming a square of more than a mile on each side, its sides facing the cardinal points. The royal palace, which occupied the center of the city, and more specifically the seven-tiered tower over the throne in the great audience hall, was identified with Mount Meru. There were three gates on each side of the city, twelve in all, and they were marked with the signs of the zodiac, thereby indicating that the city was meant to be an image of heaven with its stars spread out around the celestial mountain in its center.

Cosmic Roles of King, Court and Government

Thus the stage was set for the enacting of the cosmic roles of king, court and government. We may choose Burma as an example. There, the king was supposed to have four principal queens and four queens of secondary rank whose titles, "Northern Queen of the Palace," "Queen of the West," "Queen of the Southern Apartment," etc., show that they originally corresponded to the four cardinal points and the four intermediary directions. There are indications that at an earlier period their chambers actually formed a circle around the hall of the king, thereby emphasizing the latter's role as center of the universe and as representative of Indra, the king of the gods in the paradise on the summit of Mount Meru. Sir James George Scott's observation that King Thibaw's (the last Burmese king) failure to provide himself with the constitutional number of queens caused more concern to decorous, law-abiding people than the massacre of his blood relations, shows how important this cosmic setting was considered to be.[5] There were four chief ministers each of whom, in addition to their functions as ministers of state, originally had charge of one quarter of the capital and of the empire. They obviously corresponded to the four Great Kings or Lokapalas, the guardian deities of the four cardinal points in the Buddhist system. However, the task of representing the four Lokapalas had been delegated to four special officers, each of whom had to guard one side of the palace and of the capital. They had flags in the colors attributed to the corresponding sides of Mount Meru, the one representing Dhattarattha, the Lokapala of the East, a white one, the officer representing Kubera, the Lokapala of the North, a yellow flag, etc. The cosmological principle was carried far down through the hierarchy of officialdom, as revealed by the numbers of office bearers. Thus, there were four under-secretaries of state, eight assistant secretaries, four heralds, four royal messengers, etc.

Very much the same kind of organization existed in Siam, Cambodia and Java. Again and again we find the orthodox number of four principal queens, and of four chief ministers, the "four pillars" as they were called in Cambodia. In Siam, as in Burma, they originally governed four parts of the kingdom lying toward the four cardinal points.

There are indications that in ancient time the cosmological structure of the state was carried even farther. I have already mentioned the probability that the old kingdom of the Pyu in Burma had thirty-two provinces or vassal states, their governors together with the king having corresponded to the thirty-three gods of the paradise on the summit of Mount Meru. Similarly, the kingdom of Pegu in the 14th century had thirty-two provinces. The principality of Keng Tung, one of the largest Shan states, significantly is called "The Thirty-two Towns of the Khun," the Khun being the ruling tribe in that state. A passage in the New History of the T'ang Dynasty indicates that the kingdom of Java in the 9th century was divided into twenty-eight provinces, their governors together with the four ministers again having numbered thirty-two high officials. This may have been a somewhat older form of the same system, in which the provinces corresponded to constellations, the twenty-eight "Houses of the Moon," and the four ministers to the guardian gods of the cardinal points. It is clear that in all these cases the empire was conceived as an image of the heavenly world of stars and gods.

Throughout the kingdoms of Farther India the system based on the compass was largely supplemented and modified by the division into offices of the right and left hand, right and left in this case referring to the place on the side of the king due to the respective office bearer on ceremonial occasions. As the king, when sitting on the throne, always faced the East, right corresponded to the South and left to the North. In Siam, for instance, there were a major and a lesser queen each of the right and of the left. Civilian officers had their places on the left of the king, officers of the army on his right, i.e., "in the South," because the planet Mars, connected with war, was considered to be the planet of the South. Indeed, the population of Siam was divided into two classes of the right (South) and of the left (North). The former had to render military and the latter civilian services.

Influence on Coronation Ritual

The cosmic and divine role of the king was and still is specially emphasized in the coronation ritual. In Burma the structure erected for this purpose was significantly called Thagya-nan, "Indra's Palace."[6] Even in the Buddhist kings of Farther India the ritual is conducted by Brahmans. One of its primal features consists in the king sitting on a throne representing Mount Meru and being surrounded by eight Brahmans as representatives of the eight Lokapalas, the guardian gods of the eight directions in the Brahman world system. Moreover, four maids of honor, representing the four cardinal points, render homage to the king.

An official document published on the occasion of the coronation of King Sisowath of Cambodia in 1906 gives a slightly different explanation of the role of the king. According to this document the king is identified with Mount Meru itself, his right eye representing the sun, his left eye the moon, his arms and legs the four cardinal points, the six-tiered umbrella above his head the six lower heavens, his pointed crown the spire of Indra's palace on the summit of the Meru and his slippers the earth. This means that the king is identified with the axis of the universe. The same idea seems to be expressed by the title Paku Buwono, "Nail of the World," of the Susuhunan of Solo in Java. However, the identification of the king with the Meru is in no way incompatible with that with Indra. Plural symbolism is very frequent in Buddhist Farther India. Thus in Burma, where the king has all the attributes of Indra, he was also identified with Visvakarma, the divine architect and shaper of the world. Moreover, there is strong evidence of his having been identified also with the sun.

The Cosmic State and the Divine King

The cosmic state, as it existed in Southeast Asia, was intimately bound up with the idea of divine kingship. The divinity of kings was conceived in various ways according to the prevailing religion. Where Hinduism prevailed, the king was considered to be either an incarnation of a god or a descendant from a god or both. Mostly it was Siva who was thought to incarnate himself in kings or to engender dynasties. Thus in a Cham inscription of the 9th century Uroja, the founder of the royal dynasty is said to have been a son of Siva. The Javanese poem Nagarakrtagama (14th century) says bluntly that all kings are incarnations of Siva. The same poem tells us more specially that King Rajasanagara of Majapahit (1350–1389 AD), as proved by various portents which occurred about the time of his birth, among others a volcanic eruption, was an incarnation of Bhatara Girinatha, i.e., Siva as "Lord of the

Mountain." In the Javanese chronicle Pararaton, King Krtajaya of Kadiri (13th century) on one occasion even shows himself in the superhuman form of Siva with four arms and a third eye in the middle of the forehead and floating in the air. In ancient Cambodia and Champa the monarchy was intimately bound up with the cult of a Lingam which was considered the seat of the divine essence of kingship. As we have seen, in Cambodia this Lingam, representing the Devaräja, the "God King," was adored in the temple in the center of the capital. The actual king was considered to be a manifestation of divine power of the Devaräja and therefore, as the latter's visible form, the Lingam, implies, obviously of Siva himself.

However, Siva was not the only god to incarnate himself in kings. King Airlangga of Java (11th century) considered himself an incarnation of the Vishnu. His memorial monument shows him in the form of Vishnu riding on the latter's man-eagle Garuda. Another noteworthy example of an incarnation of Vishnu was King Suryavarman II of Cambodia (12th century) who erected his own memorial monument as a gigantic temple of Vishnu: the famous Angkor Vat. We find further the idea of plural incarnation, also known from ancient India. Thus the Pararaton tells us that Angrok (13th century), the founder of the dynasty of Singasari and ancestor of the kings of Majapahit, was an incarnation of Vishnu, begotten by Brahma from a mortal woman, and at the same time a son of Siva. King Krtarajasa (died 1316 AD), the founder of the empire of Majapahit, is immortalized by a statue representing him as Harihara, a compound of Vishnu and Siva. Even the simultaneous incarnation of Hindu and Mahayana Buddhist deities occurs. Thus, to quote only one example, the Javanese king Krtanagara (killed 1292 AD) was considered as an incarnation of Siva as well as of the Dhyani Akshobhya. Accordingly, he became known in Javanese tradition under the name of Siva-Buddha.

It may be added that the theory of divine incarnation could be used not only as a means to exalt the position of the legitimate king, but equally well as a justification for usurpation of the throne. Thus the above-mentioned Angrok, the founder of the kingdom of Singasari, was a usurper with a long criminal career as embezzler, robber and murderer. Yet, in spite of his criminal past, he became king, according to the Pararaton, because he was an incarnation of the gods.

The theory of divine incarnation as found in Hinduism and Mahayana Buddhism is incompatible with the doctrine of the Buddhism of the Hinayana. This difference in tenets is clearly expressed even in the lay-out of capital cities. In ancient Cambodia a temple formed the center of the capital and thus the Mount Meru of city and empire. In Burma the center of the capital is invariably occupied by the royal palace, and it is this latter which identified with

Mount Meru. In ancient Cambodia either Siva in his form as Devarāja, the eternal essence of kingship, or the Bodhisatva Lokesvara, the "Lord of the Universe," inhabited the "central mountain" and from there pervaded the empire. Hinayanist Buddhism does not recognize an eternal deity. Indra is but the king of one of the lowest heavens, the second one from the earth. He is as little exempt from death and rebirth as any human being, except that his life lasts longer. The same may be said of the inhabitants of the higher heavens. All these "gods" of Hinayana Buddhism should more appropriately be called angels. They have no temples and no cults. Thus it is easy to understand why in Burma no temple could be set in the center of the capital city. The adaptation to cosmological principles and the deification of the king here had to be attempted by other means. By erecting the palace in the center of the city and by identifying it with Mount Meru, the lord of the palace, i.e., the king, became automatically the representative of Indra. We might even say that he was "the Indra" of this smaller universe, the Burmese empire, but he held his place only by the magic parallelism, and he was no incarnation of the real Indra as the ancient Javanese and Cambodian kings had been incarnations of Siva and Vishnu.[7] The scheme explains the great sanctity in which the royal palace was held in the Buddhist empires of Farther India. The palace was the symbol of the celestial mountain, nay, more than a mere symbol: it was "the Mount Meru" of the microcosmos Burma, or Siam, or Cambodia. Anybody nearing the palace had to show his reverence by dismounting from his horse, by shutting his parasol, by bowing to the palace spire or even kneeling down. Attempts to exact the same expressions of reverence from British envoys led to endless negotiations and frictions as the latter refused to comply with a demand which they considered humiliating. "King of the Golden Palace" was one of the most important titles of Burmese monarchs. Yet, the fact that the king was Indra and therefore ruler of the country only as possessor of the empire's Meru, the palace, involved great dangers. It worked as a constant temptation for would-be usurpers, be it from the ranks of the royal family or outsiders, the occupation of the palace might be achieved by a coup-de-main with relatively small forces and usually meant the conquest of the whole empire. Many Burmese and Siamese kings therefore were virtual prisoners in their palace which they did not dare to leave for fear it might be seized by a usurper. The last king of Burma, Thibaw, preferred even to forego the important coronation ritual of the circumambulation of the capital to offering one of his relatives a chance to make himself master of the palace while he was away.

In Hinayana Buddhism the idea of divine incarnation as justification of kingship is replaced by that of rebirth and of religious merit. It is his good karma, his religious merit acquired in previous lives, which makes a man born a king or makes him acquire kingship during his lifetime, be it even by rebellion and murder. A typical instance is that of King Nyaung-u Sawrahan (10th century) as told in the Glass Palace Chronicle of the Kings of Burma. Nyaung-u Sawrahan, a farmer, kills the king who has trespassed on his garden and whom he had not recognized. Thereupon he is himself made king against his wish. So strong is his karma that, when one of the ministers objects to his installation, the stone statue of a guardian deity at the palace door becomes alive and kills the minister. The chronicle's comment is significant:

"Although in verity king Sawrahan should have utterly perished, having killed a king when he was yet a farmer, he attained even to kingship simply by strong karma of his good acts done in the past." But the moment the karma of his past good acts is exhausted, that same stone statue which formerly had killed his adversary becomes alive again and hurls him from the palace terrace.

No merit could exceed that of a service rendered to the Buddha himself. Thus the Glass Palace Chronicle tells us that the ogre-guardian of a mountain, who had shielded the Buddha from the sun with three leaves, had received from the latter a prophecy that he would thrice become the king of Burma. In the 10th century, he is reborn in lowly surroundings as Saleh Ngahkwe, who later becomes king by murdering his predecessor and "being reborn from the state of an ogre, was exceedingly wrathful and haughty," indulging in gluttony and sadistic murder, till he is at last killed by his own ministers. One should think that the merit of having shaded the Buddha would have been exhausted by a life full of crimes. However, according to the Burmese chronicles, this is not so. The former mountain spirit is reborn in the 12th century as Prince Narathu who becomes king by murdering his father and brother and throughout his reign excels by bloody deeds, and in the 13th century as King Narathihapate. This leads us to a very characteristic conception of historical events as based on the enormous importance attributed to the prophecies and portents. Indeed, one could say that, especially as far as alleged prophecies of the Buddha are concerned, in the view of Burmese historians, events are not prophesied because they will happen, but they happen because they have been prophesied. The "discovery" of ancient prophecies and the "observation" of contemporary portents was a generally used expedient in Burmese politics and still forms a potent factor in what we may call political folk-lore.

The whole idea and outward form of kingship in Southeast Asia, and specially in the Buddhist kingdoms of Farther India, was of course based on the conception of the Chakravartin, the Universal Monarch. Now it is known that a Chakravartin is the worldly alternative to a Bodhisatva, a future Buddha. Under these circumstances the theory of rebirth and of karma was bound to induce monarchs with a very high idea of their religious merits to consider themselves as Bodhisatvas. Thus, Oung Zaya, the founder of the last dynasty of Burma, took as king the name Alaungpaya which designated him as an Embryo Buddha. His son, King Bodawpaya (1782–1819), claimed outright to be the Bodhisatva Maitreya. However, his claim was rejected by the clergy and he dropped it. A similar claim was put forth by King Taksin of Siam (1767–1782).

The theory of vocation to kingship either on the basis of divine incarnation, as in Java and ancient Cambodia, or by karma acquired in former lives as in Burma, Siam and modern Cambodia, did not deprive that of the heredity of the right to the crown of its importance. Again and again usurpers have striven for a semblance of legitimacy by construing genealogies linking themselves either to the dynasty they had overthrown or to a dynasty which in an earlier period had governed the country. Occasionally, fantastic genealogies were constructed deriving native Southeast Asiatic dynasties from some famous dynasty of ancient India. The best known case is that of the recent kings of Cambodia who claim descent from the ancient kings of Indraprastha (Delhi). The last Burmese dynasty, founded by a village headman in the 18th century, claimed descent from the Sakya kings of Kapilavatthu, a claim which would have made them blood relatives of the Buddha himself. One type of such fictitious genealogies deserves special attention as it has a deeper meaning than merely to serve the glorification of the dynasty. The kings of Funan (3rd to 7th centuries AD) and those of ancient Cambodia were said to descend from a Brahman who had come from India and from the daughter of the serpent king of the country. The legend is still alive in Cambodia, the Brahman being replaced in the modern version by a prince of Indraprastha. It seems that similar dynastic legends existed in most parts of Southeast Asia. The meaning is clear. The Nagas, the serpent demons, are the original masters of the soil. By his descent from the daughter of the Naga king, the monarch had a legitimate claim to the soil of his kingdom which, in theory at least, thereby became his personal property. A Chinese report tells us that in the 13th century the people of Cambodia believed that the king nightly cohabited with the serpent goddess of the soil who visited him in his palace in human form. Obviously he was thought thereby to renew the connection between himself and the soil of his kingdom. Thus the king in ancient Cambodia, as an incarnation of the Devarāja and as a descendant and at the same time spouse of the goddess of the soil, formed a real magic center linking the empire to the divine forces of the heavens as well as of the earth.

Any account of the conceptions of state and kingship in Southeast would be incomplete without at least mentioning the great importance of regalia.

Some of these, as the umbrella and the crown, have cosmological meaning as noted above. Moreover, the umbrella was thought to be the seat of a protective genius who favored the king with his advice and who in critical moments might even actively intervene on behalf of the dynasty. Other regalia are thought to be possessed of magic forces, such as the royal sword of Cambodia which it is believed, if drawn from its scabbard without the prescribed ritual, would bring disaster upon the country. This magical character of the regalia is even more stressed in the Malay Peninsula and in Indonesia. It culminates in the curious conception prevalent among the Bugis and Macassarese of Celebes, according to which it is really the regalia which reign, the prince governing the state only in their name.

The deification of the king, while raising him to an almost unbelievably exalted position with regard to his subjects, has in no way succeeded in stabilizing government, rather the contrary. As explained above, the theory of divine incarnation and even more so that of rebirth and of karma, provided an easy subterfuge for usurpers. The fact that the relatively easy task of seizing the palace, as in Burma and Siam, or of seizing the regalia as in certain parts of Indonesia, often sufficed to be accepted as king by the whole nation was bound to act as an additional incitement to rebellion. Moreover, the immense power and the lack of restrictions which the king enjoyed invited abuses which in the end made the monarch obnoxious to his subjects and hastened his downfall. To this came the vagueness of the rules of succession. Sometimes the king himself chose his successor. Sometimes the ministers appointed a prince as king. Then again the queens unofficially but efficiently exercised their influence in favor of a prince of their choice. Often the crown simply fell to the prince who was the quickest to seize the palace and to execute his brothers. Under these circumstances it is no wonder that the empires of Southeast Asia from the very beginning were torn by frequent rebellion, often resulting in the overthrow of kings and even dynasties. The earliest reports we have, those from Chinese sources on the kingdom of Funan, reveal such conditions to have existed as early as the 3rd century AD. If there was a long period of oppression and unrest, rebellion and its concomitant, dacoity, could become practically a popular tradition which it was difficult to eradicate. Such was the case, for instance, in Burma during the 18th and 19th centuries, and it is in the light of such a past that recent events in that country ought to be seen.

Survival of Traditions

In order to realize how deeply the populations of Farther India were affected by the cosmological structure of the state, one need only think of the division of the Siamese people into the classes of the right and of the left which, not long ago, determined the services each person was obliged to render to the state. Moreover, it must not be forgotten that the cosmo-magic principle as applied to the state really forms only part of a much wider complex and resulted from a conception of the universe and of human existence which regulated, and to a large extent still regulates, also the private lives of individuals. When in Siam and Cambodia people wear clothes of different color on different days of the week according to the color ascribed to the planet for whom the day is named, or when in Burma before any important undertaking they examine their horoscope and the lore of lucky and unlucky days, or when they kneel down for prayer on that side of the pagoda which in the cosmological system corresponds to the planet of the weekday on which they were born, they act on the same principle which governed the structure of their empires, their ideas of king-ship and the ritual of their royal courts. It is clear then that the cosmo-magic ideas, until a very recent past, had an extremely strong hold on the minds of the people.

Is all this a crumbling structure, giving way under the impact of modern civilization or may it still influence the political activities of the peoples concerned? The question is not easily answered. Information on this point is scarce. There are, however, a few indications.

We have it on the authority of H. G. Quaritch Wales that the people of Siam, around 1930, still held the ancient state ceremonies in high esteem, those ceremonies which to a large extent are governed by cosmological ideas. One may ask oneself, how much of this old tradition may have been at the bottom of the royalist rebellion of 1933.

In Burma the following cases may be considered as significant. In 1897, twelve years after the annexation of Upper Burma by the British, a Buddhist, monk, U Kelatha, fell in love with a princess of the dethroned dynasty who promised to marry him if he became king of Burma. There followed the dreams or visions which revealed to him that in a former life he had been a Burmese prince and, moreover, that he would be king the moment he sat on the throne of the palace in Mandalay. With eighteen followers, all armed with swords only, he rushed through the city gates and tried to reach the royal palace, at that time seat of the English club. A few English officers armed with hunting rifles made an end to his attempt. The incident proves the extreme vividness of cosmo-magic ideas at the close of the 19th century. As we have seen, whoever held the palace, the Mount Meru of the Burmese empire, thereby became the representative of Indra and king. It is completely in accord with the cosmo-magic way of thinking that U Kelatha and his followers believed the mere occupation of the throne would make him automatically lord of the whole empire.

Unfortunately, very little authentic information is available on the Burmese rebellion of 1930–31, however, the following detail, as revealed at the time by newspaper dispatches, is significant. One of the first actions of Sanya San, the leader of the rebellion, was to build a "palace," in reality a bamboo hut somewhere in the jungle, with an inscription designating it as the "Palace of the Buddhist King." It is, of course, very easy to ridicule such pretensions, but it is more important to understand them. We have seen how inseparable king and palace were according to Burmese ideas. No kingdom could exist without a palace representing Mount Meru and forming its magic center, and the king, the "Lord of the Golden Palace," was king in the first line by his possession of the palace. Saya San's action in building a palace, a magic center for his embryonic empire, therefore corresponds closely to that of U Kelatha when he wanted to seat himself on the throne of the palace in Mandalay.

The story of the Myinmu rebellion of 1910, as told by Paul Edmonds in his book *Peacocks and Pagodas,* if it does not directly contribute to our knowledge of cosmo-magic ideas, at least gives a significant instance of the power of the belief in rebirth, prophecies and portents. A young man of eighteen years, Maung Than, was returning from work in the fields smoking a cigar. Some people who passed him thought they saw smoke issuing from his arms. They talked about it in the village, and the rumor reached some elders who were familiar with an old tradition according to which a former king of Burma, Chanyeiktha, would be reborn in the shape of a youth who had the power of making smoke issue from his arms. "Other signs and portents were looked for. Needless to say, they were forthcoming. The griffins at the foot of an old pagoda were seen to shake; gold showers fell on another pagoda; and everywhere omens multiplied which pointed to young Maung Than as the long-foretold reincarnation of king Chanyeiktha." Maung Than entered into the spirit of the game and put forth the usual claims of being invulnerable and of possessing the power to make himself invisible. With a crowd of a thousand followers armed with swords and spears he attacked the police station at Myinmu but was repulsed and eventually captured.

These incidents may suffice to show how lively the ideas of cosmic state and kingship, of rebirth and prophecy, still are in Burma. I have little doubt that they played a role in the events accompanying the Japanese invasion. It can easily be predicted that whatever government will exist in Burma after the war, will have to reckon with these ideas and with the possibility of similar outbreaks as those mentioned above, perhaps even on a larger scale owing to the emotions stirred up by the present turmoil.

While certain dangers for peace and order inherent in the cosmo-magic conception thus must be said to persist, one may ask whether there is any possibility of this same conception becoming the basis of future constructive developments. The question is difficult to answer. Orientals with western education, and above all the leaders of nationalist movements, tend to disregard and to despise the "superstitions" which governed their nations in the past. Yet, there is the vast mass of the common people, grown up in the old traditions, people to whom the modern ideas of democracy and representative government mean little or nothing and who cannot be educated overnight. A sudden complete break of cultural traditions has almost always proved disastrous to national and individual ethics and to the whole spirit of the peoples affected. A compromise between old and new conceptions therefore would seem desirable. Many, at least, of the outward expressions of the old ideas could easily be kept intact and gradually filled with new meaning, without in the least impairing educational and material progress. After all, the case of Japan shows that an idea decidedly more primitive than that of the cosmic state and less adaptable to ethical reinterpretation than the latter, the belief in the descent of the Mikado from the Sun Goddess (or at least the fiction of such belief) may very well survive and coexist with all the refinements of modern science and technique. The current problems of Southeast Asia hitherto have been discussed almost exclusively from the point of view of economics and political science. It would be a grave mistake to disregard the importance of native culture and tradition for a future satisfactory reorganization of that region.

A FEW BOOKS AND ARTICLES PERTAINING TO THE SUBJECT

F. D. K. Bosch. "Het lingga-heiligdom van Dinaja." *Tjdschrift voor Indische taal, land- en vollkunde,* 64 (1924): 227–291.

George Coedès. "Note sur l'apothéose au Cambodge," *Bulletin de la commission archeologique l'Indochine* (1911): 38–49.

Louis Finot. "Sur quelques traditions Indochinoises." *Bulletin de la commission archeologique l'Indochine* (1911): 20–37.

Karl Döhring. *Siam,* 2 vols. Darmstadt, 1923.

The Glass Palace Chronicle of the Kings of Burma. Translated by Pe Maung Tin and G. H. Luce. London, 1923.

Robert Heine-Geldern. "Weltbild und Bauform in Südostasien." *Wiener Beitrage zur Kunst-und Kulturgeschichte Asiens,* 4 (1930): 28–78.

Adhémard Leclère. *Recherches sur le droit public des Cambodgiens.* Paris, 1894.

Adhémard Leclère. "Cambodge: Fêtes civiles et religieuses." *Annales du Musée Guimet: Bibliothèque de vulgarisation*, 42 (Paris) 1917.

Paul Mus. *Barabudur: Esquisse d'une histoire du Bouddhisme fondée sur la critique a archeologique des textes.* 2 vols. Hanoi, 1935.

J. George Scott, assisted by J. P. Hardiman. *Gazetteer of Upper Burma and the Shan States*, Part I, Vol. I, pp. 85–195, "Palace customs and Burma under native rule"; pp. 469–515, "Government and administration under the Burmese kings." Rangoon, 1900.

Walter William Skeat. *Malay Magic.* London, 1900.

H. G. Quaritch Wales. *Siamese State Ceremonies.* London, 1931.

H. G. Quaritch Wales. *Ancient Siamese Government and Administration.* London, 1934.

NOTES

1. However, it must be taken into account that Burmese, Mon and Thai literatures are still very imperfectly known.

2. There usually are twenty-six heavens in all, including those on Mount Meru, but the number occasionally varies.

3. Although Brahman and Buddhist cosmologies usually ascribe to the world a circular shape, the "cosmic" cities of Southeast Asia, with rare exceptions, affect the square form. It would take long to explain this apparent, but not very important, discrepancy.

4. In the original myth, Mount Meru is used as a churning stick. In Southeast Asiatic variants of the myth, Mount Meru usually takes its place.

5. Similarly, H. G. Quaritch Wales comments on the bad impression created among the people by the abolition of the harem system by King Rama VI of Siam.

6. Thagya is the Burmese form of Sakra, the Buddhist designation for Indra.

7. However, strong traces of the belief that Siva and Vishnu incarnate themselves in the king survive in the coronation rituals of Siam and Cambodia.

4

Some Travelers from China in Southeast Asia

FA-HSIEN, CHAU JU-KUA, AND MARCO POLO

Apart from the Chinese official court records centered on the tribute-bearing delegations from the Southeast Asian kingdoms over the centuries, there are numerous valuable eye-witness accounts of travelers from China to Southeast Asia. Among these were Fa-hsien in the fourth century AD, Chau Ju-kua, and Marco Polo in the thirteenth century. The first was a scholar-pilgrim, the second a Chinese official, and the last the world-famous Venetian who along with his father and uncle spent more than two decades at the court of Kublai Khan, the Mongol emperor of China.

~

*Fa-hsien**

In 399 AD, Fa-hsien, at the age of sixty-five, set out westward from central China across the Taklamakan Desert, over the Pamirs to India to visit the sacred sites of Buddhism. After nearly ten years in India, he left by sea for his homeland, reaching there in 413 AD. On the way, he spent three years in Sri Lanka and Sumatra, which were then famous centers of Buddhist schol-

---

*Fa-hsien, *A Record of the Buddhist Countries,* trans. Li Yung-hsi (Beijing: The Chinese Buddhist Association, 1957), pp. 87-88.

arship. Fa-hsien carried with him to China a large number of Buddhist images as well as books of the Buddhist canon.

His *Record of the Buddhist Countries*, also known as the *Travels of Fa-hsien*, is an invaluable account, in topographic and ethnographic terms, of the countries through which he passed. Below is a portion of his account, which throws light on the conditions of maritime travel at the time and on Yavadvipa, or Sumatra.

~

The hurricane lasted for thirteen days and nights, but finally they reached the shore of an island. When the tide ebbed, they found the leak and repaired it, then sailed on again. That sea is infested with pirates, and none who meet them can escape alive. The great ocean stretches on every side without end, and one cannot tell east from west. Only by looking at the sun, the moon and the stars, can mariners tell their direction. On dull or rainy days, their vessel simply drifted before the wind. On dark nights, all they could see were great billows beating one against the other and shining like fire, with huge turtles, sea monsters and other amazing creatures in them. The bewildered seamen did not know in what direction they were sailing, but since the ocean was unfathomable there was nowhere to cast anchor; so not until the weather cleared could they distinguish the direction and set the right course. Had they happened to strike a reef, they would have been lost. After voyaging in this way for about ninety days, they reached the country called Yavadvipa [Sumatra] . . . .

In this country heretical Brahmanism flourishes, and there are very few Buddhists. After staying here for five months, Fa-hsien embarked on another great merchant ship which also carried about two hundred men. They provided themselves with fifty days' provisions, and set sail on the sixteenth day of the fourth month. Fa-hsien observed the summer retirement [Buddhist monks observe four months of "retirement" every year] on board this vessel, which sailed towards the northeast, bound for Kwangchow.

After sailing for about one month, at the second watch one night it suddenly blew a black squall, and the rain pelted down. Sailors and passengers alike were terror-struck. Once more Fahsien in all sincerity invoked Avalokitesvara [Bodhisatva] and the monks in China, and thanks to their protection he was able to live through that night . . . . Owing to the continuous rain, the pilot charted a wrong course.

Thus they sailed for more than seventy days till their provisions and water were nearly exhausted. They had to use salt water from the sea for cooking, and each man's ration of fresh water was two pints. Soon the fresh water was nearly used up, and the seamen took counsel together.

"Usually," they said, "it takes only fifty days to reach Kwangchow. But we have been sailing now for many more days than that. We must have been off our course." So they steered towards the northwest to look for land.

Chau Ju-kua*

The second major Chinese traveler who left an account of Southeast Asia was Chau Ju-kua, a Chinese official with the title of Superintendent of Maritime Trade in the second half of the thirteenth century AD. He wrote *Chu-fan-chi* or *A Description of the Barbarian Peoples*, a Chinese term that broadly included the people on China's periphery. Of the three accounts, this was the only one with references to the Philippine Islands. For quite some time, references to Sanfotsi, Ma-i, and Toupo in the accounts of Chau Ju-kua were identified with parts of Sumatra, Java, and Malaya. In the opinion of some scholars, such as Austin Craig and D'Harvey de St. Denis, at least some of these locations were part of the Philippines. The great Filipino nationalist leader and scholar, José Rizal, asked for a copy of Chau Ju-kua's book from his prison in Dapitan in 1894 because it spoke of "my country."

~

The country of Ma-i is to the north of P'o-ni [Borneo]. Over a thousand families are settled together along both banks of a creek (or gully). The natives cover themselves with a sheet of cotton cloth, or hide the lower part of the body with a loincloth.

There are bronze images of gods, of unknown origin, scattered about in the grassy wilderness. Pirates seldom come to this country.

When trading ships enter the anchorage, they stop in front of the officials' place, for that is the place for bartering of the country. After a ship has been boarded, the natives mix freely with the ship's folk. The chiefs are in the habit of using white umbrellas for which reason the traders offer them as gifts.

The custom of the trade is for the savage traders to assemble in crowds and carry the goods away with them in baskets; and, even if one cannot at first know them, and can but slowly distinguish the men who remove the

---

*Chao Ju-kua, *His Work on the Chinese and Arab Trade in the Twelfth and Thirteenth Centuries, entitled Chu-fan-chi*, trans. F. Hirth and W. W. Rockhill (St. Petersburg: Printing Office of the Imperial Academy of Sciences, 1911), pp. 159–162.

goods, there will yet be no loss. The savage traders will after this carry these goods on to other islands for barter, and, as a rule, it takes them as much as eight or nine months till they return, when they repay the traders on ship-board with what they have obtained (for the goods). Some, however, do not return within the proper term, for which reason vessels trading with Ma-i are the latest in reaching home. . . .

The products of the country consist of yellow wax, cotton, pearls, tortoise-shell, medicinal betel-nuts and yu-ta cloth [abaca textiles]; and (the foreign) traders barter for these porcelain, tradegold, iron censers, lead, coloured glass beads, and iron needles.

The San-su (or "Three Islands") belong to Ma-i; their names are Kia-ma-yen [Calamián Island Group between Mindoro and Palawan], Pa-lau-yu [Palawan], and Pa-ki-nung [Busuanga Island, largest of the Calamián Is-lands], and each has its own tribes scattered over the islands. When ships ar-rive there, the natives come out to trade with them; the generic name (of these islands) is San-su.

Their local customs are about the same as those of Ma-i. Each tribe con-sists of about a thousand families. The country contains many lofty ridges, and ranges of cliffs rise steep as the walls of a house.

The natives build . . . huts perched in lofty and dangerous spots, and, since the hills contain no springs, the women may be seen carrying on their heads two or three jars one above the other in which they fetch water from the streams, and with their burdens mount the hills with the same ease as if they were walking on level ground.

In the remotest valleys there lives another tribe called Hai-tan [negritos]. They are small in stature and their eyes are round and yellow [brown], they have curly hair and their teeth show [between their lips]. They nest in tree tops. Sometimes parties of three or five lurk in the jungle, from whence they shoot arrows on passers-by without being seen, and many have fallen victims to them. If thrown a porcelain bowl, they will stoop and pick it up and go away leaping and shouting for joy.

Whenever foreign traders arrive at any of the settlements, they live on board ship before venturing to go on shore, their ships being moored in mid-stream, announcing their presence to the natives by beating drums. Upon this the savage traders race for the ship in small boats, carrying cot-ton, yellow wax, native cloth, cocoanut-heart mats, which they offer for barter. If the prices (of goods they may wish to purchase) cannot be agreed upon, the chief of the (local) traders must go in person, in order to come to an understanding, which being reached the natives are offered presents of silk umbrellas, porcelain, and rattan baskets; but the foreigners still retain on board one or two (natives) as hostages. After that they go on shore to traffic, which being ended they return the hostages. A ship will not remain at anchor longer than three or four days, after which it proceeds to another place; for the savage settlements along the coast of San-su are not connected by a common jurisdiction (i.e., are all independent).

The coast faces south-west and during the south-west monsoon the surge dashes against the shore, and the rollers rush in so rapidly that vessels cannot anchor there. It is for this reason that those who trade to San-su generally prepare for the return trip during the fourth or fifth moon (i.e., in May or June). . . .

P'u-li-lu [Polillo Island near Luzon] is connected with San-su, but its settlements are more populous; most of the people are of a cruel disposition and given to robbery. The sea thereabout is full of bare ribs of rock with jagged teeth like blasted trees, their points and edges sharper than swords and lances; when ships pass by they tack out in time in order to steer clear of them . . . .

Marco Polo*

The third well-known traveler from China to Southeast Asia was Marco Polo, the Italian trader/traveler who accompanied the famous Polo brothers, his father and uncle, to the court of Kublai Khan, the Mongol emperor of China. Marco won the trust of the emperor and was made governor of the city of Yang-chow, and the Polos were sent on several missions in West Asia, Burma, Cochin-China, and Ceylon. After more than two decades at the Khan's court, the Polos sought, and with great difficulty obtained, permission to return to their homeland. They set sail with a fleet of fourteen four-masted ships and were charged with the escort of an imperial princess betrothed to the Khan of Persia. Below is an account of the countries the Polos visited in Southeast Asia during their voyage, which concluded in Venice in 1295.

The Book of Marco Polo was presented by Marco Polo in 1307 to Prince Charles of Valois in Venice. The book is "regarded as one of the most important in the history of geographical discoveries . . . because it contains an exact description by an intelligent and well-informed witness of all the countries of the Far East." There are some eighty-five versions of the book in a variety of European languages. The English translation with commentary by the English scholar/traveler Sir Henry Yule and revised by the

*Henry Yule, trans., *Book of Ser Marco Polo* (London: John Murray, 1903), vol. 2, pp. 264–268, 272–274, 284–285.

French scholar Henri Cordier is regarded as the most authentic in the English language.

~

... You must know the Sea in which lie the Islands of those parts is called the SEA OF CHIN, which is as much as to say "The Sea over against Manzi." For in the language of those Isles, when they say Chin, 'tis Manzi they mean. And I tell you with regard to that Eastern Sea of Chin, according to what is said by the experienced pilots and mariners of those parts, there be 7459 Islands in the waters frequented by the said mariners and that is how they know the fact, for their whole life is spent in navigating that sea. And there is not one of those Islands but produces valuable and odorous woods like the lignaloe, aye and better too, and they produce also a great variety of spices. For example in those Islands grows pepper as white as snow, as well as the black in great quantities. In fact the riches of those Islands is something wonderful, whether in gold or precious stones, or in all manner of spicery but they lie so far off from the main land that it is hard to get to them. And when the ships of Zayton and Kinsay do voyage thither they make vast profits by their venture.

It takes them a whole year for the voyage, going in winter and returning in summer. For in that Sea there are but two winds that blow, the one that carries them outward and the other that brings them homeward and the one of these winds blows all the winter, and the other all the summer. And you must know these regions are so far from India that it takes a long time also for the voyage thence.

Though that Sea is called the Sea of Chin, as I have told you, yet it is part of the Ocean Sea all the same. But just as in these parts people talk of the Sea of England and the Sea of Rochelle, so in those countries they speak of the Sea of Chin and the Sea of India, and so on, though they all are but parts of the Ocean.

Now let us have done with that region which is very inaccessible and out of the way.... And let me tell you the Great Kaan has nothing to do with them, nor do they render him any tribute or service.

Of the Great Country called Chamba [Champa]

You must know that on leaving the port of Zayton you sail west-south-west for 1,500 miles, and then you come to a country called CHAMBA, a very rich region, having a king of its own. The people are Idolaters and pay a yearly tribute to the Great Kaan [Emperor of China], which consists of elephants and nothing but elephants. And I will tell you how they came to pay this tribute.

It happened in the year of Christ 1278 that the Great Kaan sent a Baron of his called Sagatu with a great force of horse and foot against this King of Chamba, and this Baron opened the war on a great scale against the King and his country.

Now the King (whose name was Accambale) was a very aged man, nor had he such a force as the Baron had. And when he saw what havoc the Baron was making with his kingdom he was grieved to the heart. So he bade messengers get ready and despatched them to the Great Kaan. And they said to the Kaan: "Our Lord the King of Chamba salutes you as his liege-lord, and would have you to know that he is stricken in years and long hath held his realm in peace. And now he sends you word by us that he is willing to be your liege-man, and will send you every year a tribute of as many elephants as you please. And he prays you in all gentleness and humility that you would send word to your Baron to desist from harrying his kingdom and to quit his territories. These shall henceforth be at your absolute disposal, and the King shall hold them of you."

When the Great Kaan had heard the King's ambassage he was moved with pity, and sent word to that Baron of his to quit that kingdom with his army, and to carry his arms to the conquest of some other country; and as soon as this command reached them they obeyed it. Thus it was then that this King became vassal of the Great Kaan, and paid him every year a tribute of 20 of the greatest and finest elephants that were to be found in the country.

But now we will leave that matter, and tell you other particulars about the King of Chamba.

You must know that in that kingdom no woman is allowed to marry until the King shall have seen her; if the woman pleases him then he takes her to wife; if she does not, he gives her a dowry to get her a husband withal. In the year of Christ 1285, Messer Marco Polo was in that country, and at that time the King had, between sons and daughters, 326 children, of whom at least 150 were men fit to carry arms.

There are very great numbers of elephants in this kingdom, and they have lignaloes [fragrant wood] in great abundance. They have also extensive forests of the wood called Bonus [ebony], which is jet-black, and of which chessmen and pen-cases are made.

Concerning the Great Island of Java

When you sail from Chamba, 1,500 miles in a course between south and south-east, you come to a great Island called Java. And the experienced mariners of those Islands who know the matter well, say that it is the greatest Island in the world, and has a compass of more than 3,000 miles. It is subject to a great King and tributary to no one else in the world. The people are Idolaters. The island is of surpassing wealth, producing black pepper, nutmegs, spikenard, galingale, cubebs, cloves, and all other kinds of spices.

This Island is also frequented by a vast amount of shipping and by merchants who buy and sell costly goods from which they reap great profit. Indeed the treasure of this Island is so great as to be past telling. And I can assure you the Great Kaan never could get possession of this Island, on account of its great distance, and the great expense of an expedition thither. . . .

Concerning the Island of Java the Less.
The Kingdoms of Ferlec and Basma

When you leave the Island of Pentam and sail about 100 miles, you reach the Island of JAVA THE LESS. For all its name 'tis none so small but that it has a compass of two thousand miles or more. Now I will tell you all about this Island.

You see there are upon it eight kingdoms and eight crowned kings. The people are all Idolaters, and every kingdom has a language of its own. The Island hath great abundance of treasure, with costly spices, lignaloes and spikenard and many others that never come into our parts.

Now I am going to tell you all about these eight kingdoms, or at least the greater part of them. But let me premise one marvelous thing, and that is the fact that this Island lies so far to the south that the North Star, little or much, is never to be seen!

Now let us resume our subject, and first I will tell you of the kingdom of FERLEC. This kingdom, you must know, is so much frequented by the Saracen merchants that they have converted the natives to the Law of Mahommet—I mean the towns-people only, for the hill-people live for all the world like beasts, and eat human flesh, as well as all other kinds of flesh, clean or unclean. And they worship this, that, and the other thing; for in fact the first thing that they see on rising in the morning, that they do worship for the rest of the day.

Having told you of the kingdom of Ferlec, I will now tell of another which is called BASMA. When you quit the kingdom of Ferlec you enter upon that of Basma. This also is an independent kingdom, and the people have a language of their own; but they are just like beasts without laws or religion. They call themselves subjects of the Great Kaan, but they pay him no tribute; indeed they are so far away that his men could not go thither. Still all these Islanders declare themselves to be his subjects, and sometimes they send him curiosities as presents. There are wild elephants in the country, and numerous unicorns, which are very nearly as big: They have hair like that of a buffalo, feet like those of an elephant, and a horn in the middle of the forehead, which is black and very thick. They do no mischief, however, with the horn, but with the tongue alone for this is covered all over with long and strong prickles [and when savage with any one they crush him under their knees and then rasp him with their tongue]. The head resembles that of a wild boar, and they carry it ever bent towards the ground. They delight much to abide in mire and mud. 'Tis a passing ugly beast to look upon. . . . There are also monkeys here in great numbers and of sundry kinds; and goshawks as black as crows. These are very large birds. . . .

5

Interstate Relations

in Java

PARARATON*

Although composed in the sixteenth century, the Pararaton, a major text composed in the medieval language Kawi, concerns itself with events in the thirteenth and fourteenth century Indonesian archipelago, particularly Java. The only other text rivaling its importance as a quasi-historical account of the times is Nagarakrtagama, also in the Kawi language and in the verse form. The Pararaton begins with the emergence of Ken Angrok (Rajasa) as the founder of the kingdom of Singosari and his successful conquest of Daha or Kediri. It provides not only the details of the interstate conflicts but also deep insights into the socio-political structure of the time and the magico-religious basis of interstate relations.

～

King Angrok then set out for Mount Leyar, and when Black Wednesday . . . had arrived, he went to the meeting place. He hid in a refuse pile, where he was covered with grass. . . . Then the seven sounds let themselves be heard: rolling peals of thunder and short ones, earthquake, lightning, heat-lightning, whirlwinds and wind storms; rain fell at a time when it could not be expected; rainbows were constantly to be seen in the east and at the same time in the west, and after that, without any lapse of time, voices were heard, noisy and boisterous. "Who shall make the island of Java firm and

---

Pararaton (Javanese Chronicle), ed. and trans. L. A. Brandes; English translation by Margaret W. Broekhuysen (The Hague: Martinus Nijhoff, 1920).

strong?" . . . and "Who is to become king of the island of Java?" they [the gods] asked. Bhatâra Guru [the god Brahma] answered: "Know, ye gods, that I have a son who was born a human being of a woman of Pangkur; he shall make the land of Java firm and strong." Now King Angrok emerged from the refuse pile, and when they had seen him the gods approved of him and confirmed that his name as king was to be Bhatâra Guru; thus they decided amidst loud and general acclaim.

Now it so happened that as by God's direction, the king of Daha [Kediri], Prince Dangdang Gendis, said to the clergy in Daha, "Clerical gentlemen of the Civaite [followers of Shiva] doctrine as well as of the Buddhist doctrine, how is it that you do not make a *sembah* [obeisance] before me, since I am Bhatâra Guru?" The clergy, not a single one of those from Kediri excepted, answered, "Lord, there has never been a cleric yet who made a *sembah* before a king." Thus all of them spoke. Dangdang Gendis said, "Well, if this has not been done so far, you make a *sembah* before me now; if you do not realize my magic power I shall give you proof of it." He placed a spear with its stem into the ground, sat down on its point and said, "See, you gentlemen of the clergy, what magic power I possess," and he showed himself with four arms and three eyes, just like Bhatâra Guru. But the clergy of Daha, now obliged to make a *sembah* before him, still did not wish to perform it, but resisted and fled to King Angrok at Tumapel. This was the beginning of Tumapel's withdrawal from [the control of] Daha.

Then King Angrok was recognized as the Prince of Tumapel which is another name for the realm of Singosari [Simhasari], and homage was paid him by the Civaite and Buddhist clergy from Daha. . . .

Singosari was very prosperous, [and] general peace was enjoyed there. After the rumor had been spreading for some time that Ken Angrok had become king, a report was brought to Prince Dangdang Gendis that Ken Angrok wanted to march against Daha. Prince Dangdang Gendis said, "Who could destroy my country? Only if Bhatâra Guru himself were to descend from heaven, it could perhaps be achieved." This was reported to Ken Angrok. The latter then said, "Approve, gentlemen of the clergy, that I assume the name of Bhatâra Guru." He then called himself thus with their approval. Then he attacked Daha. Prince Dangdang Gendis said, "Woe unto me, for Angrok has the favor and the support of the gods." Between the armies of Tumapel and Daha it came to an encounter. An equally heroic battle was waged on both sides and considerable losses were sustained, but Daha lost. A younger brother of Dangdang Gendis, the *kshatriya* [warrior] Raden Mahisa Walungan, died a hero's death, as did one of his *mantris* [ministers] called Gubar; they were both overpowered by the people of Tumapel, but the fighting was furious. When their chief had been overpowered, the Daha army took to flight; they fled like bees. . . . It was impossible to remedy the situation. Then also Prince Dangdang Gendis withdrew from battle; he fled to a place of worship and hanged himself up in the air with [his] horse and shield bearer with [his] *payung* [umbrella] bearer and *sirih* [betel] bearer, his water page and the page who carried his mat. And when his wives, Dewi Amisani, Dewi Hasin and Dewi Paya, learned that Prince Dangdang had lost the battle and was adrift in the realm of the gods, they, too, disappeared with the *kraton* [royal palace] and everything else, becoming invisible.

Ken Angrok's victory over Daha was complete. Now that he had vanquished his adversary he returned to Tumapel, having changed the state of affairs on Java.

6

Protocol at the
Malaccan Court

SEJARAH MELAYU*

The Sejarah Melayu (the Malay Annals) may lack historical accuracy in terms of exact chronology, but they are an excellent description of the social mores of all levels of people in Malacca from the fifteenth century to the early seventeenth century. The Malay Annals were written around 1535 (after Tome Pires's Suma Oriental) and were later updated in the first quarter of the seventeenth century by a descendant of a Bendahara (chief minister) of Malacca.

Below is an account of the protocol at the Malacca court, which set the pattern for the courts of the other Malay rajas (sultans) on the Malay Peninsula. Although the Malacca court was opulent, its prosperity depended on at least four diverse communities—Chinese, Javanese, Bengalis, and Gujaratis—who traded at this greatest emporium in Southeast Asia. Therefore, the court protocol was devised not to offend their religious or cultural sensitivities. These were important communities who resided in their own quarters of the city in a semi-autonomous fashion. The court ritual was a mixture of the old Hindu customs and the more recent Muslim practices. Note, for instance, the use of umbrellas of different colors by the royalty and high officials, signifying their status and authority—a distinct Hindu-Buddhist practice. Even after Malacca's conversion to Islam, the Hindu ceremonies associated with coronation, in-

*C. C. Brown, trans., "The Sejarah Melayu," *Journal of the Malayan Branch of the Royal Asiatic Society* 25, parts 2&3 (October 1952): 54–59.

stallation of high officials, and recognition of foreign envoys were practiced by the Muslim rulers for centuries.

∽

It was he [Sultan Muhammad Shah] who first instituted royal privileges in regard to yellow, *viz.* that it could not be worn by commoners or used for cloths, for curtain fringes, for bolster ends, for mattresses or any kind of wrapping. "You may not use it for stringing jewels, for the adornment of your houses or for any other purpose." It was only for three things, *viz.* sarongs, jackets and handkerchiefs that it could be used. It was also a royal privilege to have enclosed verandahs, pillars that hung down not reaching the ground, posts that went right up to the roof-beam in summer-houses, while on boats only royalty could have windows and reception cabins. In regard to umbrellas, white was more strictly a royal privilege than yellow, for white umbrellas were reserved for rulers while yellow umbrellas could be used by princes. Commoners might not have metal casing on the sheath of the creese, whether covering it entirely or even going only half way up the sheath. Nor was it permitted to any commoner, however high his rank, to wear anklets of gold; even with silver knobs gold anklets were a royal privilege. Any one who disobeyed this ordinance was guilty of *lèse majesté* and the penalty was death. No one who possessed gold, however rich he might be, was permitted to wear it unless it was a present from the Raja, [king] when he might wear it in perpetuity. No person, whoever he might be, might enter the palace without wearing his sarong in the overlap fashion, his creese in front and a scarf over his shoulders. Any one wearing his creese behind would have it confiscated by the gate-keeper. The penalty for disobedience of this order was death.

When the king gave audience, principal ministers, senior war-chiefs and courtiers occupied the body of the hall of audience; princes of the blood royal occupied the body of the hall of audience; princes of the blood royal occupied the gallery on the left and knights the gallery on the right; heralds and young war-chiefs stood at the foot of the dais bearing swords, the heralds on the left being descendants of ministers eligible for the appointments of Bendahara, Treasurer or Temenggong, and the chief herald on the right being descended from a war-chief eligible for the appointment of Laksamana or Sri Bija diraja; he who bore the title of Sang Guna was Laksamana-designate; and he who bore the title of Tun Pikrama was Bendahara-designate. At the paying of homage the chief of the four or five heralds took precedence of the courtiers who sat in the body of the audience hall and of everybody except principal ministers. Cham shipmasters of high standing and young nobles (who held no office) occupied the balcony of the hall of audience. The Raja's personal requisites, such as his cuspidore, goblet and fan (and shield and bow) were put in the passage, though the betel set was placed in the gallery. The sword of state was borne by the Laksamana or the Sri Bija diraja, whose position was in the gallery on the left. If envoys came, the letter was received by the chief herald on the right, while the Raja's reply to the envoys was announced by the herald on the left. The ceremonial prescribed for the arrival or departure of envoys was that a large tray and a salver were to be brought in by a slave from the palace; and the large tray was to be received by the herald on the right and set down as near to the throne as the Bendahara's seat. The shoulder-cloth and the salver were given to the bearer of the letter. If it was a letter from Pasai, (or from Haru ?) it was received with full ceremonial equipment (big drum, trumpet, kettledrums and two white umbrellas side by side), and the elephant was brought alongside one end of the audience hall. For the Rajas of those two countries (Pasai and Haru) were regarded as equal (to the Raja of Malaka) in greatness and however they (the three) might stand to each other in point of age, it was "greetings" (not "obeisance") they sent to each other. To a letter from any other state less respect was accorded, only the big drum, the clarionet and a yellow umbrella being used. The letter was borne on elephant or on horseback as circumstances might demand, and it was taken down (from the elephant or horse as the case might be) outside the outer gate. If (it was a letter from) a Raja of some standing, the trumpet might be used and two umbrellas, one white and one yellow, and the elephant made to kneel outside the inner gate.

Foreign envoys, even those from Rekan, were given robes of honor on departure, as were our own envoys when departing on a mission.

For the installation of a chief the Raja would give an audience such as was customary on the arrival of an envoy. The man to be installed was fetched from his house with due ceremony. If he was of the standing of a chief, he was fetched by some one of high degree; if he was of lesser status, by a man of medium standing. If he was of a rank to be borne by elephant, he was brought by elephant; if he was of the rank to be borne by horse, he was brought on horseback. If he was not of the rank to be borne by horse, he came on foot, with umbrella, drum and clarionet. As regards the umbrella, however, some were entitled to have a green umbrella, some a blue, some a red. The highest grade was the yellow, as yellow umbrellas are the umbrellas of princes and major chiefs, while a purple or red umbrella is that of courtiers, heralds and war-chiefs. A blue umbrella could be used by any one who was being installed.

When the man who was to be installed arrived, he was halted and the *chiri* was read by an officer of the court before the Raja. After it had been read it was taken outside, to be received by one of the relatives of the man who was being installed: he wore the shoulder cloth. Then the officer who read the *chiri* put it on the head of the man who was being installed and the latter was brought into the hall of audience, where a mat was laid for him at such place as the Raja wished, so that thereafter that should be his place in the hall. Robes of honor were then brought. If it was a Bendahara (who was being installed), five trays were used for the robes of honor: the jacket was laid on one, the head-kerchief on another, the scarf on another, the waistband on another and the sarong on another. In the case of a minister or a knight, there were only four trays, the waistband being omitted. For a herald, courtier or war-chief there were three trays only—one for the sarong and the other for the jacket and the head-kerchief. In some cases all the articles of raiment were put on one tray, while in others there was no tray at all and the sarong, jacket and the head-kerchief were just heaped together and borne on the raised and upturned hands of the slave who carried them. When they reached the man who was being installed, he folded his arms around them and took them outside. The procedure was the same in regard to robes of honor for envoys, each envoy being treated according to his rank.

When the robes of honor were brought, the man to be installed went out and put them on. He then came in again and was invested with frontlet and armlets, for anyone installed wore armlets, but they varied with rank; some had armlets with dragon and clasp, some had jeweled armlets, some had armlets made in the shape of aroid fronds, some had armlets of silver. When that had been done, the man who was being installed did homage and then went home, escorted by the man who had fetched him or someone else of appropriate rank. He was taken home in procession; in some cases the only instruments used were the drum and clarionet, in others the trumpet was added, and in yet other cases there were the kettledrums and white umbrellas as well though in former days it cost money to get white umbrellas and kettledrums; even yellow umbrellas and trumpets were hard to procure.

If the Raja left the palace, on days that the litter was used the Treasurer held the head of the litter, with the Temenggong holding it on the right and the Laksamana on the left, while the rear end of the litter was held by the two chief heralds. Opposite the chain near the Raja's knee the Laksamana held the litter on the right and the Sri Bija diraja held it on the left. Heralds and war-chiefs marched in front of the litter, each carrying the insignia assigned to him. The regalia were borne by men marching in front of the Raja; and there was one state lance on the right and one on the left. In front of the Raja went . . . the heralds bearing the swords of state (and?) in front (of them?) those who carried spears. What was called the "standard" was in front of the Raja, as were the drums and kettledrums on the Raja's right and the trumpets on his left. For in a procession the right ranked higher than the left, whereas in regard to seating the left ranked higher than the right, which applied also when an audience was given. (In a procession), of those who marched in front of the Raja it was those of lower rank who led the way. In front of all went the lances and pennons followed by the musical instruments of every description. Behind the Raja went the Bendahara with the chief ministers and judges.

If the Raja went by elephant, the Temenggong rode on the elephant's head, while the Laksamana or Sri Bija diraja, bearing the sword of state, rode on the croup. At courts when the drum of sovereignty was beaten the major chiefs were on the left of the drum and the minor chiefs on the right. The *sireh* at such a court was given in the following order: first members of the ruling house; then (the Bendahara ?; then) the Treasurer, then the Temenggong; then the four chief ministers; then the Laksamana; then the Sri Bija diraja; then the principal courtiers; then the knights. But it was only if the Bendahara was present that *sireh* was given: if he was not present the *sireh nobat* was not given even though members of the ruling house were there.

If royal celebrations were being held, it was the Treasurer who was master of ceremonies and directed the laying of mats in the hall of audience, the decoration of the inner hall and the hanging of ceiling-cloths. He inspected the food that was to be served and gave orders for the proclaiming of people by name and summoning them to the throne. For all servants and clerks of the Raja were under the Treasurer's control. Under him too were the Shabandar and all those in charge of the revenues of the state. It was the Treasurer who gave orders for the summoning of people, while it was the Temenggong who arranged the guests for feeding in the inner hall. There were not more than four people to a dish, and this applied from the top downwards. If one of the four to share the dish was missing, three were left to share it; if there were two missing, two remained to share the dish; and if there were three missing, the one man had the dish to himself. People from below could not be brought up to fill the missing places; still less could people from above be moved down for that purpose. But ceremonial custom prescribed that the Bendahara should have the dish to himself or share one with members of the ruling house. Thus was the ceremonial custom in the days of (the) Malacca (sultanate). And there is much more that could be told; but to go into every detail would be bewildering to the listener.

For the festival of the night of the twenty-seventh of Ramdhan, the following was the procedure. While it was still day, the Laksamana took the royal praying-mat in procession to the mosque, the Temenggong sitting on the head of the elephant. To the mosque too were taken the betel bowl and other personal requisites of the Raja, and the drums. Then when night had fallen, the Raja proceeded to the mosque, the ceremonial being as for the days when the Raja assisted at evening prayers, followed by the special vespers, of the fasting month. When the prayers were concluded the Raja returned to the palace. On the following day the Laksamana took the royal turban in procession, for it was the custom that Malay Rajas going to the mosque should wear the turban and the cassock. These were the privilege of royalty and could not be worn for weddings except by special permission of the Raja, when they might be worn. Similarly dressing in the Kalinga fashion for weddings or Hari Raya prayers was permitted (only?) to those whose national dress such apparel was.

On the lesser Hari Raya or the greater, the Bendahara and the chiefs went into the palace, and the royal litter was brought into the palace domain in procession from the house of the Treasurer. As soon as they saw the litter taken into the palace all those in the audience hall came out. The Raja then appeared and was taken in procession, mounted on an elephant, to the royal dais, which he ascended. When the people saw the Raja, they all sat on the ground and the litter was brought alongside the dais. The Bendahara thereupon ascended the dais to conduct the Raja to the litter, which he mounted, and he was then borne to the mosque, with the procedure already described. That was the approved ceremonial. If there are errors in the description, it is the duty of anyone who remembers the history to correct them; and your humble servant trusts that he will not incur censure.

Throughout his long reign Sultan Muhammad Shah showed a high degree of justice in his treatment of his subjects, and Malaka became a great city. Strangers flocked thither and its territory stretched westward as far as Bruas Ujong and eastward as far as Trengganu Ujong Karang. And from below the wind to above the wind Malaka became famous as a very great city, the Raja of which was sprung from the line of Sultan Iskandar Dzu'l-Karnain: so much so that princes from all countries came to present themselves before Sultan Muhammad Shah, who treated them with due respect bestowing upon them robes of honor of the highest distinction together with rich presents of jewels, gold and silver.

PART II

THE COLONIAL
INTERLUDE

7

The Position of the Native Regents

BERTRAND JOHANNES SHRIEKE*

The Dutch, whether under the aegis of the East India Company or under the Crown, exploited the Javanese people for the benefit of the Netherlands. In doing so, they had a choice: to take over the administration of Java directly or to run it as if the indigenous sultans and chiefs were still in authority. A review of the records of the East India Company and those of the government would not reveal the truth, which was camouflaged by the official recognition of the "authority" of the native regents. Bertrand Shrieke (1890–1945), a leading Dutch scholar on the colonial system of the Netherlands in Indonesia, reveals how Dutch officials, whether on the East India Company's payroll or on the government's roster, continued to maintain the fiction of indirect rule, while mindful of their paramount objective of making Java financially profitable for the Netherlands. This was particularly the case during the oppressive "culture system" introduced by Governor-General Van den Bosch in 1830. The fiction of native authority continued until at least 1917 with the establishment of coffee plantations.

~

The regents of Priangan received a certificate of appointment and had to see to deliveries. Daendels put an end to this distinction. However, he main-

*Bertrand Johannes Shrieke, *Indonesian Sociological Studies* (The Hague: W. van Hoeve, 1955), vol. 1, pp. 202–221.

tained the so-called "Priangan system," which the Company had inaugurated, as did also the English interim government. Even after the introduction of land rent in other areas, the system remained unaltered in principle, until 1871. (Van den Bosch's culture system of 1830 was inspired by it.) In the main the Priangan system amounted to the following: the government levied no taxation in Priangan, but the population there was obliged to cultivate and deliver supplies of coffee to the government at a price the government itself fixed; the native regents received no salary but were authorized to raise taxes from the population on condition that they paid the salaries of the subordinate native heads.

In the days of the Company, the disparity between the legal position of the regents of the northeast coast of Java and of those of Priangan, to which disparity Daendels put an end, did not however make any practical difference in the government's attitude towards the regents nor in the way in which they were treated by government officials. In what follows I shall, however, be speaking primarily of the regents of Priangan, concerning whom Dr. Haan has collected such an abundance of information in his standard work *Priangan*.

Initially, trade remained the prime object—the Company wanted products. If the delivery of the products was irregular, the procedure was to "exhort" the regents to deliver. It was not long, however, before stronger language was being used. The Javanese heads, who, in spite of earnest recommendations and satisfactory payment, [remained disinclined] to collect in the animals and bamboo required, must be told in severe terms that they are liable by virtue of the Company's sovereignty to provide those services they had been obliged to render under the Javanese kings without, in those days, receiving anything in return.

Whereas the prices paid for products were originally fixed by negotiation with the regents, these were soon being determined by the government alone and forced on the regents as unilateral regulation. The government decided what and how much had to be delivered and the regents had to see that everything was done as required.

The compulsory cultures which resulted from this procedure soon called for inspection and improvement and were therefore subjected to supervision. Tours of inspection were made for the purpose. The Company took upon itself more and more the allure of a sovereign power. At periodic intervals the regents were obliged to come and pay their respects at Batavia. Moreover, disputes between the regents themselves induced the Company to intervene and settle matters. It hesitated all the same to punish regents for neglect of their duties. For whereas economic motives forced the Company to interfere within the province of the regents' authority, political considerations caused it to abstain. The more the Company's authority established itself (1705), however, the more economic interests secured the upper hand. For that matter, the Company's local officials already allowed themselves to go further in dealing with the native heads than the government in Batavia dared. From December 1704 onwards the Priangan regents received certificates of appointment, but their instructions remained vague. In those days the regents were in practice only dimly aware of their subordination to a sovereign, supervising power. Gradually, however, their powers were curtailed. They were no longer permitted to appoint the district chiefs themselves, even though they had to provide their salaries.

Van Imhoff concerned himself with the internal administration of the regencies. First the resident of Cheribon and later the government interfered energetically even with the reserved right of the regents to administer justice, so that nothing remained, for instance, of their judicial powers in penal affairs. They were treated more and more as officials. With the requisitioning of compulsory deliveries of coffee at a greatly reduced price by the Company, the government's voice had, indeed, already become more commanding. In 1726 the native heads were forbidden "most strictly, on pain of being put in chains" to uproot coffee bushes "since they were rooted on Company land which they have in their possession only by virtue of the Company's goodwill until further notice, and whose usufruct they enjoy." "The decline in cultivation, which resulted from the reduction in price, was attributed to the extortions of the native rulers. The appointment of European overseers was therefore considered. When, a few years later, a surplus was feared, the native rulers were then compelled to destroy the coffee bushes and to switch over to the cultivation of pepper instead. In 1789 they were issued instructions for cultivation and overseers carried out inspections to see that those instructions were adhered to, their income being made partly dependent upon the output of coffee. In the meantime the regents were falling ever more deeply into the Company's debt, in part because of the system of advances. In 1800 they were informed of "the government's legitimate displeasure" at the small coffee crop, which was attributed to carelessness in plucking, collection, and delivery. The regent of Chianjur was threatened with the government's wrath if he failed to do his best "to make good the past by energetic action." The regents were made responsible and threatened with punishment in the event of failure. Regents were now on repeated occasions even dismissed. Supervision and inspection were intensified. Action had to be taken against extortionist practices on the part of the regents. With the introduction of annual inspections the expressions of dissatisfaction and serious reprimands became more frequent. The Priangan regents were entirely dependent upon the commissioner for native affairs, whom they are used from childhood to respecting as their God and whom they obey blindly while he is in office, never uttering a word against him. . . . The slavish subjection of the native regents to the commissioner is only too well known.

They were often obliged to suffer the grossest discourtesies. Moreover, fines were imposed upon them "for their omissions" (which fines found their way into the commissioner's pocket) in order "to keep them under a bond of obedience which was reasonable and absolutely essential."

A commissioner can prove anything by means of the Javanese, for their fate lies in his hands. It depends chiefly on him whether an ordinary headman is promoted to the rank of regent or whether a regent shall be subjected to lifelong banishment or pine away in chains.

The number of European overseers (usually ex-soldiers with the rank of sergeant) was increased and their income made entirely dependent upon the production of coffee in their area. It goes without saying that these men, too, often interfered quite freely in the affairs of the regents, even though they were officially their subordinates. The instruction of 1789, meanwhile, went as far as to make the overseers responsible for the general supervision of the regents' official conduct. Arbitrary action on their part against lower native officials, without consultation of the regents themselves, was far from uncommon.

The government was not much given to theorizing about the actual nature of its position. It wanted, as far as possible, to remain simply a merchant and to involve itself as little as it could with administrative affairs. It preferred to regard even the compulsory cultivation and delivery of coffee in Priangan as a commercial transaction. As late as 1802 Commissioner Nederburgh stated that its further activities in that region were to be confined to "supervision and inspection" of the regents' doings, "contenting itself with the benefits of trade." However, during the governor-generalship of Van Imhoff (1742–1750), it was said that the produce supplied to the Company by the northeast coast of Java represented a substitute for the former capitation tax. Even after the rule of Daendels, who regarded the deliveries and quotas as a tax in the form of labor and equated them to compulsory services rendered to the government, opinion remained vague as to their true character. It was only in 1793, when plans came up for bringing about reforms in the Company system, that people began to theorize. That theorizing from the very outset lacked all relation to historical fact, and its proponents used it merely to give a legal foundation to their own proposals for reform or for preserving the old system. People theorized about the Javanese land tenure system without possessing even the most elementary knowledge of the subject. Men like Engelhard, who prompted Nederburgh from behind the scenes, forgot in the process what they had themselves written only a short while before, even forgot their own daily conduct; they produced only those archival documents which could serve to substantiate their "theoretical" views.

Thus in 1726 the Company had, for instance, termed itself "the lawful master and owner" and the regents "the vassals who enjoy the usufruct of their regencies only by virtue of the Company's favor until further notice" but whom it did not wish to "restrict in the effective government and jurisdiction of their territories and subjects" (1712). Yet at the same time the Company regarded them now as "the Company's subjects and allies," now (and preferably) as the suppliers of compulsory products, which they chose on other occasions to regard as a vassal's "tribute." At the end of the eighteenth century there were some, Nederburgh, for instance, who doubted if the Company was really "their legal master and sovereign in the strictest sense of the word," concluding from the regents' rights and authority that "they could in no wise be regarded as equivalent to the servants and officials of the Company, but were rather the true sovereign rulers of their lands." Muntinghe entertained the same fiction as late as 1821. Nevertheless, for more than a century the government had made the regents subordinate to an official, subjected them to its own jurisdiction, appointed and dismissed them at its pleasure, supplied them with instructions, and set limits upon their traditional powers.

Indeed the subsequent hesitation equally about the legal character of the compulsory cultures—whether they were to be regarded as a commercial transaction, compulsory service rendered to the government, taxation in kind, feudal dues, or rent on land according to civil law—constituted no difficulty whatsoever when the government came to determine its practical attitude towards the regents. It had no need of any theory—it had only its own interests in mind. It acted as the circumstances seemed to demand, or permit, desiring to remain a merchant yet being forced by circumstances to assume the trappings of a sovereign, whether it would or not. It was, in reality, two things in one, without being aware of the fact.

Although minors under the tutelage of guardians often succeeded their fathers in the office of regent, the government by no means regarded itself bound to observe the principle of heredity. Thus, in 1770, in the matter of succession on Madura, which island was at the time of the greatest importance politically, it declared that "there is no right of succession, the Company having a free choice in the matter." In 1780 it was of the opinion that "the rule of survivorship is alien, unnecessary, and inappropriate in the regencies." In the second half of the eighteenth century succession was, for that matter, all too subject to the sale of office, the evil which radically undermined the whole Company system. It is said of the regents of the northeast coast of Java at the end of the eighteenth century that they paid the governor for their appointment and that "it took them many long years before they had repaid the debt so contracted." According to Dirk van Hogendorp the supreme regent of Semarang at the time had paid the governor fifty thousand Dutch dollars for this appointment, as a result of which all his predecessor's children were excluded from the succession. In his memorandum of 15 April, 1805, Nicolaas Engelhard writes:

> When I accepted office [as governor of the northeast coast of Java], I was given no peace with all the requests now for this district chief's post, now for that, one offering a hundred Dutch dollars, the other two hundred, five hundred, and up to a thousand, and so on; and this habit, I was assured, had been introduced many years ago.

Of the regents Engelhard says that his predecessor Van Reede had appointed sixteen, receiving in return:

> fifteen, twenty, or twenty-five thousand dollars, according to what His Excellency was able to obtain, and besides this His Excellency always managed by some pretext or other to arrange matters so that whenever there was a vacancy in a regency he could always obtain double the amount, that is to say, not fifteen, twenty, or twenty-five thousand dollars, but thirty, forty, or fifty, on the occasion of the transfer of a regent from one regency to another or of the promotion of the sub-regent to the position of supreme regent.

Daendels states bluntly that "the regents were appointed by the governor in return for payments ranging from ten to twenty thousand piastres." These sums had of course to be exacted from the people, yet in his memorandum of 10 October, 1802, Van Ijsseldijk, though being Van Hogendorp's keenest supporter in the administration of the time and disapproving the fact that the appointment of a regent should be so costly for the inhabitants of the northeast coast of Java, was of the opinion that

> there was no question of abolishing the practice in its entirety, for the common man should not be made too independent and thereby encouraged to abuse his freedom.

The attitude of the administration itself to the regents was wholly determined by the prevailing circumstances. The line of conduct adopted by the officials, on the other hand, displayed more continuity, insofar as their number was such as to permit active intervention and laxity on their part did not prevent it; also insofar as the disturbed political situation admitted such action, though their intervention did not exactly reinforce the regents' independence. In times of supposed danger, such as during the days of the revolution in Europe or of the Cheribon riots, or when a sudden attack by the English was feared, the government felt it should respect the regents; at other times, however, it adopted a different attitude. All the same, in his function as an official, a commissioner, Engelhard, who had imprinted in Nederburgh the idea that the Priangan regents were the "sovereign rulers of their territories and peoples," had in the same period severely curtailed the power and competence of the regents, without considering it necessary to give any justification for his action. The government, however, still had in mind the idea of making use of the regents as a barrier against the influence of the principalities, until Daendels and Raffles removed all cause for fear of that nature.

In the report of 5 December, 1818, that is to say, after the Daendels and Raffles periods, Van Lawick and Van de Graaff write:

> In every regency there is a European official who according to his title should only be an inspector of the coffee plantations, but who in fact is the man who governs the regency with the regent.

The title of *controleur* was not used until 1827.

As regards Daendels' relationship with the regents it can be said that pursuant to the wishes of the government in the Netherlands, and also in order to obtain more light on the matter and to prevent serious mistakes, he instructed the commissioner to collect and hand over within a period of six months replies from the respective overseers to twenty-one questions, which replies were to be as complete as possible and also verified by the commissioner himself, while they were to make clear the manner in which the state could derive greater profit from Priangan. Here we note that these questions made no single reference to the position of the native rulers, the services they were to receive, and so on, whereas according to the instructions Daendels had received, "the most suitable means of subjecting to definite regulations the incomes the regents enjoy according to the custom of the country were to be devised in consultation with the regents themselves." In consultation with the regents!—while in point of fact the questions were submitted to the overseers alone and afterwards to the governors of other districts in Java. Even in the days of the Company it had long been unusual to allow the regents a hearing on proposed regulations, for instance as regards the settlement of the price to be paid for products, as regards their judicial functions, the internal administration of the regencies, and similar matters.

Daendels did, however, consult the regents of the northeast coast of Java, where he found authority to be in the hands of an almost independent governor whose field of office extended from the frontiers of Cheribon to the eastern tip of Java, and whose arbitrary example was taken as a model by the residents serving under him. He abolished the office of governor and placed the residents, who had up to that time been subordinate to the governor, under the immediate control of the governor general. He then conferred together with the regents at Semarang in 1808, writing on the discussions as follows:

> And however difficult and distressing it may be to carry out any negotiations with the timorous Javanese, even, indeed, with the most considerable and enlightened among them, and to get them to talk about matters, even when this is solely to serve their own interests and lighten their burdens, I have nevertheless finally succeeded—after having exercised the necessary patience for more than one month—in obtaining sufficient information from each regent individually, both as regards their complaints and objections and as regards their revenues and expenditures, and have subsequently been able to form a plan of improvement which is entirely satisfactory to every one of them, which will relieve the ordinary Javanese from his heaviest burdens and bring a considerable sum extra into the government's treasury.

It is easy to imagine the difficulty of consultations aimed at persuading the regents to undergo a painful bloodletting; easy, too, to visualize the regents' "satisfaction." Daendels' will was law. Limits were also imposed on the regents' pomp and ceremony.

> Having in this manner sufficiently preserved the authority of the native regents in the eyes of the ordinary Javanese, I have nevertheless made them completely subordinate and subservient to the aims of the government.
> That is to say, taking advantage of the favorable impression the institution of a monarchy in Holland had made upon the minds of the Javanese nobles and the greater respect and trust they display towards the government on that account, I have deemed it necessary to do away with the ideas they still harbored to the effect that they exercised a certain independent and autonomous government over their subjects in order to make room for their complete submission to the royal government, which they respect, knowing it to be now set over them. Having flattered and excited their ambition to

this end, by conferring upon them the title of "the king's servants" and granting them the right to use the state seal with the name of their respective regency underneath it in all public affairs, I have, on the other hand, declared the so-called contracts concluded between the former government and themselves, which contracts they regarded as the sole basis of their obligations, null and void, and have borne in upon them that just as they could, in their quality as officials of the king, lay claim to great privileges, so, too, in their quality as His Majesty's subjects, they were called upon to show unconditional obedience to the orders of the government, not only to those of the governor general himself, but also to the orders of all those who were placed above them in rank and authority.

In order to lend the necessary force to such words Daendels did not hesitate to sign many a notice of dismissal with a flourish of the pen and to introduce large-scale changes in the grouping of the regencies, by amalgamation and so on. The provision making the regents responsible for the supervision of the Mohammedan religion also dates from Daendels, he having borrowed the idea from Napoleon's Concordat.

It was in this manner that, in 1808, Daendels completely transformed the regents into officials. He ordered that the native regents, "both those of the uplands of Jakarta and Priangan and those of Java and Cheribon," should as from 1 January 1809 "make use of the state seal in their official dealings." When the government of the northeast coast of Java was organized, the regents "were treated as officials of His Majesty the King of Holland and made responsible for carrying out the orders of the prefects." They were issued with a somewhat detailed set of instructions. Daendels would not hear of flattering the regents. On the analogy of the regents of Madura, who had a real military function, they were accorded military rank, thereby acquiring a definite position in the general hierarchy of officials. It was the commissioners general who finally had them swear an oath of allegiance. Their settlement of ranks and titles was based on Daendels' scheme.

The lower native heads also received their government appointments as state officials from Daendels and could only be dismissed by the governor general. So far, however, the regents were granted no fixed salary, while the salaries of the lesser heads continued to come out of the regents' pockets; Daendels maintained the principle of "a tenth part of the rice crop and other incomes of the regent authorized by ancient custom, insofar as these were fair and equitable." He did not, however, trouble himself with the principle of the hereditary right of certain families to the office of regent. The Dutch government agreed to the measures taken by Daendels. Thus a letter from the minister of naval and colonial affairs dated 24 July 1809 reads:

it is to be hoped above all that the regents, who appear to be very pleased [with the arrangement], are sincere in their expressions of devotion and subordination. Whatever their attitude may be, it would not be advisable to abandon the vigilance and the strict control which their simulating nature has so far caused us to adopt.

In the margin opposite these words, Daendels added a note to the effect that "Your Excellency can set his mind at rest on this score; I am taking especial care to appoint good prefects."

Raffles' policy followed the same line, that of restricting the power of the regents. He, too, considered the possibility of making the regents salaried officials, but saw no chance of doing so for the time being. The payment of emoluments in the form of land was all he was able to achieve, but that still did not put an end to the rendering of services as was his intention. However, as the result of the introduction of the system of land rent, with its own staff of officials, the regents ceased to be the persons around whom everything revolved, through whose mediation planting was decided upon, matters arranged, and payments made. Their influence was now restricted to the native police. Raffles hoped to bring the European administration into direct contact with the people to the exclusion of the heads. It was this policy of the British governor's, among other things, which his adversaries, Secretary General Blagrave and Major General Gillespie, opposed. At first his Dutch adviser Muntinghe also regarded such an undermining of the traditional authority of the heads as too radical. The directors of the Company associated themselves with the sentiments of Raffles' accusers on this point, but no fundamental alteration was made in the system. Raffles dismissed Blagrave from his post, while Gillespie resigned.

In 1813 Raffles stated that:

The Regent himself may, in like manner, be retained as a public officer at the Residence of the European authority, and under his immediate orders. . . . An arrangement of this nature may be considered a political mode of employing many persons of influence, and now in authority, who otherwise require to be pensioned, and who would not experience, under these circumstances, the disgust that might follow a removal from office. . . . It will evidently be prudent not to abolish the rank, title, or state of the present natives.

Moreover, Raffles considered his interference with the power of the regents justified in the interests of the people, quite apart from the financial interests of the state treasury. . . . In his instructions to Hopkins, he decreed that the Regents are, in future, to be considered as the chief native officers in their respective districts; but it will be obvious, that by the new arrangement they must be effectually deprived of all political or other undue influence: and as the tranquility of the country is an essential and necessary object in establishing the new order, it is presumed they may be most advantageously employed in the department of police, while it must not be forgotten, that the watchful attention of the Resident must ever be directed to their conduct in the execution of this duty.

In 1817 the commissioners general also pursued this policy of restricting the regents' power. On 14 October 1817 Van der Capellen wrote:

> The regents, who were formerly despots of the same order as the rulers of the Confederation of the Rhine under Napoleon, and who have now been reduced to the position of dependence upon more regulated incomes as ordinary officials, are naturally dissatisfied with their new status and would gladly recover their former influence. The government must, however, make it its duty to be continually on the watch against this.

Nevertheless, like Raffles, the commissioners general wished to retain the regents for the time being. . . . In 1832, however, Van den Bosch revised this decision, in connection with his policy regarding the native heads, and it was not until the days of Van de Putte's ministry that the abolition was again brought into effect; and it was not made absolute until 1887. . . .

By this time the Java War was over and the culture system had already been introduced, both being reasons for the administration to wish to strengthen the position of the regents. The former event had caused it to guarantee various regents that their office would remain hereditary in their families, while the regents' authority was regarded as indispensable for the introduction of the culture system. According to the report on his activities in the Indies during the years 1830 to 1833, it seemed to Commissioner General Van den Bosch

> that the heads, and the regents in particular, were not always treated with the respect and justice which they could rightfully claim, and that their hereditary rights were not always respected; the government's proper interest, however, demands that the upper class should be bound to it.
>
> It was thought possible that the people could, as it were, be won over by protecting them against their heads, by taking action against the latter's so-called oppression and by inspiring in them a spirit of independence in their attitude towards their heads. But this view was mistaken, it seems.
>
> In my opinion, therefore, we must ally the heads to ourselves by every appropriate means, and this I have tried to do by respecting their hereditary

rights wherever possible, by seeing that they are treated with due deference, with kindness even, by lending them cautious aid when they were in monetary difficulties, by granting them the ownership of land when they wanted it, and finally by treating them in general in such a manner that they have reason to feel more content under our administration than under that of their own princes.

The more we show respect for the family rights of the heads, the more they will cling to them, for it is precisely the preservation of these rights which they cannot hope for under their own princes and on which, as a matter of fact, they lay so much store. . . .

. . . [The government's] attitude was based on the conception of the Indies as conquered territory which besides continuing to provide for the welfare of the native population had also to continue to supply the Netherlands with the material benefits which had been the aim of conquest, all of which was to be accomplished by peaceful means. In order to reach this the *status quo* had to be preserved as far as possible: it was necessary that the native population should continue to be governed in accordance with its ancestral institutions and customs ("insofar as they do not conflict with the immutable precepts of justice"), that it should be left as far as was practical under the immediate leadership of its own heads (without prejudice to the necessary precautions against abuse and neglect), and that the devotion of the heads to the Netherlands administration should be maintained and confirmed. Everything, that is to say, was to remain as it was.

This briefly sums up the views of Van den Bosch and Pahud. Although the "colonial opposition" did not agree with this objective of colonial policy, and although the Constitutional Regulation represents a compromise between the two schools of thought, the principle of heredity as such met with little, or, at least, with no fundamental opposition from the liberals. It was simply regarded as undesirable to lay down the principle in so many words in the Constitutional Regulation—out of opportunist considerations. When, however, the minister toned down the wording of the article in question, there was no longer any objection to the principle. It was honored later on by progressive statesmen such as Fransen van de Putte, and included in the instructions issued to the governor general.

8

The Philippines Before the Spanish Conquest

MIGUEL DE LOARCA*

When the United States took over the Philippines from Spain in 1898, there was very little information about the new acquisition available to Americans. Before leaving, the Spanish authorities deliberately destroyed most of the archives. Two Americans, Emma Helen Blair and James Alexander Robertson, took upon themselves the editorial responsibility of putting together a comprehensive history of the Philippines in fifty-five volumes, under the title, *The Philippine Islands, 1493–1898,* comprising about 20,000 pages of materials, a large part of which was translated from Spanish into English. Rarely available except in major libraries, this work is now made accessible thanks to the issue of a set of two CD-Roms in 2005 by the Bank of the Philippine Islands to mark the 150th anniversary of its founding.

The volumes are a treasure house of information about the Philippines since 1493, the year after Columbus reached the New World. Below is an account by Miguel de Loarca, an early Spanish settler, who wrote it for the King of Spain and the Royal Council for the Indies. It describes life on the island of Cebu in the years 1582–1583.

~

Although the chief settlement of the Spaniards in these islands is the city of Manila, and the island of Lucon, wherein it is situated, is the finest and rich-

---

*Emma Helen Blair and James Alexander Robertson, eds. and annotators, *The Philippine Islands, 1493–1803,* vol. 5 (Cleveland, Ohio: Arthur H. Clark, 1903).

est of all the islands discovered, . . . yet, since the island of Cubu [Cebu] was the first to be settled, and served as the starting-point for the conquest of all the others . . . I shall commence with the island of Cubu and those adjacent to it, the Pintados. . . .

Inheritances

It is their custom to share inheritances in the following manner. If a man died and left four children, the property and the slaves were divided into four equal parts, and each one of the children took his own share. If the dead man left a bastard child, the latter would receive only what the brothers were pleased to give him; for he had no right to one of the shares, nor could he take more than what his brothers voluntarily gave him, or the legacy made by his father in his favor. If the father chose to favor any of his children in his will, he did so. If the dead man left no children, all his brothers inherited his property, having equal shares therein; and if he had no brothers, his cousins-german [sic] would inherit; if he had no cousins, all his kinsmen. His property, then, went to the children, if he had any; if not, his brothers were necessarily the heirs; if he had no brothers, his first cousins; and in default of these, all his relatives shared the estate equally.

Marriage of the Chiefs

Great mistakes have been made regarding the marriages formed among the natives of this country since they have become Christians, because the marriage customs once observed among the natives have not been clearly understood. Therefore some religious join them in marriage, while others release them, and others reestablish the marriage, thus creating great confusion. For this reason, I have diligently endeavored to bring to light the way in which they observed the marriage ceremonies, which are as follows. When any man wishes to marry, he, since the man always asks the woman, calls in certain *timaguas* who are respected in the village. (This is what the chiefs do. For there appear to be three ranks of men in these islands—namely, chiefs, *timaguas*, who are freemen, and slaves—each class having different marriage customs.) The chiefs, then, I say, send as go-betweens some of their *timaguas*, to negotiate the marriage. One of these men takes the young man's lance from his father, and when he reaches the house of the girl's father he thrusts the spear into the staircase of the house; and while he holds the lance thus, they invoke their gods and ancestors, requesting them to be propitious to this marriage. If the marriage takes place, the lance belongs to the go-between, or it is redeemed.

After the marriage is agreed upon—that is to say, after fixing the amount of the dowry which the husband pays to the wife (which among the chiefs of these islands is generally the sum of one hundred *taes*, in gold, slaves, and jewels, and is equivalent to one hundred pesos)—they go to bring the bride from the house of her parents. One of the Indians takes her on his shoulders; and on arriving at the foot of the stairway to the bridegroom's house, she affects coyness, and says that she will not enter. When many entreaties have proved useless, the father-in-law comes out and promises to give her a slave if she will go up. She mounts the staircase, for the slave; but when she reaches the top of the stairway and looks into her father-in-law's house and sees the people assembled within, she again pretends to be bashful, and the father-in-law must give her another slave. After she has entered, the same thing takes place; and he must give her a jewel to make her sit down, another to make her begin to eat, and another before she will drink. While the betrothed pair are drinking together an old man rises, and in a loud voice calls all to silence, as he wishes to speak. He says: "So-and-so marries so-and-so, but on the condition that if the man should through dissolute conduct fail to support his wife, she will leave him, and shall not be obliged to return anything of the dowry that he has given her; and she shall have freedom and permission to marry another man. And therefore, should the woman betray her husband, he can take away the dowry that he gave her, leave her, and marry another woman. Be all of you witnesses for me to this compact." When the old man has ended his speech, they take a dish filled with clean, uncooked rice, and an old woman comes and joins the hands of the pair, and lays them upon the rice. Then, holding their hands thus joined, she throws the rice over all those who are present at the banquet. Then the old woman gives a loud shout, and all answer her with a similar shout; and the marriage contract or ceremony is completed. Up to this time, her parents do not allow the young couple to eat or sleep together; but by performing this ceremony they deliver her up as his wife. But if, after the marriage contract has been negotiated by a third party, the man who seeks marriage should repent of the bargain and seek to marry another woman, he loses the earnest-money that he has given, even if he has had no intercourse with the former; because when they commence negotiations for the marriage they begin to give the dowry. If a man say in conversation, or at a drunken feast, "I wish to marry so-and-so, daughter of so-and-so," and afterward break his promise and refuse to marry her, he is fined for it; and they take away a great part of his property.

In regard to the dowry, neither the husband nor the wife can enjoy it until they have children; for until then it belongs to the father-in-law. If the

bridegroom is not of age to marry, or the bride is too young, both still work
in the house of the father-in-law until they are of age to live together.

Marriage Among the Timaguas

The *timaguas* do not follow these usages, because they have no property of
their own. They do not observe the ceremony of joining hands over the
dish of rice, through respect for the chiefs; for that ceremony is for chiefs
only. Their marriage is accomplished when the pair unite in drinking *pitar-
rilla* from the same cup. Then they give a shout, and all the guests depart;
and they are considered as married, for they are not allowed to drink together until late at night. The same ceremony is observed by rich and respectable slaves.

Marriage Among the Slaves

But the poor slaves, who serve in the houses, marry each other without
drinking and without any go-between. They observe no ceremony, but simply say to each other, "Let us marry." If a chief have a slave, one of his *ay-
oiys*, who serves in the house, and wishes to marry him to a female slave of
the same class belonging to another chief, he sends an Indian woman as
agent to the master of the female slave, saying that her master wishes to
marry one of his male slaves to the other's female slave. After the marriage
has been arranged, he gives his slave an earthen jar, or three or four dishes,
and there is no other ceremony. Half of the children born to this couple will
belong to the master of the female slave, and the other half will belong to
the master of the male slave. When the time comes when their children are
able to work for their masters, the parents are made *tumaranpoques,* as we
have said; because when a male slave of one chief marries the female slave of
another chief, they immediately receive a house for their own use, and go
out to work for their masters. If a freeman marries a female slave, or *vice
versa,* half of the children are slaves. Thus, if there are two children, one is
free and the other a slave, as the parents may choose.

In one thing these natives seem to go beyond all reason and justice. It is
usage among them that, if an Indian of one village owes twenty pesos . . . to
an Indian in another village, and when asked for the money refuses to repay
it, when any Indian of that village where the said twenty pesos is due is
caught, they seize him—even if he is in no way related to or acquainted
with the debtor—and compel him to pay the twenty pesos. It is their custom that he who first owed the twenty pesos must return to him who paid
that sum forty pesos instead, on account of the violence used against him.

They say that they act thus in order not to use the mailed hand for collecting from the other in that village, since that would result in war. . . .

Witches and Sorcerers; Physicians

In this land are sorcerers and witches—although there are also good physicians, who cure diseases with medicinal herbs; especially they have a remedy for every kind of poison, for there are most wonderful antidotal herbs. The natives of this island are very superstitious; consequently, no native will embark for any voyage in a vessel on which there may be a goat or a monkey, for they say that they will surely be wrecked. They have a thousand other omens of this sort. For a few years past they have had among them one form of witchcraft which was invented by the natives of Ybalon after the Spaniards had come here. This is the invocation of certain demons, whom they call *Naguined, Arapayan,* and *Macbarubac.* To these they offer sacrifices, consisting of cocoanut-oil and a crocodile's tooth; and while they make these offerings, they invoke the demons. This oil they sell to one another; and even when they sell it they offer sacrifices and invoke the demon, beseeching him that the power which he possesses may be transferred to the buyer of the oil. They claim that the simple declaration that one will die within a certain time is sufficient to make him die immediately at that time, unless they save him with another oil, which counteracts the former. This witchery has done a great deal of harm among the Pintados, because the demon plays tricks on them. The religious have tried to remedy this evil, by taking away from them the oil and chastising them. . . .

The God Batala

According to the religion formerly observed by these Moros, they worshiped a deity called among them *Batala,* which properly means "God." They said that they adored this *Batala* because he was the Lord of all, and had created human beings and villages. They said that this *Batala* had many agents under him, whom he sent to this world to produce, in behalf of men, what is yielded here. These beings were called *anitos,* and each *anito* had a special office. Some of them were for the fields, and some for those who journey by sea; some for those who went to war, and some for diseases. Each *anito* was therefore named for his office; there was, for instance, the *anito* of the fields, and the *anito* of the rain. To these *anitos* the people offered sacrifices, when they desired anything—to each one according to his office. The mode of sacrifice was like that of the Pintados. They summoned a *catalonan,* which is the same as the *vaylan* among the Pintados, that is, a priest. He offered the sacrifice, requesting from the *anito* whatever the people desired him to ask, and heaping up great quantities of rice, meat, and fish. His invocations lasted until the demon entered his body, when the *catalonan* fell into a swoon, foaming at the mouth. The Indians sang, drank, and feasted until the *catalonan* came to himself, and told them the answer that the *anito* had given to him. If the sacrifice was in behalf of a sick person, they offered many golden chains and ornaments, saying that they were paying a ransom for the sick person's health. This invocation of the *anito* continued as long as the sickness lasted.

When the natives were asked why the sacrifices were offered to the *anito*, and not to the *Batala*, they answered that the *Batala* was a great lord, and no one could speak to him. He lived in the sky; but the *anito*, who was of such a nature that he came down here to talk with men, was to the *Batala* as a minister, and interceded for them. In some places, and especially in the mountain districts, when the father, mother, or other relative dies, the people unite in making a small wooden idol, and preserve it. Accordingly there is a house which contains one hundred or two hundred of these idols. These images also are called *anitos;* for they say that when people die, they go to serve the *Batala*. Therefore they make sacrifices to these *anitos,* offering them food, wine, and gold ornaments; and request them to be intercessors for them before the *Batala,* whom they regard as God.

Government of the Moros

Among the Moros there is precisely the same lack of government as among the Pintados. They had chiefs in their respective districts, whom the people obeyed; they punished criminals, and laid down the laws that must be observed. In the villages, where they had ten or twelve chiefs, one only—the richest of them—was he whom all obeyed. They greatly esteem an ancient lineage, which is therefore a great advantage to him who desires to be a lord. When laws were to be enacted for governing the commonwealth, the greatest chief, whom all the rest obeyed, assembled in his own house all the other chiefs of the village; and when they had come, he made a speech, declaring that, to correct the many criminal acts which were being committed, it was necessary that they impose penalties and enact ordinances, so that these evils might be remedied and that all might live in peace. This policy was not in vogue among the Pintados, because no one of them was willing to recognize another as his superior. Then the other chiefs replied that this seemed good to them; and that, since he was the greatest chief of all, he might do whatever appeared to him just, and they would approve it. Accordingly, that chief made such regulations as he deemed necessary; for these Moros possess the art of writing, which no other natives of the islands have. The other chiefs approved what he ordained. Immediately came a public crier, whom they call *umalahocan*, who is properly a major-domo, or steward; he took a bell and went through the village, announcing in each district the regulations which had been made. The people replied that they would obey. Thus the *umalahocan* went from village to village, through the whole district of this chief; and from that time on he who incurred the penalties of law was taken to the chief, who sentenced him accordingly. If the penalty be death, and the condemned man say that he prefers to be a slave, he is pardoned, and becomes a slave. All the other chiefs are also judges, each in his own district; but when any important case arises the head chief calls all the others together, in order to decide it, and the affair is settled by the vote of all. The chiefs are accustomed to impose the taxes; but there is no fixed amount for these, save what the proper judge decrees shall be paid.

This relation was written by order of the governor of these islands. MIGUEL DE LOARCA of the town of Arevalo.

9

The Hispanization of the Philippines

JOHN LEDDY PHELAN*

In 1521, Ferdinand Magellan, a Portuguese explorer in the service of Spain, reached the Philippines (he was killed there by the local people), thus opening the way for the Spanish king to lay claim to those islands. After the Spanish conquest of Cebu in 1565 and Manila six years later, the Spaniards accessed the islands through Hispanic America. In most cases, the Spanish missionaries who went to the Philippines had spent several years in Central America, where Hispanic Christianity had already integrated several indigenous practices into Spanish Catholicism. In their efforts to introduce Hispanic Catholicism to the Filipinos, the missionaries further accommodated the Filipinos' age-old religious beliefs or deliberately turned a blind eye to Filipino religious practices. This accommodation enabled the conversion of the Filipino masses, eventually making the Philippines the only country in Asia to have a majority Christian population.

John Leddy Phelan has extensively sifted through missionary records to uncover the process of Hispanization and Christianization of the Filipino population in the sixteenth and seventeenth centuries. Even though his book was published in 1959—nearly a half century ago—most of his analysis and observations are still valid.

～

*John Leddy Phelan, *The Hispanization of the Philippines* (Madison: University of Wisconsin Press, 1959), 53–89.

The Imposition of Christianity

Spanish missionaries viewed themselves as soldiers of Christ waging with
spiritual weapons a war to overthrow tyranny over pagan peoples. They
envisaged their work as a "spiritual conquest" of the minds and hearts of
the natives, a supplement to, and the ultimate justification for, the military
conquest. A superb iconographical expression of the Spanish view of the
complementary nature of the temporal and the spiritual conquests can be
found in Friar Gaspar de San Agustín's chronicle of 1698....

Christianity was presented to the infidels not as a more perfect expression of their pagan beliefs but as something entirely new. Any resemblance
between the two religions was dismissed as a diabolical conspiracy in
which the devil deceived unbelievers by mimicking the rituals and the beliefs of Christianity. The policy of breaking abruptly with the pagan past
explains the vigor with which temples and idols were destroyed. The Spanish missionaries have been much criticized for this practice. Yet the religious were not modern archaeologists. In their eyes pagan artifacts were
but the visible symbols of the devil's tyrannical dominion, and hence they
merited destruction.

In the Philippines there were no temples to demolish. But sacred groves
were cut down by zealous Spanish religious who were determined to break
the magic sway such groves exercised over the Filipinos. And pagan idols
by the thousands were committed to the flames by iconoclastic religious in
the presence of bewildered and fascinated Filipinos.[1] The dismantling of
outward pagan observances was but the first step in the introduction of
Christianity.

Baptism

In most cases the missionaries were preceded by the *encomenderos.* The latter were supposed to teach their wards the rudiments of the Christian religion and to build chapels. That most *encomenderos* poorly performed their
quasi-missionary responsibility is abundantly clear. Their principal concern
was to pacify their wards in order to collect tribute taxes from them. The
religious, fearing that the conquered would be repelled by the religion of
the conquerors, often decried the forceful methods with which the *encomenderos* went about their tasks. Such fears, although plausible, proved
in fact groundless. Actually by their very blood and fire methods the *encomenderos* rendered a service to the religious by breaking the backbone of
native resistance. The indigenous peoples with whom the Spaniards came in
contact seldom showed any desire to abandon voluntarily their own reli-

gious values. Compulsion of some sort had to be employed. Given their Christian humanitarianism, the clergy usually protested against the use of force; but without coercion, or the threat of it, the natives in many cases would have rejected the appeals of the religious to discard paganism.

Sullen distrust but not armed defiance usually greeted the newly arrived missionary. More than one friar woke up in the morning to a deathly silence only to discover that his would-be flock had stolen away to the mountains during the night. One Augustinian not only had his hut burned but also suffered from attempts to poison his drinking water. In some localities the distrustful inhabitants refused to supply the clergy with the necessities of life.

Wherever the religious met morose distrust, they did not attempt to impose themselves on the elders of the community. What the religious usually requested was that some of the children be committed to their care. The chieftains might shun the monastery for some time, but out of a combination of curiosity and fear they would hand over some of their children to be educated by the religious. Evangelization followed a standard pattern. The children of the chieftains were first indoctrinated, and then the chieftains themselves were persuaded. With the conversion of the leaders of the community the baptism of their followers came as a matter of course. Although rite indoctrination of ex-pagan adults was conscientiously pursued, it was realized that their adjustment to Christianity would be incomplete. Special attention, therefore, was concentrated on the children. The children proved enthusiastic and effective auxiliaries of the religious in winning over the parents to the new religion, reporting clandestine pagan rituals, and in catechizing the older generation.

A substantial aid to the early missionaries in removing the barrier of distrust was the impression which rapidly gained currency among the Filipinos that baptism not only wiped away the sins of the soul but also helped to cure the ailments of the body. The ecclesiastical chronicles are full of accounts of ill people who made "miraculous" recoveries after receiving baptism and cases of converts who "miraculously" avoided catching a local epidemic. Since their pagan cults had stressed the cures of illness, the popular conviction that baptism was corporeally efficacious did much to attract the Filipinos to the new religion.

The missionary enterprise in Mexico provided the Philippine clergy with a wealth of experience upon which to draw. Baptism without benefit of some preliminary instruction was seldom performed in the Philippines except in cases of serious illness. The early Franciscans in Mexico had been sharply criticized for administering baptism without benefit of prior instruction. From this controversy emerged an ideal definition of the content

of pre-baptismal instruction. Converts were expected to repudiate paganism and to affirm their belief in the efficacy of the sacrament. The marriage
of a convert was required to be monogamous. Adult converts were supposed to be able to recite by memory the Pater Noster, the Credo, the Ave
Maria, and the Ten Commandments. Finally, some idea of the meaning of
the other sacraments and an awareness of the principal obligations of a
Catholic (attendance at Mass on Sundays and holy days and mandatory annual confession) were considered desirable baptismal conditions. These
standards were not always observed in the Philippines, but they did provide
a yardstick which was often enforced.

The missionary enterprise got off to a very slow start between 1565 and
1578. During the first five years there were not more than one hundred
baptisms. In 1576 there were only thirteen Augustinian friars, and their
baptisms had been confined mostly to children. Linguistic ignorance,
paucity of priests, and the missionary interest in China account for this lack
of progress. The coming of the Franciscans in 1578 and the arrival of large
contingents of Augustinians and Franciscans after 1578 produced a change
in the scope and tempo of evangelical operations. The Franciscans were
soon followed by the Dominicans and the Jesuits. The decisive decade was
the one between 1576 and 1586. During this period the number of missionaries rose from 13 to 94 and by 1594 there were 267 regulars. The number
of baptisms rose proportionately to the increase in missionary personnel, as
the following approximate figures suggest:[2]

1583	100,000	baptisms
1586	170,000	"
1594	286,000	"
1612	322,400	"
1622	500,000	"

Thus it took some fifty years of intensive missionary activity to lay the
foundation of Philippine Christianity.

The sacrament was seldom granted to anyone who expressed strong an-
tipathy to the new religion. According to Catholic doctrine, the efficacy of
the sacrament depended upon a sincere act of repentance on the part of the
convert. Many indifferent Filipinos probably were, however, swept along in
the baptismal current, which flowed swiftly during the 1580s and 1590s. Although there are some examples of obdurate natives refusing baptism, such
cases were rare. Most religious held that infidels could be compelled only to
listen to the preaching of the gospel. Bartolome de las Casas (1484–1566),
the famous sixteenth-century Dominican priest and human rights activist

who exposed the unconscionable treatment meted out to natives in the New World and fought for their rights, rejected even this proposition, but his opinion was shared by few missionaries. No responsible Spaniard argued that pagans could be compelled to believe.

The religious may have respected the ultimately voluntary nature of baptism, but they did exert various forms of individual and social pressure which few Filipinos were able to resist. As one Jesuit observed in 1604: "It seems to me that the road to the conversion of these natives is now smooth and open with the conversion of the chiefs and the majority of the people, for the excuse which they formerly had saying, 'I will become a Christian as soon as the rest do' has now become their incentive toward conversion and they now say, 'We desire to become Christians because all the rest are Christians.'"[3] With the achievement of a Christian majority, serious outward opposition vanished.

The Catechism

The effectiveness of pre-baptismal instruction depended upon subsequent indoctrination in the catechism. The Christian doctrine taught to the Filipinos was dogmatic Catholicism reduced to its essential minimum. The Tagalog-Christian Doctrina of 1593, the first book printed in the Philippines, included the following: Pater Noster, the Ave Maria, the Credo, the Salve Maria, the fourteen articles of the Faith, the seven sacraments, the seven capital sins, the fourteen works of mercy, the Ten Commandments, the five commandments of the Church and the act of general confession.[4]

The Doctrina of 1593 closely followed the Nahuatl catechisms previously compiled for the Mexican Indians. In the century, however, the majority of the Philippine doctrinas were adaptations or translations of the much used Doctrina Christiana (1597) edited by the prominent Jesuit theologian, Robert Cardinal Bellarmine. The overwhelming popularity of the Bellarmine catechism in the Philippines is an indication of the success of the Holy See in standardizing catechismal instruction throughout the Catholic world.[5]

The catechisms published in the various Philippine languages were not meant to be distributed to the Filipinos themselves, although they possessed a long tradition of literacy. The high costs of printing and the use of fragile rice paper ruled out the feasibility of instruction by means of written materials. Indoctrination was oral, and the catechisms were for the Spanish clergy, who required accurate translations into heretofore unfamiliar languages of complex doctrinal concepts which medieval theologians had taken centuries to define. In conformity with the policy of deliberate rupture with the pagan past, the key concepts of Christianity were never translated into the Philippine tongues. Lest the converts confuse or identify the Christian with the pagan, such terms were ordinarily left in the Spanish form. Sometimes the Latin term was used.[6]

The religious organized and instructed the first catechismal classes. They were usually held on Sundays in the *cabecera* villages and in the outlying *visitas* at whatever time the itinerant priest happened to be there. In response to the shortage of priests, all the orders devised some system in which the brighter students taught the less advanced. In this method the Spanish religious foreshadowed by three centuries the Lancastrian system of instruction. The Jesuits, for example, cast the prayers, the Creed, and the commandments into Bisayan verse adapted to the traditional planting and rowing chants of the region.[7]

The sons of the chieftains might board for a few years at the parish residence, called the *convento* in the Philippines, where they were given a more intensive training in the doctrine. Reading, writing, and music as well as Spanish were also on the curriculum. In contrast to the practice in Mexico, the Filipinos were seldom taught Latin. The aim of these monastic schools was to train an elite class who could act as intermediaries between the Spaniards and the Filipino masses. Although primary schools were founded by all the orders, the Franciscan institutions were the most effective. Such had previously been the case in Mexico. Primary education flourished from the 1580s onwards, but after the intensification of the Dutch war from 1609 onward, the quality of instruction fell off noticeably.[8]

During the seventeenth century the burden of organizing and supervising catechismal instruction fell increasingly on the *fiscales*. An important personage in the community, the fiscal was more than a sacristan. He was the intermediary between the clergy and their parishioners. Among his other duties were those of organizing the village's patronal fiesta, arranging for the ornamentation of the church, and cajoling, if not compelling, his scattered charges to attend Mass and catechismal classes.

The *fiscales* were brought to the Philippines from Mexico, where they were sometimes called *mandones*. The role of the *fiscales* reflects the inalterable conviction of the Spanish clergy that the Filipinos required external discipline to compel them to perform their religious obligations. As one Jesuit observed: "They readily receive our religion. Their meager intelligence does not permit them to sound the depths of its mysteries. They also have little care in the fulfillment of their duties to the Christianity which they have adopted; and it is necessary to constrain them by fear of punishment and to govern them like school children."[9]

Informed observers agreed that most Filipinos had memorized, parrot-like, the catechism and the prayers. Reflective missionaries sometimes expressed doubts about the degree of the natives' comprehension. Alcina, for example, was discouraged in the face of his repeated failure to explain to his Bisayan parishioners the meaning of paradise. The brighter ones, he wrote, were willing to grant the plausibility of a heaven for the Spaniards, but they refused to believe that the Bisayans would be allowed to share it with the Spaniards. The Christian notion that worldly differences of race, wealth and education did not exist in the sight of the Almighty shocked the earthy realism of the Bisayans. For them the inequalities of the world would be perpetuated in the next. Alcina confessed that after sixty years of missionary activity in the Bisayas very few of the converts had acquired a clear comprehension of the basic mysteries of the Catholic creed. Other thoughtful missionaries expressed equally searching doubts.[10]

The degree to which the Filipinos understood the meaning of the doctrine was often in proportion to the density of population. The inhabitants of the maritime provinces of Luzon were settled in larger units and were cared for by a greater number of priests than were those of the Bisayan islands. Hence the former tended to be better indoctrinated than the latter. On Luzon itself the Tagalog provinces, Pampanga and the Camarines, were better instructed than the outlying provinces of Ilokos, Pangasinan, and Cagayan. Natives living nearer the *cabecera* church, where there was a resident priest, usually acquired a firmer grasp of the doctrine than those living in the vicinity of the outlying *visita,* serviced only by an itinerant priest.

Although the methods of indoctrination varied considerably from order to order, these variations were not always exactly reflected in the quality of instruction in particular areas. The Augustinians, for example, were the least effective teachers of the doctrine, a fact which may be ascribed to the prolonged disciplinary crisis in that order. Yet the level of instruction in their Tagalog and Pampangan parishes was not appreciably inferior to that in the parishes administered by the other orders. These Augustinian parishes were some of the most compactly settled in the archipelago. The Augustinian parishes in Ilokos and the Bisayas, however, were probably the worst instructed in the islands, for in addition to the mediocre quality of the clergy there was widespread rural decentralization. Of all the orders, the Jesuits had developed the soundest pedagogical methods. Nevertheless, the scattered population of their Bisayan parishes were no more intensively indoctrinated than the Tagalog and Pampangan parishes of the Augustinians. Not more, and often fewer, than thirty itinerant Jesuit priests administered to between 50,000 and 70,000 Bisayans.[11] Where Jesuit pedagogical skill did produce impressive results, however, was in their residences of An-tipolo and Silan adjacent to Manila, where there was considerable density of population. The Dominicans in their parishes in Cagayan and Pangasinan faced the same handicaps of rural decentralization confronting the Jesuits in the Bisayas. Given the obstacles, the sustained zeal of the Dominicans achieved maximum results with the limited means available. Instruction in the Franciscan parishes was of the highest quality in the islands. Not only did the Franciscans retain a respectable degree of discipline among them-selves, but also they enjoyed the good fortune of holding a series of popu-lous and compactly organized parishes in the Tagalog and Bikol country. All of which suggests that the level of instruction depended not so much on the quality of the clergy as it did on the density of the population. Given the difficulties involved in maintaining ecclesiastical discipline, and the de-centralized character of settlement patterns, catechismal instruction could only meet minimum standards. But this result was remarkable in view of the internal and external obstacles confronting the clergy.

The Sacraments

By virtue of baptism the Filipinos entered the Church. Instruction in the catechism gave them a modicum of knowledge about the doctrine of their new religion. The reception of three other sacraments was necessary before the Filipinos could become practicing Catholics. They were matrimony (for the married ones), penance, and Holy Eucharist.

Polygamy and the prevalence of divorce among the Filipinos were obsta-cles to the introduction of the Catholic sacrament of matrimony. Both cus-toms were the prerogatives of chieftains. And both traditions created hindrances to the spread of Christianity in that missionary policy was to concentrate initially on the conversion of the chieftains. Since polygamy was a custom derived from recent Muslim influence in the Bisayas (Samar, Leyte, and Cebu), it was easily liquidated.[12] More formidable, however, was the task of the missionaries to teach the Christian doctrine of the indissolu-bility of marriage to the members of a society accustomed to the principle of divorce.

The first problem confronting the missionaries was to Christianize those marriages already performed according to pagan usages. Recognizing the existence of natural marriages among the Indians, Pope Paul III, in his bull *Altitudo divini consilii* (1537), declared that the legitimate wife was the first woman that a man had espoused. In case of doubt as to which one was the first, the Indian might choose any one of his wives and be married to her in *facie ecclesiae*.[13] The Holy See's dictum had as one aim to prevent natives from becoming Christians in order to exchange an older wife for a younger one.

The papal solution proved unworkable in the Philippines, and some of its provisions were quietly disregarded. Converts were allowed to choose for a Christian spouse any one of their present or former wives. In practice, this meant the present wife and her children. Hence few Filipinos were compelled to exchange a younger wife for an older one and thus leave the children of the younger wife fatherless and destitute. The Philippine religious flexibly interpreted canonical principles in order to avoid undue economic and emotional hardships on the neophytes.[14] Later on in the seventeenth century, after the majority of Filipinos had become Christian, a more literal interpretation of Paul III's bull prevailed. The right of choice could be exercised only in cases where the first pagan wife had disappeared or had refused baptism.[15]

The penchant of the Filipinos for divorce was a habit not easily suppressed. On occasion they displayed considerable ingenuity in exploiting canon law to gratify their desire for a marital change. In 1621 the archbishop of Manila was plagued by numerous requests for annulments. These petitions bore a suspicious resemblance to one another. They all alleged that the interested parties had had intercourse before marriage with relatives of their wives. The archbishop accused the plaintiffs of intentionally concealing these facts, which canon law recognized as an obstacle, until the husband desired to marry someone else. The archbishop urged the king to request from the Pope a bull giving the Philippine prelates broad powers to grant absolution for this type of impediment in cases where a marriage had already been performed.[16] The monarch instructed his ambassador to the Roman curia to make such a request. Mentrida's manual, published in Manila in 1630, granted parish priests the very authority that the archbishop had requested in 1621.[17]

This episode illustrates the degree to which functional Hispanization had progressed within fifty years of the conquest. These Filipinos were sufficiently Hispanized to attempt to continue inside the framework of canon law the pre-conquest tradition of easy divorce.

The transition from the pagan marriage pattern to the Christian one was not always smooth. Many marriages violated some principle of canon law. There were cases of baptized natives marrying infidels according to pagan rites, or of a man marrying his widowed step-mother, or of someone else marrying a cousin within the prohibited third degree, without securing a prior dispensation.[18]

The actual sacrament of matrimony did not have to be performed inside the church itself. A priest could marry a couple in the parish residence or in the home of the bride, but the solemnities of the nuptial Mass, followed by the nuptial blessing, could be performed only inside the church, at any time of the year but during the season of Lent. Such services were, however, rare. Some contemporaries blamed the relative infrequency of nuptial Masses on the high fees charged by the clergy.[19] Although such fees were a standard custom throughout Catholic Europe, the Crown sought to delay their introduction into the Indies. It was thought that these fees might discourage the Indians from receiving the sacraments and that the Indians might be confused about the spiritual nature of the sacraments. In 1596 Philip II ordered that no sacramental fees he collected from the Filipinos.[20]

These mandates went unheeded. Nor would the regulars abide by a set of tariffs, one drawn up by Bishop Salazar in the 1580s and another by Archbishop Camacho in 1698.[21] As we have already observed in the last chapter, the religious defied Episcopal authority with impunity. The Augustinians and the Franciscans, but not the Jesuits and the Dominicans, charged substantial sacramental fees. In short, most Filipino Christians were married in the Church but not inside the churches. Nuptial blessings were for the well-to-do.[22]

The introduction of Catholic matrimony implied certain changes in sexual mores. Some erotic practices, which provoked vehement opposition among the Spaniards, were gradually suppressed.[23] In discussing changes in sexual mores following the conquest, another issue is pertinent. Did the Chinese, who did not settle in the islands until after the arrival of the Spaniards, introduce sodomy to the Filipinos? Although this allegation was made by observers whose testimony on other matters has proved reliable, the evidence they adduce on the question of sodomy is something less than convincing.[24]

Spanish policy was to tolerate many indigenous mores which did not brazenly conflict with basic precepts of Spanish Christian morality. As early as 1599, Tagalog dowry and inheritance practices as codified in Plasencia's study received recognition in the Spanish law courts as customary law in all inter-Filipino litigations.[25] The Spaniards did not object to the pre-Hispanic tradition of the groom providing the dowry, although this custom differed from Spanish usage. The Spaniards did, however, view with hostility the twin customs of bride-gift and bride-price, in which the groom rendered either labor services or a payment to his future father-in-law. To the Spaniards it smacked of fathers selling their daughters, perhaps against the latter's will, to the highest bidder. Although it was the accepted practice in Spain for parents to arrange the marriage of their children, Catholic doctrine insisted that the ultimate decision to marry must be a voluntary act of the couple concerned.[26] Bride-service also aroused the suspicions of the clergy. The engaged couple living under the same roof might have opportunities for premarital sexual relations.

Plasencia's study did not mention bride-service and bride-price. Hence these customs did not come under the protection of the Spanish law courts. In 1628 a *cedula* of Philip IV ordered that no Indian in any part of the empire should make a payment or provide free labor services to his future father-in-law.[27] This legislation was not vigorously enforced in the Philippines. At the beginning of the eighteenth century Governor Zabalburu and Archbishop Camacho did in fact launch a campaign to wipe out bride-service and bride-price,[28] but just how successful they were cannot be determined until the manuscript sources for the eighteenth century are examined. For our immediate purposes the important conclusion is that many of the socioeconomic aspects of the marriage pattern in pre-Hispanic society were not materially altered during the first century of Spanish rule.

The spread and the eventual acceptance of the Christian ideal of matrimony among the Filipinos represents one of the most enduring achievements of the Spanish religious. A new standard of premarital and marital morality was set up. Like all such norms, this one was not always observed, but it was a standard destined to exercise continuing influence through the coming centuries.

The next step in the spread of Christianity was the introduction of the sacraments of penance and Holy Eucharist. Penance provided the Church with a potent weapon in the enforcement of moral and ethical standards. Nor could the introduction of this sacrament be long delayed, for all Catholics were required to confess once a year.

This sacrament could not be properly administered unless the clergy acquired a solid linguistic training. There are few references to Filipinos confessing through interpreters, as was sometimes done in Mexico. Hence a characteristic publication of the Philippine presses was the *confessionario.* These *confessionarios* were bilingual texts designed to aid the priests in asking the pertinent questions and in eliciting truthful answers. The first of these texts was published circa 1610 by the prolific Dominican Tagalist, Francisco de San José. By the end of the seventeenth century similar manuals circulated in several of the major languages of the archipelago.[29]

The shortage of ecclesiastical personnel was always a handicap. In the Jesuit church in Manila, for example, Filipinos had to wait from ten to fifteen days in spite of the formidable array of priests hearing confession.[30] In contrast to the concentration of people in the vicinity of Manila, the dispersal of the population in the provinces posed another set of problems. Three years might elapse before Christians had their confessions heard.[31]

The principle of Confession was entirely new to the Filipinos. In their pagan cults there was nothing even remotely analogous to it. Many Filipinos first viewed the sacrament with some misgivings. They had to be persuaded that the confessor would not be angry with them if they recited all their sins.[32] Frequent rotation of regular priests, usually every three years, avoided the awkward situation of someone being compelled or refusing to confess to a priest whom he feared or with whom he had quarreled.[33] Under those circumstances a Filipino was apt to become reticent and thus endanger the validity of that particular confession. The religious scrupulously avoided imposing heavy penances, lest the people's initial distrust of the sacrament harden into opposition. Typical penances were hearing a few Masses, reciting a few Rosaries, or visiting a sick person.[34]

Once accustomed to the idea of confession, the Filipinos took to it with characteristic enthusiasm. Sharp differences of opinion, however, were expressed about whether they understood it. Ribadeneyra, the sanguine spokesman of the first generation of Franciscan missionaries, claimed that the Filipinos usually needed no prodding from their confessors. They came to confession with their consciences well examined. They recited their sins with a clarity based on a firm grasp of the doctrine. The chronicler recounted with zest cases of Filipinos not satisfied with the rigor of the penance assigned.[35] The more sophisticated Jesuit historian Pedro Murillo Velarde, writing around 1750, was more skeptical than Ribadeneyra. He wearily complained that the inclination of the Filipinos toward quibbling and contradictions created labyrinths which confused even the most experienced confessors.[36]

In order to overcome the Filipinos' fear and embarrassment, the missionaries developed a simple question and answer technique. Brief questions were phrased, and the confessors sought to elicit truthful and succinct answers. Placing no faith in the veracity of their parishioners, and experienced in handling primitive peoples, the confessors asked the same question in a variety of ways. An example of this technique is Fernando Rey's Ilokano confessional. The manual is divided into ten sections, one for each of the commandments, with a series of simply phrased questions for each section.

Evidently it was in the enforcement of the Sixth Commandment that the religious encountered their greatest difficulties. Intercourse with in-laws and future in-laws, incest according to canon law, seems not to have been uncommon. The Filipinos apparently could not be made to take very literally the prohibitions of the Sixth Commandment, and they sought to conceal such conduct from their confessors.[37] From a canonical point of view such prodding was necessary, for a confession in which some capital sins are deliberately concealed is not valid.[38] What all conscientious religious fought to overcome was the popular conviction that an annual absolution in the confessional gave the Filipinos license to gratify their passions and appetites during the rest of the year.[39] In enforcing standards of premarital chastity, the clergy had more success among the women than the men. The efforts of the religious were sometimes undercut by that minority in their own ranks who openly violated clerical celibacy.

The administration of penance was complemented by the introduction of the sacrament of the Eucharist. In the case of this sacrament the Mexican background must be taken into account. There was a spirited controversy in Mexico about the desirability of allowing the Indians to receive Communion. Many Spanish laymen voiced doubts as to whether the Indians were able to appreciate its spiritual meaning. Some Spanish colonists accused the Indians of being stupid, infamous sinners, and chronic alcoholics. Their understanding of the Christian doctrine was said to be insufficient. The regular clergy, on the other hand, were partisans of a course of action which avoided extremes. They did not refuse the Sacrament to all Indians, and yet the friars would not grant it indiscriminately to everyone. Candidates were carefully screened. The religious were particularly anxious that the candidates know the difference between ordinary and sacramental bread, and between the non-consecrated and the consecrated Host. Ordinarily, a convert was not allowed to receive Communion until he had been confessing for four or five years. The selective policy of the Mexican friars received vigorous endorsement from Pope Paul III in 1537. Although the Mexican synods of 1539 and 1546 confirmed this course of action, latent opposition continued. As late as 1573 the Augustinian canonist, Pedro de Agurto, found it necessary to publish in Mexico City a treatise whose thesis was the obligation of the Church to grant Communion discriminately to qualified Indians.[40]

This same Pedro de Agurto was presented by Philip II in 1595 as the first Bishop of Cebu. He died in his see in 1608. Two years before that event his Mexican treatise was reprinted in the Philippines.[41] This may not have been a casual circumstance, for the viewpoint expressed in Agurto's work coincided with the policy that the Philippine religious followed. Communion was not refused to all converts, nor was it granted to everyone. The Dominicans defined the course of action of the other missionary orders when, at their chapter meeting held in April of 1597, they resolved to administer the Eucharist "in good time" to those Filipinos "sufficiently well indoctrinated."[42]

The religious sought to impress upon the Filipinos the meaning of the Sacrament, so that they could derive the maximum spiritual benefit from it. It was also hoped that as a result of preliminary preparation desecrations, or the Sacrament's misuse, might be avoided. Incidents recounted in the chronicles about misfortunes befalling natives who received Communion without making a worthy confession had an obvious didactic purpose.[43] Parish priests were admonished not to allow the keys of the tabernacle where the consecrated Host was kept to fall into the hands of any Filipino lest some desecration result. For the same reason the Host was never kept in the *visita* chapels, where there were no resident priests.[44]

There was striking uniformity among the orders in their methods. By the 1590s confession was open to most converts, but only a small minority received Communion, usually during the season of Lent. Only the seriously ill received the Sacrament during the rest of the year. As in Mexico, candidates were screened as to their habits and their knowledge of the catechism. During the week prior to taking Communion, those chosen heard Mass daily. Sometimes the men lived in the monastery during that week, participating in its liturgical exercises, including the midnight matins [sic]. Some religious fostered the custom that during the week prior to taking Communion husbands and wives not cohabitate. This act of abstinence, of course, was not obligatory.[45] As the seventeenth century advanced, more and more Filipinos were receiving Communion. With the falling off of missionary enthusiasm, however, the quality of preliminary instruction declined.

The introduction of the Eucharist into the Philippines did not provoke the lively controversy accompanying its previous introduction into Mexico. For that matter the same is true for the sacraments of baptism, matrimony, and penance. Sufficient precedents had already been established in Mexico so that these sacraments could be introduced into the Philippines with only a minimum of dispute.

Not many Filipinos received the sacrament of confirmation, whose administration was an episcopal prerogative. The frequently long vacancies in the suffragan sees, as well as the extensive areas covered by each diocese, made this sacrament an occasional occurrence. In the populous Laguna de Bay district adjacent to Manila no confirmations were administered for a period of twenty-six years.[46] On the islands of Samar and Leyte there were no confirmations for a span of twenty-six years.[47] The regulars were indifferent if not actively hostile to the spread of confirmation. Some bishops had used the administration of confirmation as a preliminary to enforce episcopal visitation.[48] The consequences for the Filipinos were not grave. Theologically, confirmation is a supplement to baptism. As such it is desirable but not essential for participating in the sacramental life of the Church. Much more serious was the fact that few Filipinos received either the sacraments of holy orders or extreme unction, a condition whose ultimate consequences will be examined in the next chapter [of the original document].

The Christianization of the Philippines falls into three periods. The years between 1565 and 1578 were preparatory and exploratory. There was a scarcity of missionary personnel, and those available were without adequate linguistic training. The decades from 1578 until 1609 after which date the Philippines began to feel the full impact of the Dutch war, were the "golden age" of the missionary enterprise. Fired with apostolic zeal, this generation of missionaries was inspired by a seemingly boundless enthusiasm. A modest program for training a native elite was launched. Once the initial misunderstandings and the economic dislocations provoked by the conquest receded, the Filipinos in the main responded enthusiastically to the appeal of the new religion. The chronicles of the Franciscan Marcelo de Ribadeneyra (1601), and the Jesuit Pedro Chirino (1604), eloquently reflect the optimism animating this first generation of missionaries.

Juan de Medina's Augustinian chronicle provides a foil to the accounts of Ribadeneyra and Chirino. Serving in the Philippines from 1610 to 1635, Medina had what we might call a "second-generation complex." He suffered from an acute disappointment born of his conviction that the sanguine if somewhat unrealistic hopes of the preceding generation were not materializing. Among the Augustinians the lowering of morale took place as early as the 1590s. In the other orders the falling off of enthusiasm never was as pronounced as it was with the Augustinians, but there was a decline in the seventeenth century.

The general pattern of missionary activity in the islands was similar to what had previously occurred in Mexico. The zeal of the first generation of missionaries gave way to a spirit of apathy, routine, and discouragement. The net result was the same in both regions, but the causes were dissimilar. The decline of missionary morale in Mexico was largely the result of the losing battle the regular clergy were waging with the bishops and the secular clergy.[49] In the Philippines, the falling off of missionary enthusiasm set in as the regular clergy became increasingly aware of the limits of their resources and the magnitude of their task. The crushing burdens of the Dutch war weakened Spanish resolve to push forward the ambitious program of cultural reorganization originally contemplated.

As the seventeenth century wore on, the inadequacies of the missionary effort became increasingly apparent. Three sacraments—confirmation, extreme unction, and holy orders—were of slight importance in the spiritual life of the Filipinos. In the case of penance and the Eucharist only the minimum requirements established by the Church were met. The same situation, we observed, existed for the instruction in the catechism. Yet the Filipinos were Christianized in the face of the severe handicaps of a shortage of priests and a dispersed population speaking a bewildering variety of languages.

The "Philippinization" of Spanish Catholicism

Given the disadvantages under which the Spanish clergy had to operate, their efforts would have proved abortive if the Filipinos had not voluntarily responded to some features of Christianity. As it happened, the Filipinos endowed certain aspects of the new religion with a ceremonial and emotional content, a special Filipino flavor which made Catholicism in the archipelago in some respects a unique expression of that universal religion. In this process of "Philippinizing" Catholicism the major role belonged to the Filipinos. They showed themselves remarkedly selective in stressing and de-emphasizing certain features of Spanish Catholicism.

The Societal and Ritualistic Character of Philippine Christianity

Before the conquest, sacred and profane were often indistinguishable. The pagan religion permeated all phases of life. One of the aims of the Spanish religious was to create a Catholic community consciousness in which the teachings and the spirit of the Church would penetrate into the daily lives of the converts. The religious fostered a series of pious customs to provide daily reminders to their parishioners. The women and the children, for example, were gathered every day at the foot of the large wooden cross erected in the main plaza of each village to chant the Rosary, and in many parishes the children walked through the streets at sunset chanting the Rosary. In other parishes one of the altar boys rang a bell as he walked through the street at sunset, to remind the faithful to say one Our Father and one Hail Mary for the souls in Purgatory.[50] But these measures proved effective only in the *cabecera* villages, where there was a constant community. The majority of the Filipinos lived at some distance from the parish church.

The fiesta system and the founding of sodalities, on the other hand, reached out to embrace the whole scattered population of the parish. Although the majority of Filipinos preferred to live near their rice fields, they could be lured periodically into the *cabecera* village. The enticement was the fiesta. There were three fiestas of consequence to the Filipinos, namely, Holy Week, Corpus Christi, and the feast in honor of the patron saint of the locality. The parishioners flocked to the *cabecera* villages for these occasions. Not only did the fiestas provide a splendid opportunity to indoctrinate the Filipinos by the performance of religious rituals, but they also afforded the participants a welcome holiday from the drudgery of toil. The religious processions, dances, music, and theatrical presentations of the fiestas gave the Filipinos a needed outlet for their natural gregariousness. Sacred and profane blended together.[51]

The periodic visits which the provincial superior was obligated to make to the parishes administered by his order were usually the occasion of another elaborate celebration. The visiting prelate and his retinue made an *entrée joyeuse* into the *cabecera* village.[52] The European origins of this ceremony, the liturgical prototype for which was Christ's entry into Jerusalem on Palm Sunday, go back to the Middle Ages.[53] It is highly doubtful that the Filipinos were aware of the ceremony's elaborate liturgical symbolism, but they evidently relished the pageantry involved.

The founding of confraternities or sodalities of laymen and laywomen also contributed to the formation of a Christian community consciousness. Here is another example of a medieval Spanish institution which served different ends overseas. In the late Middle Ages confraternities (*cofradias* in Spanish) were voluntary associations whose religious function was the practice of piety and the performance of works of charity. Under the patronage of a particular saint or the Virgin these associations also provided a wide range of mutual aid benefits. Requiem Masses were sponsored for the deceased, their funerals paid for, and their widows and orphans assisted.

Confraternities were founded in many Indian parishes in America whence they were introduced into the Philippines.[54] In the islands the mutual aid benefits, a prominent feature of the institution in Spain, were deemphasized. The Jesuits skillfully used their sodalities as instruments to consolidate Christianization. The members performed two acts of charity. The first was to visit the sick and the dying to urge them to receive the sacraments and to persuade the infidels to request baptism. The purpose of these visits was to discourage the ill from appealing to clandestine pagan priests for consolation. The other act of charity was for members to attend funerals. The presence of sodality members, it was hoped, might discourage ritual drinking, a custom which the clergy was anxious to suppress.[55]

The Filipinos did not respond to all forms of social indoctrination. The attempt of the Franciscans and the Jesuits to introduce processions of flagellants during the Holy Week ceremonies enjoyed, because of its novelty, some initial success. But since the principle of corporeal mortification was alien to their previous religious traditions, the Filipinos only occasionally showed any sustained enthusiasm for that typical expression of Spanish asceticism.[56] What the Filipinos did accept with gusto were the more sensual and graphic aspects of traditional Spanish observances during Holy Week. Candlelit processions of penitents dressed in hood and gown, large floats depicting scenes from the Passion, the thick aroma of incense, and noisy music were some of the colorful externals of Spanish Catholicism which flourished in a Philippine setting.

Another act of penitence to which the Franciscans sought to persuade the Filipinos was to deprive themselves periodically of their daily bath. Ribadeneyra, the first Franciscan chronicler, quoted with approval the pious legend that Apostle St. James the Younger, never bathed during his lifetime, but he ruefully admitted that the Filipinos all too infrequently showed signs of emulating that Apostle's example. No amount of ecclesiastical eloquence could induce the Filipinos to give up their daily bath at sunset, which they took for pleasure as well as for bodily hygiene. In spite of their prejudice against bathing, the clergy had the good sense not to interfere with this Philippine custom.[57]

Accustomed to the water since infancy, the Filipinos did, however, take enthusiastically to another aspect of Catholicism, that is, the use of holy water. Their faith in its efficacy was almost boundless, and their demand for it was insatiable.[58]

It is apparent that one of Catholicism's strongest appeals was its splendid ritual and its colorful pageantry. In this respect the Filipino attitude was not substantially different from most other indigenous peoples of the Spanish empire. But there are special features to the Filipino response. Singing played a prominent role in the pre-Hispanic culture, hence the Filipinos proved eager and talented pupils of liturgical music. They soon acquired proficiency in singing Gregorian chants. They learned to play European instruments like the flute, the violin and the flagcolet with remarkable skill.[59] The Filipino love of pageantry expressed itself in a variety of ways, one of which was the popular custom of shooting off firecrackers as the Host was elevated at Mass.[60]

The pomp and pageantry of the Church's ritual contrast with the simple edifices in which these ceremonies were ordinarily performed. Only in Manila and its environs were there many elaborate stone churches constructed in the baroque style. In the provinces the majority of the cabecera churches and virtually all the visita chapels were plain, wooden structures built according to the principles of the folk architecture of the Filipinos rather than the monumental architecture of the Spaniards.[61] As a protection against the hot and humid climate these churches were built elevated on thick timbers. The walls were made of bamboo, and nipa palm leaves provided the material for the roofing. The unpretentiousness of these churches apparently did not dampen the enthusiasm of the Filipinos for the colorful rituals of the Church.

The acceptance on the part of the Filipinos of the Catholic ritual pattern had much to do with the eventual suppression of pre-Hispanic ritual drinking. Without being outright hypocrites the Spanish clergy could not oppose moderate drinking as such. Excessive indulgence they could attack as a threat to public morality. What aroused their hostility was that drinking was identified exclusively with the pagan religious observances of betrothals, weddings, and funerals. The missionaries took vigorous measures to wipe out this custom. One method was to denounce offenders from the pulpit. The culprits were ostracized for a certain period of time.[62] Often less drastic measures sufficed. In order to disentangle betrothals from ritual drinking, the religious fostered the custom that the fiscal conduct the ceremony in the presence of the two families, without benefit of alcoholic stimulation.[63] The sodalities contributed to the undermining of ritual drinking at the celebration of funeral rites, as we recently observed. Such a tradition could not be suddenly abolished by ecclesiastical fiat, but gradual progress was registered. Ritual drinking survived longest in the less Hispanized regions of the archipelago such as the Bisayas and Cagayan, but even there the custom was on the decline during the second half of the seventeenth century.[64] But the remarkable fact is that ritual drinking was eventually eliminated among the Christianized peoples of the islands. Ceremonial drinking disappeared after the suppression of the pagan rituals with which, in the minds of the Filipinos, it had come to be identified. The custom withered away as the pagan ritual complex was overwhelmed by the elaborate ceremonies of Spanish Christianity, in which alcoholic stimulation had no necessary function. Thus the acceptance of the Catholic ritual pattern had much to do with making the Filipinos the sober people they remain to this day.

Since Philippine society before the conquest was kinship-oriented, the Catholic custom of ritual co-parenthood provided an opportunity, which the Filipinos eagerly grasped, namely, to bring kinship relations into the circle of Christianity. According to the Catholic ritual, each person at baptism is required to have two sponsors, a godfather (a *compadre* or *padrino*) and a godmother *(madrina)*. Godparents were also required for confirmation, on the assumption that confirmation was a completion of baptism. At weddings, godparents were optional. The notion of sponsorship does not have a Biblical but rather a customary basis, according to canon law. Baptism was traditionally regarded as a spiritual rebirth at which ceremony spiritual, as opposed to natural, parents were considered necessary. Thus a spiritual and mystical relationship was formed between the godparents and the godchild. No marriage, for example, between them was possible.

Some interesting innovations resulted when ritual co-parenthood *(compadrazgo)* spread to America and to the Philippines. In contrast to Spain, the tendency overseas was to expand the number of people involved. The "blanketing in" of relatives of the participants was common. The relationship between godparents and parents rather than between godparents and godchildren was stressed, by creating a functional relationship between age equals rather than an unbalanced relationship between two generations. In the colonies there were sometimes as many as twenty occasions when godparents were chosen, in contrast to the two obligatory occasions fixed by the Council of Trent. Co-parenthood was often extended to include such mundane events as serious illness, the first shave of a youth, or the building of a new house. The trend was to choose godparents from a superior social stratum, for the participants in the relationship were under some moral obligation to aid each other. Ritual co-parenthood promoted social stability, especially in regard to interclass and interracial relations.[65]

Compadrazgo rapidly spread in the Philippines. *Conquistadores* and early *encomenderos* frequently served as godfathers to native chieftains and their relatives. Magellan was Humabon's sponsor.[66] Legazpi was Doña Isabel's godfather. He also served in the same capacity at the baptism of Tupas, and the Adelantado's grandson was the godfather of Tupas' son.[67] During the first generation of missionary activity, the *compadrazgo* served a symbolic purpose, a visible act of reconciliation between the conquerors and the conquered.

The actual spread of *compadrazgo* is exceedingly difficult to trace. The available sources contain very little information on the subject. A tantalizing indication of the rapid spread and the social significance of ritual co-parenthood can be found in an ordinance of the Audiencia (May 17, 1599) prohibiting Chinese converts from serving as godparents. The edict accused the Chinese of "having a great number of godchildren, both Christian and infidel, in order to have them ready for any emergency that may arise, and to employ them as false witnesses—to which they lend themselves with great facility, and at little cost—and for other evil purposes and intents, exchanging with them favors and assistance in their affairs. . . ."[68] If more information of this sort were readily available, it would be possible to reconstruct the historical process by which ritual co-parenthood blended into or destroyed pre-conquest kinship relations or created new kinship ties. Since this is not possible with the sources available, *compadrazgo* must be studied in a contemporary setting, with the tools available to the social anthropologist.

Syncretic Elements in Philippine Christianity

The Filipinos' lack of a solid grasp of Catholic doctrine threatened to cause native Christianity to degenerate into outward ritual formalism. The line between veneration of the saints and idolatry was often crossed, and belief in miracles sometimes provoked a relapse into magic and superstition.

There emerged no one single cult of mass appeal comparable to the celebrated apparition of the Indian Virgin of Guadalupe in Mexico. Although there was no Philippine Virgin of Guadalupe, the Filipinos' belief in miracles was boundless and virtually uncontrollable. Few of these "miracles" received any official recognition from the Church, but such ecclesiastical discouragement did little to dampen the simple faith of the Filipinos in the ever-present powers of the supernatural. And to this day in the rural Philippines an atmosphere of the miraculous and the supernatural permeates popular Catholicism.

The suppression of outward pagan rituals did not entail the abolition of a whole accretion of superstitious customs of pre-Hispanic origin. Rather these folk customs were gradually if only superficially Christianized. Friar Tómas Ortiz's *Practica del ministerio*, published in Manila in 1731, is an invaluable source for observing the development of this "Christianizing" process. Father Ortiz commented:

> the Indians very generally believe that the souls of the dead return to their houses the third day after their death in order to visit the people in it, or to be present at the banquet, and consequently, to be present at the ceremony of the *tibao.* They conceal and hide that by saying that they are assembling in the house of the deceased in order to recite the Rosary for him. If they are told to do their praying in the church, they refuse to comply because that is not what they wish to do. . . . They light candles in order to wait for the soul of the deceased. They spread a mat on which they scatter ashes, so that the tracks or footsteps of the souls may be impressed thereupon; and by that means they are able to ascertain whether the soul came or not. They also set a dish of water at the door, so that when the soul enters it may wash its feet there.[69]

One method for apprehending a thief turns out to be a classic example of the coexistence of pagan and Christian elements in which sacred and profane are interwoven. "It is reduced to placing in a *bilao,* sieve or screen some scissors fastened at the point in the shape of the cross of St. Andrew, and in them they hang their rosary. Then they repeat the name of each one of those who are present and who are assembled for this. If, for example, when the name Pedro is mentioned, the *bilao* shakes, they say that Pedro is the thief."[70]

The densely populated spirit world of pre-Hispanic Philippine religion was not swept away by the advent of Christianity. Some Filipino Catholics continued to ask permission from the spirits before doing certain things. The *nonos* had to be propitiated on occasions, such as before taking fruit from a tree or before crossing a river. Added Father Ortiz: "When they are obliged to cut any tree, or not to observe the things or ceremonies which they imagine not to be pleasing to the genii or the *nonos*, they ask pardon of them and excuse themselves to choose beings by saying among many other things that the Father commanded them to do it, and that they are not willingly lacking in respect to the genii, or that they do not willingly oppose their will, etc."[71] Thus did some Filipinos seek to reconcile their pagan superstitions with their Christian beliefs.

Father Ortiz's observations point up the syncretic element in Philippine Christianity during the early Spanish period; it would, however, be rash to postulate a "mixed religion" hypothesis by claiming that the Filipinos worshipped idols behind altars, adopting from Christianity only those elements which harmonized with the pre-conquest religion. Those pre-conquest rituals and beliefs which survived the conquest eventually lost their pagan identity and blended into popular or folk Catholicism. With the passing of time this process acquired increasing intensity. In the seventeenth century syncretic elements are often apparent, but in the nineteenth century they are much less so.

Toward the Spanish clergy the Filipinos were capable of showing on occasion a remarkable solidarity, even to the extent of burying, temporarily, personal animosities among themselves. An informal conspiracy of silence operated at times to keep the religious ignorant of the existence of some scandals or the continuance of clandestine pagan rituals. A Filipino who passed on such information to the priest was called a *mabibig*, a Tagalog word meaning informer or spy.[72] If his identity became known, ostracism by his fellow countrymen was apt to be his lot.

Various means of breaking through the conspiracy of silence were devised. One method was for the *fiscales* to keep the religious informed. But the *fiscales* could also be parties to the silent conspiracy. The clergy initially encouraged the writing of anonymous letters. This procedure proved not very helpful; charges made under the cover of anonymity often turned out to be false.[73]

The conspiracy of silence began to lose its effectiveness gradually, as the daily lives and customs of the Filipinos became somewhat more Christianized. The silent conspiracy continued longest in that sphere where Spanish Christianity could offer no satisfactory substitute for traditional pagan observances. Pre-conquest religion, for example, stressed the causes and cures of illness. Catholicism offered little specific help in this regard. There was no Catholic ritual for curing illness, other than the appeal to prayer. The

Church could only provide sacramental consolations to the ill and the dying. But the majority of Filipinos died without receiving the sacraments of penance, Holy Eucharist, and extreme unction. The absence of the Church when death loomed was a salient characteristic of Philippine Christianity. Its causes and its consequences merit some attention.

The Last Rites

Of all the sacraments that of extreme unction caused the greatest amount of controversy. Basic to an understanding as to how this controversy developed must be an awareness of the fact there were usually less than four hundred priests ministering to about 600,000 Filipinos. Furthermore, the majority of the natives did not live in compact villages but in small scattered units near their rice fields. The shortage of clergy and the dispersal of the population were the two basic arguments that the regular clergy invoked to justify their refusal to administer the last sacraments in the dwellings of the Filipinos. They argued that a priest would not be justified in spending, for example, three days traveling to and from a sick person's home located in an inaccessible part of the parish, thereby depriving the remainder of his parishioners of his ministrations. In the early 1680s, Archbishop Pardo vigorously sought to enforce compliance with the canon of the Mexican Council of 1585 which ordained that the last rites be administered in the homes of the dying. That prelate's efforts, however, proved to be fruitless.

In their correspondence with Archbishop Pardo, the provincial superiors contended that they had trained the chieftains and the *fiscales* to bring the sick in hammocks to the *cabecera* church before illness had progressed too far. The provincial superiors concluded that few Filipinos died without the sacraments unless death occurred suddenly, in which case a priest could scarcely be expected to be present.[74] Independent evidence does not corroborate this claim. Not laboring under any such compulsion to rationalize as were the provincial superiors in the controversy with Archbishop Pardo, Alcina candidly admitted to his Jesuit superiors in Rome that seven out of every ten Filipinos died without the sacraments.[75]

The religious were sensitive to the charge that they had abandoned their parishioners on their deathbeds. The vacuum created by the scarcity of priests and the dispersal of the population was eventually, but only partially, filled by the growth of a custom peculiar to the Philippines. Specially trained natives visited the seriously sick and, reciting the Rosary and performing other pious devotions, did bring the ill some spiritual consolation to prepare them for possible death. These visitors were called *magpapahesus*, which in Tagalog means "one who makes another call on Jesus." The genesis of this custom goes back to the seventeenth century, but it was not prevalent then. The religious superiors in their correspondence with Archbishop Pardo did not mention it. It is inconceivable that they would have neglected to do so if this practice had then been customary. Such a makeshift substitute for the last rites certainly would have eased the task of justifying their refusal to administer the last sacraments in the homes.

The *magpapahesus* evidently had a Jesuit origin. One of the duties of the Jesuit sodality members was to visit the seriously ill. This obligation was originally envisaged as a means of destroying the influence of the pagan priests rather than as an imperfect substitute for the last rites.[76] Yet this substitute is precisely what it became in the eighteenth century and afterward when the religious, sensitive about the accusations made in the Pardo period, felt compelled to do something toward consoling the sick and the dying.

The theological consequences of this neglect of the last rites may have been grave for many Filipinos. According to Catholic doctrine, a person dying in a state of mortal sin is destined for eternal damnation. In view of the fact that Filipinos ordinarily confessed only once a year, it is reasonable to suppose that some of the seriously ill were not in a state of grace. The most certain and direct means of winning grace is through the sacrament of penance. Because of the situation described above, this easier route was closed to most Filipinos. While it is true that even without the benefit of penance a believer can acquire grace by making what the theologians call an act of perfect contrition—an act of sorrow for sin based on the love of God—still, this act is a more difficult accomplishment for most people than is the act of imperfect contrition. The latter is an act of sorrow for sin motivated by fear of divine chastisement.[77] Considering the inadequacy of the average Filipino's doctrinal knowledge, it is certainly permissible to doubt whether many of them were capable of grasping the theological distinction between an imperfect and a perfect act of contrition. But here is where the task of the historian ends and that of the theologian begins. What can be said with certainty is that without the sacraments a believer's chances for salvation are made considerably more difficult but by no means impossible.

The more mundane consequences for the majority of Filipinos were as lamentable as were some of the theological implications. The dying and their relatives, on the other hand, were deprived of the ceremonial consolations of their faith. Furthermore, the dead were usually buried without benefit of sacerdotal benediction. The dispersal of the population and the exorbitant fees charged by many priests made this ecclesiastical ceremony a privilege of the relatively wealthy. Burial fees often ranged from fifty pesos to five hundred pesos, varying according to the estimated wealth of the deceased.[78]

The Question of a Filipino Clergy

Many of the characteristics of Philippine Christianity—outward ritual formalism rather than solid doctrinal knowledge, the tendency toward idolatry, superstition, and magic, the conspiracy of silence, and the infrequency
of the sacraments, especially the last rites—are largely explainable in terms
of two factors. There were not enough Spanish priests to administer the
sacraments and the population was highly dispersed. These conditions enabled the Filipinos to be selective in their response to Christianity and to
endow the new religion with a unique emotional and ceremonial content.
From the viewpoint of the Spanish clergy, the "Philippinization" of
Catholicism departed too often from the norms laid down by the Church.
There was only one feasible means of checking this trend, namely to train
carefully some Filipinos for the priesthood. Six or eight hundred well-
trained Filipino clergymen obviously could have rendered invaluable assistance in consolidating the Church's hold over the people.

In principle, the Church recognized that one of its major responsibilities
in a recently converted land was to train a native clergy which in time
would be able to assume the administration and propagation of the Faith
among their own people. And the Crown, from 1677 onward, urged that
steps be prudently taken to train a Filipino clergy. But the Spanish regular
clergy adamantly refused to grant ordination to any appreciable number of
Filipinos.[79] This hostile attitude of the Spanish regulars rested on a selfish
desire to preserve their privileges as well as upon genuine scruples of conscience. A numerous Filipino clergy obviously would have undermined the
dominant position of the Spanish regulars. According to the administration
of the *Patronato*, title to the parishes was vested in the name of the various
orders. The regulars could only be ousted from their benefices by the determined action of the civil authorities. Such a drastic step no governor of the
Philippines would undertake, for everyone was aware that the religious
were a potent factor in maintaining Spanish hegemony in the provinces.
Furthermore, there were no available replacements for the regulars.

The majority of the Spanish regular clergy genuinely believed that the
Filipinos were congenitally unfit for the full responsibilities of the sacerdotal state. Friar Gaspar de San Agustin voiced the sentiments of many of his
brethren when he wrote:

Rather, their [the Filipinos'] pride will be aggravated with their elevation to
so sublime a state; their avarice with the increased opportunity of preying on
others, their sloth with their no longer having to work for a living; their van-
ity with the adulation that they must needs seek, desiring to be served by

those whom in another state of life they would have to respect and obey. . . .
For the *Indio* who seeks holy orders does so not because he has a call to a
more perfect state of life, but because of the great and almost infinite advantages which accrue to him along with the new state of life he chooses. How
much better to be a Reverend Father than to be a yeoman or a sexton! What
a difference between paying tribute and being paid a stipend! Between being
drafted to cut timber and being waited on hand and foot! Between rowing a
galley and riding in one! All of which does not apply to a Spaniard, who by
becoming a cleric deprives himself of the opportunity of becoming a mayor,
a captain or a general, together with many of the comforts of his native land,
where his estate has more to offer than the whole nation of *indios.* Imagine
the airs with which such a one will extend his hand to be kissed! What an in-
cubus upon the people shall his father be, and his mother, his sisters, his female cousins, when they shall have become great ladies overnight, while
their betters are still pounding the rice for their supper! For if the *indio* is in-
solent and insufferable with little or no excuse, what will he be when elevated to so high a station? . . . What reverence will the *indios* themselves have
for such a priest, when they see he is of their color and race? Especially when
they realize that they are the equals or betters, perhaps of one who managed
to get himself ordained, when his proper station in life should have been that
of a convict or a slave.[80]

An enlightened Spanish Jesuit, Juan Delgado, answered these declama-
tions with wit and skill. Delgado's apologia for the Filipinos is permeated
with the atmosphere of the Age of Reason. Like his contemporary Montesquieu, Delgado stressed that the character of men is molded in large measure by their environment. Men do not inherit vices and errors but acquire
them from experience. Hence such defects are susceptible to rational cor-
rection. After urbanely demolishing Gaspar de San Agustin's dismal charac-
terology, Delgado concluded that whatever vices and defects the Filipinos
might possess had an environmental rather than a congenital origin. Give
some Filipinos a sound and well-supervised education and a conscientious
and well-trained native clergy would emerge, according to him.[81]

Delgado's reasoned defense of the Filipinos was not shared by the majority of the Spanish religious. In the eighteenth century pressure from the
Crown and the growth of the population compelled the regulars to use
some native priests. Filipinos were not admitted into the regular orders, but
some received training as secular priests in seminaries operated by the regulars. The Filipino priesthood, who numbered 142 in 1750, were trained to
fill in subordinate positions as secular coadjutors to the religious.[82] These
Filipino clergymen did a great deal of the laborious work of the parish, but

they were denied the emoluments and the prestige of heading a parish. The regulars, believing the Filipinos were fit only for subordinate positions, gave them only a minimum of training.

The growth of a native clergy sustained a severe reverse during the administration of Archbishop Basilio Sancho de Santa Justa y Rufina, who arrived in Manila in 1767. In his attempt to enforce episcopal visitation, the archbishop ousted many of the religious orders from their parishes. He replaced them with Filipino priests. He also had to fill the parishes of the Jesuits, left vacant by the expulsion of the Society from the Spanish dominions in 1767. Poorly trained and half-educated, the Filipino clergymen rendered a deplorable account of themselves. Manila wits quipped "that there were no oarsmen to be found for the coastal vessels, because the archbishop had ordained them all."[83] The most lurid fears of Gaspar de San Agustin seemed to come to pass when these semi-literate priests were suddenly put into positions of authority which their lack of sound training did not qualify them to fill. The result of the fiasco was a restoration of the old order. The Spanish religious returned to their parishes, with Filipino priests merely serving as assistants.

In the eighteenth century the Spanish clergy rationalized that the Filipinos were temperamentally unfit for the full responsibilities of the priesthood. The justification for the perpetuation of the system in the nineteenth century was a political consideration. In the face of rising Filipino nationalism aiming at independence, Filipino priests were regarded as potentially if not actively disloyal. The task which the Spanish clergy should have undertaken was not begun until after 1898. Under the American regime, church and state were separated. This change paved the way for undertaking that arduous task of training a competent Filipino clergy, an enterprise supervised by the Catholic hierarchy of the United States.

The Spanish missionaries were not unmindful of the universal character of their own religion, a universality based on the premise that all men are created equal in the image of God, endowed with a common origin and with a common end. It was in the service of this ideal that the religious went to the Philippines in the first place. Nor did the Spanish clergy believe that God spoke only in Spanish. They preached the gospel in many Philippine languages. Catholic equalitarianism and universalism however, were essentially other-worldly. All men were created equal in the sight of God but certainly not in the sight of their fellow men. The worldly inequalities in wealth, status, and intelligence were justified as a necessary consequence of man's imperfect and sinful nature. In the Middle Ages the concept of social inequalities was applied to individuals but not to whole races as such. So it was with Thomas Aquinas, for example. Dante, both one of the last exponents of medieval universalism and one of the first spokesmen of modern statism and imperialism, extended the concept of social inequalities from individuals to races and nations by setting up a hierarchy of races, with Rome at the top of the pyramid. The Spanish humanist Sepulveda molded this Dantesque argument into a justification for Spanish imperialism overseas—the Spanish race was congenitally superior and the Indians congenitally inferior.[84] This idea became a characteristic feature of the colonial mentality. Few Spanish religious in the Philippines could discard this colonialist notion that subject peoples were congenitally inferior. In deliberately stunting the growth of a Filipino clergy, they allowed their Spanish ethnocentricism to override the universal spirit of their creed.

The consequences for the character of Philippine Christianity were momentous. A well-trained Filipino clergy could have done a great deal to root out superstitions, to promote a firmer grasp of the doctrine, and to administer the sacraments with much greater frequency. As it was, there were virtually two religions. One was the Catholicism of the Spanish clergy and the Spanish colonists, and the other was the folk Catholicism of the Filipinos, a cleavage which was sharply delineated along racial and linguistic lines. A numerous Filipino clergy certainly could have done something to bridge the gap between these two expressions of Christianity. The Spanish clergy paid a heavy price for opposing the growth of a Filipino clergy. A trend toward "Philippinization" set in over which the Spanish clergy had little or no control.

If "Philippinization" was unfortunate from a Spanish and Catholic viewpoint, it had much to recommend it in a strictly Filipino context. It meant that the Filipinos absorbed as much Catholicism as they could easily digest under prevailing conditions but not as much as the Spaniards would have wanted them to do. That limited portion of Catholicism which the Filipinos did digest became an integral part of their way of life, and they found in the Church a new sense of human dignity. Catholicism forged powerful bonds of social unity, thereby creating a much-needed cushion against the severe economic stresses and strains whose exact character will be discussed in subsequent chapters [of the original document].

NOTES

1. A graphic description of iconoclastic activity on the part of the religious is in Francisco de Santa Ines, *Cronica*, II, 177ff.

2. For the documentation regarding the introduction of baptism see my article, "Pre-Baptismal Instruction and the Administration of Baptism in the Philippines during the Sixteenth Century," *The Americas*, XII (July, 1955), 3–23.

3. Pedro Chirino, *Relacion*, 233.

4. *Doctrina Christiana: The First Book Printed in the Philippines,* Manila, 1593, Edwin Wolf, editor (Washington, D.C.: Library of Congress, 1947). Friar Juan de Plascencia (see Chapter II, note 1) is the probable author, according to Wolf's introductory essay. For background material about this *Doctrina* see my article, "Philippine Linguistics," 155–156.

5. *BR*, XXIV, 268. Geronimo de Ripalda's well-known catechism, first published in Burgos in 1591, was printed in the Philippines in only one Tagalog edition during the seventeenth century (see J. T. Medina, *La imprenta*, II, 21). Hence it was no serious rival in popularity to the Bellarmine text.

6. In the *Doctrina* of 1593 the following key concepts were kept in Spanish: God, Trinity Holy Ghost, Virgin Mary, Pope, grace sin, cross, hell, church, Sunday and the names of the sacraments. This principle of missionary policy was established in Mexico after a spirited controversy, decades before the conversion of the Filipinos. Robert Ricard, *La "conquete spirituelle" du Mexique* (Paris: Institute d'ethnologie, 1933), 72–75.

7. *Archivo Ibero-Americano* II (May-June 1915), 393–394. Chirino, *Relacion,* pp. 67–70, 97, 120, 123, 151, 184, 185, 231. Colin-Pastells, *Labor Evangelica,* II, 118, 399, 409, 411.

8. For the Jesuit sources, see Colin-Pastells, *Labor Evangelica,* II, 127, 137, III, 135. Chirino, *Relacion,* 242. For the Franciscans see Ribadeneyra, *Historia,* 54–55. San Antonio, *Chronicas,* II, 12–18. For the Dominicans see Adurate, *Historia,* 64. For the Augustinians, see Juan de Medina. *Historia,* 75. Also see Morga-Retana, *Sucesos,* 206.

9. Diego de Bobadilla, S. J., "Relation of the Philippine Islands": 1640, *BR*, XXIX, 295.

10. Alcina, *Historia,* Bk. III, ch. 12.

11. There is a detailed census taken by the Jesuits of their Bisayan missions in *ARSI,* roll 158.

12. Chirino, *BR*, XII, 291–93, 295, 296, 299, 301, 317, 318, XIII, 52–54, 98–100, 134, 162, 163. Also, *ibid.*, XXI, 21, 210, 221.

13. For a Latin text of the bull, see Geronimo de Mendieta, O.F.M., *Historia eclesiastica Indiana* (Mexico: 1870), 269–271.

14. Pablo de Jesus, O.F.M., to Pope Gregory XIII: July 14, 1580, *BR*, XXXIV, 323–324.

15. Alonso de Mentrida, O.S.A., *Ritval,* 92–98. His interpretation of Paul III's bull was derived from Alonso de Veracruz's *Speculum conjugiorum* (Mexico: 1556) written as a guide to aid the clergy unravel some of the matrimonial tangles created by the shift from pagan polygamy to Christian monogamy.

16. Archbishop Garcia Serrano to Philip III: July 30, 1621, *BR*, XX, 86–87. Also see Fiscal to Philip III: July 1606, *BR*, XIV, 158–159.

17. Mentrida, *Ritval,* 88 ff. According to Rey's manual for confessors published in 1792 illicit intercourse with future in-laws continued to be not uncommon. Fernando Rey, O.S.A., *Confessionarios,* 271 ff.

18. Colin-Pastels, *Labor evangelica,* II, 404–405.

19. *Ibid.*, I, 450; *BR*, VII, 317–318.

20. *BR*, IX, 225–226.

21. Camacho investigation of 1697–98, AGI/AF 302. For the tariff itself, see *BR*, XLII, 56 ff. The Augustinians ordinarily charged two pesos for a simple marriage without the nuptial blessing. According to the Episcopal tariff no fees were to be charged for this ceremony.

22. *AGI/AF* 302.

23. The most celebrated example of Philippine erotica was one first described by the famous chronicler of the Magellan expedition: "The males, large and small, have their penis pierced from one side to the other near the head, with a gold or tin bolt as large as a goose quill. In both ends of the same bolt, some have what resembles a spur, with points upon the ends; others are like the head of a cart nail. I very often asked many, both young and old, to see their penis, because I could not credit it. In the middle of the bolt is a hole, through which they urinate. The bolt and the spurs always hold firm. They say that their women wish it so, and that if they did otherwise they would not have communication with them. When the men wish to have their communication with their women, the latter themselves take the penis not in the regular way and commence very gently to introduce it into their vagina with the spur on top first, and then the other part. When it is inside it takes its regular position; and thus the penis always stays inside until it gets soft, for otherwise they could not pull it out. Those people make use of that device because they are of a weak nature." Pigafetta, *Magellan's Voyage*, I, 166–169. Also see Loarca, *BR*, V, 117, and Morga-Retana, *Sucesos*, 196.

24. Morga, Ribadeneyra, Archbishop Benavides, Archbishop Santibanez, and Alcina, some of our most informative sources, claimed that the Chinese introduced sodomy to the Filipinos. Their principal argument was a linguistic one. They claimed that there was no word in the native languages for sodomy. The absence of a word does not necessarily prove the nonexistence of this practice, as the Spanish sources seemed to imply. Furthermore it is unprovable whether there was or was not a word for sodomy in preconquest times. The early seventeenth-century dictionaries are not now extant; and even if they were, the first vocabularies were certainly incomplete. Circa 1750 there was a Tagalog word for sodomy, *binabae,* meaning like a woman. Whether this word was of preconquest origin cannot be demonstrated. The few men who entered the pagan priesthood were effeminates or transvestites, but the Spanish sources deny that they were overt homosexuals. The linguistic argument is inconclusive, but the claim of these Spanish observers is suspect on other grounds: (1) if there was no sodomy in the Philippines before the conquest, that archipelago was one of the few regions in the world where it was unknown; (2) among the modern Filipino pagans sodomy is not unknown; (3) these Spanish observers were vituperative Sinophobes who hated the Chinese as intensely as they were dependent on them for certain economic services. Spanish Sinophobia may be unconsciously responsible for inventing the charge that the Chinese introduced sodomy to the Filipinos. A more plausible conclusion might be

that the incidence of homosexuality increased among the Filipinos as a result of the coming of the Chinese. Archbishop Santibanez to Philip II: June 24, 1598, *AGI/AF* 74; Benavides to Philip III: July 5, 1603, and February 3, 1605, *BR*, XII, 107; XIII, 274, 278; Morga-Retana, *Sucesos*, 196; Ribadeneyra, *Historia*, 37; Alcina, *Historia*, Bk. III, ch. 21. Although placing the primary responsibility on the Chinese, Alcina does admit that a few Spaniards who "ya no se contenta con la Venus ordinaria" were as guilty as the Chinese in introducing sexual deviations to the Filipinos.

25. Ordinance of the Audiencia: January 7, 1599, *BR*, XI, 31–32.

26. Mentrida, *Ritval,* 86.

27. *Recopilacion*, Bk. VI, tit. I. law 6.

28. *BR*, L, 216–217.

29. For a list of these confessionals, see J. T. Media, *La imprenta.*

30. Pedro Murillo Velarde, S. J., *Historia*, 5–6.

31. *Ibid.*, p. 28. Colin-Pastells, *Labor evangelica*, II, 409.

32. Aduarte, *Historia,* 156–157.

33. Domingo Fernandez Navarrete, O. P. *Tratados historicos*, 317.

34. Rey, *Confessonarios*, 344.

35. Ribadeneyra, *Historia,* 51–52.

36. Murillo Velarde, *Historia*, 5.

37. Rey, *Confessonarios*, 170, 208–210, 276–280, 284–287, 351–352.

38. Colin-Pastells, *Labor evangelica*, II, 409. Diaz, *Conquistas*, 239. Murillo Velarde, *Historia*, 36.

39. Rey, *Confessonarios,* 221–224.

40. Ricard, *La "conquete spirituelle,"* 148–152.

41. J. T. Medina, *La imprenta*, 4–6. I consulted a photostat copy of the 1573 edition of Agurto's treatise.

42. Aduarte, *Historia,* 121.

43. Colin-Pastells, *Labor evangelica*, III, 113; Diaz, *Conquistas*, 239; Murillo Velarde, *Historia*, 36.

44. Mentrida, *Ritval,* 48 ff.

45. Ribadeneyra, *Historia*, 67; Aduarte, *Historia*, 74, 121, 158–59; Chirino, *Relacion*, 140; Colin-Pastells, *Labor evangelica*, I, 361; II, 295, 343, 411.

46. *Ibid.*, III, 687–88. Bishop Salazar introduced confirmation as early as 1583. *BR*, V, 216–217.

47. Alcina's letter of 1660, *ARSI*, roll 165.

48. Colin-Pastells, *Labor evangelica*, III, 688. The infrequent references to confirmation in the chronicles of the regular orders suggests the relative lack of importance placed on this sacrament by the religious.

49. Ricard, *La "conquete spirituelle,"* 285 ff; Charles Gibson, *Tlaxcala in the Sixteenth Century*, 28 ff. Also see my *Millennial Kingdom*, 52–55.

50. Ribadeneyra, *Historia*, 57, 67; Chirino, *Relacion*, 70.

51. On June 18, 1677, Charles II dispatched a cedula to the Jesuit provincial superior (presumably to the superiors of the other orders also) ordering that each Philippine community have not more than patron saint for whose festivities the natives were obligated to contribute. Pastells collection, St. Louis University, Microfilm roll 28. This cedula apparently meant that the Filipinos should not be required to contribute to the patronal fiesta of both *cabecera* and the *visita*-barrio. Every male was required to make an annual contribution for this purpose at the time he made his obligatory annual confession. In 1697 this tax was fixed at three reales. *BR,* L, 218. For a description of how Holy Week was celebrated in a Jesuit parish, see Chirino, *Relacion,* 178.

52. Morga's letter to Philip II: June 8, 1598; Morga-Retana, *Sucesos,* 248.

53. Ernest Kantorowicz, "The 'King's Advent' and the Enigmatic Panels in the Three Doors of Santa Sabina," *The Art Bulletin,* XXVI (December, 1944), 207–231.

54. For general background see George M. Foster, "Cofradia and Compadrazgo in Spain and in Spanish America," *Southwestern Journal of Anthropology,* IX (Spring, 1953), 10 ff.

55. Colin Pastells, *Labor evangelica,* II, 117; Murillo Velarde, *Historia,* 219. Although generally well-informed, Morga showed no understanding of the effectiveness with which the religious used sodalities and fiestas as agencies of indoctrination and the enthusiastic response of the Filipinos to these techniques. Morga-Retana, *Sucesos,* 248.

56. The early Franciscan and Jesuit sources (Ribadeneyra and Chirino) claimed that the Filipino response was positive. This statement may be true, but the virtual absence of any references to flagellants in the later sources (San Antonio, Santa Ines, Martinez, and Colin) suggest that Filipino interest rapidly abated. Chirino, *Relacion,* 94, 137, 147, 176, 178, 186, 245; Ribadeneyra, *Historia,* 49–50; Murillo Velarde, *Historia,* 780–781.

57. Ribadeneyra, *Historia,* 49–50.

58. *BR,* XXXIV, 380.

59. Ribadeneyra, *Historia,* 54–55; San Antonio, *Chronicas,* II, 12–18; Chirino, *Relacion,* 242; Colin-Pastells, *Labor evangelica,* II, 127, 137; III, 135.

60. Acts of the First Provincial Council of Manila 1771, ms. At the Library of Congress, Manuscripts Division, Philippine Islands, Accession No. 6106-A, Box 1. Regarding the ms, see Schafer Williams, "The First Provincial Council of Manila, 1771," *Seminar,* XIII (1955–56), 33 ff. The Spaniards actually introduced a version of this theatrical custom into the Philippines. During the first Mass celebrated on Philippine soil, the guns of Magellan's ships roared a salute as the Host was elevated. Pigafetta, *Magellan's Voyage,* I, 121.

61. In the Manila area by 1620 there were only three wooden churches and twenty-seven stone churches. *BR,* XIX, 161–163. In the provinces the vast majority of *cabecera* churches and all the *visita* chapels were of wood. Alonso Sandin, O.P. to Charles II: May 20, 1685. AGI/AF 76. As of 1649 the Franciscans had some thirty-five *cabecera* churches in the Laguna de Bay area adjacent to Manila, eighteen of which were made of

stone. The Jesuits constructed three magnificent baroque churches of stone at Silang, Antipolo and Taytay near Manila. Murillo Velarde, *Historia*, 143–145. In the Bikol country, on the other hand, only three of the twenty-one parishes had stone churches. *BR*, XXXV, 278–287. Stone churches in the Bisayas and northern Luzon were uncommon, judging by the absence of references to such buildings. A few stone churches were built in the Bisayas during the eighteenth century.

62. See Chapter II [of source text] for a discussion of ritual drinking in pre-conquest times. Aduarte, *Historia*, 65.

63. Colin-Pastells, *Labor evangelica*, II, 117.

64. Alcina, *Historia*, Bk. III, ch. 22. As late as 1739 *alcades* were warned to be on the alert for clandestine ritual drinking, but even in that isolated province the custom was evidently on the wane. "Ordenanzas de alcades" (Cagan, 1739), ms. in possession of Professor Lesley Byrd Simpson, p. 6.

65. For the necessary background see Sidney W. Mintz and Eric R. Wolf, "An Analysis of Ritual Co-Parenthood *(Compadrazgo),*" *Southwestern Journal of Anthropology*, VI (Winter, 1950), 341–348. George Foster, "Confradia and Compadrazgo," *ibid.*, IX (Spring, 1953), 1–28.

66. Pigafetta, *Magellan's Voyage* I, 153–155.

67. Juan de Grijalva, O.S.A., *Cronica de la orden de n.p.s. Augustin en las provincias de la Nueva Espana en quarto edades desde el ano de 1533 hasta el de 1592* (Mexico: 1624), 125.

68. *BR*, XI, 75–76.

69. *BR*, XLIII, 105–106.

70. *Ibid.*, 109.

71. *Ibid.*, 105.

72. Letter of Gaspar de San Augustin published in Juan Delgado, S. J., *Historia sacro-profana*, 284.

73. *Ibid.*, pp. 314–315.

74. For the correspondence of the Dominican, Augustinian, and Jesuit superiors with the archbishop, see Colin-Pastells, *Labor evangelica*, III, 115 ff. For the letters of the Franciscan and Recollect superiors, see Pastells collection, St. Louis University, microfilm roll 14.

75. Alcina to General of Society, 1660, *ARSI*, roll 165.

76. Colin-Pastells, *Labor evangelica,* II. 117; Murillo Velarde, *Historia*, 28. Both Archbishop Camacho in 1697 and Simon de Anda in his memorial of April 12, 1768, criticized the religious for their refusal to administer the last sacraments in the homes of the sick. *BR*, XLIII, 55 and L, 175–176.

77. Hieronymous Noldin, S. J., *De sacramentis*, 3 vols. (Rome: 1927), III, 253–255; Henry Davis, S. J., *Moral and Pastoral Theology*, 4 vols. (London: Sheed and Ward, 1945), III, 335–357.

78. Camacho investigation of 1697–98, *AGI/AF* 302.

79. Cedula of August 22, 1677, Pastells collection, St. Louis University, microfilm roll 8. Archbishop Pardo opposed the growth of a Filipino clergy, alleging "their evil customs, their vices and their preconceived ideas which made it necessary to treat them as children even when they were fifty or sixty years old." *BR*, XLV, 182–183.

80. The translation is from Horace de la Costa, S. J., "The Development of the Native Clergy in the Philippines," *Theological Studies*, VIII (July, 1947), 235–236.

81. For San Augustin's letter and Delgado's reply see Delgado, *Historia sacro-profana*, 273 ff. Delgado's "environmentalist" explanation of the character of the Filipinos is similar to the defense of the Mexican Indians formulated by Clavigero (1731–87). Francisco Javier Clavigero, S. J., *Historia Antigua de Mexico*, 4 vols. (Mexico: 1945), IV, 259. Both Jesuit historians were evidently under the spell of Enlightenment environmentalism, whose most articulate spokesman was Montesquieu.

82. A. Brou, S. J., "Notes sur les origins du clerge philippin," *Revue de l'histoire missionaire*, IV (1927), 546–547.

83. De la Costa, in *Theological Studies*, VIII, 242. For the archbishop's melodramatic confession of failure, see his pastoral letter of June 14, 1772, in Ferrando and Fonseca, *Historia de los pp. dominicos en las islas filipinas*, 6 vols. (Madrid, 1870–72), 54–59.

84. For some remarks on the Spanish and late medieval origins of this colonialist mentality, see my *Millennial Kingdom*, 61–63.

10

Javanese Aristocracy
and the Dutch

RADEN ADJENG KARTINI*

Kartini, whose name is identified with the feminist movement in Indonesia (her birthday, April 21, is celebrated as the day of women's emancipation), was, along with her sister, among the first women in the Indonesian aristocracy to have had the advantage of a Western education. Her father was a liberal, an aristocrat who held an important position in the Dutch "indirect" administration.

Although Kartini died at the young age of twenty-five, she nonetheless had a prolific correspondence with a number of Dutch individuals, most notably two women. Mevrouw Ovink-Soer, wife of the Assistant Resident at Japara, was, in the words of the noted anthropologist Hildred Geertz, a "highly cultured" woman, "a fervent socialist and feminist" who had published a number of articles and was later to publish a book, *Women's Life in the Javanese Village.* Stella Zeehandelaar was "another radical feminist," whom Kartini had "met" through an advertisement she placed in a magazine inviting someone to correspond with her. Stella played, in Geertz's words, "the role of Kartini's ideological conscience."

Kartini's letters, written between 1899 and 1904 from the time she was twenty until her death, and translated by Agnes Louise Summers, caught the attention of Eleanor Roosevelt, who found them "fascinating for the picture they give of the life and spirit of the times." In the extracts below,

---

*Raden Adjeng Kartini, *Letters of a Javanese Princess* (Lanham, MD: University Press of America, 1985), pp. 55–64.

Kartini describes the humiliating encounters between the Javanese and the Dutch colonial officials.

~

And now about the people, about the inhabitants of Java in general. The Javanese are grown-up children. What has the government done to further their development? For the noble sons of the country, there are so called high schools, normal schools, and the Doktor-djawa School [the medical school for native Indonesians]; and for the people, there are various elementary schools—one in each district, though the Government has divided these latter institutions into two classes. The first class, composed of schools which are situated in the provincial capitals, are conducted just as they were before the division, but in the schools of the second class, the children learn only Javanese, reading, writing and a little reckoning. No Malay is taught as formerly—why, it is not made clear. The Government believes, to my thinking, that if the people were educated, they would no longer be willing to work the land.

Father sent a note to the Government on the subject of education. O Stella, I wish that you could read it. You must know that many of the native rulers rejoice at the actions of the Government. The Javanese nobles are in favor with the Government here and in the Motherland, and everything possible is done to help them and to make them blossom to perfection.

The aristocracy sees with sad eyes how sons of the people are educated and often even elevated to their ranks by the Government because of knowledge, ability and industry. Sons of the people go to European schools and compare favorably in every respect, with the high and honorable sons of the noble. The nobles wish to have rights for themselves alone, they alone wish to have authority and to make Western civilization and enlightenment their own. And the Government helps and supports them in this, for it is to its own advantage to do so. As early as 1895 there was a decree, that without the special permission of his Excellency the Governor General no native child (from six to seven years old) who could not speak Dutch would be admitted to the free grammar school for Europeans. How can a native child of six or seven years learn Dutch? He would have had to have a Dutch governess, and then before he is able to learn the Netherlands language, the child must first know his own language, and necessarily know how to read and write. It is only regents who do not have to ask permission for their families to go to the European schools, most of the native officials are afraid of receiving a "No" in answer to their request and therefore do nothing. Is it presumptuous of Father to call attention to the fact that African and Am-

bonese children may go directly to the European schools, without understanding a word of Dutch? Stella, I remember well from my own school
days many European children went to school who knew as little Dutch as I,
and I hardly knew any.

Father says in his note that the government cannot set the rice upon the
table for every Javanese, and see that he partakes of it. But it can give him
the means by which he can reach the place where he can find the food. That
means is education. When the Government provides a means of education
for the people, it is as though it places torches in their hands which enabled
them to find the good road that leads to the place where the rice is
served. . . .

Father is very proud of his ancient noble race, but right is right, and justice is justice. We wish to equal the Europeans in education and enlightenment, and the rights which we demand for ourselves, we must also give to
others. This putting of stumbling blocks in the way of the education of the
people may well be compared to the acts of the Tsar, who while he is
preaching peace to the world, tramples under foot the good right of his own
subjects. . . . The Europeans are troubled by many traits in the Javanese, by
their indifference and lack of initiative. Very well, Netherlander, if you are
troubled so much by these things why do you not do something to remedy
the cause? Why is it that you do not stretch forth a single finger to help
your brown brother? Draw back the thick veil from his understanding,
open his eyes, you will see that there is in him something else besides an inclination for mischief, which springs principally from stupidity and ignorance. . . . Here before you lie the innermost thoughts of one who belongs
to that despised brown race. They are not able to judge us, and the things
that we do, and leave undone. Do they know us?

No, even as little as we know them. . . .

If you are interested in this subject, get the October number of *Nee-
landia*. It contains an address delivered by my brother in the Dutch language at the literary congress at Ghent. Professor Kern took him there and
asked him to speak. The sentiments to which he gives utterance are also
mine; they are ours. . . . The Hollanders laugh and make fun of our stupidity, but if we strive for enlightenment, then they assume a defiant attitude
toward us. What have I not suffered as a child at school through the ill will
of the teachers and of many of my fellow pupils? Not all of the teachers and
pupils hated us. Many loved us quite as much as the other children. But it
was hard for the teachers to give a native the highest mark, never mind how
well it may have been deserved. . . .

There is too much talk about the word "prestige," through the imaginary
dignity of the under [lower] officials. I do not bother about the prestige. I

am only amused at the manner in which they preserve their prestige over us Javanese.

Sometimes I cannot suppress a smile. It is distinctly diverting to see the great men try to inspire us with awe. I had to bite my lips to keep from laughing outright when I was on a journey not long ago, and saw an assistant resident go from his office to his house under the shade of a gold umbrella [the gold umbrella is a part of the formal regalia of the highest Javanese nobility, the princes and their immediate family], which a servant held spread above his noble head. It was such a ridiculous spectacle! Heavens! If he only knew how the humble crowds who respectfully retreated to one side before the glittering sunshade, immediately his back was turned, burst out laughing.

There are many, yes very many Government officials, who allow the native rulers to kiss their feet, and their knees. Kissing the foot is the highest token of respect that we Javanese can show to our parents, or elderly blood relatives, and to our own rulers. We do not find it pleasant to do this for strangers; no, the European makes himself ridiculous in our eyes whenever he demands from us those tokens of respect to which our own rulers alone have the right.

It is a matter of indifference when residents and assistant residents allow themselves to be called *Kandjeng* [Javanese title meaning, roughly, "Lord," originally applied only to the indigenous ruling elite], but when overseers, railroad engineers (and perhaps tomorrow, station-masters too) allow themselves to be thus addressed by their servants, it is absurdly funny. Do these people really know what Kandjeng means?

It is a title that the natives give to their hereditary rulers. I used to think that it was only natural for the stupid Javanese to love all this flim-flam, but now I see that the civilized, enlightened Westerner is not averse to it, that he is daft about it. . . .

With heavy hearts, many Europeans here see how the Javanese, whom they regard as their inferiors, are slowly awakening, and at every turn a brown man comes up, who shows that he has just as good brains in his head, and a just as good heart in his body, as the white man.

But we are going forward, and they cannot hold back the current of time. I love the Hollanders very, very much, and I am grateful for everything that we have gained through them. Many of them are among our best friends, but there are also others who dislike us, for no other reason than we are bold enough to emulate them in education and culture.

In many subtle ways they make us feel their dislike. "I am a European, you are a Javanese," they seem to say, or "I am the master, you the governed." Not once, but many times, they speak to us in broken Malay; although they know very well that we understand the Dutch language. It would be a matter of indifference to me in what language they addressed us, if the tone were only polite. Not long ago, a Raden Aju was talking to a gentleman, and impulsively she said, "Sir, excuse me, but may I make a friendly request, please, speak to me in your own language. I understand and speak Malay very well, but alas, only high Malay. I do not understand this pasar [market] Malay." How our gentleman hung his head!

Why do many Hollanders find it unpleasant to converse with us in their own language? Oh yes, now I understand; Dutch is too beautiful to be spoken by a brown mouth. . . . Oh, now I understand why they are opposed to the education of the Javanese. When the Javanese becomes educated then he will no longer say amen to everything that is suggested to him by his superiors. . . .

Still this is only a beginning, and it is splendid that men of influence and ability are supporting our cause. The strife will be violent, the combatants will not have to fight against opposition alone, but also against the indifference of our own countrywomen, in whose behalf they would break their lances. While this agitation among the men is on the tapis, that will be the time for the women to rise up and let themselves be heard. Poor men—you will have your hands full.

Oh, it is splendid just to live in this age, the transition of the old into the new! . . . I find such great sympathy in you; you have told me that you and I were kindred spirits, and even as such have I considered you. I am no Javanese, no child of the despised brown race to you; and to me you do not belong to that white race around us that holds the Javanese up to scorn and ridicule. You are white to me in your understanding of the truth, white in heart and soul. For you I have a great admiration. I love you with my whole heart, and many of my fellow countrywomen would do likewise if they knew you. O that all Hollanders were like you and some of my other white friends.

PART III

NATIONALIST RESPONSE

11

Mi Ultimos Adios

JOSÉ RIZAL*

José Rizal is arguably the most loved and respected individual in the history of the Philippines. A scholar and linguist, Rizal was also a novelist and a poet. His books were banned for their anti-colonial seditionist content. In 1892, days after he established the Liga Filipina (The League of the Philippines), he was deported to remote Dapitan at the northwestern tip of Mindanao. In August, he was tried and ordered to be executed on December 30, 1896. Rizal's last piece of writing was an emotional poem, which he managed to smuggle out of his prison cell by placing it in the bottom of a kerosene lamp. His friend Mariano Ponce gave the poem the title of "Mi Ultimos Adios." As the Philippines National Historical Commission said on the occasion of the centenary of Rizal's martyrdom: "Here the poet and martyr bids farewell to his country, his family, and his friends in lines of dignity and grace devoid of bitterness. This poem has not failed to move to tears those who have heard it recited."

~

Farewell, my adored Land, region of the sun caressed,
Pearl of the Orient Sea, our Eden lost,
With gladness I give you my Life, sad and repressed;
And were it more brilliant, more fresh and at its best,
I would still give it to you for your welfare at most.

---

*José Rizal, *Rizal's Poems* (Manila: National Historical Commission, 1972), pp. 160–162.

On the fields of battle, in the fury of fight,
Others give you their lives without pain or hesitancy,
The place does not matter: cypress, laurel, lily white,
Scaffold, open field, conflict or martyrdom's site,
It is the same if asked by the home and Country.

I die as I see tints on the sky b'gin to show
And at last announce the day, after a gloomy night;
If you need a hue to dye your matutinal glow,
Pour my blood and at the right moment spread it so,
And gild it with a reflection of your nascent light!

My dreams, when scarcely a lad adolescent,
My dreams when already a youth, full of vigor to attain,
Were to see you, gem of the sea of the Orient,
Your dark eyes dry, smooth brow held to a high plane,
Without frown, without wrinkles and of shame without stain.

My life's fancy, my ardent, passionate desire,
Hail! Cries out the soul to you, that will soon part from thee;
Hail! How sweet 'tis to fall that fullness you may acquire;
To die to give you life, 'neath your skies to expire
And in your mystic land to sleep through eternity!

If over my tomb some day, you would see blow,
A simple humble flow'r amidst thick grasses,
Bring it up to your lips and kiss my soul so,
And under the cold tomb, I may feel on my brow,
Warmth of your breath, a whiff of your tenderness.

Let the moon with soft, gentle light me descry,
Let the dawn send forth its fleeting, brilliant light,
In murmurs grave allow the wind to sigh,
And should a bird descend on my cross and alight,
Let the bird intone a song of peace o'er my site.

Let the burning sun the raindrops vaporize
And with my clamor behind return pure to the sky;
Let a friend shed tears over my early demise;
And on quiet afternoons when one prays for me on high,
Pray too, oh, my Motherland, that in God may rest I.

Pray thee for all the hapless who have died,
For all those who unequalled torments have undergone;
For our poor mothers who in bitterness have cried;
For orphans, widows and captives to torture were shied,
And pray too that you may see your own redemption.

And when the dark night wraps the cemet'ry
And only the dead to vigil there are left alone,
Don't disturb their repose, don't disturb the mystery:
If you hear the sounds of cithern or psaltery,
It is I, dear Country, who a song t'you intone.

And when my grave by all is no more remembered,
With neither cross nor stone to mark its place,
Let it be plowed by man, with spade let it be scattered
And my ashes ere to nothingness are restored,
Let them turn to dust to cover your earthly space.

Then it doesn't matter that you should forget me:
Your atmosphere, your skies, your vales I'll sweep;
Vibrant and clear note to your ears I shall be:
Aroma, light, hues, murmur, song, moanings deep,
Constantly repeating the essence of the faith I keep.

My idolized Country, for whom I most gravely pine,
Dear Philippines, to my last goodbye, oh, harken.
There I leave thee all: my parents, loves of mine,
I'll go where there are no slaves, tyrants or hangmen,
Where faith does not kill and where God alone does reign.

Farewell, parents, brothers, beloved by me,
Friends of my childhood, in the home distressed;
Give thanks that now I rest from the wearisome day;
Farewell, sweet stranger, my friend, who brightened my way;
Farewell, to all I love. To die is to rest.

12

Theses on Nationalism and Colonialism

V. I. LENIN*

According to Ho Chi Minh, he came to Marxism in the summer of 1920 after reading V. I. Lenin's "Theses on Nationalism and Colonialism." He had read Marxist works before, but Lenin's theses impressed him because of the links the author established between imperialism and capitalism on the one hand and imperialism and nationalism on the other. The theses provided a very potent argument for supporting nationalist movements in Asia and Africa. Lenin endorsed a communist-nationalist nexus on a tactical level, while the transformation of the world to communism remained the strategic goal. In William Duiker's words, reading the theses "transformed him [Ho Chi Minh] from a simple patriot with socialist leanings into a Marxist revolutionary." Ho told the Fifth Congress of the Communist International, "The national question, as Lenin taught us, forms a part of the general problem of proletarian revolution and proletarian dictatorship." The "theses" had a general applicability to nationalist movements everywhere, including all of the countries of Southeast Asia.

~

The Communist Party, as the conscious champion of the struggle of the proletariat for the overthrow of the bourgeois yoke, must base its policy on

*V. I. Lenin, "Preliminary Draft of Theses on the National and Colonial Questions," in *Selected Works,* vol. 2 (Moscow: Foreign Languages Publishing House, 1947), pp. 654–658.

the national question too, not on abstract and formal principles, but, firstly, on an exact estimate of the specific historical situation and, primarily, of the economic conditions; secondly, on a clear distinction between the interests of the oppressed classes, of the toilers and exploited, and the general concept of national interests as a whole, which implies the interests of the ruling class; thirdly, on an equally clear distinction between the oppressed, dependent and subject nations and the oppressing, exploiting and sovereign nations, in order to counter the bourgeois-democratic lies which obscure the colonial and financial enslavement—characteristic of the era of finance capital and imperialism—of the vast majority of the world's population by an insignificant minority of rich and advanced capitalist countries.

The imperialist war of 1914–18 very clearly revealed the falsity of the bourgeois-democratic phrase-mongering to all nations and to the oppressed classes of the whole world by practically demonstrating that the Versailles Treaty of the famous "Western democracies" is an even more brutal and despicable act of violence against weak nations than was the Brest-Litovsk Treaty of the German Junkers and the Kaiser. The League of Nations and the whole post-war policy of the Entente reveal this truth more clearly and distinctly than ever; they are everywhere intensifying the revolutionary struggle both of the proletariat in the advanced countries and of the masses of the working people in the colonial and dependent countries, and are hastening the collapse of the petty-bourgeois national illusion that nations can live together in peace and equality under capitalism.

It follows from the above-enunciated fundamental premises that the cornerstone of the whole policy of the Communist International on the national and colonial question must be closer union of the proletarians and working masses generally of all nations and countries for a joint revolutionary struggle for the overthrow of the landlords and the bourgeoisie; for this alone will guarantee victory over capitalism, without which the abolition of national oppression and inequality is impossible.

The world political situation has now placed the dictatorship of the proletariat on the order of the day, and all events in world politics are inevitably revolving around one central point, viz., the struggle of the world bourgeoisie against the Soviet Russian Republic, around which are inevitably grouping, on the one hand, the movement for Soviets among the advanced workers of all countries, and, on the other, all the national liberation movements in the colonies and among the oppressed nationalities, whom bitter experience is teaching that there can be no salvation for them except in the victory of the Soviet system over world imperialism.

Consequently, one must not confine oneself at the present time to the bare recognition or proclamation of the need for closer union between the

UCCS BOOKSTORE
PROTECT YOUR INVESTMENT
All refunds require the
original cash register receipt

TEXTBOOK REFUND DEADLINES
* **Fall & Spring Semesters:** 2 weeks from the date of purchase*
* **Summer Semester:** 2 weeks from the date purchase*
* **Interim Sessions:** first 2 days of class for courses 2-6 weeks in length
* **Classes 2 weeks or less in length:** books are non-returnable
* After Census date, as stated in UCCS schedule of courses, books are non-returnable.

New books must be in new selling condition, free from any marks or other signs of wear, and, if shrink-wrapped, the shrink-wrap must still be intact. All accessory items (CD, information cards etc.) originally included must also be returned undamaged.

GENERAL MERCHANDISE REFUNDS
Merchandise, General Books and Nursing Reference Books may be returned within 2 weeks (5 days for software and electronics) from the date of purchase and must be in original (new) condition.

1. Software must be in its original, sealed container.
2. Defective merchandise returned in (with) original packaging will be exchanged for the identical item.
3. All items on CLEARANCE are considered final sales and may not be returned
4. Computers carry the manufacturer's warranty.

SPECIAL ORDER ITEMS, STUDY AIDS, TEST PREPARATIONS, STUDY NOTES, BACKPACKS AND COMPUTER working people of the various nations; it is necessary to pursue a policy that will achieve the closest alliance of all the national and colonial liberation movements with Soviet Russia, the form of this alliance to be determined by the degree of development of the Communist movement among the proletariat of each country, or of the bourgeois-democratic liberation movement of the workers and peasants in backward countries or among backward nationalities.

With regard to the more backward states and nations, in which feudal or patriarchal and patriarchal-peasant relations predominate, it is particularly important to bear in mind:

First, that all Communist Parties must assist the bourgeois-democratic liberation movement in these countries, and that the duty of rendering the most active assistance rests primarily upon the workers of the country upon which the backward nation is dependent colonially or financially;

Second, that it is necessary to wage a fight against the clergy and other influential reactionary and mediaeval elements in backward countries;

Third, that it is necessary to combat Pan-Islamism and similar trends which strive to combine the liberation movement against European and American imperialism with the attempt to strengthen the positions of the khans, landlords, mullahs, etc.;

Fourth, that it is necessary in the backward countries to give special support to the peasant movement against the landlords, against large landownership, and against all manifestations or survivals of feudalism, and to strive to lend the peasant movement the most revolutionary character and establish the closest possible alliance between the West-European Communist proletariat and the revolutionary peasant movement in the East, in the colonies, and in the backward countries generally;

Fifth, that it is necessary to wage a determined struggle against the attempt to paint the bourgeois-democratic liberation trends in the backward countries in Communist colors; the Communist International must support the bourgeois-democratic national movements in colonial and backward countries only on condition that, in all backward countries, the elements of future proletarian parties which are Communist not only in name shall be grouped together and trained to appreciate their special tasks, viz., to fight the bourgeois-democratic movements within their own nations; the Communist International must enter into a temporary alliance with bourgeois democracy in colonial and backward countries, but must not merge with it and must under all circumstances preserve the independence of the proletarian movement even if in its most rudimentary form. . . .

The age-old oppression of colonial and weak nationalities by the imperialist powers has not only filled the working masses of the oppressed countries

with animosity towards the oppressing nations but also with distrust of
them in general, even of the proletariat of those nations. The despicable betrayal of Socialism by the majority of the official leaders of the proletariat
of the oppressing nations in 1914–19, when "defense of the fatherland" was
used as a social-chauvinist cloak to conceal the defense of the "right" of
"their" bourgeoisie to oppress colonies and rob financially dependent
countries, could not but enhance this perfectly legitimate distrust. On the
other hand, the more backward a country is, the stronger is the hold within
it of small agricultural production, patriarchalism and ignorance, which
inevitably lends particular strength and tenacity to the deepest of petty-
bourgeois prejudices, national egoism and national narrowness. As these
prejudices can disappear only after imperialism and capitalism have disappeared in the advanced countries, and after the whole foundation of the
economic life of the backward countries has radically changed, these prejudices cannot but die out very slowly. It is therefore the duty of the class-
conscious Communist proletariat of all countries to treat with particular
caution and attention the survival of national sentiments among the countries and nationalities which have been longest oppressed, and it is also necessary to make certain concessions with a view to hastening the extinction
of the aforementioned distrust and prejudices. Unless the proletariat, and,
following it, all the toiling masses, of all countries and nations all over the
world voluntarily strive for alliance and unity the victory over capitalism
cannot be successfully achieved.

13

Vietnam's Declaration of Independence

HO CHI MINH*

In the short interregnum between the withdrawal of the Japanese forces from Vietnam and the arrival of Allied forces in August/September 1945, the Viet Minh declared on September 2 the birth of the Democratic Republic of Vietnam. In Hanoi Square, before a crowd estimated at half a million people, Ho Chi Minh read out the "Declaration of Independence." Despite the Viet Minh's leadership being predominantly communist, the Vietnamese Declaration drew heavily from the American Declaration of Independence. If the United States had then extended a hand of friendship and support to Ho Chi Minh, would it have wooed the Vietnamese communists away from the Soviet Union and (after 1949) the People's Republic of China to become, like Tito's Yugoslavia, "our communists," to quote Stanley Karnow? One can only speculate.

∼

All men are created equal; they are endowed by their Creator with certain unalienable Rights; among these are Life, Liberty, and the pursuit of Happiness.

This immortal statement was made in the Declaration of Independence of the United States of America in 1776. In a broader sense, this means: All the peoples on the earth are equal from birth, all the peoples have a right to live, to be happy and free.

---

*Ho Chi Minh, "Declaration of Independence of the Democratic Republic of Vietnam," in *Selected Works* (Hanoi: Red River Publishing House, 1960–1962), pp. 17–21.

The Declaration of the French Revolution made in 1791 on the Rights of Man and the Citizen also states: "All men are born free and with equal rights, and must always remain free and have equal rights."

Those are undeniable truths.

Nevertheless, for more than eighty years, the French imperialists, abusing the standard of Liberty, Equality, and Fraternity, have violated our Fatherland and oppressed our fellow citizens. They have acted contrary to the ideals of humanity and justice.

In the field of politics, they have deprived our people of every democratic liberty.

They have enforced inhuman laws; they have set up three distinct political regimes in the North, the Center, and the South of Viet-Nam in order to wreck our national unity and prevent our people from being united.

They have built more prisons than schools. They have mercilessly slain our patriots; they have drowned our uprisings in rivers of blood.

They have fettered public opinion; they have practiced obscurantism against our people.

To weaken our race they have forced us to use opium and alcohol.

In the field of economics, they have fleeced us to the backbone, impoverished our people and devastated our land.

They have robbed us of our rice fields, our mines, our forests, and our raw materials. They have monopolized the issuing of bank notes and the export trade.

They have invented numerous unjustifiable taxes and reduced our people, especially our peasantry, to a state of extreme poverty.

They have hampered the prospering of our national bourgeoisie; they have mercilessly exploited our workers.

In the autumn of 1940, when the Japanese fascists violated Indochina's territory to establish new bases in their fight against the Allies, the French imperialists went down on their bended knees and handed over our country to them.

Thus, from that date, our people were subjected to the double yoke of the French and the Japanese. Their sufferings and miseries increased. The result was that, from the end of last year to the beginning of this year, from Quang Tri Province to the North of Viet-Nam, more than two million of our fellow citizens died from starvation. On March 9 [1945] the French troops were disarmed by the Japanese. The French colonialists either fled or surrendered, showing that not only were they incapable of "protecting" us, but that, in the span of five years, they had twice sold our country to the Japanese.

On several occasions before March 9, the Viet Minh League urged the French a tolerant and humane attitude. Even after the Japanese *Putsch* of March, 1945, the Viet Minh League helped many Frenchmen to cross the frontier, rescued some of them from Japanese jails and protected French lives and property.

From the autumn of 1940, our country had ceased to be a French colony and had become a Japanese possession.

After the Japanese had surrendered to the Allies, our whole people rose to regain our national sovereignty and to found the Democratic Republic of Viet-Nam.

The truth is that we have wrested our independence from the Japanese and not from the French.

The French have fled, the Japanese have capitulated, Emperor Bao Dai has abdicated. Our people have broken the chains which for nearly a century have fettered them and have won independence for the Fatherland. Our people at the same time have overthrown the monarchic regime that has reigned supreme for dozens of centuries. In its place has been established the present Democratic Republic.

For these reasons, we, members of the Provisional Government, representing the whole Vietnamese people, declare that from now on we break off all relations of a colonial character with France; we repeal all the international obligation that France has so far subscribed to on behalf of Viet-Nam, and we abolish all the special rights the French have unlawfully acquired in our Fatherland.

The whole Vietnamese people, animated by a common purpose, are determined to fight to the bitter end against any attempt by the French colonialists to reconquer their country.

We are convinced that the Allied nations, which at Teheran and San Francisco have acknowledged the principles of self-determination and equality of nations, will not refuse to acknowledge the independence of Viet-Nam.

A people who have courageously opposed French domination for more than eighty years, a people who have fought side by side with the Allies against the fascists during these last years, such a people must be free and independent.

For these reasons, we, members of the Provisional Government of the Democratic Republic of Viet-Nam, solemnly declare to the world that Viet-Nam has the right to be a free and independent country—and in fact it is so already. The entire Vietnamese people are determined to mobilize all their physical and mental strength, to sacrifice their lives and property in order to safeguard their independence and liberty.

14

Indonesian Independence and Pancasila

S U K A R N O *

On June 1, 1945, in his address to the Independence Preparatory Commit-tee, Indonesia's foremost leader of the nationalist movement, Sukarno, enunciated the five principles, or Pancasila (Panca = five; sila = foundations or principles), that were to form the foundation of the country's constitu-tion: belief in one supreme God, humanitarianism, nationalism expressed in the unity of Indonesia, consultative democracy, and social justice. The speech was dubbed "The Birth of the Pancasila."

Although the Pancasila (also spelled *Pantja Sila*) provided for a modern, free, secular society with guarantees of freedom of religion, democracy, and equal justice for all citizens, it also incorporated traditional practices such as the age-old custom of consensus decision-making, or *musyawarah,* and the organization of the economy on the basis of mutual self-help, or *gotong royong.* Unfortunately, the "general nature" of the five principles allowed both Sukarno, in his later years, and his successor, Suharto, to use the Pancasila to support their authoritarian power and to promote their political agenda.

~

Three days have passed during which the members of the Investigating Committee in Preparation for Independence have made known their opin-

---

*President Sukarno, "The Birth of *Pancasila,*" speech on June 1, 1945 (Jakarta: Ministry of Information, Republic of Indonesia, 1952).

ions, and now I have from the Chairman the honor of stating my opinion also. I will comply with the Honorable Chairman's request. What is that request of his? The Honorable Chairman asked this gathering of the Investigating Committee in Preparation for Independence to draw up a draft of the basic principles for Free Indonesia. . . .

What is it that is called freedom? In the year 1933 I wrote a booklet called "Kearah Indonesia Merdeka." In that booklet of 1933, I stated that freedom, political independence, was nothing more than a bridge, a golden bridge. I said in that booklet that on the far side of that bridge we would rebuild our society . . . I remind you once again, Free Indonesia, political independence, is nothing more than, and does not differ from a bridge! . . .

There are two millions of youths, whose single slogan is: "A Free Indonesia, Now." If, for instance, the Japanese Army today were to surrender affairs of state to you, would you decline it, saying, just a moment, wait a while, we ask that this and that be finished first, and only then we will dare accept the affairs of state of Free Indonesia? (Cries of No! No!)

If, for instance, at this very moment the Japanese forces were to transfer state responsibilities to us, then we would not hold back for one minute, we would at once accept these responsibilities, we would at once begin with the independent Indonesian state! (Thundering applause)

We are today facing an all important moment. Do we not understand, as declared by dozens of speakers, that in very truth international law simplifies our task? For the organization, the establishment, the recognition of an independent state, there need not be any condition which is complicated, which is hairsplitting. The only condition is a territory, a people, and a stable government. This is sufficient in international law. . . . As soon as there is a territory, a people, a government, recognized by one other free state, there is already what is termed: freedom. No matter whether the people can read or not, no matter whether the people have a good economy or not, no matter whether the people are stupid or clever, if according to international law, the nation possesses the conditions for a free state, that is, a people, a territory, and a government, it is free. Do not let us waver or be ponderous, and wanting to finalize beforehand a thousand and one imaginary matters! Once again I ask: Do we want to be free or do we not? Do we want to be free or do we not? (Reply from audience: We want to be free!)

Gentlemen! Now that I have spoken about the matter of "freedom," I will proceed to speak of the matter of principles. . . .

First principle: nationalism. To begin with, I ask: Do we intend to set up Free Indonesia for one particular individual, for one particular group? To set up Free Indonesia, which in name only is Free Indonesia, but in reality is only something to crown some individual, to bring power to a wealthy group, to give power to a group of nobles?

Is our objective like that? Certainly not! Our compatriots the "nationalists," who are present here, as well as our compatriots the "Moslems," have all agreed that no such state is our goal. We intend to establish a state "all for all." Neither for a single individual, nor for a group, neither for a group of nobles, nor a group of wealthy people—but "all for all." This is one of the principles which I will explain again. And so, what I always have at heart, not only in these days of this session of the Investigating Committee, but ever since the year 1918, for more than 25 years, is this: The first principle, best to become the foundation for the State of Indonesia, is the principle of nationalism. We will establish an Indonesian national state. . . .

What is it that is termed nation? What are the requirements for a nation? According to Renan, the requirement for a nation is "the will to unite." It is necessary that the people feel themselves united and wish to be united.

Let us consider a definition by another person, namely the definition by Otto Bauer in his book, *Die Nationalitatenfrage,* where the question is raised: *"Was ist eine* Nation?" and the answer was: "A nation is a unity of conduct which comes into being because of unity of destiny." This, according to Otto Bauer, is a nation. . . .

Men and place cannot be separated! Impossible to separate people from the earth under their feet. Ernest Renan and Otto Bauer only looked at men alone. They thought only about their *Gemeinschaft* and the feeling of men, *"L'âme et le désir."* They were only thinking of character, not thinking of the earth, the earth inhabited by those people. What is that place? That place is a country. That country is one entity. God Almighty made the map of the world, created the map of the world. If we look at the map of the world, we can show where are the "entities" there. Even a child, if he looks at the map of the world, can show that the Indonesian Archipelago forms one entity. On the map can be shown an entity of a group of islands between two big oceans, the Pacific Ocean and the Indian Ocean, and between two continents, the continent of Asia and the continent of Australia. Even a child can see that the islands of Java, Sumatra, Borneo, Celebes, Halmahera, the Lesser Sunda Islands, the Moluccas, and the other islands in their midst are one entity. Similarly any child can see on the map of the world that the islands of Japan stretching on the eastern brink of the continent of Asia, as a breakwater of the Pacific Ocean, are one entity. . . .

And so, what is it that is called the Land of our Birth, our country? According to geopolitics, Indonesia is our country. Indonesia in its entirety, neither Java alone, nor Sumatra alone, nor Borneo alone, nor Celebes alone, nor Ambon alone, nor the Moluccas alone, but the whole archipelago ordained by God Almighty to be a single entity between two continents and two oceans, that is our country. . . .

Briefly speaking, the people of Indonesia, the Indonesian Nation is not only a group of individuals who, having "the will to unite," live in a small area like Minangkabau or Madura or Jogja or Pasundan or Makassar, but the Indonesian people are all the human beings who, according to geopolitics ordained by God Almighty, live throughout the entity of the entire archipelago of Indonesia from the northern tip of Sumatra to Irian! All, throughout the islands! The Indonesian nation, the people of Indonesia, the Indonesian human beings numbering seventy million persons, but seventy million who have already become one, one, once again one! (Loud clapping.)

This is what we should all aim at: the establishment of one National State based on the entity of one Indonesian soil from the tip of Sumatra right to Irian. I am confident that there is not one group amongst you which does not agree, neither the Moslems nor the group called "the Nationalist Group." This is what all of us should aim at.

Let no one think that every independent country is a national state. Neither Prussia nor Beieren, nor Saxony, is a national state, but the whole of Germany is a national state. Not the small areas, neither Venice, nor Lombardy, but the whole of Italy, the entire peninsula in the Mediterranean bounded to the north by the Alps, is the national state. Neither Bengal, nor Punjab, nor Behar and Orissa, but the entire triangle of India must become a national state.

Similarly, neither were all the states of our homeland, which were independent in the past, national states. Only twice have we experienced a national state; that was in the time of Sriwijaja and in the time of Modjopabit. Apart from those, we have never experienced a national state. I say with full respect for our former Rajas, I say, with a thousand respects to Sultan Agung Hanjokrokusumo, that Mataram, although independent, was not a national state.

With a sense of respect towards Prabu Siliwangi of Pejajaran, I say that his kingdom was not a national state. With a sense of respect towards Prabu Sultan Agung Tirtayasa, I say that his kingdom in Banten, although independent, was not a national state. With a sense of respect towards Sultan Hasanuddin in Celebes where he erected the Kingdom of Bugis, I say that the independent land of Bugis was no national state.

The national state is only Indonesia in its entirety, which was set up in the time of Sriwijaja and Modjopabit, and which now we also ought to establish together. Therefore, if you, gentlemen, are willing, let us take as the first principle of our state Indonesian Nationalism. Indonesian Nationalism in

the fullest sense! Neither Javanese Nationalism, nor Sumatran Nationalism
nor the Nationalism of Borneo, or Celebes, Bali, or any other, but the Indonesian Nationalism which at one and the same time becomes the principle of one National State. . . .

Second principle: internationalism. But . . . but . . . undoubtedly there is a
danger involved in this principle of nationalism. The danger is, that probably men will narrow down nationalism to chauvinism, the creed of "Indonesia *über Alles.*" This is the danger. We love one homeland, we feel
ourselves one nation, we possess one language. But our homeland Indonesia is only a small part of the world. Remember this.

Gandhi said, "I am a nationalist, but my nationalism is humanity." The
nationalism we advocate is not the nationalism of isolation, not chauvinism,
as blazoned by people in Europe who say *"Deutschland über Alles,"* who
say that there is none so great as Germany, whose people they say are su-
permen, corn-haired and blue-eyed *"Aryans,"* whom they consider the
greatest in the world, while other nations are worthless. Do not let us abide
by such formulas, gentlemen, do not let us say that the Indonesian nation is
the noblest and most perfect, whilst belittling other people. We should aim
at the unity and brotherhood of the whole world.

We should not only establish the state of Free Indonesia, but we should
also aim at making one family of all nations. It happens that this is my second principle. This is the second principle of philosophy I propose to you,
gentlemen, to which I give the name of "internationalism." But when I say
internationalism, I do not mean cosmopolitanism, which does not recognize nationalism, which says there is no Indonesia, no Japan, no Burma, no
England, no America and so on. Internationalism can not flower if it is not
rooted in the soil of nationalism. Nationalism cannot flower if it does not
grow within the garden of internationalism. Thus, these two, gentlemen,
principle one and principle two, which I have first proposed to you, are
dovetailed together.

Third principle: representative government. Well then, what is the third
principle? That principle is the principle of consent, the principle of representative government, the principle of consultation. The Indonesian State
shall not be a state for one individual, neither a state for one group, nor for
the wealthy. But we are to establish a state "all for all," "one for all, all for
one." I am convinced that the necessary condition for the strength of the
Indonesian state is conferring, is representative government.

For Islam, this is the best condition for the promotion of religion. We
are Moslems, myself included—a thousand pardons my Islamism is far
from perfect—but if you open up your breast, and look at my heart, you
will find it none other than Islamic. And this Islamic heart of Bung

Karno hopes to defend Islam by agreement, through discussion! By means of agreement, we shall improve all matters, we shall promote the interest of religion, that is, by means of talks or discussions in the House of Representatives. . . .

Therefore, I ask you gentlemen, both those that are not Moslem, and in particular those who are, to accept this principle number 3, that is, the principle of conferring, of representative government. In the House of Representatives there will be great conflicts of opinion. There is not one state truly alive, if it is not as if the cauldron of Tjondrodimuko burns and boils in its representative body, if there is no clash of convictions in it. Both in an Islamic state and also in a Christian state, there is always a struggle. Accept principle number 3, the principle of consent, the principle of people's representation!. . .

Allah, God of the Universe, gave us the capacity to think, so that in our daily intercourse we might constantly burnish our thoughts, just like the pounding and husking of paddy to obtain rice, in turn to become the best Indonesian food. Accept, gentlemen, then, principle number 3, which is the principle of conferring!

Fourth principle: social justice. Principle number 4, I will now propose to you. During these three days I have not yet heard of that principle, the principle of prosperity. The principle: there shall be no poverty in Free Indonesia. Our principles should be: Do we want a free Indonesia whose capitalists do as they wish, or where the entire people prosper, where every man has enough to eat, enough to wear, lives in prosperity, feels cherished by the homeland that gives him sufficient keep? Which do we choose, gentlemen? Do not imagine, gentlemen, that as soon as the People's Representative body comes into being, we shall automatically achieve this prosperity. We have seen that in the states of Europe there are representative bodies, there is parliamentary democracy. But is it not precisely in Europe that the capitalists are the bosses?. . .

I suggest: if we are seeking democracy, the need is not for the democracy of the West, but for conferring, which brings life, which is politico-economic democracy, able to bring about social prosperity! The people of Indonesia have long spoken of this matter. What is meant by *Ratu Adil?* What is meant by the conception of *Ratu Adil* is social justice. The people wish for prosperity. . . . Therefore if we truly understand, remember, and love the people of Indonesia, let us accept this principle of social justice which is not only political equality, gentlemen. In the field of economics, too, we must create equality, and the best common prosperity.

The body for consultation which we will establish should not be a body for the discussion of political democracy only, but a body which, together with the community, will be able to give effect to two principles: political justice and social justice. . . .

Fifth principle: belief in God. Gentlemen, what is the fifth principle? I have already expounded 4 principles:

1. Indonesian nationalism.
2. Internationalism—or humanism.
3. Consent, or democracy.
4. Social prosperity.

The fifth principle should be: To set up Free Indonesia with faith in God the Almighty.

The principle of Belief in God! Not only should the people of Indonesia have belief in God, but every Indonesian should believe in his own particular God. The Christian should worship God according to the teachings of Jesus Christ, Moslems according to the teachings of the Prophet Mohammad, Buddhists should discharge their religious rites according to their own books.

But let us all have belief in God. The Indonesian state shall be a state where every person can worship God in freedom. . . .

Let us observe, let us practice religion, whether Islam or Christianity, in a civilized way. What is that civilized way? It is the way of mutual respect. (Clapping amongst the audience.) The Prophet Mohammad gave sufficient proofs of tolerance, and of respect for other religions. Jesus Christ also showed that tolerance. Let us within the Free Indonesia which we are going to organize along those lines, let us declare that the fifth principle of our state is belief in God, belief in God with a high code of honor, belief in God which has respect for one another. I shall be glad indeed if you agree that the state of Free Indonesia shall be founded upon belief in God the Almighty. . . .

Gentlemen: I have already proposed to you "The principles of the State." There are five. Is this *Pantja Darma*? No. The name *Pantja Darma* is not suitable here. *Darma* means duty, whereas we are speaking of principles. . . .

The name is not *Pantja Darma*, but I call it according to the advice of a linguist, a friend of ours: *Pantja Sila. Sila* means basis or principle, and upon those five principles we shall build Free Indonesia, lasting and age-long. (Loud applause.)

As I said a while ago, we are establishing an Indonesian state, for which all of us should be responsible. All for all. . . . If I compress what was five to get three, and what was three to get one, then I have a genuine Indonesian term, the term *gotong rojong* (mutual cooperation). The State of Indonesia, which we are to establish, should be a state of mutual cooperation. How fine that is! A *Gotong Rojong* state! (Loud applause on all sides.)

The principle of *Gotong Rojong* between the rich and the poor, between the Moslem and the Christian, between those not originating from Indonesia and their children who become Indonesians. This, gentlemen, is what I propose to you. . . .

Principles such as I have proposed to you, gentlemen, are the principles for a Free Indonesia which will endure. For decades has my breast burned fiercely with these principles. But do not forget that we live in a time of war, gentlemen. During this time of war we are going to establish a state of Indonesia—in the midst of war's thunder. I even render thanks to the Divine God that we are to establish an Indonesian state not under the full moon, but with the sound of the drums of war and in the fury of war. Free Indonesia shall emerge a tempered Free Indonesia, Free Indonesia tempered in the fury of war, and a Free Indonesia of that kind is a strong Indonesian state, not an Indonesian state which would turn soft after some time. It is because of that, that I thank God Almighty. . . .

If the people of Indonesia desire that the *Pantja Sila* I propose become a reality, that is, if we wish to live as one nation, one free nationality, if we wish to live as a member of a free world imbued with humanism, the principle of conferring, to live in complete social justice, to live in peace and prosperity, if we desire to live in the belief of God in the fullest and completed sense, we must not forget the conditions for its realization, and that is struggle, struggle, and once again struggle.

Do not imagine that with the existence of the state of Free Indonesia, our struggle is at an end. No! I even say: Within that Free Indonesia our struggle must continue. The struggle, however, must be of a different nature from what we have been carrying on so far. Then we, as a united people, shall continue our struggle to bring realization to our ideals contained in *Pantja Sila.* And, particularly in this time of war, have faith, cultivate in your hearts the conviction that Free Indonesia cannot come if the people of Indonesia do not dare take a risk, do not dare dive for pearls into the depths of the ocean. If the people of Indonesia are not united, and are not determined to live or die for freedom, the freedom of Indonesia will never be the possession of the Indonesian people, never, until the end of time! Freedom can only be achieved and owned by a people whose soul is aflame with the determination of *"Merdeka, —freedom or death!"*

15

Burma Under the Japanese

U NU*

U Nu (1907–1995) first came to be known as the student leader who organized a massive strike in 1936 as part of Burma's struggle for independence
from British colonial rule. When Burma was under Japanese occupation
from 1942 to 1945, a puppet government was established under Dr. Ba Maw
as prime minister. In his memoirs, originally written in the Burmese language, U Nu described the delicate and difficult relationship between
Burmese leaders and the Japanese military occupiers. While serving briefly
as foreign minister in Ba Maw's puppet government, he organized an anti-
Japanese guerrilla movement.

After the war, U Nu helped secure his country's independence from
Britain in 1948 and then became Burma's first prime minister, serving from
1948 to 1956. He resigned in 1957 but returned as premier later that year.
However, he was forced to step down by the army, led by General Ne Win,
in the following year. After the elections in 1960, he became prime minister
again but was deposed two years later by Ne Win. Released from jail in
1966, he led an anti-Win movement from his exile in Thailand. In 1980, he
was allowed to return to his country; from 1989 to 1992 he was placed under house arrest for establishing a parallel provisional government under his
premiership in opposition to Ne Win's. He wrote his autobiography during
his exile in Thailand. The narrative is often in the third person, with U Nu
being called "Thakin" meaning "Teacher."

*U Nu, *Saturday's Son: Memoirs of the Former Prime Minister of Burma* (New Haven:
Yale University Press, 1975), pp. 102–113.

~

Having escaped from Mandalay jail, Thakin Nu and his friends found signs of great excitement at the first village they entered. Men and women, boys and girls were out on the street, talking animatedly. Soon two monks appeared and the villagers, unrehearsed, fell in behind them in a procession obviously headed for Mandalay. Two old women distributed sprigs of thayeban (eugenia) and these were seized with practised ease even by those balancing bowls of rice and fruit on their heads. Other old women, with scarves round their breasts, as though bound for a place of worship, were dancing madly to the strains of a popular ditty that is sung whenever the victory flower appears. All were exulting in the thought that Burma would at last be free.

The air was thick with rumours: The Japanese were arriving as friends. They had the same war aims as the Burmese: they were ready to die for Burma. The most persistent rumour was that a Burman prince rode in the Japanese vanguard.

Thakin Nu met some of these same people later that afternoon. They were no longer marching in procession but straggling back in clumps of three or four. They had obviously met with some Japanese but did not seem inclined to relate their experiences. Pressed by Thakin Nu for details, a surly voice said: "The Japanese commander was less than grateful for our rice. When he took his hand out of his pocket it was to greet us with a hard slap in the face." And then he broke out laughing.

The face slapping had apparently been the prelude to a work detail that involved clearing logs and endlessly drawing water. Finally, the Japanese had, without so much as a "thank you," taken not only all the rice and curry but the bowls as well. . . . From that moment onward the news spread rapidly from one village to another that the Japanese were a coarse, hard crowd.

Dr. Ba Maw Forms a Government

Some time elapsed, and Thakin Nu was invited by Dr. Ba Maw to join the Preparatory Committee which was to fashion the form and content of the Burma government. Thakin Nu's initial reaction was to refuse, but Dr. Ba Maw had his name on his list and would not be gainsaid. He pointed out to Thakin Nu that, along with Bo Aung San and Thakin Than Tun, he must equip himself for responsibility and leadership. Dr. Ba Maw, as a much older man, would soon shed his mantle but only upon a successor he had trained. He was willing to be Thakin Nu's mentor.

Thakin Nu's rejoinder to this was that Dr. Ba Maw should go ahead and train Bo Aung San and Thakin Than Tun, but he himself was "not interested in that kind of thing.". . .

The upshot was a compromise. Thakin Nu would serve on the Preparatory Committee, but implicit in this acceptance was agreement on the part of Dr. Ba Maw to drop him when the government was formed. The next day they all went to the Japanese army headquarters in Maymyo. . . .

It occurred to Dr. Ba Maw that Thakin Nu had perhaps suffered a loss of esteem in the eyes of the Japanese military police because of a visit he had made to China in 1940 as a member of a Burmese goodwill mission. Therefore it would be necessary for Nu to redeem himself by making a public pronouncement of Japanese probity and invincibility. Thakin Nu was to develop the theme of an East-West conflict in a historical context, with the Russo-Japanese War of 1905 as the fifth in a series of confrontations. Dr. Ba Maw himself dictated an account of these five wars, and Thakin Nu sallied forth to do justice to his thesis. The occasion chosen was the East Asia Youth Conference, presided over by Ko Ba Gyan. At the end of the lecture, when questions were invited, up spoke an Arakanese lawyer: "Will Japan give Burma independence?" Thakin Nu felt vexed. What was the man up to? He must know the room was full of Japanese spies and informers. "Of course they will," he replied. The lawyer was on his feet again. "I don't believe a word of it," he said. The emotions Thakin Nu felt were mixed: he could not help admiring the man for his courage, but there was also pain at the thought of what the military police might do to the intrepid lawyer.

About two months after the formation of the Preparatory Committee Dr. Ba Maw received approval for the setting up of a Burmese government subordinate to the Japanese command . . . to take effect from 1 August. . . . In accordance with the previous arrangement in Maymyo, Dr. Ba Maw agreed to omit Thakin Nu's name. By this time the extent of Japanese perfidy in regard to the future of Burma was widely manifest, and a Burmese resistance movement had already started, almost from the very first days of the Japanese occupation. General Aung San and Thakin Than Tun had begun to organize for the tasks that lay ahead, and were indefatigable in bringing about reconciliation between Burmans and Karens.

Thakin Nu's being excluded from the Cabinet, logical though it might have been in the light of the "gentlemen's agreement" with Dr. Ba Maw, did not fail to arouse the suspicions of the Japanese spies, and at a dinner given by the Japanese commander-in-chief, Colonel Nasu asked pointedly if it meant that Thakin Nu did not wish to collaborate with the Japanese. On the contrary, Thakin Nu assured him, it would mean full-time participation in the promotion of good relations between the Burmese and the Japanese.

Under the Kempeitai

With his coming into power, Dr. Ba Maw fused his own Dama organization with the thakins' party. The result was the Dobama Sinyetha Party, an amalgam of the words meaning "We Burmans" and "Poor." The latter word did not signify "proletariat" or the industrial working class but simply meant people without any means. Nevertheless, such was the atmosphere of suspicion that the very title gave rise to conjecture, and the Japanese, through their agents, were soon inquiring if "sinyetha" was synonymous with "communist." Communism was the special bugbear of the dreaded Kempeitai, or Japanese military police, which went to great lengths to gather reports that might somehow incriminate individuals, either as communist sympathizers or as malcontents whose disenchantment with the new order might be expected to lead to trouble. In addition to Burmese agents and special newspaper reporters appointed by the military command, Japanese soldiers were found to be mingling with the people, castigating the Kempeitai and deploring injustices against the communists. They dug little verbal canals into which the responses of the naive, the innocent, and the unsuspecting might flow. Thakin Nu, like many others, was continually finding such traps set before him, but he managed to escape the ordeals by water or electrodes, the nail plucking, and the emasculation that others less fortunate than he had to endure.

Even as he felt besieged and beset by the Japanese Inquisition, Thakin Nu was startled out of his wits to discover that the Kempeitai had closed in on the thakins in Toungoo. All the thakin leaders were in custody, except one who had been executed by the Kempeitai chief. Upon receiving this news Thakin Nu sent Ko Hla Maung to Colonel Hiraoka, while he himself sped to the Japanese headquarters to see Colonel Nasu, the chief of staff. He found General Aung San already there. Since the message from Toungoo explicitly said that all the arrested men had been condemned to death, the first step was to send a reprieve order by wireless. Colonel Nasu rose to the occasion. An aide was dispatched to wait on Major-General Matsuoka, commander of the Kempeitai, and an appointment was made for Thakin Nu to see the major-general. By the time this interview took place, Thakin Nu had learnt that Colonels Nasu and Hiraoka had prevailed upon the Kempeitai to stay the executions in Toungoo. But the matter was far from ended. At Colonel Nasu's suggestion, Thakin Nu went to Toungoo to clear up the misunderstanding.

Everyone knew Bo Saing-gyo, the head of the Kempeitai in Toungoo. The interpreter from the Japanese War Office who accompanied him told Thakin Nu that Bo Saing-gyo was more of an ogre than a man, and the description was not exaggerated. Bo Saing-gyo was angry even in repose. With him to suspect was to torture. One of his suspects, accused of theft, was strung up on a beam, his collarbone broken. The next day the real thief was caught, and the innocent one was fortunate to get out alive. If time hung heavy on him Bo Saing-gyo would look out into the street and arrest the first passer-by. The pedestrian was expected to know that the kicks and blows he received were delivered in fun.

If the thakins in Toungoo remained alive, it was largely owing to the pluck and pugnacity of Thakin Than Pe, who would not break under torture. Repeatedly beaten and kicked in the head, twice rendered unconscious, he still refused to sign a confession which would have been a death warrant for all the thakins. Thakin Than Pe, with a blindfold over his eyes, was actually on his way to execution when the stay order arrived. By the time Thakin Nu arrived in Toungoo his friends had already been released.

A Cabinet Post for Thakin Nu

On the evening of 30 July 1943, Dr. Ba Maw summoned Thakin Mya, Thakin Than Tun, and Thakin Nu to Government House. Thakin Nu was asked if he had quite made up his mind not to enter the government, and he said, "Yes, long ago." Wearily, Dr. Ba Maw explained to the company that he had done everything in order to persuade Thakin Nu to accept office but had failed. . . . The meeting ended . . . and Thakin Nu went home. But then the top thakin leaders descended on him and bitterly reproached him. It was just like him, they complained, to make decisions without thought of consulting them. They too would like to stand aside and ignore the call of duty. One said that he had a good mind to resign, if only to get even with Thakin Nu. Another taunted him with the charge that it was mere pretence, that he was playing hard to get. Assailed on all sides, Thakin Nu's defences weakened and crumbled. He held out the white flag in unconditional surrender, and Thakin Mya, General Aung San, and Thakin Than Tun appointed themselves an allied victory council to make the capitulation complete. The choice lay between the Home Office and the Foreign Office. It was General Aung San who opined that the Foreign Office was the more important of the two, so the following day Thakin Nu went to Dr. Ba Maw and accepted this portfolio.

An Embarrassing Incident

The cars of Cabinet ministers came equipped with a flagstaff, and regulations called for flying the national flag whenever a minister was riding in the car. Thakin Nu regarded this as ostentation and refused to display the flag, to the immense sorrow of his faithful driver, who felt demeaned in the eyes of his peers. At length Thakin Nu gave in, and up went the flag. The first time out with the flag flying, a Burmese policeman saluted smartly and Thakin Nu called out to the driver: "Hey, you're quite right; we are more important with a flag." But a little further on, a Japanese military policeman ordered the car to stop. It seemed a Japanese general was expected to pass that way at any moment. Thakin Ba Hein, who was riding with Thakin Nu, had been to Japan and spoke the language fluently. "This is the foreign minister," he said, "on his way to office." "Is that so?" replied the policeman, "Good, good; then you can just stay where you are." So there they sat, covered with shame, in full view of the Kamayut police station. Just then a breeze sprang up and, when their flag fluttered before it, Thakin Nu felt even angrier and more ashamed. . . . He vented his anger on the hapless man [the driver] and shouted to him to drive straight home. Nor would he ride in the car that day, but went to his office by rowing across the lake.

Leaving the Foreign Office

After a year at the Foreign Office, Thakin Nu asked Dr. Ba Maw to let him resign or transfer to another department. As foreign minister, besides sending telegrams, he was expected to greet foreign visitors upon arrival and departure. He found all this very trying. Among friends he was capable of talking freely and volubly, but in the presence of strangers he was often tongue-tied. . . .

Thakin Nu thus found himself relying more and more on U Tun Aung to deal with visitors. . . . The truth was that he found the Japanese attitude towards his office degrading. In independent countries, a deputy minister or permanent secretary could summon a foreign ambassador. But he, as foreign minister, was obliged to go to the Japanese embassy if he had anything to discuss. The Japanese ambassador had called on him twice: once upon his arrival in Burma, and only once more since then. On all other occasions he had sent a deputy or subordinate. The ambassador made a habit of going over the minister's head direct to Dr. Ba Maw. The position had become intolerable to Thakin Nu.

Not long afterwards Thakin Nu was transferred to the Greater Burma Department but, owing to some disagreement, he moved on again to the Information Department. At his first press conference he discommoded his audience of Japanese reporters by saying something like this: "Burma and Japan are geographically far apart. We are even further apart spiritually. When the war began, Burmans had a great respect for the Japanese and looked up to them in every way. Your former commander-in-chief, General Iida, has acknowledged that Burmese support contributed to the success of the Burma campaign. In the short time that has elapsed since then, 95 percent of our population has lost its fervour, and something radical will have to be done if Japan's good image is to be restored. It is not enough for the Japanese to proclaim 'We're on the side of the Burmans.' If they want true Burmese regard they must change their whole attitude. So long as your military police continue to be so rough and your traders so greedy there will be no accord between us."

Thakin Nu did not know if he was expected to talk a lot of nonsense about Burma doing its best to help Japan win the war. In any case, having said what he had said, platitudes about the war effort would have come as an anticlimax. It was left to Secretary U Tun Sein to somehow mollify the Japanese by explaining that the minister was a blunt man who liked to speak his mind, but that underlying the outburst that day was a passion for improving relations between the Burmese and the Japanese. The cover-up was not totally effective. Major-General Ichida, successor to Isamura, had reservations which he brought to the attention of Dr. Ba Maw.

The Resistance

Thakin Nu, although his thoughts were charged with hatred for the Japanese, was incapable of expressing them other than in words. It took a man of action like Thakin Than Tun to find ways and means of getting rid of the Japanese. First he sent a secret mission to the Chinese army, which failed because the Burmese messenger contracted malaria on the journey. Next, he turned to India, and Thakin Nu was made privy to his plans only after initial success. . . .

General Aung San Leads an Uprising

One night a conference was held at Thakin Nu's house. Present were members of the thakin inner circle: General Aung San, Thakin Mya, Thakin Than Tun, and Thakin Chit. The general read out a long proclamation he had prepared entitled "Rise and Attack the Fascist Dacoits!" Everyone present signified approval and support, whereupon it was decided that the Burmese army would print the proclamation and send copies of it to revolutionaries everywhere for the widest possible circulation. From that day forward the Burma Defence Army linked itself indissolubly to the resistance and spearheaded the uprising that would follow.

Events moved fast thereafter until one day, in March 1945, General Aung San, Bo Let Ya, Thakin Than Tun, Ko Kyaw Nyein, and Thakin Soe arrived at Thakin Nu's house to apprise him of the latest situation. Thakin Soe alone was carrying a weapon, a tommy-gun. Thakin Than Tun produced a flimsy piece of paper with English writing on it. According to this message, Thakin Than Tun was to rendezvous with an English major called Carew near Toungoo. It would not be possible for him to return to Rangoon, so Thakin Than Tun would have to go underground.

Once Thakin Than Tun disappeared, General Aung San and Thakin Nu would have to follow suit. Than Tun's meeting with Carew was fixed for 18 March, so on that day Thakin Nu would go into hiding, leaving his family in Bo Let Ya's care. For Thakin Nu to take up arms was out of the question. When it came to shock action he would be worse than useless, because he would be a hindrance to the others. Since the purpose of his disappearance was simply to put him out of harm's way, Thakin Soe's plan was to use his wireless to make arrangements for Thakin Nu to be airlifted to India or elsewhere beyond reach of the Japanese. Three or four days later Thakin Soe sent a messenger to pick up Thakin Nu's bags in preparation for his departure.

When the time came for Thakin Nu to vanish, he hesitated. Just recently he had been discussing the general situation with Dr. Ba Maw, and the latter had told him even the Japanese had noticed how close they were to each other—that Nu, a thakin, was more in his confidence than one of his own party. The thought of leaving, without a word of warning, a man to whom he had pledged his loyalty went against Thakin Nu's grain. So when Bo Let Ya arrived to spirit him away, he asked him to wait a couple of days. . . .

In his present dilemma U Nu decided he must confide in Dr. Ba Maw. Dr. Ba Maw heard him out; then, with gaze averted, he sighed deeply before he spoke. He said, "I suppose you'd better go into hiding. As things are, I'm hardly in a position to protect you, and before long it will be as much as I can do to protect myself. So there you are! If you wish to go into hiding, do so. As for any sort of pledge made to me, I free you of it."

"But if I go into hiding, won't the Japanese be doubly suspicious of you?" Thakin Nu asked.

"They won't trust me any more because you remain," was the retort.

. . . A few days later, Thakin Nu was called out of bed at two o'clock in the morning. With a start he recognised the voice of a Japanese summoning him downstairs to see Major Takashita. Saying to himself, "Now they've got me," Thakin Nu threw on some clothes and woke up Ko Chit, who was sleeping in the same room. Downstairs, standing at the door, were the major, an interpreter, two military policemen with fixed bayonets, and another in Burmese dress. The major held a note written in English, apologizing for the lateness of the hour but asking him to go at once to the Japanese army headquarters as they feared for his life. Simultaneously, that same night, Dr. Ba Maw and all the other ministers received the same message offering them protection. According to the Japanese, Dr. Ba Maw was so much against Japanese soldiers entering his house that he would not tolerate them even for his own protection. So this time the Japanese had acted without consulting him.

The Japanese Withdraw

On 22 April [1945], Dr. Ba Maw met with his ministers. Thakin Nu, who saw him alone ahead of the others, was told the Japanese were withdrawing and would abandon Rangoon on the following evening. Dr. Ba Maw would be leaving Rangoon with the Japanese, but Thakin Nu was not expected to do so since he did not seem to get along with the Japanese. However, he must not tell this to the other ministers. Thakin Nu at once rejected this advice. He would accompany Dr. Ba Maw, as he was certain there would be many thakins caught and held on the Moulmein side for whose safety he held himself responsible. He announced this decision to the other ministers when they came in. The only thing Thakin Nu refused to do was to leave the confines of Burma.

Some of the ministers followed Thakin Nu's example and accompanied Dr. Ba Maw to Mudon, a small town near Moulmein. There, on the evening of 14 May, Dr. Ba Maw called all the ministers to his house and read them a letter from the Japanese ambassador telling them of the atomic bomb, the entry of Russia into the war, and the Japanese intention to surrender. Thakin Nu was thrilled to know that the war and all its dangers had come to an end but saddened at the same time by the thought that thirty resistance leaders had been executed only ten days before.

The ambassador's note warned the ministers that the news was very secret as it had not yet been communicated to the troops, and Dr. Ba Maw impressed this on his hearers. However, Thakin Nu felt compelled to confide in his wife. There had earlier been an assassination attempt on the life of Dr. Ba Maw, which the Japanese had been at pains to hush up but which had all but shattered Ma Mya Yee's nerves. So, as soon as he got home, Thakin Nu whispered to her, "Ma Mya Yee, the Japanese have surrendered; the war is over." She was overjoyed. But it was not because the war had ended; it was because this was the first time in her life that Thakin Nu had told her a political secret.

16

Indonesian Nationalists and the Japanese

ELLY TOUWEN-BOUWSMA*

It is an established fact that during the years of Japanese occupation of the Dutch possessions in the Indian Archipelago from 1942 to 1945, Japan helped to establish an indigenous government, consisting of well-known nationalist leaders such as Sukarno and Hatta. While Harry Benda's classic, *Crescent and the Rising Sun: Indonesian Islam Under the Japanese Occupation* (The Hague, W. van Hoeve, 1958) is still regarded as one of the best accounts of that period, there were gaps in information about some nationalist groups.

In 1994, thanks to generous funding by Japan, a "Peace, Friendship and Exchange Initiative" was launched to exchange historical materials between Japan and the states of the Asia-Pacific region that would help foster a better understanding of Japan's relations with the region in one of the most troubling periods in Japanese history. In 1996, the project included the Netherlands due to the availability there of a large amount of documentation in regards to its interaction with Japan in Java during World War II. A number of Indonesian scholars, including Dr. E. Touwen-Bouwsma (Head of Information and Documentation and Chair of the Advisory Committee), were associated with the project. The article reprinted below is the first major study to appear, throwing light on an underground

---

*Elly Touwen-Bouwsma, "The Indonesian Nationalists and the Japanese 'Liberation' of Indonesia: Visions and Reactions," *Journal of Southeast Asian Studies* 27 (March 1996): 1–18.

organization that was operating to sabotage Dutch defenses before the Japanese occupation of Java.

~

It is generally assumed that most of the Indonesian population, including the nationalists, resigned themselves passively to the threat of an imminent war with Japan. There were no large-scale preparations on the side of the Indonesians either to help the Japanese army of invasion find its way or to sabotage the Dutch.[1] This is especially true of Java, the political heartland of Indonesia, where the evidence would seem to point to the fact that no pro-Japanese underground movement existed.[2] Only in Aceh among the Minangkabau in Sumatra had the Japanese found Indonesian allies willing to organize anti-Dutch activities.[3] In Palembang in South Sumatra there was also an espionage organization established by the Japanese themselves probably in order to prevent the destruction of the oil refineries at Playu and Sungai Gerong.[4] In the strongly Islamic region of Gorontalo in North Sulawesi, the local nationalists actually succeeded in taking over the European administration. They arrested the Dutch and proclaimed the Republik Gorontalo on 23 January 1942, just before the Japanese reached their area.[5]

In Java, where the repressive policy adopted by the Dutch government towards the nationalists was most severe, the Dutch seem to have had everything under control on the eve of the outbreak of the war with Japan. Nevertheless, there is some information available which suggests that there could have been an anti-Dutch oriented underground organization in Java. In this context George Kanahele[6] mentions the Sumatran Jusuf Hasan who returned to Java early in 1941 as a Japanese agent.[7] He collaborated with several Japanese, including Nishijima Shigetada,[8] Ishii Taro, Maeda and Machida. Kanahele claims that their specific assignment was to collect information on Dutch military and defence installations and to set up a fifth column. In the summer of 1941, Jusuf Hasan and his Japanese accomplices organized a group of Indonesian nationalists in a conspiracy to sabotage the Dutch defence efforts in the event of a war with Japan. Among those whom he names as belonging to Jusuf's fifth column group are Achmad Subardjo,[9] Maramis, a close friend of Subardjo and of Jusuf Hasan himself, Tadjuddin Noor (member of the People's Council) and Dr. Samsi Sastrowidagdo, a prominent nationalist. The others are unnamed. Kanahele treats seriously the possibility that there was indeed a real attempt made by Jusuf Hasan to set up a fifth column. He concludes, however, that as events turned out the group had no real opportunity to operate against the Dutch because of the sudden collapse of the colonial defence forces a week after the Japanese landed in Java.

The NEFIS collection, held by the Dutch Ministry of Foreign Affairs in The Hague, contains some documents classified under different headings which seem to support George Kanahele's presumption that there was a kind of underground organization operating in Java some months before the Japanese landed there. The documents, written in Indonesian, were found in December 1945 by the Dutch in the former building of the Gunseikanbu in Jakarta, where they were part of the archive of Sudjono,[10] who worked during the war with the Japanese Ministry of General Affairs. Most of these documents are classified under the heading "Organization Subardjo," even though most of the reports do not actually refer to this organization. Some of the 30 or so reports are dated March, April and May 1942, but the bulk of them are dated July 1942. All give an overview of the local situation and the activities of the members involved in the organization just before and just after the arrival of the Japanese Army. During the eight-day battle for Java they were among the first to form Merdeka committees to welcome the victorious Japanese army and offer their help.[11] Achmad Subardjo is named as one of the leaders of the Central Committee in Jakarta which coordinated the activities of the local Merdeka committees.[12]

In the first part of this paper I will pay attention to an underground organization directed by nationalists in Java which prepared anti-Dutch activities before and during the war, examining what preparations they made and what activities they undertook. Going one step further, another question is what were the motives of the local nationalists who set up Merdeka committees for becoming supporters of the Japanese, rather than striving for independence for Indonesia? In order to gain an insight into the activities of the nationalists, including the preparations they made and the actions they carried out, these must be analyzed against the background of the continuously changing political context: the Dutch colonial regime, which was in full control before the outbreak of the war on 8 December 1941; the brief interregnum when the battle for Java was waged; the vacuum of authority in the first week after the invasion of Java by the Japanese army; and the policy of the Japanese military regime towards the nationalists in the first four months of the occupation.

Japan: The Liberator of Indonesia

One crucial point which caused many nationalists to look to Japan as the power that could help them to gain their Indonesia Merdeka was the introduction of the Native Militia Bill by the Dutch government in July 1941. Although they had been requesting the setting up of an Indonesian Militia for years, the nationalists in the People's Council unanimously rejected the bill. They did so because the Dutch, thus far, had refused to recognize the right of the Indonesian people to defend their own country and, moreover, no concessions for any political reforms were being granted.[13] Another point which influenced some nationalists was the failure of the economic negotiations between the Dutch and the Japanese governments in June 1941. They supported Japan 100 per cent because it represented a source of cheap commodities for the Indonesian people and could change the economic structure.[14]

The Dutch refusal to grant any political reforms strengthened solidarity among the nationalists and led to the establishment of the Council of the Indonesian People, Madjalis Rakyat Indonesia, in September 1941, as a representative body of the people whose aim was to strive together for an Indonesian parliament.[15] Quite apart from these disappointments, there were signs that nationalist sympathy for Japan was also gaining ground in the same period. The Japanese propaganda "Asia for the Asians" was increasingly seen as an ideal solution to a political situation which seemed to have reached an impasse. Only the Gerindo (Gerakan Rakjat Indonesia/the Indonesian People's Movement), the leftwing of the nationalist movement, still saw the struggle for national independence as dependent upon the outcome of the world-wide struggle between the forces of Fascism and anti-Fascism. The Parindra (Partai Indonesia Raya/the Greater Indonesia Party), the largest nationalist party, was becoming steadily more pro-Japan minded. The popularity of Japan intensified as one aspect of the growing anti-Dutch animus, which was a projection of the frustrated desire for freedom. The idea took hold that the liberation of Indonesia would begin with the expulsion of the Dutch by the Japanese. According to the Jayabaya myth, the Dutch would be driven out of Indonesia by a yellow race which would come from the north, and the ordinary people interpreted this to refer to the Japanese. After a hundred days of occupation, the promised days of freedom would be at hand.[16] The Japanese propaganda made very good use of this material. Since 1939, Radio Tokyo had been broadcasting daily programs to the Indies in Malay,[17] but from September 1941 the tone of the Japanese broadcasts changed, growing more anti-Dutch, and stressing that Japan would liberate the Indonesians and bring prosperity. Each transmission ended with the national anthem, Indonesia Raya.[18] The independence of Indonesia was, so to speak, just around the corner.

This was the political climate in which an anti-Dutch underground organization took shape. The first information available about the existence of such a kind of organization dates from September 1941. In that month, Achmad Subardjo proposed to the writer of the relevant report that he join the underground movement active against the Dutch government in Batavia. The aims of the organization were to stimulate the population to help the Japanese in their landings in Java, to prevent the Dutch from pursuing a scorched-earth policy, to maintain order among the population and to stockpile food supplies. The contacts in Japan mentioned were Jusuf Hasan and one of his fellow-workers. They worked for Radio Tokyo and would give instructions. Much later, the writer of this report heard that he was supposed to co-operate with Subardjo, Maramis, Tadjuddin Noor and Hindromartono.[19] Other nationalists named as members of this organization were Sartono (Buitenzorg), Dr. Boentaran (Semarang), Dr. Samsi (Surabaya),[20] Latuharhary and Soenarko (Malang).[21] Most of the above-mentioned people were friends of Achmad Subardjo. Dr. Samsi and Dr. Boentaran knew Subardjo from their university days in the Netherlands, where they used to meet each other at the Indonesian Student Association (Perhimpunan Indonesia). This was also the case with Maramis and Latuharhary. Tadjuddin Noor was a friend of Subardjo whom he had met in Malang when he was gravely ill.[22] Subardjo probably met Jusuf Hasan during his visit to Japan in 1935. Jusuf Hasan is also mentioned as one of the people who sought contact with nationalists in Blitar in October 1941, declaring that they were prepared to work in the interests of Japan. He is only mentioned once, probably because he returned to Tokyo to support the organization by means of Radio Tokyo in November 1941. It was, however, not Subardjo himself who travelled through Java to recruit supporters for anti-Dutch underground activities, but one of his fellow-workers; Ismangoenwonoto spent October and November 1941 on the road in Java, visiting nationalists in Yogyakarta, Kertosono and Semarang.[23] Ismangoenwonoto instructed the nationalists to incite anti-Dutch feelings among the Indonesian people, in particular among Indonesian members of the Royal Netherlands Indies Army and the police, and advise them not to fight against the Japanese. Further instructions would be given by Radio Tokyo.[24] In Semarang, he co-ordinated the activities of three small groups of nationalists already established there to undermine Dutch authority. The tasks were shared out, with one group responsible for propaganda among the Indonesian soldiers, one for work among the common people and the third for infiltration of the upper echelons of society—intellectuals and government officials.[25] These local nationalists, in their turn, sought contact with like-minded people in their neighbourhoods and passed on instructions from Batavia. In places as far apart as Tuban, Demak and Jember local nationalists joined the underground organization.[26] Some of these nationalists were members of various political parties like Parindra, Gerindo and Partindo, but others had not aligned themselves with any political party.

The motive spurring most of the local nationalists to join the underground movement and support the Japanese was a conviction that the

Indonesian people would never achieve prosperity as long as the Dutch were in power. They also believed that the Indonesians did not themselves possess the power to unseat the Dutch and that only changes in international politics could help them to reach their goal for their homeland: a free Indonesia.[27] This mixture of left and right wing ideologies among the nationalists is characteristic of their hitherto forlorn attempts to gain independence and freedom for Indonesia. The hope of changes in the international political arena was a mainstay of Gerindo, while support for the Japanese as a direct means of helping the Indonesians was more in line with the thinking of the Parindra. However, according to Nishijima, Achmad Subardjo was convinced that independence would be achieved once the Japanese landed in Java.[28]

The actual activities undertaken by the local nationalists in the period just before the outbreak of the war with Japan remain fairly obscure. Probably they did no more than encourage and stimulate anti-Dutch feelings, trying to convince the people that the Japanese would liberate them from the Dutch. They had to tread very warily because the police and the Political Intelligence Service (PID) kept a watchful eye on the nationalists, in particular on those who were suspected of having contacts in Japan. Even a prominent nationalist and member of the People's Council like Thamrin was suspected of pro-Japanese activities, and was put under house arrest shortly before he died of heart failure and malaria in January 1941.[29] The chances of being able to meet one another were very few and far between. Following the outbreak of the war in the Netherlands in May 1940, all political meetings had been banned by the Dutch government. Some nationalists involved in the underground organization managed to meet each other at the Gerindo Congress held in Batavia in October 1941,[30] but more often they met informally as friends to discuss their activities pending the advent of the Great East Asian War that would liberate them from the yoke of the Dutch.

After the declaration of war with Japan, on 8 December 1941, the first thing the Dutch government did was to arrest all the Japanese in Java, about 2,000 persons in all,[31] and to place Indonesians known to have relations with Japanese under strict police surveillance. One of Achmad Subardjo's sisters[32] and her family, who lived in Batavia, were put under house arrest, accused of harbouring sympathy for the Japanese because they had a son in Formosa and a son-in-law in Japan. Sometime later the family was taken to a camp at Cibadak, a hill station in the interior.[33] Even Indonesians who had been friendly with Japanese living in their neighbourhoods ran the risk of being arrested by the PID. The Indonesians taken into custody by the Dutch were transported to Garut on 15 January 1942, where they were liberated by the Japanese army on 11 March 1942. In all, about 600 persons accused of being pro-Japan were interned there, including 100 Chinese.[34]

The strained political climate prevailing after the outbreak of the war made it virtually impossible for the local nationalists involved in underground activities to contact each other. Their only source of information seems to have been Radio Tokyo, and this was crucial because it had been impressed on them that Radio Tokyo would issue instructions. Although the Dutch had placed a ban on listening to Radio Tokyo, they waited daily for messages from Tokyo. It was Jusuf Hasan who broadcast appeals to the people back home. He would sing Indonesia Raya and speak passionately about the country's imminent liberation by Japan.[35]

Preparations and Mounting Expectations

Once the war began, the Dutch government created facilities to help eventual victims of war among the people in the Indies. Several civil front organizations were set up by and for the Europeans, and other population groups like the Indonesians and the Chinese were given permission to form their own civil front organizations. The Indonesians set up the Penolong Korban Perang (Pekope) to help potential Indonesian victims of war.[36] Strangely enough, rather than entrust the task of forming Pekope to the Indonesian civil service, the Dutch turned to local nationalists. Enthusiasm for the civil front organization waxed strong, and the Indonesian press fervently supported it.[37] This organization gave local nationalists a perfect instrument to carry out underground activities. It seems that Parindra, by far the largest party of the time with 20,000 members,[38] was especially active in setting up local Pekope branches.[39] All over the country Parindra endeavoured to organize Pekope in the kampongs, and instructed the people in what they should do if the war reached their villages. Wherever possible nationalists involved in underground activities infiltrated Pekope and sometimes, as in Semarang, succeeded in taking it over completely.[40] Although Pekope was meant for Indonesians only, in some localities Chinese seem to have joined as well. For instance, in Godong and in Salatiga, Chinese are mentioned as members of this organization.[41] A Dutch civil servant in Batavia, however, saw the Pekope as nothing more than a front organization. He believed that the Indonesians were apparently already counting upon the capitulation of the Netherlands Indies, after which they would be able to take over control.[42]

It is not known if local nationalists involved in underground activities actually received any instructions from Radio Tokyo.[43] Most of their activities during the early days of the war had to do with preventing the implementation of a scorched-earth policy by the Dutch. The Dutch had formed a demolition corps to destroy vital objects like oil refineries, factories, bridges and rice-mills. The nationalists saw the scorched-earth policy as being directed more against the Indonesian people than against the Japanese. In the words of an upper middle class Indonesian woman in Batavia: "It seems that the Dutch begrudge our having their factories and bridges. Why do they want to destroy them? Those who will suffer most are the Indonesians, because the people on those burnt out estates will be without employment and will starve."[44] To spread propaganda among those Indonesians who participated in the demolition corps urging them to sabotage the orders of the Dutch was one of the priorities of the local nationalists active in the underground organization,[45] alongside the guarding of such vital targets to prevent their destruction.[46] Nationalists also urged the Indonesian soldiers serving in the local Dutch forces, the KNIL, not to fight against the Japanese. The Japanese were not fighting the Indonesians, so why should Indonesians retaliate against them? Some went so far as to exhort the soldiers to kill their commanders first.[47]

By the time Japanese troops landed in Java, a frantic atmosphere of welcome had overwhelmed the island, arising from the expectation on the part of the Indonesians that prosperity and independence, about which they had been dreaming for so many years, would soon be achieved with the help and assistance of Japan. During the landing of the Japanese army in Java on the night of 1 March 1942, all over the island planes dropped leaflets bearing the slogan, "One colour, one race," with the two flags (Japanese and Indonesian) printed on the reverse sides.[48] Members of the underground organization were given instructions to make the mark of Hinomaru, a red ball, on the left palm of their hands. Should they meet Japanese soldiers, they would only have to show the symbol of the sun to let them know that they were friends.[49] But, to their disappointment, the Japanese soldiers seemed to be unaware of the meaning of the sign.[50]

In the chaotic days between the Japanese invasion of Java and the capitulation of the Dutch on 9 March 1942, local nationalists seized the opportunity to set up so-called Merdeka committees. They instructed the people to greet the Japanese with cries of "Banzai!" and to carry a handkerchief in the likeness of the Japanese flag with them. In Magelang and Jember thousands of people did indeed welcome the Japanese with cries of "Banzai," "Hidup Indonesia" and "Selamat Nippon datang."[51] Among the first to set up such committees were the nationalists involved in the underground network. As mentioned above, some committees like those in Semarang had already been formed before the Japanese invasion under the guise of Pekope. Now they lost no time in changing their designation from Pekope to Komite Indonesia Merdeka. In Blitar, Madiun, Batavia, Magelang, Semarang, Yogyakarta,[52] Kroya, Kendal, Salatiga, Jember and Ambarawa committees were formed under different names, such as Komite Nasional Indonesia, Komite Indonesia Merdeka and Komite Barisan Rakyat Indonesia (Indonesian People's Army Committee). In Magelang a prominent Chinese was also asked to sit on the committee, but as a rule committee members were Indonesian.[53] Although the names differed, the aims of the committees were virtually the same, to support the Japanese in order to achieve the East Asia Co-Prosperity Sphere; to destroy the power of Western nations; to maintain law and order until there was a new administration; and to recognize Dai Nippon as the leader and protector of Asia. Lurking behind these aims lay the expectation that the committees would be given a say in the local administration and the economy.

The newly formed committees often tried in vain to maintain order among the population pending the arrival of the glorious Japanese army. They were powerless to prevent the chain of banditry, looting and arson which welled up in the wake of the Dutch scorched-earth policy and the subsequent invasion of the Japanese army. On 28 February the Dutch government gave orders to the demolition corps to do their job. All over Java bands of robbers plundered stores of food, pawn shops and depots at railway stations. They regarded Dutch and Indonesian civil servants, not to mention the Chinese, as their legitimate targets. In Jombang, according to a Dutch police report, the Parindrists stirred up anti-Dutch feelings. "The natives must have no sympathy for the Dutch. They had tyrannized and exploited the Indonesian people. The Indonesians should help the Japanese to murder the Dutch."[54] In Yogyakarta the house of the Assistant Resident was attacked,[55] while in Pare the Wedana had to hand over control to the local Parindrists,[56] and in Kendal, the members of the newly formed committee also tried to seize control of the administration.[57] Even more extreme measures were taken at Kesamben, near Blitar, where men armed with cudgels and knives attacked the home of the Assistant Wedana planning to murder him, but he escaped.[58]

However, the main target of the bands were Chinese living in rural areas. In East Java all the rice mills in the vicinity of Jombang were ransacked, and Chinese men were forcibly circumcised by the Nahdatul Ulama. Chinese shops were looted, and some of their owners were killed.[59] The plundering of Chinese property, factories and rice-mills also occurred in Central Java. In Demak the looting began in the Chinese kampong. One report says that the Indonesians were shot at by the Chinese who had been armed by the Dutch. Thereupon members of the underground organization arrested all the Chinese and threw them into the local prison.[60] It is striking that several nationalists involved in underground activities claimed that they had prevented the murder of hundreds of Chinese. In Ambarawa the Komite Indonesia Merdeka succeeded in preventing a clash between Indonesians and Chinese. In Godong, where about 900 Chinese were locked up in the local pawnshop, Pekope took care of them, giving them food and protection. The members of the committee of Kendal district, originally nationalists attached to the underground organization who included Parindrists and young people from the Surya Wiryawan, Parindra's Youth Association, were able to evacuate the Chinese before the looting began. This pattern was repeated in Boja where Chinese shops were plundered, but the Chinese had been evacuated to Semarang and escaped personal harm. Around Semarang as well the committee evacuated the Chinese from rural areas into the city.[61]

On 7 March 1942, 18 Japanese officers, representing the army, arrived in Semarang where they were received by the Dutch Resident and the mayor of the city. Members of the Komite Indonesia Merdeka tried in vain to join in the welcome.[62] Nor were they the only ones who complained that they were obstructed in their activities by Dutch and Indonesian civil servants, who were then still at their posts. In the eyes of the Dutch and Indonesian civil servants, these elements were not the upholders of law and order but were in fact perpetrators of the plundering and looting. Eight members of committees were arrested by the Assistant Wedana in Wates in East Java.[63] There were also arrests in Kertosono. The supporters and helpers of the Japanese army were branded robber-chiefs by the Indonesian civil servants and held responsible for the looting and arson, for which they were imprisoned.[64] The nationalists, in their turn, were convinced that the looting of Dutch and Chinese property was the consequence of the centuries of exploitation of the people. It was clear that the people hated both the Dutch government and their alleged accomplices, the Chinese. It was also obvious to them that the Indonesian civil servants, the representatives of the Dutch, did not want to submit to the Japanese, but were pretending to do so for the time being.[65]

The rivalry between the local nationalists on the one hand and the Indonesian civil service and the Chinese on the other now emerged as a leading point of friction. Under the pretext of helping to maintain law and order, nationalists staged takeovers of local administrative functions and, ostensibly to take care of the welfare of the people, Pekope and the committees attempted to get a grip on the food distribution system, which was mainly in Chinese hands. They were convinced that as soon as the Japanese controlled Indonesia they, as leaders of the people, would be chosen to improve the welfare of the people, who were still suffering from abuses under the former Dutch regime.

Illusions and Disenchantments

The Japanese invasion evoked tremendous excitement not only in the countryside of Java but also in the political centre of the island, Batavia. Here, as elsewhere, the nationalists expected not only to be liberated from Dutch imperialism but to be able to achieve independence as a consequence of the invasion. There were rumours from Semarang that in their first contacts with nationalists the Japanese officers, who arrived in Demak between 2 and 4 March, had given voice to such ideas as "We shall drive out the Dutch. You try to govern your own country."[66] Expectations that the nationalists would gain control of the administration of their country were rising high. Directly after the capitulation of the Dutch, the Japanese authorities in Batavia sought contact with some prominent nationalists in order, so it was said, to consult with them on the organization of the new administration. However, the rivalry among the nationalists increased apace with the steadily rising expectations of an Indonesia Merdeka. In the course of five days, three different blueprints for the composition of an Indonesian cabinet were proposed by the nationalists. Subardjo's name was mentioned in one of the lists as deputy-minister for Foreign Affairs, with Sudjono as secretary of state and Tadjuddin Noor as deputy-minister.[67] The Japanese authorities speedily rejected the proposals and made it quite clear that any political concessions were out of the question.[68] In his autobiography Subardjo states that, even before the landing of the Japanese, he had written a blueprint for a provisional constitution for Indonesia in conjunction with Maramis and Supomo. The blunt rejection of the proposals for a transitional Indonesian government by the Japanese army authorities made this completely irrelevant.[69] Moreover, by Ordinance no. 3, dated 20 March 1942, the Japanese authorities in Java prohibited any kind of discussion, suggestions or propaganda about the political organization of the country. Within a fortnight the disillusioned nationalists were forced to give up their dreams. Even the word Indonesia in a political sense was no longer permitted. On the same day, in Ordinance no. 4, displaying the Indonesian flag was banned.[70] In Batavia the Japanese authorities were quick to smash the hopes and expectations of the nationalists in the centre, but it took more time to make it clear to the local nationalists in the countryside that there could not be any talk of independence and freedom for Indonesia. Ordinance no. 3 does not seem to have affected the local committees in Java directly. In the course of March and April 1942 in several other places, especially in Central Java, local nationalists freely continued to set up committees, for example, in Surakarta, Kebumen, Karanganyar, Sumpiuyuh,

Probolinggo and Purworejo.[71] These committees were managed by nation-alists from different nationalist parties and unions who were eager to offer their services to the Japanese. In several localities members of the Parindra took the initiative in forming committees, for instance in Bangil, where a Komite Keamanan Rakyat (People's Security Committee) was set up,[72] but elsewhere Gerindo and Partindo members were in the forefront. There were also places, such as Surakarta, where the Barisan Rakyat Indonesia (Indonesian People's Army) worked alongside the Komite Nasional In-donesia helping to maintain law and order.[73]

The Komite Indonesia Merdeka in Semarang functioned as the central or-ganization for most of the local committees in Central Java.[74] It was subor-dinate to the Central Committee in Batavia, which was run by Subardjo and others. The members of the Semarang committee believed that the ban is-sued by the Japanese commander on the holding of meetings and the under-taking of political action did not apply to them, because the Komite Indonesia Merdeka was a working committee and not a political party or association.[75] The committee in Semarang continued its activities and even organized a conference on 21 March 1942 at which representatives from Surakarta and Yogyakarta were present. At this conference the aims of the committees were laid down: first, an independent Indonesia and, second, the realization of a Greater Asia under the leadership of Japan. Moreover, the delegation decided that the Central Committee in Batavia should try to establish close contacts with the Japanese authorities there, but on the con-dition that the local committees would retain the right to keep in touch with the local Japanese administration. Subardjo and his committee in Batavia would be asked to set up a mediation committee, which would maintain direct contact with the supreme Japanese authorities.[76]

The working programs of the local committees reveal a large degree of similarity. All of them recognized Dai Nippon as the leader and protector of Asia and formed contact committees to inform the Japanese commander and the civil service about their activities. Besides this, propaganda and informa-tion sections were set up in order to inform the people about the changes in the administration. Most of the committees also had an intelligence section which gathered information about arms, oil and petrol stores, Dutch soldiers who were in hiding, and the subversive activities of foreign nationals, as well as a section whose aim was to liberate the Indonesian economy from the hands of foreigners and plan a new system of economic organization.[77]

In the city of Surabaya the Parindrists arranged a meeting with a repre-sentative of the Japanese army commander during which they discussed the re-division of the provincial administration and the police, and presented an economic plan which would give Parindra the opportunity to help villagers by means of consumer co-operative societies, such as Rukung Tani, Lumbung and credit banks.[78] The Komite Nasional Indonesia in Magelang took on a security function, obtaining authorization from the Japanese Army authorities to impound goods, conduct house-searches and call on the police for help. The chairman of this committee was a member of the former Communist Party of Indonesia (PKI) who had been interned for four years at Digul. Members collected arms from the town guard and searched the Dutch barracks as well as those of the military and police for arms, which they then handed over to the local Japanese army authorities.[79]

The most important aims of the nationalists, however, seem to have been to wrest local administrative authority from Indonesian civil servants and to pry the local economy out of the hands of the Chinese. Committee representatives generally operated as follows: men—usually young and sometimes armed—would use force or the threat of force to try to remove administrative officials. These takeovers were carried out under the pretext of helping to maintain law and order.[80] The same argument was used to gain control of food storage and distribution. Chinese were locked up in jails or other secure buildings, ostensibly to protect them from the fury of the people. In the meantime, committee members used their own organizations to appropriate the distribution of food and set up co-operatives. In Magelang and Semarang, the local Pekope coordinated the rice supply,[81] while in Krawang rice was distributed among the population and the essential components of the rice-mills, all owned by the Chinese, were removed and hidden.[82] In Blitar the Rukun Penduduk Indonesia Blitar (United Indonesian Citizens of Blitar) helped the people to organize the local economy.[83]

Within a month, however, the local Japanese authorities forced the nationalists to surrender local control of the administration to them and reinstated both Dutch and Indonesian civil servants.[84] The Indonesian civil servants and police, now supported by the Japanese, struck back at the committees, branding members as leaders of robber gangs and arresting them for disturbing the peace.[85] Parindra also found itself in deep trouble. Some of its local members in East and Central Java were arrested by the Kempeitai, accused of robbery and sowing discord in wartime. After the reinstatement of Dutch civil servants on 3 April, members of the local board of the Parindra in Malang were arrested by the Kempeitai. In all about 85 persons were taken, among them 11 Parindrists including Latuharhary, who had joined the underground organization in Malang.[86] Other arrests took place in Bangil, when nine people, including prominent Parindrists and the local leader of the Arab minority, were jailed for looting Dutch and Chinese properties. In June, most of those arrested were released, but 18 people, including 15 Parindrists, remained in detention.[87]

In Surakarta, where the Komite Nasional Indonesia and the Barisan Rakyat Indonesia were embroiled in fierce competition with the Chinese civil front organization, the chairmen of both groups were arrested along with 55 youths. To the dismay of the nationalists, the Chinese civil front worked for the Japanese and guarded their offices, whereupon the nationalists accused the Chinese of manufacturing weapons and of being involved in black marketeering. To their disappointment, the Japanese did not take any notice of their accusations, and one night when a Chinese guard spied some members of the Barisan Rakyat guarding the residential neighborhood in the city, they were arrested on suspicion of being involved in looting. They were set free some days later, with the exception of the committee chairmen who were still in jail at the beginning of May.[88]

Meanwhile, the nationalists in the political center in Batavia, who were still confused by the measures taken by the Japanese authorities, tried to find out what was going on elsewhere in Java. Under the guise of visiting their families in Central Java, Sukarto, deputy-secretary of the GASPI (Gabungan Sarekat Sekerdja Partikulir Indonesia/Federation of Private Workers) and Hindromartono, a prominent member of the PVPN (Persatoean Vakbonden Pegawai Negeri/League of Civil Servants' Unions)[89] left Batavia at the end of March and visited several branches of the GASPI and local committees during April 1942. Afterwards Sukarto reported his findings to Subardjo. He hoped that the report would stimulate the Japanese authorities to take appropriate action and that they would gain confidence in the committees set up by the Indonesian people.[90] In this he was disappointed, for the measures taken by the Japanese authorities were quite different from those anticipated by the nationalists. The Indonesian civil service and the Indonesian police continued to be used by the Japanese, while prominent members of local committees and Parindrists remained in jail. In the eyes of the nationalists, nothing had changed since these elements were the same people who had oppressed them and the public at large before the outbreak of war.

In May 1942 the deeply chagrined committee in Semarang adjusted its objectives. Under pressure from the local Japanese authorities it admitted that Indonesia was now subject to the power of Japan, and that gaining independence did not mean winning it (that would have meant fighting), but receiving it which implied acquiescing to the wishes of Japan. The Indonesians had to prove that they possessed the necessary competence to undertake the job, otherwise they had no right to be independent. Japan wanted Indonesia to become independent under the leadership of Japan. In the opinion of the committee, however, to be independent implied first the existence of a Greater Indonesia, as expressed in the anthem Indonesia Raya, and second the right to raise the Indonesian flag. But the Japanese army decreed otherwise. The red and white Indonesian flag was banned, Indonesia Raya could not be sung and the words Indonesia Merdeka could not be uttered. Instead, there had to be an Asia Raya (Greater Asia) under the leadership of Japan and once the goal of Indonesia Merdeka was no longer a possibility, it became obvious that the committee had to be dispensed with.[91]

It is not known when the other local committees were abolished, but it is almost certain that all surviving committees were eliminated in July 1942, when Ordinance no. 23 required all political parties and other associations to disband. One of the reasons behind this ban on committees was probably that the Japanese authorities were no longer prepared to tolerate any interference in the economic sphere. In particular, they wanted to prevent the nationalists from leading any agrarian resistance to their measures.[92] In June, the Japanese authorities had ordered the reopening of the rice-mills, and forced the rice co-operatives set up by the local committees to stop their work. Farmers had to sell their rice to the Chinese mill-owners for a fixed price. To ensure that all the rice went to the rice-mills, even the traditional pounding of rice was forbidden.[93]

In June, the Parindra was also ordered to desist from its economic activities. During the first months of the Occupation Parindra had set up shops in almost every town in Java which sold food and other related articles but only to Parindra members. After several months, when food shortages began to occur everywhere, the people could buy food in the Parindra shops but only on condition that they join the association.[94] The Japanese authorities, however, wanted to have complete control of both the food supply and the food distribution, and at the same time to disembarrass themselves of the Parindra, their most fervent supporter.

In July the Japanese authorities put Parindra under severe pressure to cease its activities immediately. At that point Parindra had still not succeeded in freeing its members arrested in April, although it had made representations about this several times. On 26 June 1942 a member from Malang went to Batavia to speak to Subardjo, who was then working in Hatta's office in the Department of Economic Affairs of the Gunseikanbu, concerning the Parindra members who were still in jail in Malang.[95] The Parindra board in Surabaya also sent representatives to Batavia for consultation with the Japanese authorities.[96] The Japanese announced that they were willing to release Parindra members on condition that the party be dissolved, and the Parindrists concerned affirm under oath ten conditions imposed by the Japanese. Besides the dissolution of the Parindra, most of these conditions referred to general matters such as submission to Dai Nippon and the ban on any kind of discussion or organization, and only two applied specifically to Parindra: namely, that the name Parindra on buildings had to be taken down and, probably the most remarkable, that in future only the Indonesian language would be permitted.[97] In view of the relatively high educational level of prominent nationalists, it is likely they used to communicate with each other in Dutch, a language that most Indonesians and Japanese had not mastered. The Parindra was dissolved as from the end of July. In August 1942 the last Parindrists still imprisoned were released.[98] By then the Japanese had the local administration and the economy completely under their control, and the influence of the nationalists in the rural areas of Java had been definitively curbed. The best that remained for them was membership in one of the many advisory councils which the Japanese authorities were to set up during the occupation.

Conclusion

Have we sufficient evidence to conclude that there was a kind of underground organization in Java before and during the initial stages of the war? The reports provide a picture of a loosely knit underground group, based in the first instance on the network of personal relations of Subardjo and his friends. They belonged to the upper echelons of the nationalist elite who were aspiring to gain freedom and independence for Indonesia, directly below Sukarno, Hatta and Sjahrir. Pertinently, these three prominent nationalists had been interned by the Dutch in Bengkulen and on the island of Banda respectively and were not available to lead the nationalist movement. In the eyes of the local nationalists, Subardjo and his friends were obviously the most appropriate leaders to set them on the road to freedom with the aid of Japan, being preferable to those nationalists who were involved in the Madjalis Rakyat Indonesia and other large political federations endeavoring to negotiate their freedom from the Dutch. The fact that Subardjo had been in Japan and had contacts and friends there, as did Jusuf Hasan, strengthened their position.

Under the influence of Japanese propaganda, groups of nationalists whose aim was to support Japan as a way of gaining independence for Indonesia were set up here and there. They made contact with one of Subardjo's fellow-workers who visited several of his friends in October and November 1941. There was, however, no direct contact between the members, and the different groups were unacquainted with each other before the outbreak of the war with Japan. All these small groups were looking for leaders who could give guidance in the imminent independence of Indonesia, and such leaders were Subardjo and his friends. The activities the different groups, consisting of two or at most four people, claimed to have undertaken before the war were so general—to propagate anti-Dutch sentiments and listen to Radio Tokyo—that everyone who was expecting the war could be said to have taken part. One very important instrument in making preparations for the new Indonesia was Pekope. This civil front organization provided the local nationalists with the means to make close contact with the people. Under the pretext of organizing aid to civilian war victims, they set up provisional networks to take over the local administration and economy. The bitterness of the local nationalists about the scorched-earth policy of the Dutch must be seen against this background.

During the invasion of the Japanese these different groups came to the fore and set up Merdeka committees. From that point on a kind of organization began to take shape with Subardjo as the behind-the-scenes organizer. Convinced of the imminent independence of Indonesia once the Japanese had arrived, Subardjo in collaboration with Maramis and Supomo drew up a blueprint for a provisional constitution for Indonesia. There is no evidence that Subardjo's other friends knew about this blueprint. Whatever the case may be, Subardjo and Maramis became the leaders of the Central Committee in Batavia, which functioned as a mediation group between the Japanese authorities and the local committees, at least in Central Java. Moreover, Subardjo was well informed about the activities the local committees had undertaken in the first two months after the capitulation of the Dutch, thanks to Sukarto's report.[99] Under the pretext of supporting the Japanese, the committees then started a social revolution in order to realize their idea of a free Indonesia in which they would be the leaders assigned to guide the people to a prosperous future. In their vision there was no place in the new Indonesia for collaborators with the Dutch or for capitalists like the Chinese who had exploited the people for so long. Pending the arrival of their liberators, they took over the local administration and tried to implement their plans to control the food production and distribution.

However, within a month, the Japanese had restored the Indonesian civil servants to their posts, and thrust aside the local nationalists, who were branded as agitators and accused of disturbing the peace. Arrests followed and the bewildered nationalists, who could not believe that the former oppressors of the people had been put back in power by their putative liberators, directed their energy towards the development of food and other production co-operatives. Momentarily, the Japanese authorities turned a blind eye to nationalist activities in the agrarian sector. In view of the destruction of the estates and rice-mills by the Dutch and by plundering bands, the Japanese needed some support at least from the local nationalists to be able to secure the production and distribution of food. Besides the committees, the Japanese depended in particular on Parindra, although they did not trust it completely, and as soon as the Japanese had restored the damage to the factories and rice-mills, they ordered the Chinese to resume operations. The committees and Parindra were forced to abandon their activities in this sphere as well.

The local Merdeka committees set in motion the first social revolution in Java, a forerunner of the large-scale social revolution which erupted directly after the capitulation of Japan in August 1945. In the frantic atmosphere of freedom that seized them during the first weeks after the arrival of their assumed liberators, they gave no thought to the possibility that their revolution might be stillborn. They believed that their liberators intended to grant them political independence. After all, had the prophecy of Jayabaya not foretold that their liberators would remain for only three months? Japan's attitude to the demands of the nationalists, however, was governed by immediate plans for the exploitation of the resources and manpower of Java. The nationalists found themselves involved in a serious conflict with the Japanese authorities and the social revolution they set in motion rebounded on them.

Within four months the nationalists' aspirations had been completely crushed. The local nationalists felt badly betrayed by the Japanese refusal to grant Indonesia its independence. They had co-operated with the Japanese, having taken the latter's claim that they would grant independence to Indonesia at face value. The nationalists were expelled from the rural areas in Java, and the Japanese kept a close eye on them to make sure that they did not have a chance to maintain contact with the common people. The organizations the Japanese set up during the occupation to mobilize the manpower in Java such as the Seinandan, the Keibodan, PETA and the Jawa Hokokai were put unequivocally under the control of the Indonesian civil servants, which was tantamount to being under the control of the Japanese. The nationalists were co-opted into countless advisory councils, where they bided their time waiting for the moment when they could seize freedom and independence for Indonesia.

NOTES

1. An overview of anti-Dutch activities in the Netherlands East Indies before the invasion of Japan is given in E. Touwen-Bouwsma, "De Indonesische nationalisten en de oorlog met Japan: houding en reacties," in *Nederlands-Indie 1942. Illusie en ontgoocheling*, ed. P. Groen and E. Touwen-Bouwsma (Den Haag: SDU Uitgeverij, 1992), pp. 57–75.

2. H. J. Benda, "The Beginning of the Japanese Occupation of Java," *Far Eastern Quarterly* 15 (1956): 544; B. Bouman, "Een veelzijdige waarneming. Japan in Indonesische ogen in het tijdvak 1930–1942," in *Beelden van Japan in her vooroorlogse Nederlands-Indie*, ed. E. Locher-Scholten (Leiden: Werkgroep Europese Expansie, State University of Leiden, 1987), p. 230.

3. See for anti-Dutch activities in Aceh, A. J. Piekaar, *Atjeh en de oorlog met Japan* (Den Haag: Van Hoeve, 1949). For a detailed account of the role the Japanese played in the so-called F-organization in Aceh, see Fujiwara Iwaichi, "Fifth Column Work in Sumatra," in *The Japanese Experience in Indonesia: Selected Memoirs of 1942–1945*, ed. Anthony Reid and Oki Akira (Athens: Ohio University Monographs in International Studies, Southeast Asia Series No. 72, 1986), pp. 9–31. Benda states that among the Minangkabau there were two groups who fought against the Dutch: Indonesia Bergerak and Islam Raja. See "The Beginning of the Japanese Occupation of Java," p. 544.

4. M. Zed, *Kepialangan Politik dan Revolusi: Palembang 1900–1950* (Amsterdam: Centrale Huisdrukkerij VU, 1991).

5. For more information on the Republik Gorontalo, see Republik Indonesia, *Propinsi Sulawesi* (Jakarta: Kementerian Penerangan, 1953), pp. 202–207.

6. G. S. Kanahele, "The Japanese Occupation of Indonesia: Prelude to Independence" (Ph.D. diss., Cornell University, 1967), pp. 17–18, 35.

7. Jusuf Hasan was a Sumatran who went to Japan in 1930 to study economics at the Meiji University, where he joined the ultra-nationalist Black Dragon Society. He was probably the most active Indonesian propagandist in Tokyo, taking part in establishing the Kainan Ryo Centre for overseas students. In 1941 he returned to Indonesia as a secret Japanese agent. See Nishijima, "The Nationalists in Java, 1943–1945," in *The Japanese Experience in Indonesia*, ed. Reid and Oki, p. 262. At the end of November 1941, just before the outbreak of the war with Japan, he returned to Tokyo, where he worked with the short-wave radio transmitter of the Japanese navy to broadcast appeals to his people back home. See K. Goto, "Life and Death of 'Abdul Rachman' (1906–49): One Aspect of Japanese-Indonesian Relationships," *Indonesia* 22 (1976): 66.

8. Nishijima had lived in Java before the war and was sympathetic to the nationalists cause. He was close friends with outstanding nationalists and spoke Malay fluently. He was one of the Japanese who had been interned by the Dutch at the outbreak of the war with Japan and was transported to Australia. In August 1942, he returned to Java where he remained in close contact with his nationalist friends.

9. Achmad Subardjo had studied at the Universities of Utrecht and Leiden. In the Netherlands, he had been an active member of the Indonesian Student Association/Perhimpunan Indonesia. He returned to Java in 1934, and earned his living as a self-employed lawyer, as he did not want to work for the Dutch government. He went to Japan in September 1935 as a correspondent for the Indonesian journal *Matahari*, issued in Semarang. After returning to Java in 1936, he earned a living in Bandung. In 1939 he moved to Jakarta where he arranged programmes for Radio Ketimuran, a branch of the Netherlands Indies Radio Network Company/NIROM. He also worked with Sam Ratulangi writing a newspaper column called "National Comments." He was a non-co-operative nationalist and apparently not a member of one of the nationalist parties. See A. Subardjo Djoyoadisuryo, *Kesadaran Nasional, Sebuah Otobiografi* (Jakarta, 1978), and *Orang Indonesia yang Terkemuka di Jawa* (Jogjakarta: Gadjah Mada University Press, 1986), p. 290.

10. Sudjono had been in Japan teaching Indonesian. He returned to Java with the Japanese army of invasion in Bantam. Sudjono was married to a niece of Subardjo, the daughter of one of his sisters. It was Sudjono who invited Subardjo to come to Japan in 1935. Subardjo, *Kesadaran Nasional*, p. 191.

11. Nishijima claims there were committees set up by Indonesians who hoped to achieve independence for Indonesia by cooperating with the Japanese. See Nishijima, "The Nationalists in Java, 1943–1945," in *The Japanese Experience in Indonesia*, ed. Reid and Oki, p. 262.

12. Sukarto Report, *Journey through East Java*, 4 May 1942. Rijksinstituut voor Oorlogsdocumentatie [henceforth RIOD] IC: 031605–031630. See also *BUZA.NEFIS/CMI:2407*. Strangely enough, Subardjo does not mention this organization in his autobiography, *Kesadaran Nasional*.

13. For a detailed overview of the attempts of the nationalists to co-operate with the Dutch government in the last year before the outbreak of the Pacific War, see S. Abeyasekere, *One Hand Clapping: Indonesian Nationalists and the Dutch, 1939–1942* (Clayton, Victoria: Monash Papers on Southeast Asia, Number 5, 1976).

14. Report on the activities before and during the Japanese invasion in Java. *BUZA.NEFIS/CMI:2717*.

15. The Madjalis Rakyat Indonesia (M.R.I.) included the Federation of Political Parties, Gabungan Politik Indonesia (GAPI); the Federation of Islamic Unions, Madjlisoel Islamil A'laa Indonesia (M.I.A.I.); and the Trade Union for Civil Servants, Persatoean Vakbonden Pegawai Negeri (P.V.P.N.).

16. S. Sjahrir, *Out of Exile* (New York: John Day, 1949), pp. 219, 233.

17. According to a Dutch publication the effect of these broadcasts was negligible. See *A Decade of Japanese Underground Activities in the Netherlands East Indies* (London: HMSO, 1942), p. 15.

18. For the impact of the transmissions from Radio Tokyo, see B. Bouman, "Een veelzijdige waarneming. Japan in Indonesische ogen in het tijdvak 1930–1942," in *Beelden van Japan in het vooroorlogse Nederlands-Indie*, ed. E. Locher-Scholten and G. S. See also Kanahele, "The Japanese Occupation of Indonesia."

19. Two of them, Maramis and Tadjuddin Noor, were also mentioned by Kanahele as belonging to the fifth column in Java ("The Japanese Occupation of Indonesia," pp. 17–18). It is known that Hindromartono, a prominent member of the Persatuan Vakbonden Pegawai Negeri (P.V.P.N.), the trade union for civil servants, made a tour through Central Java in April 1942 with Sukarto, who reported to Subardjo about how the Committees Indonesia Merdeka established by then were doing (RIOD IC: 031605–30).

20. Dr Samsi is also named by Kanahele as a member of the fifth column in Java. See "The Japanese Occupation of Indonesia," pp. 17–18.

21. Report on activities before and during the Japanese invasion of Java. *BUZA. NEFIS/CMI:2717*.

22. Subardjo, *Kesadaran Nasional*, p. 189.

23. See the following reports on Subardjo's organization: *BUZA.NEFIS/CMI:2775* (Jogyakarta), 2727 (Kertosono), 2739 (Semarang).

24. Report on Subardjo's organization. *BUZA.NEFIS/CMI:2729.*

25. Report of the Komite Indonesia Merdeka for Semarang. *BUZA.NEFIS/CMI:2739.*

26. See the reports of Subardjo's organization. *BUZA.NEFIS/CMI:2773* (Toeban), 2762 and 2769 (Djember), 2726 (Demak).

27. Report of Subardjo's organization about activities in Feb./Mar. 1942. *BUZA.NEFIS/CMI:2769.*

28. Nishijima, "The Nationalists in Java," p. 259.

29. Thamrin's funeral was attended by more than 20,000 people and became a great mass manifestation of Indonesian nationalism, which bore a clearly anti-Dutch character. See Abeyasekere, *One Hand Clapping,* pp. 77–78.

30. Report of Subardjo's organization in Magelang, Feb./Mar. 1942. *BUZA.NEFIS/CMI:2775.*

31. *A Decade of Japanese Underground Activities,* p. 30. The interned Japanese were transported to Australia before the capitulation of the Royal Netherlands Indies Army, the KNIL, on 9 Mar. 1942.

32. One of Subardjo's sisters was married to Dr. Latip (see Subardjo, *Kesadaran Nasional,* p. 195). It was this family which was interned in Cibadak by the Dutch.

33. S. Suleiman, "The Last Days of Batavia," *Indonesia* 28 (1979): 56.

34. Report of Subardjo's organization in Tegal, Mar. 1942. *BUZA.NEFIS/CMI:2760.*

35. Goto, "Life and Death of 'Abdul Rachman,'" p. 66. See also Kanahele, "The Japanese Occupation of Indonesia," p. 253, n. 22.

36. R. de Bruin, *Indonesie: De laatste etappe naar de vrijheid, 1942–1945* (Ph.D. diss., Universiteit van Amsterdam, 1982), p. 58.

37. *The Pesat* of 28 January 1942 made an urgent appeal to the nationalists to join the Pekope (*Persoverzichten,* Januari, 1942: 1312). The journal *Pesat* was Gerindo oriented.

38. Review of the Indonesian political parties in 1942. *BUZA.NEFIS/CMI:2413.*

39. Hering, "Het afscheidswoord van bet dagelijks bestuur van Parindra," *Kabar Seberang* 38 (1992): 58.

40. The head of the Pekope in Semarang was Dr. Boentaran, later on the chairman of the Komite Indonesia Merdeka, taking over this function from his wife. See report of the Komite Indonesia Merdeka for Semarang. *BUZA.NEFIS/CMI:2739.*

41. See the reports from Godong (*BUZA.NEFIS/CMI:2768*) and Salatiga (*BUZA.NEFIS/CMI:2761*).

42. Report of the Controleur, A.H.P. Regoort, in Batavia, 10 Mar. 1947. *ARA.* Alg.Secr.:4946.

43. One source claims that in its pre-invasion propaganda broadcasts Radio Tokyo encouraged Indonesian nationalists to form independence committees. Kanahele, "The Japanese Occupation of Indonesia," p. 258, n. 63.

44. Suleiman, "The Last Days of Batavia," p. 62.

45. On 28 Feb. 1942 the Dutch government gave orders for the demolition corps in Java to get on with their job.

46. How far the members of Subardjo's group succeeded in their anti-sabotage activities is not known. Several claim to have prevented the destruction of bridges and rice-mills, but they do not explain how this was accomplished.

47. Report of Subardjo's organization during the Japanese invasion in 1942. *BUZA.NEFIS/CMI*:2729.

48. Benda, "The Beginning of the Japanese Occupation of Java," p. 545.

49. See the following reports of Subardjo's organization: *BUZA.NEFIS/CMI*:2715, 2722 and 2717.

50. There seems to have been a radio message claiming that Indonesians would not be killed by Japanese soldiers when they landed if they showed the mark of the sun on their palms. See Nishijima, "The Nationalists in Java," p. 262.

51. See reports of Subardjo's organization for Magelang (*BUZA.NEFIS/CMI*:2775) and Demak (2726).

52. In the reports Yogyakarta is consistently called Mataram (2763). See also the report of Sukarto, 4 May 1942. RIOD.IC: 031605–031630. The name Mataram refers to the glorious days of Sultan Agung (r. 1613–46).

53. See report of Subardjo's organization in Magelang. *BUZA.NEFIS/CMI*:2775. The reason that a Chinese could join the Merdeka committee was that the person in question had not been a member of any Chinese association under the Dutch. He was more Indonesian than Chinese oriented and, moreover, he had been considered dangerous by the Dutch.

54. Report of Police Inspector Van Leeuwen in Djombang, 7 Nov. 1946. *ARA*.Alg. Secr.4956.

55. Report of Assistant Resident W. C. Schoevers, 7 May 1946. *ARA*.Alg.Secr.4952.

56. Report of the Dutch Police in Malang. *ARA*.Alg. Secr.4955.

57. Report of Subardjo's organization for Kendal. *BUZA.NEFIS/CMI*:2765.

58. Report on the activities in Blitar. *BUZA.NEFIS/CMI*:2722.

59. Report of Police Inspector Van Leeuwen, 7 Nov. 1946. *ARA*.Alg.Secr.4956.

60. Report of Subardjo's organization for Demak. *BUZA.NEFIS/CMI*:2726.

61. See the following reports of Subardjo's organization in Ambarawa: (*BUZA.NEFIS/CMI*:2721), Godong (2768), Kendal (2765), Semarang (2739).

62. Report of the Komite Indonesia Merdeka for Semarang. *BUZA.NEFIS/CMI*:2739.

63. Report of Subardjo's organization for Kediri. *BUZA.NEFIS/CMI*:2774.

64. Report of Subardjo's organization in Kertosono. *BUZA.NEFIS.CMI*:2727.

65. Sukarto Report, *Journey through East Java*, 4 May 1942. RIOD. IC: 031605–031630.

66. Report of the Komite Indonesia Merdeka for Semarang, *BUZA.NEFIS/ CMI*:2739.

67. See the confidential letter from Abikusno, 10 Mar. 1942, concerning two lists of candidates for the posts of ministers and deputy-ministers in an Indonesian government during the transitional period. *BUZA.NEFIS/CMI*:1972. See also L. Sluimers, "Nieuwe orde op Java," *Bijdragen tot de Taal-, Land-en Volkenkunde* 124 (1968): 336–67. In an appendix, Sluimers gives an overview of the three lists of ministerial candidates for the Indonesian government and their assistants.

68. This was in accordance with the Japanese blueprint for Indonesia determined during the Liaison Conference on 20 November 1941 in Tokyo, where it was stated that the Greater Indonesia Movement should be curbed as much as possible. See H. J. Benda and J. K. Irikura, *Japanese Military Administration in Indonesia: Selected Documents* (New Haven: Yale University Southeast Asia Studies, 1965), p. 2. See also M. Nakamura, "General Imamura and the Early Period of Japanese Occupation," *Indonesia* 10 (1970): 5.

69. Subardjo, *Kesadaran Nasional,* pp. 236–37.

70. K. A. de Weerd, *The Japanese Occupation of the Netherlands Indies.* RIOD. IC: 032759.

71. These committees are mentioned in Sukarto's report. He visited them during his trip through Central Java in April 1942. Some of the committees were formed as late as the end of that month. RIOD. IC: 031605–031630.

72. The Parindra at the Beginning of the Japanese Occupation. *BUZA.NEFIS/ CMI*:2405.

73. Sukarto Report, 4 May 1942. RIOD. IC: 031605–031630.

74. The chairman of the committee in Semarang was Dr. Boentaran (see note 40 above), a member of Subardjo's organization. Besides him there were six other board members.

75. Report of the Komite Indonesia Merdeka for Semarang, 19 May 1942. *BUZA. NEFIS*/CMI:2739.

76. Komite Nasional Indonesia in Semarang, 21 Mar. 1942. *BUZA.NEFIS/CMI*:2738.

77. Sukarto Report, 4 May 1942. RIOD. IC: 031605–031630.

78. Hering, "Het afscheidswoord van het dagelijks bestuur van Parindra," *Kabar Seberang* (1992): 60, 63.

79. Report of Subardjo's organization for Magelang, Feb.-Mar. 1942. *BUZA.NEFIS/ CMI*:2775.

80. See Kanahele, "The Japanese Occupation of Indonesia," pp. 28–29.

81. For Magelang, see *BUZA.NEFIS/CMI*:2775 and for Semarang, *BUZA.NEFIS/ CMI*:2739.

82. For Krawang, see *BUZA.NEFIS/CMI*:2711.

83. For Blitar, see *BUZA.NEFIS/CMI*:2771. After the Japanese had taken measures against the activities of the committees and their organizations in July 1942, the ROEPIB took care of the support for the unemployed Indonesians and set up a committee to organize economic requirements of the Japanese.

84. In Subang the nationalists had to turn over the local administration to the Indonesian civil servants within one week. See report on the activities for Subang in March 1942. *BUZA.NEFIS/CMI:2712.*

85. Many who could not produce a certificate from the Japanese army were arrested and put in jail. A member of the committee in Kertosono reported that he had been arrested by the Dutch commander of the field police at the end of March. Thanks to his friends, who worked with the Kempeitai, he was released from prison on 29 April 1942. He had been arrested on charges of disturbing peace. See the report of Subardjo's organization in Kertosono. *BUZA.NEFIS/CMI:2727.* According to Kanahele the arrests of nationalists may have been largely due to a misunderstanding on the part of the Kempeitai, rather than any hostile opposition ("The Japanese Occupation of Indonesia," p. 43). But this is only partly correct. It was the Indonesian civil servants in conjunction with the former Dutch PID (Political Intelligence Service), the opponents of the nationalists, who informed the Kempeitai about disturbers of peace.

86. See Kanahele, "The Japanese Occupation of Indonesia," p. 267, n. 18.

87. Parindra in the beginning of the Japanese occupation. *BUZA.NEFIS/CMI:2405.*

88. Sukarto Report, 4 May 1942. RIOD. IC: 031605–031630.

89. Hindromartono was not in Java during the Japanese invasion. He remained in New York, where he was a member of the Dutch delegation attending the Labour Conference as technical adviser on the interests of the Indonesians. He returned to Java shortly after the surrender of the Dutch, so he had good reasons for visiting his family. See *Orang Indonesia yang Terkemuka di Jawa,* p. 10.

90. Sukarto Report, 4 May 1942. RIOD. IC: 031605–031630.

91. Report of the Komite Indonesia Merdeka for Semarang, 19 May 1942. *BUZA. NEFIS/CMI:2739.*

92. See also L. Sluimers, "De Japanse bezettingspolitiek en de Indonesische elites, 1942–1943," *Bijdragen tot de taal-, Land-en Volkenkunde* 124 (1968): 364.

93. Report of Winarno Danoeatmodjo, Semarang, Aug. 1942. RIOD. IC: 039581.

94. Report of Police Inspector Van Leeuwen in Jombang, Soerabaya, 7 Nov. 1946. *ARA.* Alg. Secr.:4946.

95. Report of Subardjo's organization for Malang, Feb.-Mar. 1942. *BUZA.NEFIS/ CMI:2771.*

96. Hering, "Het afscheidswoord van het dagelijks bestuur," p. 63.

97. Parindra in the beginning of the Japanese occupation. *BUZA.NEFIS/CMI:2405.*

98. Hering, "Het afscheidswoord van het dagelijks bestuur," p. 63.

99. Sukarto Report, 4 May 1942. RIOD. IC: 031605–031630.

17

Decolonization in Malaya, 1942–1952

A. J. STOCKWELL*

After the British withdrawal in 1947 from the Indian sub-continent, it was expected that Britain would grant independence to their other colonies in Asia, notably in South and Southeast Asia. Sri Lanka (then Ceylon) and Myanmar (then Burma) became free nations in 1948. Malaya and Singapore were expected to follow suit. The process there was delayed by several factors, the chief of which was the twelve-year-long Chinese-led insurgency in Malaya from 1948 to 1960. British bureaucrats both in Southeast Asia and in London acknowledged that another major hurdle faced them in the shape of a very complex administrative structure the British had created in Malaysia: nine princely states on the Malay peninsula, of which four had been brought together as a federation; the other five were administered indirectly as individual political entities. Penang, Malacca and Singapore together constituted the Straits Settlements; until 1946, Sarawak was a personal kingdom of the Brooke family and North Borneo, a territory under a chartered company.

Professor Stockwell, currently Editor of the prestigious *Journal of Imperial and Commonwealth History*, is an acknowledged expert on Malaya during the British rule.

∼

*A. J. Stockwell, "British Imperial Policy and Decolonization in Malaya, 1942–52," *Journal of Imperial and Commonwealth History* 13 (1): 68–87.

In parliamentary statements during the inter-war years successive Secretaries of State proclaimed Britain's mission to be that of leading her dependencies to self-government in the 'fullness of time.' It was, Malcolm MacDonald put it in 1938, an 'evolutionary process' through which different colonies passed at different speeds. In the tropical empire, however, significant constitutional changes were scarcely perceptible. As for Malaya, its prosperity, strategic position and political quiescence convinced the British that they would remain in control for the indefinite future. Senior officials had no wish 'to sell the pass in the East' and were not persuaded by arguments in favour of 'graceful voluntary concession.'[1] Confident in their ability to rule well, they also felt that self-government for a society so obviously divided on ethnic lines would be a disservice to the Malayan peoples.[2]

The Second World War set Malayan policy upon a new course. In February 1942 Singapore surrendered to the Japanese. It was, said Churchill, 'the worst disaster' in Britain's history. In the depths of the war Britain lost a profitable colony, a supposedly impregnable naval base of thousands of fighting men who went into captivity. Defeat by an underrated Asian power was particularly hard to bear; the invulnerability of the white man was flawed. The whole of Southeast Asia lay at Japan's feet. India and Australia were also exposed to attack. Britain would need American help to win back lost territory.

During their exile from Malaya the British devised the Malayan Union which abandoned the old principles of the sovereignty of the Malay rulers, the autonomy of the Malay states and the special position of the Malay people. After their return in September 1945 the British acquired sovereignty from the Sultans and used it to establish a unitary government for Malaya (less Singapore) and press ahead with the creation of a Malayan nation by offering citizenship to all (Chinese and Indians as well as Malays) who regarded Malaya as home. The Malayan Union was a response to the following circumstances: (i) the administrative problem of the peninsula which before the war had been divided into Straits Settlements, Federated and Unfederated Malay States; (ii) the prospect of economic rehabilitation after the war when Britain would depend more than ever before upon the dollar-earning tin mines and rubber estates of Malaya; (iii) the need to assure the world, or at least the USA, of British progressivism by laying the foundations for a future self-governing nation.[3]

Though welcomed by some, the Malayan Union was condemned by the more vociferous as a betrayal of Britain's old allies and princes of the soil, the Malays. In response to unprecedented opposition from the Malays, who formed the United Malays National Organisation (UMNO), they decided to negotiate with their leaders. In February 1948 the Malayan Union was replaced by a federal constitution endorsing Malay sovereignty and political privileges and considerably diluting the rights promised to non-Malays. Here was an apparent return to normalcy, to Anglo-Malay collaboration.[4] It is often said that the British, in surrendering to the opponents of the Malayan Union, lost their chance to put the country on a multiracial course; never again would they dare to indulge in the progressivism of the Malayan Union which at a stroke had attempted to end the administrative and social divides for which pre-war policy had been largely responsible. 'For some members of the non-Malay intelligentsia,' the late Wong Lin Ken has written, 'the Malayan Union seems, in retrospect, to have become a historic opportunity that had been allowed to pass away with far-reaching consequences for generations.'[5]

With the inauguration of the Federation of Malaya, it is claimed, the British put constitutional issues on ice. A few months later (June 1948) the outbreak of communist insurrection reinforced Anglo-Malay collaboration and further postponed constitutional advance. Defeating the insurgents was the prime task; the British did not envisage early self-government, so this argument runs, and the Malays did not seek it at a time when the Chinese-dominated Malayan Communist Party threatened to take all. Though Attlee repeated His Majesty's Government's commitment to eventual Malayan independence, he refused to announce a constitutional review, let alone a date by which power would be transferred. Moreover, parliamentary statements with regard to Malaya's future were made as much to reassure those who accused the government of infirmity of purpose towards terrorism as to convince those who doubted the sincerity of its promise of self-government. In 1949 and 1950 Attlee insisted, lest there be a flight of planters, miners and capital from Malaya, that there would be no 'premature withdrawal.'[6]

The end of 1951 appears to mark another turning-point in the story. Onn bin Jaafar, president of UMNO and Britain's key ally, left UMNO to form another party; Anglo-Malay collaboration was jeopardized. Then, in October, High Commissioner Gurney was assassinated by insurgents, and British morale sank to its lowest ebb. In the same month, a plenary meeting of the Malayan Communist Party reviewed the campaign and 'virtually called off the shooting war'[7] to concentrate on the political front. Meanwhile in the United Kingdom, parliament was dissolved and the Conservatives were returned to office. The Conservatives were generally held to have been less disposed than were Labour towards the sentimentalism of colonial self-rule. Indeed, with Lyttelton at Colonial Office and General Templer in Malaya, firmness was injected into government. But there was

enlightenment too; Templer (High Commissioner 1952–54) is usually cred-
ited with having had the perception and energy to make political advances
as the best way of 'winning the hearts and minds of the people' in the campaign against communism. Under Templer citizenship was broadened, municipal elections were held and a commission for federal elections was
appointed. Then, with Lennox Boyd as Secretary of State and MacGillivray
as High Commissioner, Malaya achieved almost complete self government
in 1955 and independence in 1957. 'The transition,' writes Sir Richard Allen,
'from a colonial-autocratic regime to an autonomous-democratic one came
with startling swiftness and achieved remarkable success. It was all accomplished in some six years.'[8]

British policy towards Malaya in the post-war years is usually seen to
pass through the three phases which I have just outlined. The first is dominated by the supposedly aberrant and abortive Malayan Union experiment
(1945–1948); the second, from 1948 to the end of 1951, is a period of apparent drift during which, despite Labour's good intentions there is little advance either against the communist insurgents or self-government; and the
third, which gets under way with the return to power of the Conservative
Party in October 1951 witnesses new determination and clear direction in
the conduct of Malayan affairs. The combination of military vigour and political sense proved effective in combating terrorism and saving independent
Malaya for the Commonwealth.

Recently released papers at the Public Record Office enable us to review
the account which has been summarized above and to modify it in significant respects. They confirm the similarity of predicament in which governments of different political hues were placed when grappling with imperial
problems. They reveal a clear appreciation in the highest circles of the significance of Malaya in the post-war period for Britain's influence in Asia
and her recovery at home. In particular they show an essential continuity in
British strategy stretching from the so-called 'deviant' Malayan Union
through the years of apparent 'drift' to the supposedly 'new course' of
1952–57.

I

Officials and politicians who had nailed their colours to the Malayan Union
mast were loth to accept that its replacement by the Federation was anything other than a deceleration in the speed by which the new route would
be followed. Sir Edward Gent, previously Governor of Malayan Union, set
about managing its successor during the few months before his recall as if
nothing had really changed. Secretary of State Creech Jones, justifying to

Cabinet what elsewhere was regarded British *volte face,* argued that the essence of the Malayan Union, namely, a strong central government, financial stability and common citizenship was preserved in the federal constitution.[9] When Professor Silcock wrote to the Colonial Office criticizing the Federation and urging a return to Malayan Union progressivism, H. T. Bourdillon minuted, 'we have it in mind to proceed in many ways on the lines which Mr. Silcock advocates.'[10]

Indeed, after 1948 genuine efforts were made to attain the basic objectives of the Malayan Union. One of these was the further consolidation of possessions. In May 1948, shortly after the Federation had been inaugurated, the Commissioner General of Southeast Asia, the High Commissioner of Malaya and the Governor of Singapore met to discuss ways in which to create 'a climate of opinion in Malaya favourable to the inclusion of Singapore in some sort of constitutional union with the Federation.'[11] The fusion of peninsula and island had been included in the draft of the Malayan Union scheme in 1942 but, because of its implications for imperial defence and relations between the Malays and the Chinese, it had been omitted from the final version. Painstaking work for the merger went on throughout 1948–51 but it was recognized that real advance depended on communal harmony. Fostering multiracialism was the keynote of British Malayan policy from 1943 until 1955 at least. Through the unofficial Communities Liaison Committee (CLC), Malcolm MacDonald (Commissioner General, Southeast Asia) acted as a mediator between community leaders. Very largely as a result of his behind-the-scenes diplomacy, the CLC came out publicly in favour of self-government and a Malayan nationality for the long term and, for the short term, a broadening of the Federation's restrictive citizenship provisions and moves towards elections. All these points Onn, who was a member of the CLC, and UMNO found difficult to swallow but the Secretary of State congratulated MacDonald on pursuing the multiracial course and was pleased to note 'that the agreed views of the Committee are so closely in line with the fundamental aims of the policy which has been pursued by His Majesty's Government in relation to Malaya ever since the Liberation (not excluding the Malayan Union phase).'[12] The CLC's proposals were the basis for the citizenship legislation which Gurney so carefully prepared and introduced into the legislative council in 1951 and which was eventually enacted during Templer's first year in office. This ordinance opened the door to citizenship considerably wider for the non-Malays although no progress was made in solving the more fundamental problem of creating a Malayan nationality.[13]

Progress towards a broader citizenship and elections was understandably slow. The 1948 constitution left the British in control at the centre but devolved state power upon Malays; federal (British)–state (Malay) tensions hampered day-to-day administration as well as constitutional change. Malay leaders dug in on the terms of the Federal Agreement and obstructed proposals from Kuala Lumpur which modified their position. In order to associate them more closely with federal government, High Commissioner Gurney introduced the Member system, a quasi-cabinet in which Dato Onn became the Member for Home Affairs. Proposed in March 1950 and put into effect in March 1951, the Member system enabled both officials and unofficials to be appointed as ministerial heads of departments and to gain experience of policy-making before the introduction of federal elections. In compensation for the CLC's citizenship proposals, Onn was also invited in June 1950 to be Chairman of the Rural and Industrial Development Authority (RIDA), an organization to improve the economic position of the Malays. Despite his efforts, however, RIDA did little to alleviate Malay poverty.[14]

Far from being shelved, the principles of the Malayan Union guided British policy after the inauguration of the Federation. Moreover, the Emergency gave immediate impetus to constitutional advance. Although HMG feared that any commitment to a specific date for independence would both hasten the flight of western capital from Malaya and kill growth of that multiracial nation which they were nurturing, it recognized that insurgency was bringing the day of departure ever nearer. In 1948 the government were thinking rather vaguely in terms of a transition period: it was unprecedentedly liberal without being uncomfortably close. Two years later they shortened it. MacDonald told Secretaries of State for the Colonies and War (James Griffiths and John Strachey) during their visit to Malaya in June 1950 (the month the Korean War erupted) that the tempo 'will inevitably be accelerated by factors over which we shall have little or no control.' MacDonald cited the emergence of a new generation of Malayan leaders, the climate of opinion outside Malaya and the impact of the Emergency upon Asian expectations, and he argued:

> We must be mentally prepared, therefore, to accept a quickening of the pace, and if we were to resist the pace of change we should lose the present support of Asian leaders. . . . We must be in harmony with Asian leaders so that there is no discernible difference in views on which world opinion can take sides against us.[15]

Griffiths agreed and recommended to Cabinet that plans be laid for the introduction of social and constitutional reforms as soon as the Emergency ended 'to demonstrate to the workers in Malaya that a non-Communist régime offered them greater opportunities for economic and social better-

ment than any Communist régime.'[16] If the British had been defensive
about their imperial record after the fall of Singapore, by the summer of
1950 they paraded progressivism with pride. In August, as they handed to
the American Joint Staff Defense Survey Mission to Southeast Asia an extensive shopping-list for hardware necessary to counter-insurgency, Mac-
Donald and Gurney stressed that the British in Malaya were fighting
communism on the political, economic and social fronts as well as militarily. Though not, of course, prepared to name a date, MacDonald gave his
American visitors an indication of the quickening pace of decolonization.
He told them: 'Ideally the handover should take place after another generation but pressure from within and without would make the process more
rapid, unless there was a reaction because of a breakdown in Indonesia or
Burma, the transfer were more likely in 10 to 15 years.'[17]

The Foreign Secretary, Ernest Bevin, was convinced that American policy
in Asia, particularly as regards Korea and China, was neither as realistic or
as enlightened as that of Britain which he summarized in a Cabinet Paper of
August 1950 as follows:

> Since the end of the war, the policy of His Majesty's Government in South
> and South-East Asia has been to encourage the legitimate aspirations of the
> peoples of that area for independence. . . . In our dependent territories His
> Majesty's Government are pursuing an enlightened policy of progress to-
> wards self-government within the Commonwealth, while seeking to im-
> prove the social and economic welfare of the people. That the policy pursued
> by His Majesty's Government has been the right one there can be no doubt,
> and our support of nationalism in South and South-East Asia provides the
> possible counter to communist subversion and penetration.[18]

Bevin argued that help from Britain and the USA in the economic and
technical fields would be an earnest of their good intentions towards Asia
and could prompt Asians to act in their own self-interest and withstand
Cominform threats. Without a firm and comprehensive policy towards
Southeast Asia the West would, he feared, quickly lose the support of a
large part of a highly important region of the world.

During meetings with Dean Acheson in March 1949, Bevin, acting on a
brief from MacDonald, urged the US Secretary of State to plan for Southeast Asia as a whole, as did the Communists, and not simply country by
country, as appeared to be the American practice. Bevin and MacDonald
had in mind the formation of an association of Southeast Asian states mod-
elled more on the Marshall Plan than on NATO. They wanted to convene
a conference to promote Southeast Asian regionalism and cooperation

between the West (including Australia and New Zealand) and the newly independent countries of Asia (notably India and Pakistan). But Bevin found
the Americans unresponsive and the Colombo Conference of January 1950
met without them. Bevin's purpose as Bullock has put it was 'that like-
minded countries with interests in the East should act together to resist
Communism by improving the standards of the peoples of South East
Asia.'[19] To his satisfaction an aid programme—the Colombo Plan—was
launched at the conference, and this initiative was followed up by an American economic mission to Southeast Asia with a view to developing a parallel aid programme from the USA. The outbreak of the Korean War in June
1950, however, soured the good relations that had been developing between
Asia and the West.[20]

Constitutional advance in Malaya was part of a wider policy of winning
friends in a changing Asia. Of course, there were links with developments
elsewhere in the Empire (notably in the area of constitutional modelling)
but the context in which major Malayan decisions were taken was the context of Southeast Asia: it would be disastrous to lose Malaya precipitately as
the British had lost Burma or the Dutch Indonesia. It would be foolhardy
to imitate the negative attitudes of the French Indo-China. British actions
were being watched by a new generation of Asian leaders.

II

In the coordination of British policies in Southeast Asia and in the mould-
ing of post-war colonialism in Malaya, Malcolm MacDonald was central.
From 1946 to 1948 he was Governor General, Southeast Asia and answer-
able to the Colonial Secretary for the oversight of British dependencies
(Malaya, Singapore, North Borneo and Sarawak). As Commissioner General between 1948 and 1955 he continued to supervise the policies of colonial governments (though he was not responsible for direct administration),
and in addition, he reported to the Foreign Secretary with regard to the independent states of the region. A broker between colonial governors,
Whitehall departments, Britain and her allies, and Britain and the independent states of Southeast Asia, MacDonald had the job of integrating British
activities in the area. He corresponded personally as well as officially with
Creech Jones and Griffiths (Labour Secretaries of State at the Colonial Office) and with Sir Thomas Lloyd (the Permanent Secretary at the Colonial
Office), and he visited London regularly for high-level consultations. Mac-
Donald was in a more commanding position to influence the direction of
colonial, if not foreign, policy in Southeast Asia than were the governors
and ambassadors who were posted to the separate countries of the region.

Son of a prime minister and himself a former Secretary of State at both Colonial and Dominions Offices, MacDonald carried weight in London while Attlee was Prime Minister. Though some Labour politicians were suspicious of him for being the son of his father and though Colonial Office officials occasionally expressed mild irritation with his habit of appeasing firebrands like Dato Onn, MacDonald's political, departmental and diplomatic experience won him respect. His tactful and often informal handling of local leaders was generally admired and his advice until the end of 1951, usually accepted by London. His role in convincing the Cabinet in the summer of 1946 of the wisdom of conciliating the Malays and in maintaining the momentum of constitutional advance after 1948 was crucial.

MacDonald's relations with the career civil servants, who as Governors or High Commissioners dealt directly with the administration of British dependencies, varied. With Gimson (Singapore) he seems to have been correct; with Arden-Clarke (Sarawak) MacDonald, who enjoyed playing the part of white rajah on frequent visits to Borneo, was cordial; with Hone, who had been MacDonald's Secretary-General and then his Deputy, he was familiar. With Gent, however, he was increasingly at loggerheads and funnelled to London criticisms of his handling of both Dato Onn and the Malayan Communist Party. Gent was recalled to London in July 1948 ostensibly for consultations but actually for reposting. Gent's tragic death in an aircraft accident on the approaches to Norholt removed the pressure to find a successor immediately. Had they reposted Gent the government would have had to announce his successor simultaneously if only to disguise the sacking as a change of guard. As it was they could argue that thoughts of replacing Gent had been far from the official mind and that they would need to take their time in choosing a worthy successor at such a critical juncture in Malaya's history.[21]

Creech Jones favoured Henry Gurney for the vacancy. Gurney had recently acquitted himself with distinction as Chief Secretary in Palestine but was now inclined to return to Oxford. MacDonald privately objected to Gurney on the grounds that he lacked both status (he had not held a Governorship before) and Malayan experience, and hoped that Lord Millverton might be persuaded to take the job. Creech Jones had his way; Gurney accepted the High Commissionership albeit hesitantly; and MacDonald swallowed his pride, though, one suspects, he may have felt vindicated by Malay objections to yet another 'outside' appointment. Despite his initial reservations, however, MacDonald developed a close partnership with Gurney. The two men came to think alike on key issues such as citizenship, nationality, closer union between Malaya and Singapore, the Member system and preparations for local elections. After two years together, MacDonald paid

Gurney 'a quite extraordinary tribute,' describing him in a personal letter to
Sir Thomas Lloyd as 'the outstanding Colonial Governor within the whole
of his experience.'[22] MacDonald proposed that Singapore be added to Gurney's duties when Gimson came to retire in April 1952. By then, however,
Gurney was dead, and the higher ranks of colonial government had been
re-ordered by Churchill and Lyttelton.

The years 1948–51 in the history of British Malaya are the years of the
MacDonald-Gurney partnership. Efficient and a man of routine, Gurney
excelled in the secretariat; full of charm and enjoying company and conversation, MacDonald extended business to the verandah and drawing room.
Ironically, Gurney's weakness lay in his very imperturbability and in his
civil servant manner which allowed the less perceptive to underrate him and
the more flamboyant to upstage him. J. M. Gullick, who worked under
Gurney in Kuala Lumpur, states that 'there was a lot more to Gurney than
mere professional competence in a colonial secretariat.' A sense of humour
spurred him to write for *Punch* even during the stress of Palestine. His
courage was beyond dispute: he caught the last plane out of Jerusalem in
1948, and he drew the terrorists' fire away from his wife and his secretary at
Fraser's Hill in 1951. 'Above all,' writes Gullick, 'Gurney had a creative
mind. If he wrote a minute on a file in his neat, round handwriting, it added
something.' He was the author of schemes ranging from the Briggs Plan for
re-settling squatters who gave succour to insurgents to the Employee Prov-
ident Fund which helped sustain Malayan workers in old age. Gullick recalls that Templer used to express 'the greatest admiration for all that the
records showed Gurney had done.'[23]

MacDonald's métier was making friends with the up-and-coming leaders of the new Asia—what a decade or so before would have been called
'taking tea with treason.' . . . Where Governors appeared in uniform or
tropical white suits, the Commissioner General paraded short sleeves and
a bow-tie. To many Asians he represented, if not a wind of change, at least
a breath of fresh air blowing through the stuffiness of a colonial society.
To others—and there were progressives as well as reactionaries who dis-
trusted him—he was a smooth talker and mover who projected the public
persona of the approachable proconsul, but deflected to those with executive responsibilities the bleak task of putting words into action. By no
means bewildered by Britain's declining power, he hailed decolonization
as a development from which Britain would reap moral and material re-
wards. He sincerely believed in the rhetoric of transforming colonies into
self-governing nations; indeed, it was rather curious to read substantially
the same messages in his wireless broadcasts to the Malayan peoples and
his secret dispatches to Secretaries of State. Anxious to avoid at all costs

the charge of 'ganging up' with the Dutch and French against Asians, MacDonald saw 'much promising material' in moderate nationalist movements in Asia and felt that 'the whole future of Britain in Asia might depend on the attitude we adopted towards them.[24] Amongst his friends he counted Sutan Syahrir of Indonesia, Prince Sihanouk of Cambodia and Dato Onn bin Jaafar.

The British in general did not find Onn easy to handle. His mercurial temperament and continuing bitterness about British perfidy tried their patience. Gent's relations with Onn were always sour (neither could forget the Malayan Union conflict), and even Gurney at first found it hard to share MacDonald's enthusiasm for UMNO's president. Onn was, as he himself admitted, 'ever eager for a scrap,'[25] and his position in the cross fire between Malays and Britons, Malays and non-Malays, the Malay raayat and their rulers, the UMNO executive and the party rank and file encouraged him to lash out. One day the 'statesmanlike' moderate and loyal subject of his Sultan, the next he could embarrass the High Commissioner or enrage Their Highnesses.

Nevertheless, the cooperation of UMNO was essential if the Federation was to be administered, insurgency subjugated and progress made towards self-government. MacDonald insisted that Onn offered the best hope of keeping the Malays together and bridging the gulf between their and other communities. His cosmopolitanism, mixed blood and populist methods (all of which had before the war confirmed the British in their view that he was an unsuitable representative of the 'real Malay') now seemed to befit an aspiring member of that growing circle of leaders of independent Asia, and officials were encouraged when he exhibited the nationalist characteristics of an Aung San or a Sukarno. Secure in the knowledge that no UMNO leader would press for independence while there was a danger of communist (and therefore Chinese) victory, MacDonald and Gurney tried to wean UMNO from chauvinistic communalism and educate it in multiracial politics while there was still time. Creech Jones was merely echoing MacDonald and Gurney when he acknowledged that 'Onn represents the only real hope of the Malayan peoples breaking away from Race and turning to Party.'[26]

Sensing that the British would withhold power for as long as communalism bitterly divided the peoples of Malaya, Onn attempted to open up UMNO to non-Malays. Having been rebuffed, he planned the non-communal Independence of Malaya Party in June 1951. The British welcomed the multiracialism of the IMP but were anxious lest it undermine UMNO, and therefore Malay, solidarity. Gurney explained his position in a telegram to London:

Our line is to persuade him [Onn] of the advantage of continuing to lead
UMNO as well as forming new party, which is, of course, in no way an un-
healthy development, but not to be godfathered on to me except in so far as I
have never made any secret of the view that a united party [that is, multiracial party] would be a move in the right direction, getting away from communal politics.[27]

Gurney appealed to Onn not to sever his links with UMNO. His plea
was in vain; in late August Onn left UMNO and was succeeded by Tunku
Abdul Rahman. On 16 September the IMP was formally launched in a
blaze of publicity. Quite clearly MacDonald and Gurney preferred the
Datu to the Tunku. 'I am afraid,' wrote Gurney of the future Prime Minister of Malaya/Malaysia, 'that he will not be the sort of leader who will be
capable of holding UMNO together in any important controversy.'[28]
Though the divorce of Onn and UMNO cast doubts on the dependability
of either, Gurney retained some hope for Onn. 'But his decision to break
with UMNO is a major one which may have far-reaching consequences.'[29]
Indeed it did. Onn's record as saviour of the Malays during the Malayan
Union crisis could not sustain the popularity he had enjoyed since 1946. A
study of Onn's miscalculations in 1951–52 belongs more to the field of
Malayan politics than to the theme of this article.[30] None the less, it is
worth noting that, in the period before elections, Malayan leaders could
have an unrealistic view of their authority and support, and that Onn in
particular was becoming convinced that his identification with Malay chauvinism would impede his ascent as a truly 'national' figure. The defeat of
the IMP by a local alliance of UMNO and the Malayan Chinese Association in the Kuala Lumpur municipal elections of February 1952, however,
shattered Onn's career in multiracialism and initiated a different pattern in
Malayan politics marked by deals struck between mutually exclusive communal parties.

Dato Onn's decline coincides with MacDonald's decreasing involvement
in Malayan politics. Having backed a loser and given his friendship to a
man whom the Malays no longer trusted, MacDonald was neither eager nor
able to establish a similar rapport with Tunku Abdul Rahman. It is not too
fanciful to suggest parallels between the careers of Dato Onn and Ramsay
MacDonald (whose respective reputations Malcolm was keen to salvage);
one led a class party which he 'betrayed' for the National Government in
1931, the other founded a communal party which he 'deserted' for the multiracial IMP in 1951. Bereft of a secure ally in Malaya, MacDonald was also
losing the confidence of powerful men in Britain who were worried by the
slow progress of the war again the communists.

III

Nation-building was intended to prepare Malaya for self-government without endangering Britain's considerable interests in the country. It has been estimated that British investment in Malaya in 1950 was rather more than £lOOm.[31] Moreover, Malaya's dollar earnings were too important to lose. In 1947 rubber (of which Malaya was the world's top producer) led the list of colonial products that won dollars; it brought in $120m and was followed by cocoa with $50m. In 1948 the USA imported 727,000 tons of rubber, of which 371,000 came from Malaya, and 158,000 tons of tin, of which 155,000 were Malayan produced. In the same year when the sterling area suffered an overall dollar deficit of $1,800m, there were within the empire four large dollar-earners, viz., Malaya with over $170m, the Gold Coast with $47.5m, the Gambia with $24.5m and Ceylon with $23m. The boom in rubber and tin prices following the outbreak of the Korean War enlarged Malaya's surplus with the dollar area as follows: $170m (1948), $160m (1949), $271m (1950), $350m (1952). While the UK's balance of payments within the sterling area slumped from + pounds 221m in 1950 to –pounds 540m by 1952, Malaya's position held up: + pounds 60m (1950), + pounds l37m (1951) and + pounds 75m (1952).[32]

In addition to its dollar-earning capacity, Malaya's military demands made it too important a colony to be left to the Colonial Office. The Emergency was the concern of Cabinet to which the Colonial Secretary made regular reports and in which sometimes conflicting views were expressed. The Foreign and Colonial Offices, for example, differed on the Chinese question. The Colonial Office complained that British recognition of communist China had compromised the Malayan government dealing with recalcitrant Chinese. The Foreign Office accused the colonial administration of ignorance; instead of blaming interference from China for their difficulties they should, argued the FO, have got to grips much sooner with the enemy within—the Min Yuen, that network of information and food-gatherers which had been laid during the Japanese occupation and which now supplied the insurgents. The Under-Secretary who briefed Kenneth Younger (the FO Minister on the Cabinet Malaya Committee) was Robert Scott, whose immense experience of the Far East included consular service in China, Japan and Manchuria before the war, a frustrating spell on the Singapore Governor's War Council 1941–42 and a heroic record of internment during the Japanese occupation. In 1955 Scott would succeed MacDonald as Commissioner General.[33]

The Ministry of Defence, meanwhile, became worried by the Malayan drain on Britain's limited resources. In the summer of 1950 the Cabinet committed itself to a defence expenditure of £3,000m for 1951–54; averaged over the years this sum represented a 50 per cent increase compared with spending in 1950–51. By January 1951, with the Korean War in full spate, the commitment for 1951–54 had risen to £4,700m or nearly double the level envisaged before the conflict.[34] If the Korean War enhanced the value of Malaya's exports, it impeded the revival of British industry. Emmanuel Shinwell has recalled the pressures upon him as Minister of Defence in 1950:

> On one side Cripps [Chancellor of the Exchequer] used every argument he could to cut expenditure on the three services. On the other Bevin [Foreign Secretary] required strengthening of the military arm in order to support his view that more trouble was looming, not only in Europe, but in the Middle East, Malaya, and Hong Kong.[35]

In the second half of 1951 the British economy would suffer a record trade gap and current account deficit. Moreover, the guardians of the welfare state were dismayed by the government's commitment to a defence budget that made grave inroads into those of health and social security, and in April 1951 Aneurin Bevan, Harold Wilson and John Freeman would resign when Hugh Gaitskell (Cripps's successor as Chancellor) introduced certain charges into the health service. Though the Labour government accepted the need to maintain imperial defence east of Suez, it was desperate to cut its costs.

When Attlee formed his second administration after the general election of February 1950, it was clear that, if Malaya was too wealthy to lose, it was fast becoming too expensive to maintain. This had not been the case before the war when Malaya had paid for its own administration and local defence, and had made substantial contributions to imperial defence as well. Shortly after becoming Minister of Defence, Shinwell persuaded Attlee to form a Cabinet Committee on Malaya.[36] At a time when Britain was building up a strategic reserve and preparing for imminent global conflict, men and materials were being sidetracked into the Malayan theatre. The lack of obvious success against the insurgents provoked criticism of the structure, policies and personalities of the British civil authorities in Southeast Asia. Service chiefs grew impatient with the pace at which the Malayan police and civil administrators assumed responsibilities in the campaign.

General Sir John Harding (Commander-in-Chief Far East Land Forces) told Field Marshall Slim (Chief of the Imperial General Staff): 'The great need in S.E. Asia today is for really inspiring and courageous leadership at the highest level.' He suggested the creation of a supremo for the region as a whole with greater local power and more weight in the Cabinet than the Commissioner General currently enjoyed. While MacDonald was 'a great enthusiast for S.E. Asia' and had 'long experience of its problems,' Harding reckoned that he had 'too many political inhibitions and local personal ties to be sufficiently forceful and insistent on using the overriding powers he would have to exercise' were he to be upgraded to the position of supremo. Slim accepted that 'all was not with the higher overall direction of affairs in the Far East.'[37]

The Korean War, as Kenneth Morgan has put it, 'cast a sombre shadow over the last phase of the Attlee Government.'[38] In late November China entered the conflict, and on the night of 3 December Attlee, fearing that Truman was contemplating the use of the atomic bomb, flew to Washington. While he was able to reassure Cabinet on this score, ministers were still afraid that American retaliation against the Chinese could provoke them to invade Hong Kong and drive south through Indo-China and towards Malaya.[39] On the day the Prime Minister returned from Washington, John Strachey, Secretary of State of War wrote him a personal and top secret memorandum urging the thorough overhaul of the civil authorities in Southeast Asia. Simultaneously but coincidentally, religious riots (in which Europeans and Eurasians were the target of Muslim fanatics) erupted in Singapore; in addition to their misgivings about the Federation of Malaya, the military now had their doubts about the competence of the island colony's police and senior civil servants. Strachey's left-wing intellectualism did not endear him to some of his generals, but in this attack on civil rule in Malaya he did not pull his punches. Officials were, he wrote, too liberal when they should be ruthless and too conservative when they should be progressive. Strachey accepted that MacDonald—they had been up at Oxford together—had done 'an admirable job' but pointed out that he was feeling 'the strain of Malaya' and should be reposted. He did not hide his scorn for 'the middle rank of officials and administrators' and those who still 'hanker for the old colonialism.' He argued that the political and social reforms being planned for after the Emergency should be brought forward by a new supremo for the region who would combine toughness with enlightenment.[40]

Both Harding and Strachey suggested Mountbatten for the job of Southeast Asia's Governor General. Other candidates being canvassed included Alanbrooke, Auchinleck and Montgomery. Though they had the successes of General de Lattre de Tassigny in Indo-China to hand, the Imperial General Staff were not enthusiastic about the proposal to appoint a military governor-general. They insisted that the Malayan problem was 'essentially a civil administrative problem' and that 'the Army can do no more than give the civil administration the necessary support.' Slim wanted to 'instill a sense of urgency into the Colonial Office,' not take on its responsibilities.[41]

IV

In view of what we now know about the commitment of MacDonald and Gurney to social and political progress, it may seem strange that the Malayan administration was not shining like a beacon in the naughty world of old colonialism and cold war but was being taken to task, and by the military of all people, for its lack of enlightenment. To be fair, the estimable efforts of Commissioner General and High Commissioner were acknowledged, though Field Marshall Montgomery and Sultan Ibrahim of Johore had little taste for MacDonald's style. Nevertheless, one wonders whether the generals, secure in their well-defined command structure, appreciated the complexities of civil rule, of managing a federal constitution, of engineering political evolution. Indeed, Gurney complained that the federal constitution encumbered counter-insurgency and political progress, and that Malayan civil servants in Britain kept alive pre-war attitudes from which he was trying to emancipate Malaya. 'One of the difficulties I have to contend with here,' he protested to Sir Thomas Lloyd, 'is the part played by old retired Malayans, years out of date, in encouraging locally the survival of their ideas,'[42] and the Colonial Office ruefully recalled the campaign of the old Malayans against the Malayan Union in 1946. As regards the strictures against MacDonald's apparently informal methods, it should be noted that he did not have the authority to intervene directly in the administration of Malayan affairs. Moreover, he felt he functioned best as a co-ordinator of policies and as a catalyst for political consensus, and he let it be known that he did not want enlarged powers.

In response to Strachey's appeal for radical reorganization, Attlee convened a ministerial meeting for 26 February 1951 to which MacDonald was summoned from overseas. It is not entirely clear from the papers which I have seen whether this meeting met Strachey's points head-on. At any rate the highest civil command remained intact although the Colonial secretary asked MacDonald to investigate personally and in consultation with Gurney the desirability of getting rid of some of the older and less energetic officers in senior posts, a number of whom may have been suffering from the effects of wartime internment. When the Commission of Inquiry into the Singapore riots of December 1950 published its report in May, the Secretary of State accepted the need to strengthen the island's government at the highest levels and was on the look-out for a dynamic successor to Governor Gimson who was due to go on leave in November prior to retirement in April 1952.[43]

By June 1951, however, the CIGS was more optimistic about the Briggs Plan in Malaya. A year earlier General Briggs, Director of Operations, had introduced his scheme to evacuate Chinese squatters from jungle fringes to new villages in order to deprive the insurgents of their vital sources of intelligence and rice. Having started sluggishly, there was now every prospect of completing the resettlement of half a million Chinese by the end of the year. Slim was also pleased to 'have ginned up the Civil to be fairly effective' and no longer favoured 'the idea of a Military Governor General.'[44] Despite some disquiet about the flaws in the government of Singapore revealed in the Hertogh riots and their possible repercussions in Malaya, there was generally more confidence about the security situation than there had been for a long time. The Colonial Office and War Office accepted the existing structure of government and agreed on the nomination of Sir Rob Lockhart as Director of Operations. General Briggs came up for retirement towards the end of 1951.[45]

In October the assassination of Gurney and the change of government at home brought to a head this long-running review of Malayan affairs. On entering office, the Conservative Chancellor of the Exchequer, R. Butler, reported to Cabinet what Gaitskell had been forewarning colleagues, namely that Britain faced a balance of payments worse than that of 1949 and even in some respects worse than that in 1947.[46] Within a few days of being appointed Colonial Secretary, Oliver Lyttelton recognized the Malayan problem as his first priority and, in spite of the Conservatives' precarious majority in the House of Commons, forthwith asked Churchill for leave to examine the situation himself.[47] The new Minister of Defence, Churchill himself set his two questions: 'What is the cost per month or per quarter of this enormous force?' Is 'a retired Indian Army Officer [that is Lockhart] the best person to pick for a job which obviously requires intense action?'[48] The cost of the Malayan campaign to Britain was estimated at £56m per annum (there were other charges, of course, which were borne by the Malayan government). This was excessive at such a crisis in the balance of payments. As for persons, 'we need the spark,' wrote Montgomery, bombarding Churchill, Lyttelton and Slim with his view. 'We must electrify Malaya.' The 'waffler' MacDonald 'must go' as must 'duds' like the Chief Secretary (Del Tufo) and the Commissioner of Police (Gray). Montgomery called for a master-plan and urged the creation of a 'Dominion of South East Asia, under one Governor General.'[49]

The Cabinet stopped short of appointing a supremo for the whole of Southeast Asia, but they did approve Lyttelton's recommendation (presented soon after his return from his Malayan tour) that one may be appointed both High Commissioner and Director of Operations Malaya.[50]

Who should he be? It has been suggested that Montgomery himself wanted
the job. It is clear from the papers I have seen that the Imperial General
Staff considered him to be unsuitable.[51] Oliver Lyttelton in his memoirs
refers to the Field Marshal's concern about the Malayan crisis but makes no
mention of his candidature. Lyttelton's first choice was General Sir Brian
Robertson, who was reluctant to leave his post as Commander-in-Chief
Middle East Land Forces. He next considered Slim, who declined on
grounds of age. He then worked through the War Office short-list coming
to Sir Gerald Templer and 'was sure that he was the man.' Churchill took a
close interest in Malaya in the months of November 1951–February 1952
and insisted on seeing Lyttelton's nominee. Templer was flown out to Ottawa to dine with Churchill. If the General's sobriety was subjected to some
strain he none the less 'won the Prime Minister's confidence'.[52]

MacDonald was critical of the merger of civil and military responsibilities
in the person of a general, but his own position was not strong. The Commissioner General's powers in Malaya, notably in defence matters, was
clipped and the Foreign Office made it plain that it would not object to the
abolition of the Commissioner Generalship altogether since it was expensive. Lyttelton felt that the need for administrative continuity at a time
when several major changes of personnel were being made together with
MacDonald's local popularity warranted the extension of the Commissioner General's tour for three or four months beyond May 1952 when he
was due to be relieved. Ministers agreed to postpone a decision on the future of the office until the late summer.[53] As it happened, MacDonald
stayed at his post in Southeast Asia until 1955, when he was transferred to
New Delhi as British High Commissioner, and the post of Commissioner
General in Southeast Asia lasted until the formation of Malaysia in 1963.
However, although he survived the shake-up of 1952, MacDonald was
never to enjoy the same influence on Malayan policy that he had wielded
between 1946 and 1951.

In their reorganization of Malayan administration the Conservatives did
initiate a new course; they completed a review which had been going on for
at least 18 months, and they improved the means to attain objectives which
had been set by Cabinet as early as May 1944 and regularly repeated since.[54]
British successes recorded from 1952 onwards in large measure rested on
developments originating before the arrival of the Conservative government, notably the Briggs resettlement plan and the premium placed upon
constitutional developments. Though Lyttelton startled the Malayan press
by declaring on his arrival at Singapore airport in early December 1951 that
'to restore law and order is the first thing,' he later referred both those who
criticized and those who welcomed what appeared to be his reactionary

hard-headedness to the directive issued to Templer in February.[55] This directive, which the Prime Minister had personally approved, opened with these words: 'The policy of His Majesty's Government in the United Kingdom is that Malaya should in due course become a fully self-governing nation. His Majesty's Government confidently hope that that nation will be within the British Commonwealth.' Having made reference to the terms of the Federation of Malaya Agreement of 1948, the directive continued: 'To achieve a united Malayan nation there must be a common form of citizenship for all who regard the Federation or any part of it as their real home and the object of their loyalty.'[56] Like his Labour predecessors, Lyttelton looked forward to the emergence of a broader citizenship, a Malayan nationality and a multiracial political movement.

British policy towards Malaya before the fall of Singapore had rested on the assumption that British rule would endure indefinitely; after the war the government accepted that independence would come in a generation. It is, however, unlikely that the archives will reveal a clearly formulated decision to quit Malaya. I am not suggesting that Britain lost her empire in the manner that some have said she acquired it—in a fit of absence of mind—but that thinking focused upon the practicalities and the imponderables of retreat. The major issue of Britain's declining world power was not a matter for government decision; it was a trend to which wise men adjusted. By the late 1940s decolonization had entered the official mind of British Imperialism. The transformation of rhetoric into policy is beyond the scope of this article, but it will not be satisfactorily explained solely in terms of trade balances and fiscal arithmetic. There was a mental revolution; with India out of the empire and safely in the Commonwealth, Britain had breached the psychological barrier to transfer of power which the Dutch and French found so agonizing to surmount. The ideology of trusteeship, touched up with partnership cushioned British *amour propre* as they skirted the problem of why they were withdrawing in order to make the best arrangements for departure.

When the Malayan Union was drafted in 1943–45 great play was made with progressive ideas but it was then believed that Malayan independence was safely distant. Post-war events jarred this measured approach. On the one hand Malay opposition to the Malayan Union obliged the British to defer the implementation of their immediate aims (that is administrative union and a broad citizenship); on the other hand the Emergency and developments outside Malaya hastened preparations for self-government. Desiring the continued enjoyment of the fruits of Malaya without the back-breaking toil of its government, the British made a shift to lead its peoples from empire to commonwealth by transferring power to leaders who would command local support and look after British interests. Though Malayan nationhood was still accepted as the prerequisite for Malayan independence, MacDonald and Gurney (in their plans for citizenship reform, local elections and the Member system) began to juggle with both objectives simultaneously. Indeed constitutional concessions became the tools for the fabrication of the nation. During the MacDonald-Gurney partnership, and during the Lyttelton-Templer partnership too, government remained convinced that the transfer of real power to Malayans must wait upon the evolution of a multiracial political movement. In 1955–57 this progression was reversed as the British granted self-government to an ethnically divided society and went along with the politics of communalism in the hope that the challenges and responsibilities of independence would in time fashion a Malayan identity.

Although things did not turn out quite as they had hoped, in this story of apparently graceful and voluntary concession to a stable and cooperative regime MacDonald and Gurney—though impeded by the federal constitution, inhibited by Malayan politics and eventually overshadowed by the more obvious successes of Templer and MacGillivray—maintained the momentum of that new course in British Malayan policy which had been triggered by the fall of Singapore in 1942. In this account of continuity and change in British policy we have seen that while the Labour government were no less dutiful than the Conservatives in upholding Britain's world position and defending imperial outposts, the Conservatives on their return to power in 1951 followed the route towards constitutional advance and nation-building blazed by the wartime coalition and Attlee administrations.

NOTES

1. The first of these phrases is from a minute by G. Grindle about Ceylon. 23 Jan. 1927, Public Record Office, C.O. [Colonial Office] 537/692; the second is from a minute by Sir Samuel Wilson about the Federated Malay States, 2 Nov. 1927, C.O. 717/58: 29223.

2. Before 1942, British Malaya consisted of the colony of the Straits Settlements (Penang, Malacca and Singapore) and nine protected Malay States, four of which had been the Federated Malay States. According to the 1931 census the total population was 5,849,000 persons of whom 44.4% were Malays, 39.2% Chinese, 14.3% Indians and 2.1% were 'others.' The term 'Malayan' denoted either the country as a whole or the people as a whole, and in the postwar period it had connotations of multiracialism.

3. For the Malayan Union and the Malay reaction to it see A. J. Stockwell, *British Policy and Malay Politics During the Malayan Union Experiment, 1942–1948* (Kuala Lumpur, 1979); also J. de V. Allen, *The Malayan Union* (New Haven, 1967); and C. Mary Turnbull, "British Planning for Post-war Malaya," *Journal of Southeast Asian Studies*, 5, ii (1974). For the Colonial Office during the Second World War see J. M. Lee

and Martin Petter, *The Colonial Office, War, and Development Policy, Organization and the Planning of a Metropolitan Initiative, 1939–1945* (London, 1982).

4. In 1974, I wrote in this Journal: 'Despite its intent to break with the past, the British scheme for post-war Malaya was received with such hostility that policy was rapidly revised in accordance with those criteria which had commanded Anglo-Malay relations before the war.' *Journal of Imperial and Commonwealth History*, II, 3 (1974), 347. Ten years later I am not disputing that the surprising wave of Malay nationalism forced the British to water down the principles of the Malayan Union in the federal settlement of 1948. Nevertheless, examination of the papers relating to the subsequent years shows that the Colonial Office retained those principles as their ultimate goal for Malaya. During 1948–52, relying on the patient negotiation suited to a situation where Malay rights were enshrined in the 1948 constitution instead of the abrupt methods that had been employed during the reoccupation of 1945–46, they sought to achieve a coherent administrative structure and the basis for Malayan nationhood.

5. 'The Malayan Union: A Historical Retrospect,' *Journal of Southeast Asian Studies*, XII, 1 (1982), 184.

6. Great Britain. 463. H.C. *Deb*. 5s (13 April 1949), c2815 and 473 H.C. *Deb.*, 5s (28 March, 1950), cc180–1.

7. V. Purcell cited in A. Short, *The Communist Insurrection in Malaya, 1948–60* (London, 1975), 318. Though Short calls this an 'extravagant' assessment of the directives issued by the Central Committee of the Malayan Communist Party in October 1951, he none the less stresses 'the primacy of political considerations in the October Directives.' *Ibid.*, 321.

8. Sir Richard Allen, *Malaysia, Prospect and Retrospect* (London, 1968), 105.

9. Public Record Office, *PREM* 8/459, c(46)6, 29 Nov. 1946.

10. C.O. 537/3670, minute by H. T. Bourdillon, 12 Jan. 1948.

11. C.O. 537/3669, minute by O. Morris, 8 Sept. 1948. See also C.O. 537 nos. 4743, 5962 and 7251.

12. C.O. 717/183: 52928/17 (1949), Creech Jones to MacDonald, personal and private, 24 Oct. 1949. Cf. C.O. 537/6018 on the CLC.

13. K. J. Ratnam, *Communalism and the Political Process in Malaya* (Kuala Lumpur, 1965), 89.

14. On the formation of RIDA see C.O. 537 nos. 6018, 6020 and 7297.

15. C.O. 537/5970, minutes of Commissioner General's Conference, 7 June 1950; cf C.O. 537/5962.

16. Public Record Office, CAB 128/17: 37(50)1, 19 June 1950. James Griffiths in his *Pages from Memory* (London, 1969), 94–101 does not reveal much about his Malayan trip.

17. C.O. 537/5966, note on meeting between MacDonald et al. and the American Joint Staff Defense Survey Mission to Southeast Asia (led by John F. Melby), 8 Aug. 1950.

18. *PREM* 8/l171: CP(50)200, 30 Aug. 1950.

19. Alan Bullock, *Ernest Bevin: Foreign Secretary, 1945–1951* (London, 1983), 747. See also 611–12, 673, 720, 743–7.

20. See David Rooney, *Sir Charles Arden-Clarke* (London, 1982), 67–73, 80–81; and Malcolm MacDonald, *Borneo People* (London, 1956).

21. C.O. 537/3686 contains correspondence and telegrams between Creech Jones and MacDonald relating to Gent's recall and the appointment of his successor. MacDonald, looking back on Gent's regime, wrote that he had forfeited Onn's trust. (MacDonald to Creech Jones, C.O. 537/3756).

22. C.O. 537/5962, T. Lloyd to J. Paskin, 5 Oct. 1950, reporting a private letter he had received from MacDonald.

23. Letter from J. M. Gullick (formerly of the MCS) to me, 4 June 1984. I am grateful to Mr. Gullick for his comments on a draft of this paper.

24. C.O. 537/2177, minute by Bourdillon, 21 Jan. 1948, on discussions with MacDonald on the subject of Indonesian influences in Malaya. For some insight into MacDonald's methods, see his *People and Places* (London, 1969) and *Titans and Others* (London, 1972).

25. C.O. 537/6020, Onn to Gurney, 26 June 1950.

26. C.O. 537/7303, Secretary of State as reported by J. D. Higham to Gurney, secret and personal, 6 July 1951.

27. *Ibid.*, Gurney to Higham, telegram, 22 June 1951.

28. C.O. 537/7297, Gurney to Higham, confidential, 29 Aug. 1951.

29. C.O. 537/7303, Gurney to Higham, secret and personal, 13 June 1951.

30. See Gordon Means, *Malaysian Politics* (London, 1970), 124–7, 132–7; R. K. Vasil, *Politics in a Plural Society* (Kuala Lumpur, 1971), 37–82; Karl von Vorys, *Democracy without Consensus* (Princeton, 1975), 96–112.

31. Phillip Darby, *British Defence Policy East of Suez, 1947–1968* (London, 1973), 25.

32. CAB 129/48: C(51)22, 19 Nov. 1951; C.O. 8521989; F.O. 371/76049.

33. For Scott's career see his obituary in *The Times,* 2 March 1982; for his advice see Public Record Office, F.O. 371/84478.

34. For the Cabinet papers on defence expenditure in the period July 1950–February 1951, see CAB 129/41: CP(50)181 and 188; CAB 129/42: CP(50)246, 247 and 248; CAB 129/44: CP(51)16, 20, 25, 32, 34, 36, 47 and 64. See also Cabinet minutes for meetings in November 1950, CAB 128/18: CM 70(50)1, CM 72(50)7 and CM 74(50)4.

35. Emmanuel Shinwell, *I've Lived Through It All* (London, 1973), 198.

36. For the Cabinet Committee on Malaya see CAB 134/497, F.O. 371/84478, *PREM* 8/112 and *PREM* 8/1406.

37. Public Record Office, W.O. 216/835, Harding to Slim, personal and top secret, 21 Nov. 1950; Slim to Harding, top secret, 21 Nov. 1950.

38. Kenneth O. Morgan, *Labour in Power, 1945–1951* (Oxford, 1984), 422.

39. See Kenneth Harris, *Attlee* (London, 1982), 462 ff; Philip M. Williams, *Hugh Gaitskell* (London, 1979), 242 ff; and Philip M. Williams (ed.), *The Diary of Hugh Gaitskell, 1945–1956* (London, 1983), 226.

40. *PREM* 8/1406, Strachey to Attlee, top secret and personal, 11 Dec. 1950. Cf. Hugh Thomas, *John Strachey* (New York, 1973), 264. On the Maria Hertogh or Nadra riots in Singapore and the unease of the Ministry of Defence see C.O. 537/7247 and F.O. 93117.

41. W.O. 216/835, VCIGS to CIGS, top secret and personal, 24 Feb. 1951; Slim to Harding, top secret, 21 Nov. 1950.

42. C.O. 537/7257, Gurney to Lloyd, 27 July 1951.

43. C.O. 537/7247.

44. W.O. 216/394, Slim to VCIGS, 25 June 1951.

45. C.O. 537/7267 and W.O. 216/394. Sir Rob Lockhart (brother of Sir Robert Bruce Lockhart who was the writer, diplomat and author of *Return to Malaya*, 1936) stayed on in Malaya as Deputy Director of Operations when Templer was appointed Director.

46. CAB 129/47: CP (51)243, 3 Sept. l951, Memorandum by the Chancellor of the Exchequer (Gaitskell) on the balance of payments position; and CAB 129/48: C(51), 1, 31 Oct. 1951, Memorandum by the Chancellor of the Exchequer (R. A. Butler) on the economic position. Butler's memorandum was the first Cabinet paper of the new government.

47. *PREM* 11.122, Lyttelton to Prime Minister, 30 Oct. 1951; Oliver Lyttelton, *The Memoirs of Lord Chandos* (London, 1962), 362.

48. W.O. 216/446, Churchill to Sir K. McLean, 6 Nov. 1951.

49. *PREM* 11/121, private and secret letters from Montgomery to Slim, 3 Dec. 1951; to Lyttelton, 27 Dec. and 30 Dec. 1951.

50. CAB 128/23: 10(51)2, 22 Nov.1951; 20(51)1 28 Dec. 1951.

51. Short, 325–6; W.O. 216/835, VCIGS to CIGS, top secret and personal, 24 Feb. 1951.

52. Lyttelton, 379–81.

53. CAB 130/74: Cabinet Committee on Malaya, 10 Jan. 1952.

54. CAB 98/41 and CAB 65/42 WM(44) 70th conclusions, minute 3, 31 May 1944.

55. Lyttelton, 364; C.O. 1022/81.

56. C.O. 1022/102.

18

Operations at Dien Bien Phu

VO NGUYEN GIAP*

The battle of Dien Bien Phu near the Vietnam-Laos border is arguably one of the most seminal battles in modern history, deciding the fate of French rule in Vietnam, Laos, and Cambodia. The French defeat at the hands of the Viet Minh on May 7, 1954, determined the course of the negotiations at the Geneva Conference on Indo-China, which opened the following day. The agreements signed there on July 21 ended French rule in Indo-China, gave independence to Laos and Cambodia, but divided Vietnam at the 17th parallel.

The confrontation at Dien Bien Phu was sought by the French military, who challenged the Viet Minh commander-in-chief, Vo Nguyen Giap, to a conventional battle. Both the Communist Party's Politburo and Giap himself knew that the strategy required to engage a Western-trained army with air support would have to be entirely different from the guerrilla tactics employed by the Viet Minh up to that time. Giap, a former history teacher and a self-trained general who later authored *People's War, People's Army,* wrote about the tactics employed at Dien Bien Phu.

~

We have expounded the essence of the strategic direction of the 1953–1954 Winter-Spring campaign. The spirit and guiding principles of this strategic

---

*Vo Nguyen Giap, *People's War, People's Army* (New York: Praeger, 1965), pp. 166–171.

direction posed two problems to be solved for the direction of operations on the Dien Bien Phu battlefield:

1. To attack or not to attack Dien Bien Phu?
2. If we attack, how should we go about it?

The parachuting of enemy troops into Dien Bien Phu was not necessarily to be followed by an attack on the fortified camp. As Dien Bien Phu was a very strongly fortified entrenched camp of the enemy we could not decide to attack it without first weighing the pros and cons very carefully. The fortified entrenched camp was a new form of defense of the enemy developed in face of the growth in the strength and size of our army. At Hoa Binh and at Na San, the enemy had already entrenched his forces in fortified camps. In the Winter-Spring campaign new fortified entrenched camps appeared not only at Dien Bien Phu but also at Seno, Muong Sai and Luang Prabang in the Laotian theatre of operations, and at Pleiku, on the Western Highlands front.

With the enemy's new form of defense, should we attack the fortified entrenched camp or should we not?

While our forces were still obviously weaker than the enemy's we always stuck to the principle of concentration of forces to attack the points where the enemy was relatively weak to annihilate his manpower. Our position was, time and again, to pin down the enemy's main forces in the fortified camps, while choosing more favorable directions for our attack. In Spring 1952, when the enemy erected the fortified camps at Hoa Binh, we struck hard and scored many victories along the Da river and in the enemy's rear in north Viet Nam. In Spring 1953, when the enemy fortified Na San, we did not attack his position but intensified our activities in the delta and launched an offensive in the west. During the last months of 1953 and at the beginning of 1954, when the enemy set up fortified camps in various places, our troops launched many successful offensives on sectors where the enemy was relatively weak, and at the same time stepped up guerrilla warfare behind the enemy's lines.

These tactics of attacking positions other than the fortified entrenched camps had recorded many successes. But these were not the only tactics. We could also directly attack the fortified entrenched camp to annihilate the enemy's manpower in the heart of his new form of defense. Only when we had wiped out the fortified entrenched camp, could we open up a new situation, paving the way for new victories for our army and people.

That was why, on the Dien Bien Phu battlefield, the problem of whether to attack or not had been posed, especially as Dien Bien Phu was the enemy's strongest fortified entrenched camp in the whole Indochina war theatre, while our troops had, up to that time, attacked only fortresses defended by one or two companies or one battalion at most.

Dien Bien Phu being the cornerstone of the Navarre plan, we considered that it should be wiped out if the Franco-American imperialist plot of protracting and expanding the war was to be smashed. However, the importance of Dien Bien Phu could not be regarded as a decisive factor in our decision to attack it. In the relation of forces at that time, could we destroy the fortified entrenched camp of Dien Bien Phu? Could we be certain of victory in attacking it? Our decision had to depend on this consideration alone.

Dien Bien Phu was a very strongly fortified entrenched camp. But on the other hand, it was set up in a mountainous region, on ground which was advantageous to us, and decidedly disadvantageous to the enemy. Dien Bien Phu was, moreover, a completely isolated position, far away from all the enemy's bases. The only means of supplying Dien Bien Phu was by air. These circumstances could easily deprive the enemy of all initiative and force him on to the defensive if attacked. On our side, we had picked units of the regular army which we could concentrate to achieve supremacy in power. We could overcome all difficulties in solving the necessary tactical problems; we had, in addition, an immense rear, and the problem of supplying the front with food and ammunition, though very difficult, was not insoluble. Thus we had conditions for retaining the initiative in the operations.

It was on the basis of this analysis of the enemy's and our own strong and weak points that we solved the question as to whether we should attack Dien Bien Phu or not. We decided to wipe out at all costs the whole enemy force at Dien Bien Phu, after having created favorable conditions for this battle by launching numerous offensives on various battlefields and by intensifying preparations on the Dien Bien Phu battlefield. This important decision was a new proof of the dynamism, initiative, mobility and rapidity of decision in face of new situations displayed in the conduct of the war by the Party's Central Committee. Our plan foresaw the launching of many offensives on the points where the enemy was relatively weak, availing ourselves of all opportunities to wipe out the enemy's manpower in mobile warfare. But whenever it was possible and success was certain, we were resolved not to let slip an opportunity to launch powerful attacks on strong points to annihilate the more concentrated enemy forces. Our decision to make the assault on the Dien Bien Phu fortified camp clearly marked a new step forward in the development of the Winter-Spring campaign, in the annals of our army's battles and in the history of our people's resistance war.

We had pledged to wipe out the whole enemy force at Dien Bien Phu but we still had to solve this problem: How should we do it? Strike swiftly and win swiftly, or strike surely and advance surely? This was the problem of the direction of operations in the campaign.

In the early stage, when we began the encirclement of Dien Bien Phu, and the enemy, having been newly parachuted into the area, had not yet had time to complete his fortifications and increase his forces, the question of striking swiftly and winning swiftly had been posed. By concentrating superior forces, we could push simultaneously from many directions deep into enemy positions, cut the fortified trenched camp into many separate parts, then swiftly annihilate the entire enemy manpower. There were many obvious advantages if we could strike swiftly to win swiftly: by launching a big offensive with fresh troops, we could shorten the duration of the campaign and avoid the wear and fatigue of a long operation. As the campaign would not last long, the supplying of the battlefront could be ensured without difficulty. However, on further examining the question, we saw that these tactics had a very great basic disadvantage: our troops lacked experience in attacking fortified entrenched camps. If we wanted to win swiftly, success could not be ensured. For that reason, in the process of making preparations, we continued to follow the enemy's situation and checked and re-checked our potentialities again. And we came to the conclusion that we could not secure success if we struck swiftly. In consequence, we resolutely chose the other tactic: to strike surely and advance surely. In taking this correct decision, we strictly followed this fundamental principle of the conduct of a revolutionary war: strike to win, strike only when success is certain, if it is not, then don't strike.

In the Dien Bien Phu campaign, the adoption of these tactics demanded of us firmness and a spirit of resolution. Since we wanted to strike surely and advance surely, preparations would take a longer time and the campaign would drag out. And the longer the campaign went on, the more new and greater difficulties would crop up. Difficulties in supply would increase enormously. The danger increased of our troops being worn out while the enemy consolidated defenses and lined up his forces. Above all, the longer the campaign lasted, the nearer came the rainy season with all its disastrous consequences for operations carried out on the mountains and in forests. As a result, not everybody was immediately convinced of the correctness of these tactics. We patiently educated our men, pointed out that there were real difficulties, but that our task was to overcome them to create good conditions for the great victory we sought.

It was from these guiding principles that we developed our plan of progressive attack, in which the Dien Bien Phu campaign was regarded not as a large-scale attack on fortresses carried out over a short period but as a large-scale campaign carried out over a fairly long period, through a series of successive attacks on fortified positions until the enemy was destroyed. In the campaign as a whole we already had numerical superiority over the enemy. But in each attack or each wave of attacks, we had the possibility of achieving absolute supremacy and ensuring success of each operation and consequently total victory in the campaign. Such a plan was in full keeping with the tactical and technical level of our troops, creating conditions for them to accumulate experience in fighting and to ensure the annihilation of the enemy at Dien Bien Phu.

We strictly followed these guiding principles throughout the campaign. We encircled the enemy and carried out preparations thoroughly over a period of three months. Then, after opening the offensive, our troops fought relentlessly for 55 days and nights. Careful preparation and relentless fighting led our Dien Bien Phu campaign to resounding victory.

PART IV

FRUITS OF FREEDOM

19

Cambodian

Neutrality

NORODOM SIHANOUK*

Within weeks of the Geneva Agreements of July 1954, which ended French rule, brought independence to Cambodia and Laos, and divided Vietnam between the Communist-ruled North and the U.S.-supported South, the United States created the Southeast Asia Treaty Organization (SEATO) to contain communism in Southeast Asia. Cambodia under Norodom Sihanouk refused to join the organization, instead preferring to remain neutral. Sihanouk felt that his country's independence was in jeopardy, given that Cambodia's two traditionally hostile neighbors—South Vietnam and Thailand—were aligned with the United States. His policy came under severe criticism in the Western world, especially in the United States. The article reproduced below is from the prestigious *Foreign Affairs Quarterly*, wherein Sihanouk described his political predicament and defended his country's "neutralist" foreign policy.

Norodom Sihanouk has continued to play an important role in Cambodian politics over the intervening decades. He was most pre-eminent in domestic administration and in the conduct of foreign policy from 1954 to 1970.

∼

Certain misconceptions have arisen from insufficient knowledge of the true situation in my country since it attained independence in November 1953.

*Norodom Sihanouk, "Cambodia Neutral: The Dictate of Necessity," *Foreign Affairs* 36, 1/4 (1957/1958): 582–586.

Although I am convinced that the leaders of the United States Government and the State Department's experts on Southeast Asia are fully conversant with Cambodian policy, I do not feel that the public has always been accurately informed about us. Americans will have learnt, from the type of magazine that serves up complex world problems in palatable and easily digestible form, that Cambodia has more or less cast off its former friends in order to seek new ones further east, that it practices a "pro-Red neutralism," is "rotten" with Communist propaganda and constitutes a "breach" in the front of the "free nations." I have received a number of touchingly naïve letters from American citizens imploring me to end this state of affairs and warning me of the dangers that would face my country if it put its trust in a certain "bloc."

I would like our American friends to know how mistaken they are in such appraisals. I can think of no better way of convincing them than by giving a frank account of Cambodia's present situation, its difficulties and the way in which it is trying to overcome them, Cambodia is a country of six million inhabitants, including 400,000 Vietnamese and 350,000 Chinese. Our army—and this is important to remember—numbers only 25,000 men. After Laos, which has a population of two million, we are the smallest state in the Indochinese Peninsula. But at least we are united. With our long-standing tradition of monarchy, we are drawn together by the Throne. As sincere democrats, we hate disorder, and as exponents of a purely national form of socialism, we can only be indifferent to foreign ideologies. We go our own national way, unswervingly.

First and foremost we are Cambodians, and lackeys of foreign powers have no hope of success here. Since we achieved independence, our policy has always been suited to our national needs. In our foreign relations we have favored neutrality, which in the United States is all too often confused with "neutralism," although it is fundamentally different. We are neutral in the same way Switzerland and Sweden are neutral—not neutralist like Egypt or Indonesia. Let anyone examine our votes in the United Nations; they are not often "aligned" with those of the bloc of "neutralist" nations.

Our neutrality has been imposed on us by necessity. A glance at a map of our portion of the world will show that we are wedged in between two medium-sized nations of the Western bloc and only thinly screened by Laos from the scrutiny of two countries of the Eastern bloc, North Viet Nam and the vast People's Republic of China. What choice have we but to try to maintain an equal balance between the "blocs"?

Furthermore, how could our neutrality be taken seriously if we had persisted in maintaining diplomatic, commercial and other relations exclusively with the Western bloc? As it is, we have refrained from recognizing the non-unified countries. The United Kingdom has an embassy at Peking; we have not. France has a general delegation at Hanoi; we have not. Our connections with these countries are limited to economic, commercial and cultural relations.

We are receiving some $25,000,000 in economic aid from China over a period of two years, with no conditions attached. . . . Assuredly all these aid programs are of great help to us. We feel particularly indebted to the United States for underwriting a great part of the maintenance of our army; for constructing the highway which will directly connect the seaport of Kompong Som with our capital of Phnom Penh; for the teacher training school of Kompong Kantout; and for the projected Police Academy and important irrigation schemes.

It is true that we wish this aid might be less "rigid" in its conception; more flexibility is desirable so that we can face unforeseen needs and situations. Finally, why not say it? We would like to be reassured about the continuity of aid, especially for the army, which is of such vital importance to the security of our country.

Chinese aid has been granted us for only two years but it is very flexible. On a grant basis, we receive from China consumer goods which are used both to meet the requirements of the population and at the same time to provide our Government with much needed revenue. Thus, from the sale of aid goods received from China, we have been able to dig wells, build dams, furnish schools, construct administration buildings and help victims of national disasters. In addition, the Chinese are building three factories in Cambodia which they will equip and donate to us. Furthermore, the Soviet Union has promised to build a 500-bed hospital in Phnom Penh entirely equipped and provided with consultation services.

As to France, she maintains a military mission which provides advisers and instructors for our army. A French economic mission puts experts at our disposal and offers numerous scholarships to our students and military personnel. France has undertaken to provide us with a seaport at Kompong Som and a modern airport at Phnom Penh with longer and more adequate runways. Several other important projects are under study, but whether they can be undertaken depends on the French financial situation.

By far the most important aid is that from the United States, since its purpose is to provide us with the framework of a modern state. For this reason American aid is conceived in anticipation of the future. Our elite understands this. The poor, however, are less sympathetic to it because what they think about above all is the quick and easy satisfaction of their most pressing needs. This is the reason why other aid programs, more tangible because they are in response to . . . demands, perhaps bring higher returns to their authors.

We have nothing to reproach ourselves with in so far as our old friends are concerned. Most of our students and soldiers receive their basic or advanced training in the West. Our elite has retained its French culture and many of the younger generation are learning English as well. Our foreign experts and military instructors are from the West. No Westerner has ever met with the slightest hostility here and all our visitors speak favorably of our hospitality, even "Eastern" diplomats and travellers, who seem to appreciate the atmosphere of freedom they find here.

Are we "pro-Red" in our neutrality? . . . When a great Power tries to submerge us beneath a flood of propaganda or to tempt our youth away from its duty to the King and Country, we take a firm stand. . . . it will be difficult, if not impossible, to "corrupt" us.

We are taking all the necessary precautions—and we will go to considerable lengths if necessary—to prevent anything of the kind. Besides, the loyalty of our people would doom any such dividing tactics to failure from the start. As for the foreign minorities living in Cambodia, we shall, without ever repressing them, see that they respect our neutrality and security. In that regard we are far more vigilant than is generally believed.

I have sometimes been represented to the American public as trying to "flirt with the Reds." The fact is, I abdicated in 1955 to save the monarchy—not to abandon it. However strongly democratic, I am sure that the citizens of the United States can appreciate that, short of being mentally deranged, a Prince and former King must be well aware that the first concern of the Communists is to get rid of the King and natural elite of any country they succeed in laying hands on. By that I do not mean to imply that the Communists wish to take possession of Cambodia; that may not enter into their plans at all and, for the moment at least, they have far weightier matters to occupy them. But I am not overlooking any possibilities, and that one is quite enough to deter me from any "flirtation." If I have no particular liking for Communism, neither have I any cause or means to join a crusade—even a moral one—against the nations that have adopted that ideology and which since 1954 have not given my country sufficient grounds for complaint. It would be absurd to suppose that a tiny country like mine, geographically situated as it is, would risk provoking the Chinese and Soviet colossi now that planes fly so fast and rockets so far.

We are not a "breach" in the Western bloc merely because we cannot be a "rampart"; in the event of a world conflict, we might very well become one of the first victims of a harsh occupation. In that case, the "free world" would have other things to do besides undertaking our liberation—or rather the liberation of what little remained of us.

Are we selfish or "wrong-minded" in thinking as we do? I maintain that we are merely being realistic. By practicing a genuine neutrality which eliminates any pretext for aggression we have a chance of not bringing down a storm on our heads; and a storm can be dangerous where there is no lightning-conductor.

Our precautions may be to no avail, and we may one day be invaded notwithstanding them (I am not afraid of internal subversion which stands no chance here). If, in spite of our manifest good intentions and our utter propriety in respect to the blocs, one of these should attack us, then I would be the first to advocate reconsidering our policy and invoking aid from the opponents of our aggressors. I profoundly hope that our country will never have to take such a step.

20

The Birth of the NLF

T R U O N G   N H U   T A N G *

Truong Nhu Tang, the principal author of *A Vietcong Memoir,* from which this extract on the birth of the National Liberation Front (NLF) is taken, was himself a founding member of the NLF and later a minister in the Provisional Revolutionary Government (PRG) from 1969 to 1975. Before founding the NLF on December 20, 1960, Tang had held significant positions in Saigon. There he became disillusioned by Diem's excesses and decided to become a full-time revolutionary.

His memoir became quite controversial among scholars. Tang himself maintained that he was a nationalist and not a communist. His claim that his views are representative of the NLF is also widely disputed.

~

By the time 1957 merged into 1958, Ngo Dinh Diem had exhausted the patient hopefulness that had initially greeted his presidency. From the first he had moved ruthlessly to consolidate his personal power, crushing the private army of the Binh Xuyen and then subduing the armed religious sects. From there he attacked those suspected of Communist sympathies in what was called the To Cong ("Denounce the communists") campaign, jailing and executing thousands who had fought against the French. Each of these moves was carried out with surprising energy, and in their own terms they succeeded. As he surveyed the political landscape three years after assuming power, Diem could see no well-organized centers of opposition to his rule. The National Assembly was wholly dominated by his brother's National Revolutionary

*Truong Nhu Tang with David Chanoff and Doan Van Toai, *A Vietcong Memoir* (New York: Vintage Books, 1985), pp. 63–80.

Movement, the troublesome private armies had been severely handled, the communist-dominated resistance veterans were cowed and in disarray.

But Diem's successes had all been of a negative sort. Though he had asserted his authority and gained time, he had done nothing about establishing positive programs to meet the nation's economic and social needs. He had not used the time he had gained. After three years it was apparent that the new president was a power-monger, not a builder. For those who could see, the fatal narrowness of his political understanding was already evident.

In the first place, Diem's armed enemies had for the most part only been mauled but not destroyed. Elements of the defeated sect armies went underground, licking their wounds and looking for allies. Gradually they began to link up with groups of former Vietminh fighters fleeing from the To Cong suppression. The core of a guerrilla army was already in the making.

Even as old enemies regrouped, Diem was busy adding new ones. In the countryside he destroyed at a blow the dignity and livelihood of several hundred thousand peasants by canceling the land-redistribution arrangements instituted by the Vietminh in areas they had controlled prior to 1954. He might have attempted to use American aid to compensate owners and capitalize on peasant goodwill; instead he courted the large landholders. Farmers who had been working land they considered theirs, often for years, now faced demands for back rent and exorbitant new rates. It was an economic disaster for them.

In 1957 Diem promulgated his own version of land reform, ostensibly making acreage available, though only to peasants who could pay for it. But even this reform was carried out primarily on paper. In the provinces it was sabotaged everywhere by landowners acting with official connivance. The result of all this was a frustrated and indignant peasantry, fertile ground for anti-Diem agitation.

Meanwhile, the city poor were tasting their own ration of misery. In Saigon, the government pursued "urban redevelopment" with a vengeance, dispossessing whole neighborhoods in favor of modern commercial buildings and expensive apartments, which could only be utilized by Americans and the native upper classes. Not a few times, poorer quarters were completely razed by uncontrollable fires (Khanh Hoi and Phu Nuan were particularly calamitous examples). Few thought these fires were accidental; they were too closely followed by massive new construction. The displaced moved onto sampans on the river or to poorer, even more distant districts. In the slums and shanty villages resentment against the Americans mixed with a simmering anger toward the regime.

In the highland regions of the Montagnards too, Diem's policies were cold-blooded and destructive. Attempting to make the tribespeople more accessible to government control, troops and cadres forced village populations down out of the mountains and into the valleys—separating them from their ancestral lands and graves. In Ban Me Thuot and other areas, the ingrained routines of social life were profoundly disrupted by these forced relocations, which seemed to the tribespeople nothing more than inexplicable cruelty.

By the end of 1958, Diem had succeeded brilliantly in routing his enemies and arrogating power. But he had also alienated large segments of the South Vietnamese population, creating a swell of animosity throughout the country. Almost unknown at first, in a few short years he had made himself widely detested, a dictator who could look for support only to the Northern Catholic refugees and to those who made money from his schemes. Most damning of all, he had murdered many patriots who had fought in the struggle against France and had tied his existence to the patronage of the United States, France's successor. To many nationalist-minded Vietnamese, whose emotions were those of people just emerging from a hundred years of subjection to foreigners, Diem had forfeited all claims to loyalty.

In light of Diem's conduct of the presidency, two facts were clear: First, the country had settled into an all too familiar pattern of oligarchic rule and utter disregard for the welfare of the people. Second, subservience to foreigners was still the order of the day. We had a ruler whose overriding interest was power and who would use the Americans to prop himself up—even while the Americans were using him for their own strategic purposes.

As far as I was concerned, this situation was intolerable. Replacing the French despots with a Vietnamese one was not a significant advance. It would never lead to either the broad economic progress or the national dignity which I (along with many others) had been brooding about for years. Among my circle of friends there was anger and profound disappointment over this turn of events. We were living, we felt, in historic times. A shameful, century-long era had just been violently closed out, and a new nation was taking shape before our eyes. Many of us agreed that we could not acquiesce in the shape it was taking. If we were not to be allowed a say about it from within the government, we would have to speak from without.

By the end of 1958, those of us who felt this way decided to form an extralegal political organization, complete with a program and plan of action. We had not moved toward this decision quickly; it was an undertaking of immense magnitude, which would require years of effort before giving us the strength to challenge Diem's monopoly on power. To some, that prospect seemed quixotic at best. But most of us felt we had little choice.

From casual discussions, we began to meet in slightly more formal groups, sometimes only a few of us, sometimes eight or ten together. Two doctors, Duong Quynh Hoa and Phung Van Cung, took active roles, as did Nguyen Huu Khuong, a factory owner, Trinh Dinh Thao, a lawyer, and the architect

Huynh Tan Phat. We were joined by Nguyen Van Hieu and Ung Ngoc Ky, who were lycée teachers, and other friends such as Nguyen Long and Tran Buu Kiem. Our first order of business was to identify and make contact with potential allies for what we knew would be a long and bitter struggle.

To do this we formed what we called the mobilization committee, whose members were myself, Hieu, Kiem, Ky, Long, Cung, and architect Phat. Through friends, relatives, business and political contacts we began to establish a network of people who felt as we did about Diem and his policies. Phat and a few of the others were old resisters and had kept their ties with fellow veterans of the French war, many of whom were hiding with friends and family from the To Cong hunters. They too were beginning to organize, and they had colleagues and sympathizers in every social stratum throughout the country. They were natural allies.

Among us we also had people with close ties to the sects, the legal political parties, the Buddhists. In each group we made overtures, and everywhere we discovered sympathy and backing. Sometimes individuals would indicate their desire to participate actively. More often we would receive assurances of quiet solidarity. At the same time, we sent Nguyen Van Hieu to Hanoi to begin working out a channel of support from our Northern compatriots.

At each stage we discussed carefully the ongoing search for allies, wary about how to gather support and still retain our own direction and freedom of action. It was a delicate and crucial problem of the utmost complexity. The overwhelming strength of our enemy urged us to acquire whatever assistance we could from whatever source. In addition, the anti-colonial war had not simply ended in 1954; a residual Vietminh infrastructure was still in place and was beginning to come alive again. For better or worse, our endeavor was meshed into an ongoing historical movement for independence that had already developed its own philosophy and means of action. Of this movement, Ho Chi Minh was the spiritual father, in the South as well as the North, and we looked naturally to him and to his government for guidance and aid. . . . And yet this struggle was also our own. Had Ngo Dinh Diem proved a man of breadth and vision, the core of people who filled the NLF and its sister organizations would have rallied to him. As it was, the South Vietnamese nationalists were driven to action by his contempt for the principles of independence and social progress in which they believed. In this sense, the Southern revolution was generated of itself, out of the emotions, conscience, and aspirations of the Southern people.

The complexity of the struggle was mirrored in the makeup of our group. Most were not Lao Dong ("Workers' Party"—the official name of the Vietnamese Communist Party) members; many scarcely thought of themselves as political at least in any ideological way. Our allies among the resistance veterans were also largely nationalists rather than political (though they had certainly been led and monitored by the Party). But we also had Party activists among us, some open, some surreptitious. Tran Bu Kiem, the architect Phat, and the teachers Hieu and Ky I knew as political-minded individuals, who had been leaders of the New Democratic Party during their student years at Hanoi University in the early forties. This militant student union had been absorbed by the Lao Dong in 1951, some of its members enrolling in the Party, some defecting altogether, some simply accepting the change in leadership without themselves becoming Communists. What I didn't know was that Phat had been a Party member since 1940, while Hieu, Ky, and Kiem had rallied to the Party in 1951!

But I was not overly concerned at the point about potential conflicts between the Southern nationalists and the ideologues. We were allies in this fight, or so I believed. We needed each other, and the closest ties of background, family, and patriotism united us in respect for each other's purposes. This was my reading of the situation in 1959 as the yet-to-be-named National Liberation Front gathered momentum. I was not alone in drawing this conclusion. And I was not the only one whom time would disabuse.

In addition to making contacts and setting up working relationships with supporters, we also began searching for a leader. Our requirements were clear: someone who was well known and who had a reputation for integrity, someone associated with neither the French nor the Communists. This person had to strike a note of moderation and goodwill, attracting support from all sides and alienating no one. Several names kept surfacing in our discussions about this, and finally we drew up a list of four candidates.

Our first choice was Tran Kim Quan, a pharmacist who had been president of the South Vietnamese Student Association at Hanoi University and chairman of the Peace Movement in 1954. Quan met all the criteria; he had an established reputation as a patriot and was widely respected as a man of principle. Kiem was delegated to approach him for us. But though Quan turned out to be sympathetic to our goals he was unwilling to accept our offer. Perhaps he had a premonition of the tortuous course this struggle would take.

There were two second choices, Trinh Dinh Thao, already one of our colleagues, and Michael Van Vi. Thao was a high official of the Cao Dai sect and had been a minister in the old imperial cabinet. Accordingly, he was conspicuously free from any Communist taint. Van Vi, director of the Franco-Chinese Bank, was likewise distant from leftist ideology. His nonprofessional interests ran largely to culture; he chaired the Society for the Propagation of the Vietnamese Language. I was appointed to sound out Thao and Van Vi, but my luck was no better than Kiem's had been. They were willing to play a supporting role but would not assume the leadership.

By elimination our list now was narrowed to Nguyen Huu Tho, a lawyer who, with Quan, had been cochairman of the Peace Movement, a vaguely leftist group of Saigon intellectuals who had tried to encourage Diem to hold reunification elections as stipulated by the Geneva Accords. But talking to Tho would be a complicated matter. His peace activities had landed him under house arrest in Tuy Hoa, a town in the center of Vietnam. Phat, who had contacts with the resistance veterans in the area, was assigned the job of stealing Tho away from his guards.

As Phat was making his plans, we began to refine our working procedures. Up to this point we had not been terribly afraid of the police. Ours could easily be construed as just another circle of talkative Saigon intellectuals engaged in the national sport of arguing about politics. There was nothing we had actually done. But by the fall of 1959 our organization had grown considerably. As we began working toward a first large-scale general meeting, the time had come to shift over to more formal, security-conscious methods.

Now we divided up our more numerous membership into many small working groups of three, four, or five people, no single group knowing who belonged to the other groups. This cell structure is sometimes thought of as a Communist innovation, but for the Vietnamese, with their long history of secret societies, it is practically second nature. Each cell included people from different classes and backgrounds to insure a wide range of thinking. I found myself working with three others: Sau Cang, a small businessman; Le Van Phong, a resistance veteran; and Truong Cao Phouc, a schoolfellow of mine who had also fought with the Vietminh and whose family owned a large rubber plantation.

The mobilization committee also appointed a leadership group made up of Phat, Hieu, and Kiem—responsible for overseeing the details of organization and bringing together input from the different working groups. After two months or so of intense activity throughout the organization, the leadership was ready to circulate a consensus that had been generated. General agreement had been reached on the following objectives:

1. Bring a sense of unity to the different classes of people in the South, regardless of their position in society or their political or religious views.
2. Overthrow the Diem regime.
3. Achieve the withdrawal of American advisers and an end to American interference in the self-determination of the South Vietnamese people.
4. Defend and protect the rights of Vietnamese citizens, including democratic freedoms and respect for private property rights.

5. Carry out a "land to the tiller" policy.
6. Build an independent economy.
7. Establish an educational system that will protect Vietnamese traditions and culture.
8. Establish a pluralistic national government, nonaligned and neutral.
9. Unify the North and the South on the basis of mutual interest through negotiations, without war.

As we finished our broad objectives and began grappling with their ramifications, we also set a tentative date for the first general meeting: December 19 and 20 of the following year. We decided on a name for our movement: the National Liberation Front of South Vietnam. We devised a flag (later to become famous as the flag of the Vietcong) and an anthem, "Liberate the South." At the same time, Hieu was sent North again, this time for guidance from Uncle Ho on the platform we had enunciated. By the end of 1959, work was complete on transforming these general principles into a manifesto and a formal political program.

Reading through the finished documents, I was impressed by the analysis they presented of the South's political situation and the balance of forces within the country as well as in Southeast Asia and throughout the world. It was clear that these works had been finely crafted to appeal to the broadest spectrum of people in the South and to marshal the anti-colonial emotions that animated almost everyone. At the same time, the manifesto and program responded forcefully and specifically to the interests of various elements of South Vietnamese society—the intellectuals, students, middle class, peasants, and workers.

As I read, I had the distinct sense that these historical documents could not have been the work of just the leadership group. They had too much depth, they showed too expert a grasp of politics, psychology, and language. I suspected I was seeing in them the delicate fingerprints of Ho Chi Minh. There seemed nothing strange about this. Ho's experience with revolutionary struggle was not something alien, to arouse suspicion and anxiety. It was part and parcel of our own background.

We were now, in the winter of 1959–60, ready to move into the next phase of the struggle. In early March as internal tension grew, the Resistance Veterans' Association suddenly launched an appeal to the people of the South. Spread through leaflets and posters, broadcast by Hanoi Radio, it called for an armed struggle to begin. It was a signal that the political action, which had been our focus for the past two years, would now acquire a coordinated military dimension. With this step, the Northern government had reinforced the Front's credibility and had flashed its own readiness for a wider conflict.

I felt a hint of trepidation at this. For several years there had been violence in the countryside; indeed, violent conflict had been a fact of life since Diem's suppression of the sects and the former Vietminh fighters. But the struggle we were now embarked on would involve military confrontation on a different scale altogether. My colleagues and I had known from the start that moving Diem into any serious negotiations regarding political participation would require the sustained use of force. Regardless of our personal predilections, there was no choice in this. But our priorities had always been distinctly political. We envisioned as our goal a political settlement that could be brought about largely by political means. Military victory was seen neither by us nor by any one else as a serious possibility. Diem's own army was vastly superior to any forces we might deploy—and behind Diem were the Americans. A high level of warfare would bring with it the grave danger of direct American intervention, which we wished at all costs to avoid. What all this meant was that violence was called for, but a carefully controlled violence that would serve political ends. In addition, I believed that the core group of the NLF, men who felt much as I did, would act as an effective brake against those who might be tempted to look for a military solution. Nevertheless, now that the engagement was opened, there was occasion for a surge of doubt.

But events quickly pushed trepidation aside. The signal given by the Resistance Veterans' Association was loudly confirmed by the Third National Congress of the Workers' Party, which met in Hanoi during the second week of September. Proclaiming the liberation of the South as a major priority, the Northern government was formally announcing its readiness in the most unambiguous fashion. The stage was now fully set.

Meanwhile Huynh Tan Phat had organized a raid to liberate President-designate Tho from his detention in Tuy Hoa. The region around this town had been a center of Vietminh activity in the French war and was crawling with former guerrillas. From these Phat had put together a commando unit whose job was to grab Tho and spirit him away to a safe area on the Laos/Cambodia/Vietnam border. Here he could hide until preparations were completed for the general meeting scheduled for December 19. Phat's deadline was approaching fast.

Along with a number of other peace activists, Tho was being held in a loosely guarded house looked after by local soldiers. Neither he nor his fellow detainees were considered high security risks, their crimes having consisted of some relatively innocuous agitation for elections several years earlier. No one, neither Tho nor his wardens, suspected that he was about to become a prime object of guerrilla attention. Taking advantage of the relaxed atmosphere, Phat's commandos were able to lure the guards away by having relatives call them with various family emergencies that required their immediate presence. With the guards out of the way, the kidnappers simply walked into the house. Unfortunately, so unaware was Tho that anything was brewing that he had requested (and had received) permission for a private visit with his family. At the moment his would-he rescuers began looking through the house, the object of search was in a government compound on the other side of town, enjoying a reunion with his wife and children.

In a series of comic-opera mistakes, none of the commandos—all of whom were from the Tuy Hoa area—had ever actually seen Tho, though they had been provided with a picture of him as an aid to identification. Now they paraded through the house asking questions and trying to match up the various prisoners with the face in the photo. Unsure as to who was who and skeptical of the story about Tho's outing, they decided to take along the two candidates who most nearly resembled their quarry. . . .

Having liberated the wrong men, the commandos were now forced to launch a second operation, organized a little more carefully this time, and including someone who could recognize Tho by sight. But because of the first mix-up, we were still without a president as the December 19 meeting came on. . . .

[On] December 19, I was again taken to the hall, which now had acquired a different set of trappings. Over the entrance hung a red-and-white banner proclaiming "Welcome General Congress for the Foundation of the National Liberation Front for South Vietnam." Flanking this banner were two flags, red and blue with a yellow star in the center, the flag we had devised during our working meetings the previous year. Inside, last night's stage had become a dais, above which the same banner was draped. On the dais sat Phat, Hieu, and Kiem, our leadership group, together with Ung Ngoc Ky, Dr. Cung, and several others I didn't recognize. These others turned out to be representatives of various groups, youth, peasants, workers, and women— Pham Xuan Thai, Nguyen Huu The, Nguyen Co Tam, and Nguyen Thi Dinh respectively. Again I was shown into one of the curtained boxes along the side, hidden from the public delegates, who were seating themselves on the middle benches and from the other secret members occupying the adjoining boxes. There were perhaps sixty participants in all, including twenty or so behind the curtains. Over all of us a sense of expectancy began to build, as a spokesman got up to announce the agenda.

After the agenda was read, a security force representative described the safety measures that had been taken and gave instructions about what to do should there be an alarm or an attack by air or land forces. Then Dr. Cung arose for a short inaugural statement, declaring the congress in session and wishing us success in our great undertaking. He was followed by Kiem who read a report on the political situation in South Vietnam, and Hieu, who presented the manifesto and political program.

The hortatory language of these documents seemed to heighten the drama of what was happening: each individual in the hall was aware that he was participating in a historic event. Sensing the excitement, Hieu went on to explain that the name "National Liberation Front for South Vietnam" symbolized the unity of the southern people in their struggle to free the country from My Diem (America/Diem). The flag, he said, red and blue, signified the two halves of the nation, united under the star—in a single purpose. The anthem, "Liberate the South," echoed the appeal with simple clarity.

At midday when the meeting broke for lunch, the delegates were visibly moved by feelings of brotherhood and resolution. For me, though, these feelings were to remain private as, muffled in my scarf, I was led back to the cottage to eat in solitude.

After lunch, the meeting reconvened to hear statements from representatives of various social elements—the sects, the intellectuals, students, peasants—each speaking of the aspirations of his group. When these had been given, we recessed for a dinner of soup, vegetables, and rice, returning to hear statements and suggestions from those who had submitted them in writing the previous day. Near midnight we voted to accept the manifesto, program, flag, everything that was before us. There were no dissenters.

Finally, Huynh Tan Phat moved that we adopt a suggested list of names as a Provisional Committee to carry the movement forward until the next general congress could be held. Specifically, the Provisional Committee would proclaim the creation of the NLF and publicize its manifesto and program not only throughout Vietnam but internationally as well. (The diplomatic front was to open immediately.) The committee would also intensify our proselytizing efforts and make preparations for the next congress at which a regular Central Committee and organizational hierarchy would be established. It would, in addition, continue to develop our infrastructure throughout the South, with special attention to the Saigon-Cholon/Giadinh zone.

Phat's proposal was passed again unanimously, and Dr. Cung was elected chairman of the Provisional Committee with Hieu to serve as Secretary General. In the early hours of December 20, we adjourned.

Once finished with our business, the delegates dispersed as quickly as they could knowing that each moment the danger of discovery increased. . . . By the following morning . . . from Hanoi . . . a special broadcast reached every corner of the south, announcing the formation of the NLF and offering congratulations from the Workers' Party and the Northern government. It was a time for nourishing the most sublime hopes.

21

The United States
in Vietnam

LYNDON B. JOHNSON*

This extract is taken from a well-known address President Johnson gave at the Johns Hopkins University following the beginning of U.S. bombing of strategic targets in North Vietnam in February 1965. He had widened the war without any specific declaration of war, depending only on the "mandate" given by the U.S. Senate resolution in the wake of the Gulf of Tonkin incident in August 1964. The address at Johns Hopkins was the first clear enunciation of the U.S. war aims in Vietnam directed not only to the domestic audience but also to the North Vietnamese and their Chinese and Soviet supporters. Note the confident note in LBJ's speech: "We will not be defeated. We will not grow tired. We will not withdraw, either openly or under the cloak of a meaningless agreement." That confidence would progressively give way to anxiety as the build-up of U.S. troops in Vietnam and the number of U.S. and South Vietnamese casualties mounted. Below are excerpts from that crucial speech.

~

. . . Tonight Americans and Asians are dying for a world where each people may choose its own path to change.

This is the principle for which our ancestors fought in the valleys of Pennsylvania. It is the principle for which our sons fight in the jungles of Vietnam.

---

*Lyndon B. Johnson, "A Pattern for Peace in Southeast Asia," *Department of State Bulletin* 52 (April 26, 1965): 606–610.

Vietnam is far from this quiet campus. We have no territory there, nor do we seek any. The war is dirty and brutal and difficult. And some 400 young men, born into an America bursting with opportunity and promise, have ended their lives on Vietnam's steaming soil.

Why must we take this painful road?

Why must this nation hazard its ease, its interest, and its power for the sake of a people so far away?

We fight because we must fight if we are to live in a world where every country can shape its own destiny. And only in such a world will our own freedom be finally secure.

This kind of a world will never be built by bombs or bullets. Yet the infirmities of man are such that force must often precede reason, and the waste of war, the works of peace.

We wish this were not so. But we must deal with the world as it is, if it is ever to be as we wish.

The world as it is in Asia is not a serene or peaceful place. The first reality is that North Vietnam has attacked the independent nation of South Vietnam. Its object is total conquest.

Of course, some of the people of South Vietnam are participating in this attack on their own government. But trained men and supplies, orders and arms, flow in a constant stream from North to South.

This support is the heartbeat of the war.

And it is a war of unparalleled brutality. Simple farmers are the targets of assassination and kidnapping. Women and children are strangled in the night because their men are loyal to their Government. Small and helpless villages are ravaged by sneak attacks. Large-scale raids are conducted on towns, and terror strikes in the heart of cities.

The confused nature of this conflict cannot mask the fact that it is the new face of an old enemy. It is an attack by one country upon another. And the object of that attack is a friend to which we are pledged.

Over this war, and all Asia, is another reality: the deepening shadow of Communist China. The rulers in Hanoi are urged on by Peking. This is a regime which has destroyed freedom in Tibet, attacked India, and been condemned by the United Nations for aggression in Korea. It is a nation which is helping the forces of violence in almost every continent. The contest in Vietnam is part of a wider pattern of aggressive purpose.

Why are these realities our concern? Why are we in South Vietnam? We are there because we have a promise to keep. Since 1954 every American President has offered support to the people of South Vietnam. We have helped to build, and we have helped to defend. Thus, over many years, we have made a national pledge to help South Vietnam defend its independence. And I intend to keep our promise.

To dishonor that pledge, to abandon this small and brave nation to its enemy, and to the tenor that must follow, would be an unforgivable wrong.

We are also there to strengthen world order. Around the globe, from Berlin to Thailand, are people whose well-being rests, in part, on the belief that they can count on us if they are attacked. To leave Vietnam to its fate would shake the confidence of all these people in the value of American commitment, the value of America's word. The result would be increased unrest and instability, and even wider war.

We are also there because there are great stakes in the balance. Let no one think for a moment that retreat from Vietnam would bring an end to conflict. The battle would be renewed in one country and then another. The central lesson of our time is that the appetite of aggression is never satisfied. To withdraw from one battlefield means only to prepare for the next. We must say in Southeast Asia, as we did in Europe, in the words of the Bible: "Hitherto shalt thou come, but no further."

There are those who say that all our effort there will be futile, that China's power is such it is bound to dominate all Southeast Asia. But there is no end to that argument until all the nations of Asia are swallowed up.

There are those who wonder why we have a responsibility there. We have it for the same reason we have a responsibility for the defense of freedom in Europe. World War II was fought in both Europe and Asia, and when it ended we found ourselves with continued responsibility for the defense of freedom.

Our objective is the independence of South Vietnam, and its freedom from attack. We want nothing for ourselves, only that the people of South Vietnam be allowed to guide their own country in their own way.

We will do everything necessary to reach that objective. And we will do only what is absolutely necessary.

In recent months, attacks on South Vietnam were stepped up. Thus it became necessary to increase our response and to make attacks by air. This is not a change of purpose. It is a change in what we believe that purpose requires.

We do this in order to slow down aggression.

We do this to increase the confidence of the brave people of South Vietnam who have bravely borne this brutal battle for so many years and with so many casualties.

And we do this to convince the leaders of North Vietnam, and all who seek to share their conquest, of a very simple fact:

We will not be defeated.

We will not grow tired.

We will not withdraw, either openly or under the cloak of a meaningless agreement.

We know that air attacks alone will not accomplish all these purposes. But it is our best and prayerful judgment that they are a necessary part of the surest road to peace.

We hope that peace will come swiftly. But that is in the hands of others beside ourselves. And we must be prepared for a long, continued conflict. It will require patience as well as bravery, the will to endure as well as the will to resist.

I wish it were possible to convince others with words of what we now find it necessary to say with guns and planes: Armed hostility is futile. Our resources are equal to any challenge because we fight for values and we fight for principles, rather than territory or colonies. Our patience and determination are unending.

Once this is clear, then it should also be clear that the only path for reasonable men is the path of peaceful settlement.

Such peace demands an independent South Vietnam securely guaranteed and able to shape its own relationships to all others, free from outside interference, tied to no alliance, a military base for no other country.

These are the essentials of any final settlement.

We will never be second in the search for such a peaceful settlement in Vietnam.

There may be many ways to this kind of peace: in discussion or negotiation with the governments concerned; in large groups or in small ones; in the reaffirmation of old agreements or their strengthening with new ones.

We have stated this position over and over again fifty times and more, to friend and foe alike. And we remain ready, with this purpose, for unconditional discussions.

And until that bright and necessary day of peace we will try to keep conflict from spreading. We have no desire to see thousands die in battle, Asians or Americans. We have no desire to devastate that which the people of North Vietnam have built with toil and sacrifice. We will use our power with restraint and with all the wisdom we can command. But we will use it.

This war, like most wars, is filled with terrible irony. For what do the people of North Vietnam want? They want what their neighbors also desire: food for their hunger, health for their bodies and a chance to learn, progress for their country, and an end to the bondage of material misery. And they would find all these things far more readily in peaceful association with others than in the endless course of battle.

These countries of Southeast Asia are homes for millions of impoverished people. Each day these people rise at dawn and struggle until the night to wrest existence from the soil. They are often wracked by disease, plagued by hunger, and death comes at the early age of 40.

Stability and peace do not come easily in such a land. Neither independence nor human dignity will ever be won by arms alone. It also requires the works of peace.

The American people have helped generously in times past in these works.

Now there must be a much more massive effort to inspire the life of man in the conflict-torn corner of our world.

The first step is for the countries of Southeast Asia to associate themselves in a greatly expanded cooperative effort for development. We would hope that North Vietnam will take its place in the common effort just as soon as peaceful cooperation is possible.

The United Nations is already actively engaged in development in this area, and as far back as 1961 I conferred with our authorities in Vietnam in connection with their work there.

I would hope that the Secretary-General of the United Nations could use the prestige of his great office, and his deep knowledge of Asia, to initiate, as soon as possible, with the countries of the area, a plan for cooperation in increased development.

For our part I will ask the Congress to join in a billion dollar American investment in this effort as soon as it is underway.

And I hope all other industrialized countries, including the Soviet Union, will join in this effort to replace despair with hope, and terror with progress.

The task is nothing less than to enrich the hopes and existence of more than a hundred million people. And there is much to be done.

The vast Mekong River can provide food and water and power on a scale to dwarf even our own TVA.

The wonders of modern medicine can be spread through villages where thousands die every year from lack of care. Schools can be established to train people in the skills that are needed to manage the process of development.

And these objectives, and more, are within the reach of cooperative and determined effort.

I also intend to expand and speed up a program to make available our farm surplus to assist in feeding and clothing the needy in Asia. We should not allow people to go hungry and wear rags while our own warehouses overflow with an abundance of wheat and corn, rice and cotton.

I will very shortly name a special team of patriotic and distinguished Americans to inaugurate our participation in these programs. This team will be headed by Mr. Eugene Black, the very able former president of the World Bank.

In areas still ripped by conflict, of course, development will not be easy. Peace will be necessary for final success. But we cannot wait for peace to begin the job.

This will be a disorderly planet for a long time. In Asia as elsewhere, the forces of the modern world are shaking old ways and uprooting ancient civilizations. There will be turbulence and struggle and even violence. Great social change, as we see in our own country, does not always come without conflict.

We must also expect that nations will on occasion be in dispute with us. It may be because we are rich, or powerful, or because we have made mistakes, or because they honestly fear our intentions. However, no nation need ever fear that we desire their land, or to impose our will, or to dictate their institutions.

But we will always oppose the effort of one nation to conquer another nation.

We will do this because our own security is at stake.

But there is more to it than that. For our generation has a dream. It is a very old dream. But we have the power and now we have the opportunity to make it come true.

For centuries, nations have struggled among each other. But we dream of a world where disputes are settled by law and reason. And we will try to make it so.

For most of history men have hated and killed one another in battle. But we dream of an end to war. And we will try to make it so.

For all existence most men have lived in poverty, threatened by hunger. But we dream of a world where all are fed and charged with hope. And we will help to make it so. The ordinary men and women of North Vietnam and South Vietnam—of China and India—of Russia and America—are brave people. They are filled with the same proportions of hate and fear, of love and hope. Most of them want the same things for themselves and their families. Most of them do not want their sons ever to die in battle, or see the homes of others destroyed.

Every night before I turn out the lights to sleep, I ask myself this question: Have I done everything that I can do to unite this country? Have I done everything I can to help unite the world, to try to bring peace and hope to all the peoples of the world? Have I done enough?

Ask yourselves that question in your homes and in this hall tonight. Have we done all we could? Have we done enough? We may well be living in the time foretold many years ago when it was said: "I call heaven and earth to record this day against you, that I have set before you life and death, blessing and cursing: therefore choose life, that both thou and thy seed may live."

This generation of the world must choose: destroy or build, kill or aid, hate or understand.

We can do all these things on a scale never dreamed before.

We will choose life. And so doing we will prevail over the enemies within man, and over the natural enemies of all mankind.

22

The Tet Offensive

LARRY BERMAN *

On the night of January 31, 1968, the Lunar New Year, or Tet, the National Liberation Front (NLF) attacked every major city, provincial capital, and military base in South Vietnam. The targets included the U.S. embassy in Saigon. True, the NLF held most of the cities only briefly before abandoning them, and only Hue remained in their control for a month. There were heavy casualties on both sides. The offensive had a crucial impact on the U.S. resolve to continue its war effort and led to President Johnson's decision not to run for re-election. In the article reproduced below, Larry Berman discusses the debate in Washington, D.C., on whether the United States should wind down its participation in the consuming conflict. The Tet Offensive of January 1968 was clearly the turning point in the Vietnam conflict.

Professor Larry Berman, Director of the University of California Washington Center and Professor of Political Science at the University of California–Davis is one of the most eminent scholars on the American presidency, particularly in regard to foreign policy. He has written several books on the U.S. role in the Vietnam conflict. The article reproduced below is arguably the clearest analysis of the Tet Offensive, both of the event itself and its impact on the future course of U.S. engagement in Vietnam.

~

*Larry Berman, "The Tet Offensive," in *The Tet Offensive,* ed. Marc J. Gilbert and William Head (Westport, CT: Praeger, 1996), pp. 17–44.

I just don't understand it. Am I that far off? Am I wrong? Has something
happened to me? My wife said, I think so. But she said you don't know
what year you are living in. This is '68.

—Remarks by President Lyndon Johnson to a
congressional delegation in the White House, January 30, 1968

On January 11, 1968, U.S. intelligence detected a buildup of forces in the
Laotian panhandle west of the demilitarized zone, threatening the marine
base at Khe Sanh in western Quang Tri Province of South Vietnam. Khe Sanh
was located eight miles east of Laos and eighteen miles south of the DMZ
(Demilitarized Zone). The base occupied a strategically important location
for the purposes of hindering enemy infiltration down the Ho Chi Minh Trail
as well as providing a staging post for possible operations into Laos.

The enemy force buildup of two additional North Vietnamese divisions
was incontrovertible, but Hanoi's motives were wildly disputed. Prisoner
reports and captured documents revealed that a massive winter-spring offensive was being planned. Truck traffic down the Ho Chi Minh Trail had
reached massive proportions and major North Vietnamese troop reinforcements were in the border areas. Was Hanoi merely setting the stage for negotiations or was the offensive intended to topple the government of South
Vietnam? What was the enemy up to? General William Westmoreland believed a maximum military effort was under way, possibly to improve
chances of achieving an end to the war through negotiations which would
lead to a coalition government involving the NLF. Hanoi's major offensive
also might have been aimed at achieving one major psychological victory in
the United States prior to the start of the presidential campaign.

The enemy was finally coming to Westmoreland for battle. This would
not be search and destroy in the jungle. Years of waiting for the enemy were
almost over, and even though U.S. forces were significantly outnumbered,
Westmoreland cabled Wheeler on January 12 that a withdrawal from Khe
Sanh was unthinkable. "I consider this area critical to us from a tactical
standpoint as a launch base for Special Operations Group teams and as
flank security for the strong point obstacle system; it is even more critical
from a psychological viewpoint. To relinquish this area would be a major
propaganda victory for the enemy. Its loss would seriously affect Vietnamese and US morale. In short, withdrawal would be a tremendous step
backwards."

With 15,000–20,000 North Vietnamese reinforcements circling Khe Sanh,
Westmoreland hit the lure by ordering the 6,000 marine troops to defend
the garrison. General Westmoreland also set in motion plans for imple-
menting Operation Niagara (evoking an image of cascading bombs and

shells), which became the most intense and successful application of aerial firepower yet seen in the war.

During the predawn hours of January 21, 1968, Khe Sanh came under constant rocket and mortar fire. The battle was on and it appeared to President Johnson and his principal advisors that the North Vietnamese envisioned Khe Sanh as a potential Dien Bien Phu. During a January 23 White House meeting with members of the Democratic leadership, the president reported that "intelligence reports show a great similarity between what is happening at Khe Sanh and what happened at Dien Bien Phu." Johnson became preoccupied with the Khe Sanh–Dien Bien Phu analogy. He had a sand-table model of Khe Sanh plateau constructed in the bunkerlike Situation Room of the White House. He feared that Khe Sanh would be his "Dinbinphoo," as LBJ was prone to pronounce it.

The Khe Sanh–Dien Bien Phu analogy was fraught with historical misapplication. The actual siege of Dien Bien Phu had lasted fifty-six days. The French forces included Montagnards, North Africans, Vietnamese, and Foreign Legionnaires. The total force was about 13,000 and casualties amounted to 1,100 killed, 1,600 missing, and 4,400 wounded. The Viet Minh totaled 49,500 combat troops plus 55,000 support troops. At Khe Sanh, U.S. forces numbered 6,000 Americans versus an enemy strength of about 20,000. The enemy's advantage was less than four to one rather than eight to one as it was at Dien Bien Phu (including support troops). Moreover, usable supplies parachuted into Dien Bien Phu averaged about 100 tons per day; General Westmoreland had a capability of 600 tons per day. The French possessed 75 combat aircraft and 100 supply and reconnaissance aircraft. By comparison, the United States had more than 2,000 aircraft and 3,300 helicopters.

Uncertainty about the military situation at Khe Sanh led LBJ to question the Joint Chiefs. At a meeting on January 29 the president requested that each member submit "his views concerning the validity of the strategy now pursued in South Vietnam by the Free World Forces." The declassified meeting notes show that LBJ asked the Chiefs "if they were completely in agreement that everything has been done to assure that General Westmoreland can take care of the expected enemy offensive against Khe Sanh." General Wheeler and the Joint Chiefs "agreed that everything which had been asked for had been granted and that they were confident that General Westmoreland and the troops were prepared to cope with any contingency."

It was during this period that Johnson, finding it difficult to sleep, would walk the halls of the White House or call down to the Situation Room for a report on Khe Sanh. Secretary of State Dean Rusk recalled that "we couldn't break him of the habit, even for health reasons, of getting up at 4:30 or 5:00

every morning to go down to the operations room and check on the casualties from Vietnam, each one of which took a little piece out of him."

An NSC (National Security Council) staff assistant, Major Robert Ginsburgh, frequently found himself on night watch at the Situation Room in the basement of the White House. The Situation Room was actually two rooms—one windowless room with a long table for private meetings, the other an active hub of communications with AP, UPI, and Reuters teletypes. Four clocks were mounted on the wall—Washington, Greenwich mean time, Saigon, and the official presidential time which followed LBJ. The room also contained three television sets, burn gags, and other forms of technology befitting a White House communications center—especially a telephone. Ginsburgh recalled that during the battle for Khe Sanh, "I had the night-time watch. And so, every two hours I was either in touch with the President on the phone, that is, he would call me or I would have sent him a message, a little memo to try and preclude his calling. He wanted to know, how is it going, what is happening?"

Johnson wanted to know how things were going because he was running out of trust for those who had brought him to this point. Johnson later denied pressuring the Chiefs, but the declassified record contradicts his position. Meeting on February 2 with White House correspondents, the president discussed the JCS assurances about Khe Sanh. "I asked the JCS to give me a letter saying that they were ready for the offensive at Khe Sanh." Yet, when reporters wrote that Johnson had obtained these letters from the Chiefs, the president vehemently denied the claim.

The president then asked his assistant Tom Johnson to review all meeting notes to see whether there was any proof to the charge. Tom Johnson soon wrote the president:

> I have reviewed all of the notes of meetings held during the past two weeks. In addition, I have searched my memory thoroughly. . . . At no time do my notes show, or my memory recall, an incident when the President said: "I do not want any Damn Dien Bien Phu." The President said we wanted to make sure we had done everything here and the JCS had done everything to make certain there is not another Dien Bien Phu. The word "damn" was not used in any meeting I attended in this context. Never did the President say he had made each Chief sign a paper stating that he believed Khe Sanh could be defended.

LBJ could thus claim that he had neither said "damn" nor "each"; but he had made the Dien Bien Phu analogy as well as requiring "the Chiefs" to sign a paper.

During a particularly contentious morning meeting on January 30 with
the Democratic congressional leadership, Senator Byrd remarked, "I am
very concerned about the buildup at Khe Sanh. I have been told that we
have 5,000 troops there compared with 40,000 enemy troops. Are we prepared for this attack?" The president responded:

> This has been a matter of great concern to me. I met with the Joint Chiefs
> yesterday. I went around the table and got their answer to these questions. In
> addition, I have it in writing that they are prepared. I asked, "Have we done
> all we should do?" They said yes. I asked, "Are we convinced our forces are
> adequate?" They said yes. I asked should we withdraw from Korea. They
> said no, that Khe Sanh is important to us militarily and psychologically.

General Wheeler sought to provide clarification for Byrd's queries:

> On the matter of your question, Senator Byrd, about 5,000 U.S. troops ver-
> sus 40,000 enemy troops. Khe Sanh is in very rugged areas. There are 5,900
> U.S. troops in the Khe Sanh Garrison. There are support troops including
> 26th Marines and a battalion of the ARVN. . . . There are 39,968 friendly
> forces versus 38,590 enemy forces. Roughly, there are 40,000 allied troops to
> match the 40,000 enemy. We think we are ready to take on any contingency.
> In addition, there are 40 B-52 sorties and 500 tactical air sorties in the area
> Niagara each day hitting the enemy. . . . General Westmoreland is confident
> he can hold the position. To abandon it would be to step backward. The
> Joint Chiefs agree with General Westmoreland. The Joint Chiefs believe that
> he can hold and that he should hold. General Westmoreland considers it an
> opportunity to inflict heavy casualties on North Vietnam. We have 6,000
> men there, and 34,000 available. It is 40,000 versus 40,000.

A week later during a White House meeting of the principals the president again asked Wheeler, "Are you as confident today as you were yester-
day that we can handle the situation at Khe Sanh?" General Wheeler
answered, "I do not think the enemy is capable of doing what they have set
out to do. General Westmoreland has strengthened his position. He has
contingency plans and can meet any contingency. There is nothing he has
asked for that he has not been given. Khe Sanh is important to us militarily
and psychologically. It is the anchor of our defensive situation along the
DMZ." Johnson again asked General Wheeler, "Are you sure that you have
everything that is needed to take care of the situation in Khe Sanh?"
Wheeler responded, "Yes, we are. General Westmoreland has been given
everything he has requested."

Tet: Move Forward to Achieve Final Victory

During the early morning hours of January 31 approximately 80,000 North Vietnamese regulars and guerrillas attacked over 100 cities throughout South Vietnam. Tet involved enemy attacks on thirty-five of forty-four province capitals, thirty-six district towns, and many villages and hamlets. Over 80,000 enemy troops were involved in attacks directed against population centers. For weeks prior to the offensive, enemy forces had been infiltrating into Saigon in civilian clothes in preparation for a well-planned campaign of terror. The goal was to achieve a popular uprising against the GVN (government of Vietnam) and to show the American public that the very notion of security was null and void.

Communist forces were given the general order "Move Forward to Achieve Final Victory." Combat orders urged the assaulters to do everything possible to completely liberate the people of South Vietnam. The orders found on captured guerrillas described the Tet strategy as one which would launch "the greatest battle ever fought throughout the history of our country." The infiltrators were exhorted to

> move forward aggressively to carry out decisive and repeated attacks in order to annihilate as many American, Satellite and Puppet troops as possible in conjunction with political struggles and military proselytizing activities. . . . Display to the utmost your revolutionary heroism by surmounting all hardships and difficulties and making sacrifices as to be able to fight continually and aggressively. Be prepared to smash all enemy counter attacks and maintain your revolutionary standpoint under all circumstances. Be resolute in achieving continuous victories and secure the final victory at all costs.

While the attack itself did not surprise the principals, its timing during the Tet holiday truce phasedown did. In Washington, Walt Rostow was called away from a foreign affairs advisors' luncheon to receive news of the offensive. Rostow quickly returned to report, "We have just been informed we are being heavily mortared in Saigon. The Presidential Palace, our BOQ's, the Embassy and the city itself have been hit." General Wheeler did not seem very alarmed:

> It was the same type of thing before. You will remember that during the inauguration the MACV [Military Assistance Command, Vietnam] headquarters was hit. In a city like Saigon people can infiltrate easily. They carry in rounds of ammunition and mortars. They fire and run. It is impossible to

stop this in its entirety. This is about as tough to stop as it is to protect against an individual mugging in Washington, D.C. We have got to pacify all of this area and get rid of the Viet Cong infrastructure. They are making a major effort to mount a series of these actions to make a big splurge at Tet.

But General Westmoreland quickly cabled Admiral Sharp that the enemy attacks constituted more than a D.C. mugging. The enemy

appears to be employing desperation tactics, using NVA troops to terrorize populated areas. He attempted to achieve surprise by attacking during the truce period. The reaction of Vietnamese, US and Free World Forces to the situation has been generally good. Since the enemy has exposed himself, he has suffered many casualties. As of now, they add up to almost 700. When the dust settles, there will probably be more. All my subordinate commanders report the situation well in hand.

Military assessments indicated that the VC suffered a major defeat at Tet. Over half of their committed force was thought to be lost and perhaps a quarter of their whole regular force. Moreover, the Communists failed to achieve what MACV assumed to be the major goal of the attacks on urban centers: the diversion of U.S. forces from Khe Sanh or elsewhere. Nevertheless, the psychological impact of Tet was demoralizing. The enemy demonstrated a capability to enter and attack cities and towns and do vast damage. Bunker cabled Johnson on February 8 that

Hanoi may well have reasoned that in the event that the Tet attacks did not bring the outright victory they hoped for, they could still hope for political and psychological gains of such dimensions that they could come to the negotiating table with a greatly strengthened hand. They may have very well estimated that the impact of the Tet attacks would at the very least greatly discourage the United States and cause other countries to put more pressure on us to negotiate on Hanoi's terms.

The impact on the American public would indeed be great. A front-page photograph in the February 1 New York Times showed three military policemen, rifles in hand, seeking protection behind a wall outside the consular section of the U.S. Embassy in Saigon. The bodies of two American soldiers slain by guerrillas who had raided the compound lay nearby. All nineteen guerrillas had been killed, but not until they had blasted their way into the Embassy and held part of the grounds for six hours. Four M.P.'s, a marine guard, and a South Vietnamese employee were killed in the attack.

President Thieu declared a state of martial law. Yet during a news conference from the Cabinet Room, President Johnson likened Tet to the Detroit riots, asserting "a few bandits can do that in any city."

Meeting with key congressional leaders on January 31, LBJ reviewed the events preceding Tet as well as Khe Sanh:

> The Joint Chiefs, and all the Joint Chiefs, met with me the day before yesterday and assured me that they had reviewed the plans and they thought they were adequate. I told them I thought I almost had to have them sign up in blood because if my poll goes where it has gone, with all the victories, I imagine what it would do if we had a good major defeat. So General Westmoreland and the Joint Chiefs of Staff are sure that we are not anticipating some major activity there that we have not heard about.

General Wheeler then explained to the congressional leaders that Hanoi's military purpose was to draw forces away from the Khe Sanh area. The second objective seemed to be more political, to demonstrate to the South Vietnamese people and the world that the Communists still possessed considerable strength in the country and thereby to shake the confidence of the Vietnamese people in the ability of the government to provide them security, even where they were within areas held by government and U.S. troops:

> A significant thing about this attack is that in many areas, particularly in Saigon, and at Bien Hoa, the attackers were dressed in one of three types of clothing: civilian clothes, military, ARVN military police uniforms, or national police uniforms. Apparently, they gave no attention at all to whether or not they killed civilians. This is a sort of an unusual action for them because they have posed as the protectors of the civilian populace. Apparently this is the effort to reestablish by terror a degree of control over the population.

The meeting of congressional leaders was followed by a cabinet meeting which Johnson opened by acknowledging, "There is a lot of stress and plenty of overtime for us all." The president then engaged in a series of free-flowing remarks in which he came close to blaming the pope for Tet:

> I think I admired President Kennedy most during the Bay of Pigs when he said, "No one is to blame but me." I know that wasn't true. . . . We went into Rome at night and we could have been faced with two million Red demonstrators. The Pope appealed to me. We had no differences, no quarrels. He

said, "I want to do something, anything for peace—can't you give us one extra day of the holiday truce?" General Westmoreland told me how many American lives it would cost, but we did give the Pope his extra day. Now it's hard not to regret the number of boys who were killed. It is now so much worse after the Tet truce. Westmoreland cancelled the Tet truce because the house was on fire. So you look at Pueblo, Khe Sanh, Saigon and you see them all as part of the Communist effort to defeat us out there. We can dodge it by being weak-kneed if we want to. I said at San Antonio that we have gone as far as we could—farther, I might add, than the military wanted. We made it clear how much we want to talk and not bomb, just so long as there is some prompt and productive response. But if you sneak in the night and hit us, we can't stop bombing. Now we have their answer with this new offensive. It just should satisfy every dove who loves peace as much as any mother does.

The president then read excerpts from a memorandum received from Ambassador Bunker, drawing particular attention to a passage recalling Thomas Paine's remark, "[These are the] times that try men's souls. . . . What we attain too cheaply, we esteem too lightly."

Attending the annual presidential prayer breakfast at the Shoreham Hotel, the president sounded weary and burdened by events: "The nights are very long. The winds are very chill. Our spirits grow weary and restive as the springtime of man seems farther and farther away. I can, and I do, tell you that in these long nights your President prays." Indeed, as these personal pressures grew, LBJ sought private solace in late-night prayer at St. Dominic's Church, in southwest Washington. Accompanied only by the Secret Service, the president and his "little monks" would read scriptures and psalms, and sing hymns.

On February 1 Wheeler cabled Sharp and Westmoreland that if there was any validity to the Khe Sanh–Dien Bien Phu comparison, perhaps they should consider "whether tactical nuclear weapons should be used if the situation in Khe Sanh should become that desperate." While Wheeler considered that eventuality unlikely, he requested a list of susceptible targets in the area "which lend themselves to nuclear strikes," and asked "whether some contingency nuclear planning would be in order, and what you would consider to be some of the more significant pros and cons of using tac nukes in such a contingency."

Westmoreland soon responded that "the use of tactical nuclear weapons should not be required in the present situation." However, should the situation change, "I visualize that either tactical nuclear weapons or chemical agents would be active candidates for employment." Adding even more fuel to the credibility-gap fire, Johnson vehemently denied that nuclear weapons had ever been considered. During an emotional February 16 news conference, LBJ stated that it was "against the national interest to carry on discussions about the employment of nuclear weapons with respect to Khe Sanh."

The long-promised light at the end of the tunnel was about to be turned off. Satirist Art Buchwald likened administration optimism to another type of historical revision: "'We have the enemy on the run,' says General Custer at Big Horn. 'It's a desperation move on the part of Sitting Bull and his last death rattle.'" Senator George Aiken wryly remarked, "If this is a failure, I hope the Viet Cong never have a major success." Yet Rostow again wrote Johnson that the degree of Communist terrorism during the Tet period would actually strengthen the South Vietnamese resolve to get even with these terrorists. "There is a chance that South Viet Nam will emerge in the weeks and months ahead with stronger political institutions and a greater sense of nationhood and common destiny than before."

More Troops

General Wheeler understood the severity of Westmoreland's military position. His forces were stretched to their maximum extent and effectiveness. On February 3 Wheeler cabled Westmoreland that "the President asks me if there is any reinforcement or help that we can give you." Receiving no answer, Wheeler tried again on February 8: "Query: Do you need reinforcements? Our capabilities are limited.... However, if you consider reinforcements imperative, you should not be bound by earlier agreements.... United States government is not prepared to accept defeat in Vietnam. In summary, if you need more troops, ask for them."

Westmoreland now cabled Wheeler that there was cause for alarm:

> From a realistic point of view we must accept the fact that the enemy has dealt the GVN a severe blow. He has brought the war to the towns and the cities and has inflicted damage and casualties on the population. Homes have been destroyed, distribution of the necessities of life has been interrupted. Damage has been inflicted to the LOG's and the economy has been decimated. Martial law has been invoked, with stringent curfews in the cities. The people have felt directly the impact of the war.

While U.S. forces had repelled the Communist onslaught and inflicted major losses on the enemy manpower pool, Tet revealed the enemy's courage and great skill in planning and coordination. The enemy had infiltrated

previously secure population centers and exploited the GVN claim of security from attack. There was no general uprising and the enemy did not hold
a single city, although enemy units waged a fierce three-week battle at the
ancient city of Hue, where they occupied the citadel—a nineteenth-century
fortress which shielded the nation's historic imperial palace. Hue, a city of
100,000, was also the traditional center of religious and intellectual life in
Vietnam. After weeks of fighting, U.S. and ARVN forces secured Hue, but
not before some of the worst carnage of the war had been unleashed on its
civilian inhabitants.

Westmoreland cabled Wheeler that enemy activity at Hue and elsewhere
had helped Hanoi to score "a psychological blow, possibly greater in Washington than in South Vietnam, since there are tentative signs that the populace is turning against the Viet Cong as a result of these attacks." The enemy
had also succeeded in temporarily disrupting the South Vietnamese economy, and Westmoreland believed the enemy would continue to strain the
will of the people by maintaining pressure on the populated areas with his
forces already committed. The general also expected another major offensive in the Saigon area, commencing in mid-February.

Meeting with the Democratic congressional leadership at breakfast on
February 6, 1968, the president once again faced tough questions from Senator Byrd: "I am concerned about: 1. that we had poor intelligence; 2. that we
were not prepared for these attacks; 3. we underestimated the morale and vi-
tality of the Viet Cong; 4. we over-estimated the support of the South Vietnamese government and its people." Johnson shot back at Byrd: "I don't
agree with any of that. We knew that they planned a general uprising around
Tet. Our intelligence showed there was a winter-spring offensive planned.
We did not know the precise places that were going to be hit. General
Abrams said the Vietnamese are doing their best. There was no military victory for the Communists. Just look at the casualties and the killed in action."

The discussion then moved to a more general level of political discussion:

Senator Byrd: I have never caused you any trouble in this matter on the
    Hill. But I do have very serious concerns about Vietnam. I think this is
    the place to raise these questions, here in the family.
Congressman Boggs: What about Bob Byrd's charge that we are under-
    estimating the strength of the VC? I personally do not agree with that.
The President: I have never under-estimated the Viet Cong. They are not
    pushovers. I do not think we have bad intelligence or have under-
    estimated the Viet Cong morale.
Senator Byrd: Something is wrong over there.
The President: The intelligence wasn't bad.

Senator Byrd: That does not mean the Viet Cong did not succeed in their efforts. Their objective was to show that they could attack all over the country and they did.

The President: That was not their objective at all.

Senator Byrd: You have been saying the situation with the Viet Cong was one of diminishing morale. When I say you, I mean the Administration.

The President: I personally never said anything of the sort. I am not aware that anyone else has been saying that. What do you think the American people would have done if we had sent in troops and had lost 21,000 of them as the enemy has?

Senator Long: If we had planned to have an uprising in Cuba and you had caused 21,000 men to be lost as the Viet Cong did, I am sure you would have been impeached.

The President: I am of the opinion that criticism is not worth much. I look at all these speeches that are in the *Congressional Record.* I look at all the people who are going around the country saying our policy is wrong. Where do they get us? Nowhere. The popular thing now is to stress the mismanagement of Vietnam. I think there has been very little. I wish Mike (Senator Mansfield) would make a speech on Ho Chi Minh. Nothing is as dirty as to violate a truce during the holidays. But nobody says anything bad about Ho. They call me a murderer. But Ho has a great image.

Senator Byrd: I don't want the President to think that I oppose you. I am just raising these matters.

The President: I don't agree with what you say.

Senator Long: I am happy you raised the point, Bob.

The President: Everybody should say and do what they want to. But we have put our very best men that we have out there. I believe that our military and diplomatic men in the field know more than many of our Congressmen and Senators back here. Anybody can kick a barn down. It takes a good carpenter to build one. I just wish all of you would expose the Viet Cong and Ho. We have got some very crucial decisions coming up. Personally, I think they suffered a severe defeat. But we knew there would be a general uprising, and they did not win any victory. It seems to be an American trait to ask why. I just hope that we don't divert our energies and our talents by criticizing unnecessarily. We've got all we can of this "What's wrong with our country?" Fulbright, Young and Gruening haven't helped one bit.

Senator Byrd: I do not want to argue with the President. But I am going to stick by my convictions. [During a meeting the next day the president left the room to take a call from Senator Byrd. "The President returned to say that the Senator had called to apologize for his criticism at the morning leadership meeting."]

The Tuesday luncheon following Tet revealed frustration among the participants. For the departing secretary of defense, Robert McNamara, the Tet Offensive demonstrated that Hanoi had

more power than we credit them with. I do not think it was a "last-gasp" action. I do think that it represents a maximum effort in the sense that they poured on all of their assets and my guess is that we will inflict a very heavy loss both in terms of personnel and material and this will set them back some but that after they absorb the losses they will remain a substantial force. I do not anticipate that we will hit them so hard that they will be knocked out for an extended period or forced to drop way back in level of effort against us. I do think that it is such a well-coordinated, such an obviously advanced planned operation, that it probably relates to negotiations in some way. I would expect that were they successful here they would then move forward more forcibly on the negotiation front and they are thinking they have a stronger position from which to bargain.

Johnson wanted to know what should be done militarily to sock it to the enemy. McNamara argued that the Joint Chiefs possessed no answer:

I have talked to the Chiefs about some kind of a reciprocal action—retaliation for their attack on our Embassy or in retaliation for their attack across the country. There just isn't anything the Chiefs have come up with that is worth trying. They talk about an area-bombing attack over Hanoi but the weather is terrible. You can't get in there with pinpoint targeting. The only way you could bomb it at all at the present time is area bombing and I would not recommend that to you under any circumstances. They have just not been able to think of retaliation that means anything. My own feeling is that we ought to be able to depend upon our ability to inflict very heavy casualties on them as our proper response and as the message we give to our people.

But the Chiefs did have an answer. In a meeting with the president they proposed removing the restrictions around Hanoi and Haiphong, reducing the circles to three miles around Hanoi and one and one-half miles around Haiphong. Secretary of State Rusk feared that the proposed action "opens up the possibility of large civilian casualties and leads to extensive devastation of the area. From what we have seen in other areas this leads to almost total devastation. What to hit is up to the pilot." Wheeler responded, "We do not advocate attacking the population centers. We never have before, and we don't ask for that now. I admit there will be more civilian destruction, but we will be going after trucks and water craft. They are secure now, but represent genuine military targets." Secretary McNamara challenged Wheeler's logic. "Any attack of this type is very expensive both in the number of U.S. aircraft lost and in civilian destruction. I do not recommend this. The military effect is small and our night time attack capability is small. Civilian casualties will be high. In my judgment, the price is high and the gain is low. The military commanders will dispute all the points I have made except aircraft loss."

Wheeler now placed his cards on the table in a direct rebuttal of Secretary McNamara:

I do not think the effects on the civilian population will be that high. As you know, they have an excellent warning system and most of them go to shelters and tunnels. From that standpoint, civilian loss could be lower than it is in other areas. We have had nothing like this civilian destruction that took place in World War II and Korea. But the targets which are there are military targets of military value. Frankly, this [civilian casualties which might result] does not bother me when I compare it with the organized death and butchery by the North Vietnamese and the Viet Cong during the last two weeks in South Vietnam. All of this relates to the matter of pressure.

Choices had to be made. The president told the Chiefs, "I believe somebody in government should say something. I do not share the view that many people have that we took a great defeat. Our version is not being put to the American people properly. . . . What are we going to do now on these bombing targets?" It was left to the incoming secretary of defense, Clark Clifford, to recommend accepting the Chiefs' proposal. Clifford believed that the Tet Offensive constituted Hanoi's answer to the San Antonio Formula 6 [of September 29, 1967, when Johnson made an offer to halt bombing Vietnam if Hanoi agreed to negotiate]: "I am inclined to resume the bombing in North Vietnam and go ahead with the suggested three mile and one and a-half mile limits. As long as the enemy had demonstrated that they are not going to respond positively we should go ahead with this."

When Rusk and McNamara warned about the need to distinguish restricted from authorized targets, Wheeler showed his discontent: "I am fed up to the teeth with the activities of the North Vietnamese and the Viet Cong. We apply rigid restrictions to ourselves and try to operate in a humanitarian manner with concern for civilians at all times. They apply a double standard. Look at what they did in South Vietnam last week. In addition, they place their munitions inside of populated areas because they think they are safe there."

The effects of Tet were discussed at a February 7 National Security Council meeting. Dialogue among the principals revealed the continuing uncertainty concerning enemy capabilities and U.S. military strategy:

Secretary Rusk: What about the possibility of the MIGs attacking a carrier?

General Wheeler: No, I do not think this is likely. The carriers do have air caps and are distant from the MIG bases.

The President: Go in and get those MIGs at Phuc Yen.

General Wheeler: We will as soon as the weather permits.

Secretary McNamara: The MIGs would have negligible military effects but they would have spectacular psychological impact. We do get the feeling that something big is ahead. We do not exactly know what it is, but our commanders are on alert.

The President: I want all of you to make whatever preparations are necessary. Let's know where we can get more people if we need to move additional ones in.

General Wheeler: I have a preliminary list on my desk. I am not satisfied with it.

Secretary McNamara: This would include Army, Navy, Air Force and Marine units.

The President: What about the allies?

General Wheeler: The Australians are incapable of providing more troops. The problems in Korea are such that it will be hard to get the South Koreans to even send the light division they had promised. The Thai troops are in training and to move them in now would be more detrimental than helpful.

The President: So it would be only Americans? Well, I want you to know exactly where you could get them, where they are located now and what we need to do. Get whatever emergency actions ready that will be necessary.

Secretary McNamara: All we would recommend at this time are the three items we had discussed earlier. There may be some increase in draft calls but this would have no immediate effect.

The President: Do we have adequate hospitals and medical personnel?

General Wheeler: We have ample space, ample supplies, and enough doctors for the present.

Secretary McNamara: There are 6,400 military beds. Of that, 2,900 are occupied by U.S. troops and 1,100 by Vietnamese civilians. So we have an additional capacity of about 2,400.

The President: Look at this situation carefully. If we have another week like this one, you may need more.

Secretary Rusk: How do you interpret their use of tanks?

General Wheeler: They had to bring them all the way from Hanoi. This shows that this plan has been in staging since September. It represents a real logistic feat. They want to create maximum disruption.

Director Marks: Could they do anything at Cam Ranh Bay?

General Wheeler: They could. On this last attack, we caught frogmen in there. They could put rockets in the hills and fire on to the base.

The President: How many of the 25,000 killed were North Vietnamese Regulars?

General Wheeler: Approximately 18,000 were of a mixed variety of South Vietnamese enemy. Approximately 6,000 to 7,000 were North Vietnamese.

The President: How do things look at Khe Sanh? Would you expect to have to move out of Lang [Vie]?

General Wheeler: It was not planned that we would hold some of these outposts. We may have to move back that company on Hill 861.

The President: Bob, are you worried?

Secretary McNamara: I am not worried about a true military defeat.

General Wheeler: Mr. President, this is not a situation to take lightly. This is of great military concern to us. I do think that Khe Sanh is an important position which can and should be defended. It is important to us tactically and it is very important to us psychologically. But the fighting will be very heavy, and the losses may be high. General Westmoreland will set up the forward field headquarters as quickly as possible. He told me this morning that he has his cables and his communications gear in. He is sending a list of his needs, including light aircraft. We are responding to this request.

The President: Let's get everybody involved on this as quickly as possible. Everything he wants, let's get it to him.

Stalemate in Vietnam

The shocking depiction of enemy strategy for Tet led Rostow to the conclusion that "it is time for a war leader speech instead of a peace-seeker speech." The speech offered a way to "slay the credibility-gap dragon with one blow or rather with one speech." Writing to the president on February 8, Rostow made the following observations and recommendations:

> It is, I think, also the time to say plainly that hard fighting and heavy casualties lie ahead. They do, and the way to minimize their impact on American public opinion is to acknowledge them in advance and set the national tone by a call for steadiness and resolution. Finally, sooner or later, we are going to have to take on the peace issue squarely. There is a widespread assumption in the country, even among those who support our policy, that peace requires only that the right button can be found to push—the right gimmick discovered. This is, of course, naive. But it furnishes the basis for what will probably be a growing issue as the year proceeds. The serious opposition will not call for a pull-out from Vietnam. They will, instead, promise to do it better. They will say you cannot find the right button—and they will imply they can. We can defuse this issue by saying plainly that there can be no peace because the enemy still wants war. And those who talk of peace only cause the enemy to redouble his attacks on our men in Vietnam.

President Johnson would need all the help he could muster. On February 7 Major General W. E. DePuy provided General Wheeler with an assessment entitled "The Meaning of the Communist Offensive in Vietnam." In an effort to achieve a popular uprising against the government, the enemy had sent his VC main, local, and guerrilla forces against the GVN at every level simultaneously. DePuy offered a chilling analysis of the enemy manpower situation: "It seems that he is pushing all his chips into the middle of the table. Ours are there also. It is not credible to think in terms of a peak of effort followed by subsidence and a return to the status quo ante. Vietnam will never be the same again."

The Senate Foreign Relations Committee had just published Senator Joseph Clark's report based on a recent study mission to South Vietnam. *Stalemate in Vietnam* constituted a singularly powerful indictment of U.S. policy. The report concluded that "the war in Vietnam is at a stalemate which neither side can convert into a military victory without leaving the country—and perhaps the world—in ruins." America's national unity was threatened by the divisiveness of convictions on the war, creating a condition whereby "the political fabric of our society is at the tearing point." Senator Clark believed that Vietnam had become "a cancer" which threatened to destroy our country. "Never, never again," concluded the senator, "should we commit a ground army on the mainland of Asia."

The president had clearly been shaken by recent events, and during a White House meeting of the principals he told his advisors, "Well, it looks as if all of you have counseled, advised, consulted and then—as usual—placed the monkey on my back again." Johnson believed he could lose Vietnam:

> I do not like what I am smelling from those cables from Vietnam and my discussions with outside advisers. We know the enemy is likely to hit the cities again. They will likely have another big attack and there undoubtedly will be surprises. I want you to lay out for me what we should do in the minimum time to meet a crisis request from Vietnam if one comes. Let's assume we have to have more troops. I think we should now tell the allies that we could lose Southeast Asia without their help.

The president's meeting on February 8 with the Joint Chiefs revealed perceptions of a deteriorating military situation. Westmoreland needed an immediate deployment of 45,000 men to meet a similar increase in enemy strength. But if the enemy had been losing men, why did Westmoreland need the increment? Had the enemy suffered erosion over the last few months? Was Hanoi planning for a psychological victory prior to negotiations? Did the enemy have sufficient strength to renew the attacks? What strength did the ARVN possess to resist these attacks?

The president first asked Wheeler, "What is the ARVN strength?" General Wheeler responded, "Approximately 360,000 men now. Total forces about 600,000." The discussion then turned to the enemy's strength. Since it appeared that few North Vietnamese regular forces had been utilized for the Tet attack, how many guerrillas and irregulars (recently moved from OB) were still available as reserves or replacements? Secretary Rusk explained to Johnson that "I have been asking for several days if there was a new order of battle. This is the first time that I have heard of this."

LBJ instructed the Chiefs to "work up all the options and let's review them together. I want you to hope for the best and plan for the worst. Let's consider the extensions, call ups, and use of specialists. Dean, should we have more than the Tonkin Gulf resolution in going into this? Should we ask for a declaration of war?" The secretary answered, "Congressional action on individual items would avoid the problems inherent in a generalized declaration. I do not recommend a declaration of war. I will see what items we might ask the Congress to look at." President Johnson persisted, "What would be the impact internationally of a declaration of war?" Rusk responded that "it might be a direct challenge to Moscow and Peking in a way we have never challenged them before. There would be very severe international effects."

At this point in the meeting, Clark Clifford, soon to be confirmed as the new secretary of defense, interjected with a series of questions concerning what he saw as historical and institutional schizophrenia:

> There is a very strong contradiction in what we are saying and doing. On one hand, we are saying that we have known of this build-up. We now know the North Vietnamese and Viet Cong launched this type of effort in the cities. We have publicly told the American people that the communist offensive was (a) not a victory, (b) produced no uprising among the Vietnamese in support of the enemy, and (c) cost the enemy between 20,000 and 25,000 of his combat troops. Now our reaction to all of that is to say that the situation is more dangerous today than it was before all of this. We are saying that we need more troops, that we need more ammunition and that we need to call up the reserves. I think we should give some very serious thought to how we explain saying on one hand the enemy did not take a victory and yet we are in need of many more troops and possibly an emergency call-up.

The president, clearly shaken by Clifford's remarks, offered the following observation: "The only explanation I can see is that the enemy has changed its tactics. They are putting all of their stack in now. We have to be prepared for all that we might face. Our front structure is based on estimates of their front structure. Our intelligence shows that they have changed and added about 15,000 men. In response to that, we must do likewise. That is the only explanation I see."

The meeting ended with Secretary Rusk pointing out the contradiction in U.S. strategy. "In the past, we have said the problem really was finding the enemy. Now the enemy has come to us. I am sure many will ask why aren't we doing better under these circumstances, now that we know where they are."

Johnson's own frustrations were evident during his next meeting with the Joint Chiefs. In this instance LBJ appears close to the caricature of an embattled and unyielding president:

The President: All last week I asked two questions. The first was "Did Westmoreland have what he needed?" (You answered yes.) The second question was, "Can Westmoreland take care of the situation with what he has there now?" The answer was yes. Tell me what has happened to change the situation between then and now?

General Wheeler: I have a chart which was completed today based on a very complete intelligence analysis. It relates to all of South Vietnam, Laos and the area around the DMZ. It shows the following: Since December the North Vietnamese infantry has increased from 78 battalions to 105 battalions. Estimating there are 600 men per battalion that is approximately 15,000 men. This represents a substantial change in the combat ratios of U.S. troops to enemy troops. This ratio was 1.7 to 1 in December. It is 1.4 to 1 today. In the DMZ and I Corps area, there is a 1 to 1 ratio. There are 79 enemy battalions in the 1st Corps area (60 North Vietnamese and 19 Viet Cong). In the same area there are 82 Free World battalions (42 U.S.; 4 Free World; and 36 ARVN). This is about 1 to 1.

The President: What you are saying is this. Since last week we have information we did not know about earlier. This is the addition of 15,000 North Vietnamese in the northern part of the country. Because of that, do we need 15 U.S. battalions?

General Wheeler: General Westmoreland told me what he was going to put in tonight's telegram. This is the first time he has addressed the matter of additional troops.

Paul Nitze: I was not aware of this new intelligence.

General Wheeler: The last report was that there was approximately 15,000 enemy near and around Khe Sanh. As of today, our estimates range between 16,000 and 25,000. Their infantry has been built up.

During a February 10 meeting of foreign policy advisors, Secretary Rusk was still puzzled about enemy strength: "I can't find out where they say those 15,000 extra enemy troops came from. They say that these battalions came in between December and January." The president responded that "the Chiefs see a basic change in the strategy of the war. They say the enemy has escalated from guerrilla tactics to more conventional warfare." Clark Clifford added another perspective: "All we have heard is about the preparation the North Vietnamese have made for the attack at Khe Sanh. I have a feeling that the North Vietnamese are going to do something different. I believe our people were surprised by the 24 attacks on the cities last week. God knows the South Vietnamese were surprised with half of their men on holiday. There may be a feint and a surprise coming up for us."

Order of Battle

Westmoreland cabled Wheeler and Sharp concerning the high number of enemy casualties during Tet. How, for example, could the enemy have absorbed such a high number in light of their manpower shortages? The high enemy casualty figures had caused a great deal of consternation for MACV.

The enemy committed virtually every VC unit in the country regardless of combat effectiveness and regardless of normal area of operations. They were committed with do-or-die orders, forbidden to retreat, and with no withdrawal or rallying plans. The enemy attacks might be described as a country-wide series of "Loc Ninhs." The very high casualties are not strange in this light. We cannot, of course, provide a very precise breakdown of casualties by type of enemy force.

Westmoreland then tried to deflect any insinuation that irregulars might have been involved. "I do not doubt that some of the enemy's casualties were guerrillas, porters, and such, but the percentage will probably be small. Thus, the enemy obviously banked heavily on surprise in its Tet offensive. This may account for minimal participation by guerrillas."

On February 11, 1968, Rostow forwarded the most recent order of battle estimates to President Johnson. MACV's figures for the period December–January reflected "no significant change" in the confirmed strength of main force and local force combat units. Rostow explained to LBJ that changes had occurred in the listing of non-combat elements such as combat support and administrative support, which involved "a bookkeeping character which do not really reflect changes in the enemy's combat potential."

Once again, MACV's statistics proved the United States was winning the war. CIA analyst Sam Adams wrote his colleague George Carver, the CIA's primary in-house expert on Vietnam, requesting a transfer from SAVA (Special Assistant for Vietnamese Affairs):

I do not feel that SAVA has been sufficiently diligent in bringing to the attention of the intelligence community the numerical and organizational strength of our adversaries in Vietnam. . . . I feel we (the CIA in general and SAVA in particular) have basically misinformed policy makers of the strength of the enemy. The pressures on the CIA and on SAVA, I realize, have been enormous. Many of the pressures—but not all—have originated from MACV, whose Order of Battle is a monument of deceit. The Agency's and the office's failing concerning Viet Cong manpower, I feel, has been its acquiescence to MACV half-truths, distortions, and sometimes outright falsehoods. We have occasionally protested, but neither long enough, nor loud enough.

Carver shared Adams's viewpoint, and he now recommended reopening the OB [Order of Battle controversy of 1967 when the CIA estimates of enemy strength in South Vietnam challenged the much higher figure advanced by MAC–V] debate in order to realistically reassess the enemy's overall capabilities. Excluding from the numerical military order of battle all Communist components other than main and local forces, and administrative service and guerrillas, strictly defined, had been an error. CIA analysts strongly suspected that many of the Communist forces in Tet were drawn from secret self-defense components, perhaps the assault youth, and other elements written out of the order of battle because they had no military significance.

A CIA Directorate of Intelligence memorandum of February 21 which analyzed the Communist units participating in attacks during the Tet Offensive concluded that if MACV's latest estimates were correct, the enemy would have committed over 50 percent of their regular force to battle. "If the reported losses of 32,500 killed in action and 5,500 detained applied solely to the VC/NVA regular forces, the commands would have lost more than 65% of the forces committed to the Tet offensive. This would have been a devastating blow. However, there are a number of pieces of evidence which suggest that such an interpretation would overstate the Communist manpower drain." What were these factors? The VC/NVA forces participating at Tet were augmented by large numbers of guerrillas operating in independent units or integrated into local force units. Moreover, prior to Tet the VC had actively recruited additional laborers and civilians, who almost certainly constituted the higher proportion of casualties during the offensive.

Wheeler's Ploy for More Troops and Mobilization

Wheeler had twice asked Westmoreland if, in the wake of Tet, he needed more troops. On February 12, 1968, Westmoreland cabled Sharp and Wheeler with his assessment of the military situation and force requirements in Vietnam. Westmoreland emphasized that the enemy "had launched a major campaign signaling a change of strategy of protracted war to one of quick military/political victory during the American election year." The enemy had failed to secure the border areas or to initiate a public uprising.

Westmoreland now argued that since the enemy had changed his strategy,

We are now in a new ball game where we face a determined, highly disciplined enemy, fully mobilized to achieve a quick victory. He is in the process of throwing in all his "military chips to go for broke." We cannot permit this. . . . I have approximately 500,000 US troops and 60,981 free world military assistance troops. Further contributions from the Thais and Koreans are months away. I have been promised 525,000 troops, which according to present programs will not materialize until 1969. I need these 525,000 troops now. It should be noted that this ceiling assumed the substantial replacement of military by civilians, which now appears impractical. I need reinforcements in terms of combat elements. . . . Time is of the essence. . . . I must stress equally that we face a situation of great opportunity as well as heightened risk. However, time is of the essence here, too. I do not see how the enemy can long sustain the heavy losses which his new strategy is enabling us to inflict on him. Therefore, adequate reinforcements should permit me not only to contain his I Corps offensive but also to capitalize on his losses by seizing the initiative in other areas. Exploiting this opportunity could materially shorten the war.

In addition to the previously authorized 525,000, Westmoreland requested an additional six battalions (10,500) for resuming offensive operations against a weakened enemy. Wheeler wrote to President Johnson that Westmoreland "does not know how sacrosanct that (525,000) figure is." Moreover, "he does not anticipate 'defeat,' but he desperately needs the troop elements requested in order to capitalize on opportunities available to him. . . . If requested troops are not made available, he would have to undertake an unacceptably risky course of drawing additional forces from elsewhere in South Vietnam."

The Joint Chiefs rejected Westmoreland's request for the 10,500 (a request which their chairman had pressed on Westmoreland) on grounds that U.S. military manpower requirements were at their limit; any further authorizations without a mobilization of reserves might erase even minimal levels of readiness for other military contingencies. Wheeler's ploy had been to use the Tet crisis as justification for reconstituting the strategic reserve. The 10,500 was a minor issue compared to mobilization. Wheeler had tried to force Johnson's hand into accepting a reserve call-up. Having encouraged Westmoreland to make the request, Wheeler then rejected it on grounds that U.S. forces were already pushed to their limits. Wheeler's plan backfired; the commander in chief rejected the JCS recommendation and directed the deployment of the 10,500 troops to South Vietnam.

President Johnson was very worried about the political costs of mobilization. Would the new units be used as reinforcements in Vietnam, for contingencies outside Vietnam, or to reassure NATO allies that the United States would meet its military commitments? Johnson worried about the size of the call-up and whether it could be diminished by reducing overseas garrisons in Europe or Korea. What were the budgetary implications of these actions?

Before making any decisions, the president ordered Wheeler to Vietnam for an on-the-spot report of Westmoreland's manpower needs, but the general's visit was delayed one week because the Senate Foreign Relations Committee was holding hearings on the 1964 Tonkin Gulf incident and Wheeler was needed in Washington. President Johnson's political standing was now plummeting. A Gallup poll conducted in early February showed that only 41 percent of the nation's adults approved of the president's handling of his job.

Explaining the Unacceptable

It now appeared unavoidable that Johnson would have to mobilize the reserves. The enemy had shaken U.S. and world opinion with its offensive, and the government of South Vietnam was tottering on the brink of insolvency. Rostow tried to nudge Johnson toward a positive decision: "Only you can make the political assessment of what it would cost to call up the reserves; but that would be the most impressive demonstration to Hanoi and its friends." Rostow believed that the issue needed to be handled carefully, particularly with respect to explaining mobilization in terms of past statements of progress: "We are sending men to assure Westy the reserves he needs; we are calling up reserves to make sure no one gets the idea that we can't handle our other world commitments."

Doubts about military strategy were emerging from all quarters. In a message communicated directly to the president, former president Eisenhower expressed personal support for a reserve call-up. The fact that Westmoreland was only asking for 10,500 suggested to Eisenhower that MACV did not have enough troops to fight the kind of campaign necessary to win the war and that U.S. forces were so scattered and committed that "we cannot hit the enemy when he concentrates, for example, around Khe Sanh." Eisenhower asked, "Has Westmoreland really been given the forces he is asking for; if he has asked for 525,000 men why didn't we send them sooner, and are we going to have enough in the area to provide a 'corps of maneuver'?" Eisenhower continued, "He said that moving a relatively small force of this size sounds as though we have been on a shoestring, suggests weakness on our part to the enemy, and gives the critics of what we are doing in Vietnam a target."

Ambassador Taylor also possessed grave doubts on the military situation in South Vietnam, and he endorsed the Joint Chiefs' proposal on grounds that the possibilities of an unpleasant surprise in Korea or elsewhere in the Far East were sufficiently acute "that it is an act of prudence to move additional

ground forces to the area as rapidly as possible." Taylor believed a call-up
of reserves was justified by the military requirement and that, in addition,
it would have some political-psychological value in demonstrating to the
world, including Hanoi, that the United States meant business. "It would
also serve as a reminder to our people at home that, while we are not technically at war, we are in a situation of similar emergency which places on
our citizens duties and responsibilities analogous to those in a state of declared war."

General Westmoreland's decision to hold Khe Sanh now came under
careful scrutiny. The occupation of Khe Sanh had been premised on establishing a forward operating base against infiltration routes in eastern Laos.
But, there had been little effect on infiltration from Laos. Moreover, General Westmoreland did not argue strongly for the defense of Khe Sanh because of its present value in relation to impeding infiltration routes or in the
defense of major areas of the northern provinces. Instead, his cables stressed
rather the difficulty of getting out of Khe Sanh and the adverse psychological effects of a withdrawal upon South Vietnam and upon the American
people. What was the military importance of maintaining Khe Sanh? Why
not withdraw and redeploy the troops? Maxwell Taylor wrote LBJ that
"whatever the past value of the position, it is a positive liability now. We are
allowing the enemy to arrange at his leisure a set-piece attack on ground
and in weather favorable to him and under conditions which will allow us
little opportunity to punish him except by our air power."

Taylor urged LBJ to have the Joint Chiefs instruct Westmoreland to pull
out. Rostow then weighed in with the opinion "that Khe Sanh probably can
be held but that it will be at a heavy price in terms of casualties and in terms
of other ground troops necessary to support and reinforce it. I have real
doubt that we can afford such a defense in view of the limited reserves
which General Westmoreland is likely to have in the time frame during
which these events may take place."

It was evident that Westmoreland needed direction from Washington,
and Rostow explained to LBJ that "I would feel greatly relieved if the Joint
Chiefs of Staff would see fit to send General Westmoreland guidance
which would provide Westmoreland with a way out of Khe Sanh." For example, the Chiefs might suggest that "it is less clear that its present value
now justifies the cost of an all-out defense." Perhaps Westmoreland could
be persuaded to reassess the feasibility or desirability of withdrawing from
Khe Sanh.

The president decided to stand by his field commander's judgment.
Moreover, he instructed Clark Clifford to draft a statement of unequivocal

support to General Westmoreland—but support which left Westmoreland a way out of a no-win situation:

> The President wants General Westmoreland to know that he has freedom of action to conduct his military operations as he thinks wise from a military point of view without being inhibited by political or psychological factors originating in the United States. To the extent that such factors in South Vietnam itself are an important part of the struggle, General Westmoreland should take those into account in close consultation with Ambassador Bunker and President Thieu.
>
> Specifically with regard to Khe Sanh, the President does not wish to inhibit General Westmoreland's judgment as to when, where and under what circumstances he wishes to fight his battles. When the President became convinced that General Westmoreland intended to defend Khe Sanh, the President threw himself into the task of insuring that General Westmoreland had the means to do so successfully. He further sought the judgment of the Joint Chiefs of Staff both as to the desirability and capability of defending Khe Sanh. This interest on the part of the President should not be interpreted, however, as a directive from the Commander in Chief to defend Khe Sanh under all circumstances if, in General Westmoreland's judgment, it is better to have his battle somewhere else. The purpose of this message is not to export to General Westmoreland the responsibility for events which are inherent in the responsibilities of the Commander in Chief. The President just wants General Westmoreland to know the General has his fullest confidence and does not want his hands tied by the build-up of irrelevant factors on the home front in a way that would cause General Westmoreland to make military judgments which are contrary to his best thinking. If General Westmoreland wishes to defend Khe Sanh he will be supported; if he wishes to avoid a major engagement in a fixed position which does not utilize the peculiar mobility of U.S. forces, he will also be supported.

The time for reassessment was fast approaching. With the Senate Foreign Relations Committee's inquiry on Tonkin done, Wheeler flew from Washington to Vietnam. In anticipation of the visit, Maxwell Taylor wrote the president, "Reflecting on the possible objectives of General Wheeler's visit, I would hope that he would obtain answers to some of the fundamental questions which are troubling us, derived from detailed private discussions with General Westmoreland and his staff." Taylor wanted Westmoreland to answer questions on his operational plans, force requirements, and force availabilities. In particular,

What enemy units have been identified in the attacks on the cities? What un-committed units are available for a second cycle? What grounds are there for the allegation of an "intelligence failure" at the time of the first wave of attacks on the cities? How does General Westmoreland feel about the functioning of his own and the Vietnamese intelligence services in connection with this situation? What has been the nature of our psychological warfare activities directed at North Vietnam and the VC since January 30? These are all hard questions for which there are probably no final answers at this time but whatever Bus can bring back will be most helpful.

On February 24, Rostow wrote LBJ that the enemy was preparing to make a total effort "with all their capital soon. They will then try to lock us into a negotiation at their peak position before we can counter-attack." Rostow and Taylor both agreed "with Napoleon that Providence is on the other side with the last reserves. Therefore, right now we should be moving out to Westy all the ready forces we have and calling up reserves for: A Vietnam counter-attack; Korean contingency; General purposes, for our world posture." Rostow believed

we face the decisive battle of the war. They will try to dissipate Westy's reserves by simultaneous attacks at a number of places and take Khe Sanh if possible. I am uncertain about timing; but they are so obsessed with memories of 1954 I suspect they will hit soon, get a maximum position, and then force a negotiation, perhaps via the San Antonio formula before the weather opens up for us in I Corps and at Hanoi-Haiphong. The Geneva Conference of 1954 opened on April 26. Dien Bien Phu fell on May 7/8.

While in Vietnam General Wheeler concluded that the last three years had adversely impacted the U.S. worldwide military posture. Something had to be done and Wheeler took responsibility by cabling LBJ at his ranch with the tentative conclusions from his trip to Vietnam. The cable must have ruined Johnson's day. Had Westmoreland not redeployed some of his troops from border areas to urban centers in mid-January, severe setbacks would have occurred. "I will have on my return examples of how narrow the margin was between victory and defeat in certain key areas," Wheeler reported. "The enemy has suffered very substantially, but he still has sizeable uncommitted reserves. He displays a tenacity which we have not seen before in this war."

Wheeler also believed that "Westy's forces are stretched too thin . . . believe that we must reinforce him promptly and substantially." Wheeler's conclusion left Johnson on uncertain ground:

In summary, the military situation continues to be fluid; the enemy is determined and tenacious; troop morale, both U.S. and ARVN, is good; Westy's forces are stretched thin in view of the enemy threat and the courses of action open to the enemy. I do not have any apprehension that we will be run out of the country by military action, but I do believe that to achieve victory we must expand our effort substantially and promptly.

On February 27, 1968, General Wheeler sent LBJ his "Military Solution and Requirements in SVN." The report was based on three days of conferences with Westmoreland and the senior American commander in each of the four corps areas. (Clifford described Johnson "as worried as I have ever seen him," after hearing Wheeler's report.) As Major Andrew Krepinevich later observed,

Wheeler's report reflected the bankruptcy of the Army's strategy. Although in the Tet Offensive the Army had destroyed enemy forces in far greater numbers than in any other period in the war, it had had a negligible impact on the United States' prospects for victory. Hanoi had demonstrated its ability to accept extraordinary losses, without reaching its breaking point. Instead, the enemy had both the capability and the will to continue the struggle indefinitely.

Wheeler now asked for troops. Specifically, MACV needed 205,000 troops in order to regain the strategic initiative. According to Wheeler:

The enemy has undoubtedly been hurt, but he seems determined to pursue his offensive—apparently he has the capability to do so. . . . It is the consensus of responsible commanders that 1968 will be the pivotal year. The war may go on beyond 1968 but it is unlikely that the situation will return to the pre-Tet condition. The forces committed and the tactics involved are such that the advantage will probably swing one way or the other, during the current year. . . . In many areas the pacification program has been brought to a halt. The VC are prowling the countryside, and it is now a question of which side moves fastest to gain control. The outcome is not at all clear. I visualize much heavy fighting ahead.

Casualties would he high. Equipment losses would continue at a high level. ARVN would prove to be shaky under sustained pressure. "If the enemy synchronizes his expected major attacks with increased pressure throughout the country, General Westmoreland's margin will be paper thin. He does not have a theatre reserve. We can expect some cliff-hangers, and with bad luck on weather or some local RVNAF [Republic of Vietnam Armed Forces] failures he may suffer some reverses. For these reasons he is asking for additional forces as soon as possible during this calendar year."

During a February 27 White House meeting attended by Rusk, McNamara, Clifford, Katzenbach, Bundy, Rostow, Califano, and McPherson, debate focused on Westmoreland's still secret request for the 205,000. Clark Clifford, who would shortly be sworn in as secretary of defense, suggested that instead of proceeding incrementally, "another possibility that should be considered—and I am not pushing it—is announcement that we intend to put in 500,000 to a million men." Secretary McNamara responded, "That has the virtue of clarity. Obviously we would have decided to put in enough men to accomplish the job. That and status quo both have the virtue of clarity. I do not understand what the strategy is to putting in 205,000 men. It is neither enough to do the job, nor an indication that our role must change."

The discussion then focused on what really had happened at Tet:

Bundy: We must also prepare for the worst. SVN is very weak. Our position may be truly untenable. Contingency planning should proceed toward possibility that we will withdraw with best possible face and defend rest of Asia. We can say truthfully that Asia is stronger because of what we have done in past few years.

   Katzenbach took call from Habib in Hawaii. Reports Habib is "less optimistic" about political situation in Saigon than he was when he went out. Reports that there is various disagreement in American circles in Saigon over 205,000 request. Bunker has doubts about this.

Rusk: If we have to call up reserves, we should take some of our troops out of Europe. Europeans will have to put some more in for their defense.

McNamara: Agree, if we call 400,000.

State of Military Situation: Rusk, Rostow think enemy took beating in Tet Offensive. Rostow says captured documents show enemy was disappointed, may be unable to mount heavy coordinated attack on cities. Rusk reminds that enemy took 40,000 casualties. No U.S. units out of operation. Rostow says if we can re-enforce Westy now, he should be able to handle situation until good weather comes to I Corps and NVN.

McNamara: What then? Let's not delude ourselves into thinking he cannot maintain pressure after good weather comes.

(Rostow apparently had air attacks in mind. McN: We are dropping ordnance at a higher rate than in last year of WWII in Europe. It has not stopped him.)

Bundy: SVN forces uncertain, but almost certainly not as strong as were before.

Clifford: Look at situation from point of view of American public and Vietnamese. Despite optimistic reports, our people (and world opinion) believe we have suffered a major setback. Problem is, how do we gain support for major program, defense and economic, if we have told people things are going well? How do we avoid creating feeling that we are pounding troops down rat-hole? What is our purpose? What is achievable? Before any decision is made, we must re-evaluate our entire posture in SVN. Unfortunately, Pres. has been at ranch with hawks.

McNamara: Agreed. Decision must not be hasty. Will take a week at least to work out defense and economic measures, if we go big. Wheeler, Habib will meet with Secretaries Wednesday morning at breakfast with President. Decision should certainly not be announced that night.

General Impression: Prevailing uncertainty. Radically different proposals were offered and debated, more rejected out of hand. We are at a point of crisis. McNamara expressed grave doubts over military, economic, political, diplomatic and moral consequences of a large force buildup in SVN. Q is whether these profound doubts will be presented to President.

The doubts would be presented to the president but in a circuitous fashion. During a February 28, 1968, cabinet meeting President Johnson warned cabinet members that

the big problem is the impression we make with the public. . . . We have **to** be careful about statements like Westmoreland's when he came back and said that he saw "light at the end of the tunnel." Now we have the shock of this Tet Offensive. Ho Chi Minh never got elected to anything. . . . He is like Hitler in many ways. . . . But we, the President and the Cabinet, are called murderers and they never say anything about Mr. Ho. The signs are all over here. They all say "Stop the War," but you never see any of them over there. Then he launches the Tet attack, breaks the truce and escalates by firing on 44 cities, all at the time that we are offering bombing pause. It is like the country lawyer who made the greatest speech of his life but they electrocuted the client. We are like that now.

February ended with Johnson fighting back. In his first visit to Dallas since President Kennedy's assassination, he announced that the war had reached a critical turning point and said, "I do not believe we will ever buckle." Flying from his ranch near Austin to attend a convention of the

National Rural Electric Cooperative Association, the president spoke about the war: "There will be blood, sweat and tears shed. The weak will drop from the lines, their feet sore and their voices loud. Persevere in Vietnam we will and we must. There, too, today, we stand at a turning point."

Johnson would need all the help he could get because he was about to lose Middle America. CBS news anchor Walter Cronkite had told a national television audience that the war was stalemated: "We have been too often disappointed by the optimism of the American leaders, both in Vietnam and Washington, to have faith any longer in the silver linings they find in the darkest clouds. . . . For it seems now more certain than ever that the bloody experience of Vietnam is to end in a stalemate. Today, that we are mired in stalemate seems the only realistic, yet unsatisfactory, conclusion."

A television anchorman had declared the war over. After watching the broadcast Johnson concluded, "Cronkite was it." But Johnson was wrong. Cronkite mirrored public opinion; he was not ahead of it. The weeks ahead would lead the president's inner circle of advisors and then Lyndon Johnson to the same conclusions. The initial impetus would be pressure to meet General Westmoreland's troop request. Should the nation's reserves be mobilized? The president appointed his new secretary of defense, Clark Clifford, to head a task force to evaluate General Westmoreland's request. The president's initial instructions to Clifford were "give me the lesser of evils."

23

U. S. Involvement

in Vietnam

NOAM CHOMSKY*

At 8 A.M. on April 30, 1975, the last U.S. Marine helicopter took off from the roof of the American Embassy in Saigon. Less than five hours later, General Minh made the following announcement over the Saigon radio: "I, General Duong Van Minh, President of the Saigon Government, appeal to the armed forces of the Republic of Vietnam to lay down their arms and surrender to the forces of the NLF unconditionally. I declare that the Saigon Government, from central to local level, has been completely dissolved."[1]

For the United States, these events signaled the end of a quarter-century effort to maintain Western domination over all or part of Indochina. For the Vietnamese, it meant that the foreign invaders had finally been repelled and their colonial structures demolished, after more than a century of struggle.

With fitting symmetry, history had come full circle. "The first act of armed intervention by a Western power in Vietnam," according to the Vietnamese historian Truong Buu Lam, "is generally held to have been perpetrated in 1845 by a ship of the United States Navy, the Constitution"[2] in an effort to force the release of a French bishop. The skipper of "Old Ironsides" was Commander John Percival, known as "Mad Jack." Sailors under his command "disembarked at Danang and proceeded to terrorize the local population. . . . United States sailors fired on an unresisting crowd and several dozens were killed" before Mad Jack withdrew in failure.[3] A few

*Noam Chomsky, "U.S. Involvement in Vietnam," *Bridge: An Asian American Perspective* (October-November 1975): 4–21.

years later the French Navy returned and took Da Nang, and in the years that
followed, established their imperial rule over all of Indochina, bringing misery
and disaster. The agronomist Nghiem Xuan Yem wrote in 1945 that under
French colonization "our people have always been hungry . . . so hungry that
the whole population had not a moment of free time to think of anything besides the problem of survival."[4] In the northern parts of the country, two million people are reported to have died of starvation in a few months in 1945.[5]

Throughout this period, resistance never ceased. Early French eyewit-
nesses reported that

> We have had enormous difficulties in imposing our authority in our new
> colony. Rebel bands disturb the country everywhere.[6] The fact was that the
> centre of resistance was everywhere, subdivided to infinity, almost as many
> times as there were Annamese. It would be more exact to consider each
> farmer busy tying up a sheaf of rice as a centre of resistance.[7]

Meanwhile, the French complained, the only collaborators are

> intriguers, disreputable or ignorant, whom we had rigged out with some-
> times high ranks, which became tools in their hands for plundering the
> country without scruple. . . . Despised, they possessed neither the spiritual
> culture nor the moral fibre that would have allowed them to understand and
> carry out their task.[8]

A century later, the imperial overlords had changed, but their complaints
never varied.

The resistance, however, did significantly change its character over the
years:

> At first, the partisans fought to recover the independence of their country to
> avenge their king, and to safeguard their traditional pattern of life. By the
> 1900s, as the occupation developed into a systematic exploitation of the
> colony's economic resources, creating in its wake large-scale social disrup-
> tions, slogans of explicit social and political values were added to the original
> calls for independence from the French. The spontaneous reaction against
> foreigners, the armed struggle to oust them, had grown into a demand for
> revolutionary—political and later social—changes.[9]

The August revolution of 1945, led by the Viet Minh, was the culmination of a struggle of revolutionary nationalism. On September 2, President
Ho Chi Minh proclaimed the independence of Vietnam:

Our people have broken the chains which for a century have fettered us, and have won independence for the Fatherland. Viet Nam has the right to be free and independent and in fact it is so already. The entire Vietnamese people are determined to mobilize all their physical and mental strength, to sacrifice their lives and property, in order to safeguard their freedom and independence.[10]

... It is important to bear in mind that the United States Government was never in any doubt as to the basic facts of the situation in Vietnam. Intelligence reports describe the "intense desire on the part of the Annamese for independence and thorough hatred by them of the French and any other white people who happen to be in any way supporting or sympathizing with the French."[11] The Headquarters of the OSS, China Theatre reported to the Chief of the Intelligence Division on September 19, 1945, that Emperor Bao Dai, in an interview, "stated that he had voluntarily abdicated, and was not coerced by the Provisional Government" because he approved "the nationalistic action of the Viet Minh" and preferred to "live as a private citizen with a free people than rule a nation of slaves." On the same date, the same source reported an interview with Ho Chi Minh, "the president of the Provisional Government of Viet Nam," in which Ho assured him that "his people are prepared for a long struggle of ten or twenty years and are willing to fight for the freedom, not of their own, but of future generations." He reported his personal opinion that "Mr. Ho Chi Minh is a brilliant and capable man, completely sincere in his opinions," and that "when he speaks, he speaks for his people, for I have traveled throughout Tonkin province, and found in that area people of all classes are imbued with the same spirit and determination as their leader." The new government, he reported, "is an outgrowth of the controlling forces in the military resistance"; Viet Nam looks to America for moral support in their struggle, almost expect it." A "personal observation" of October 17 certifies "to the fact that the great mass of the population supports Ho Chi Minh and his party, and to the anti-Japanese action in which they have engaged. . . . In traveling through Tonkin, every village flew the Viet Minh flag . . . the women and children were also organized, and all were enthusiastic in their support." The report continues that American observers "saw how well the majority of the people follow the orders of Ho Chi Minh and the provisional Government" apart from the wealthy merchants and former high Annamese officials.

As for those at the receiving end of these communications, the State Department's assessment of Ho Chi Minh and the Provisional Government of Vietnam was summed up this way by Abbot Low Moffat, the Chief of the Division of Southeast Asian Affairs:

I have never met an American, be he military, OSS, diplomat, or journalist, who had met Ho Chi Minh who did not reach the same belief: that Ho Chi Minh was first and foremost a Vietnamese nationalist. He was also a Communist and believed that Communism offered the best hope for the Vietnamese people. But his loyalty was to his people. When I was in Indochina it was striking how the top echelon of competent French officials held almost unanimously the same view. Actually, there was no alternative to an agreement with Ho Chi Minh or to a crushing of the nationalist groundswell which my own observations convinced me could not be done. Any other government recognized by the French would of necessity be puppets of the French and incapable of holding the loyalty of the Vietnamese people.[12]

Thus, the United States committed itself with its eyes open and with full knowledge of what it was doing to crush the nationalist forces of Indochina. "Question whether Ho as much nationalist as Commie is irrelevant," Secretary of State Dean Acheson explained. Quite the contrary, he urged in May 1949 that "no effort should be spared" to assure the success of the French Quisling government since there seemed to be "no other alternative to estab Commie pattern Vietnam." And on the eve of the Korean war, in March 1950, Acheson observed that French military success "depends, in the end, on overcoming opposition of indigenous population"; we must help the French "to protect IC [Indochina] from further COMMIE encroachments."[13]

Two years earlier, a State Department Policy Statement of September 1948 had spelled out the fundamental "dilemma" which the United States faced in Indochina. It was a "dilemma" which would never cease to haunt American policymakers. The "dilemma" was this. The Communists under Ho Chi Minh had "captur[ed] control of the nationalist movement" thus impeding the "long-term objective" of the United States, namely, "to eliminate so far as possible Communist influence in Indochina." The State Department analysis added that "our inability to suggest any practicable solution of Indochina problem" was caused by "the unpleasant fact that Communist Ho Chi Minh is the strongest and perhaps the ablest figure in Indochina and that any suggested solution which excludes him is an expedient of uncertain outcome." But to the end, the United States continued to back former agents of French colonialism, easily transferred their allegiance to the successor imperial power, against the nationalist movement "captured" (by implication, illegitimately) by the Viet Minh and its successors.

This "dilemma" is absolutely central to the understanding of the evolution of American policy in Indochina. The *Pentagon Papers* historian, considering the situation after the Tet offensive of 1968, asks whether the

United States can "overcome the apparent fact that the Viet Cong have 'captured' the Vietnamese nationalist movement while the GVN [government of South Vietnam] has become the refuge of Vietnamese who were allied with the French in the battle against the independence of their nation." It does not occur to him to ask whether the United States should attempt to "overcome" this fact. Rather, the problem is a tactical one: how can the fact be overcome? In this analysis, the historian reflects accurately the tacit assumptions that were unquestioned in the extensive documentary record.

For propaganda purposes, the issue was reformulated. It was our noble task to protect Indochina from "aggression." Thus, the *Pentagon Papers* historian, in the musings just cited, continues by observing that the question he raises is "complicated, of course, by the difficult issue of Viet Cong allegiance to and control by Communist China." Again, the historian accurately reflects the mentality revealed in the documents. He does not try to demonstrate that the Viet Cong owed allegiance to Communist China or were controlled by Peking. Rather, he adopts the premise as an *a priori* truth untroubled by the fact that no evidence was ever brought forth to substantiate it.

Not that intelligence didn't try. Elaborate attempts were made to demonstrate that the Viet Minh and its successors were merely the agents of some foreign master. It was, in fact, a point of rigid doctrine that this must be true, and no evidence to the contrary served to challenge the doctrine. Depending on date and mood the foreign master might be the Kremlin or "Peiping," but the principle itself could not be questioned.

The function of the principle is transparent: it served to justify the commitment "to defend the territorial integrity of IC and prevent the incorporation of the ASSOC[iated] States within the COMMI-dominated bloc of slave states" (Acheson, October 1950) or to safeguard Vietnam from "aggressive designs of Commie Chi" (Acheson, May 1949) by support for the French puppet regime. One of the most startling revelations in the *Pentagon Papers* is that in the twenty-year period under review, the analysts were able to discover only one staff paper (an intelligence estimate of 1961) "which treats communist reactions primarily in terms of the separate national interests of Hanoi, Moscow, and Peiping, rather than primarily in terms of an overall communist strategy for which Hanoi is acting as an agent."

Intelligence labored manfully to provide the evidence required by the doctrine. But their failure was total. It was impossible to establish what had to be true, that Ho Chi Minh was a puppet of the Kremlin or "Peiping."[14] Faced with this problem, American officials in Saigon reached the following caustic conclusion: "It may be assumed that Moscow feels that

Ho and his lieutenants have had sufficient training experience and are sufficiently loyal to be trusted to determine their day-to-day policy without
supervision." In short, the absence of evidence that Ho was a puppet was
held up as conclusive proof that he "really" was an agent of international
communism after all, an agent so loyal and trustworthy that no directives
were even necessary.

The whole amazing story gives a remarkable indication of how effective
are the controls over thought and analysis in American society. It is a
gross error to describe the *Pentagon Papers* as is commonly done, as a
record of government lies. On the contrary, the record reveals that the top
policy planners and, for the most part, the intelligence agencies were prisoners of the ideology of our highly ideological society. No less than independent intellectuals in the press and the universities, they believed
precisely those doctrines that had to be believed in order to absolve the
United States of the charge of aggression in Indochina. Evidence was—
and remains—beside the point.

Not only were the Viet Minh necessarily agents of a foreign power, they
were also literally "aggressors." The National Security Council, in February 1950, held that France and the native armies it had assembled "is now in
armed conflict with the forces of communist aggression." A presidential
commission of early 1954 added that France was fighting "to defend the
cause of liberty and freedom from Communism in Indochina," while the
cause of the Viet Minh is "the cause of colonization and subservience to
Kremlin rule as was the case in China, in North Korea and in the European
satellites." Later internal documents refer generally to the VC aggression
and describe the Pathet Lao in Laos as aggressors. Indeed, the Joint Chiefs
of Staff went so far as to characterize "political warfare, or subversion" as a
form of aggression. And Adlai Stevenson informed the United Nations Security Council that "the United States cannot stand by while Southeast
Asia is overrun by armed aggressors" adding that "the point is the same in
Vietnam today as it was in Greece in 1947," where the United States was
also defending a free people from "internal aggression," a marvelous new
Orwellian construction.

By and large the New Frontiersmen were quite at home with this
rhetoric. With "aggression checked in Vietnam," writes Arthur
Schlesinger, "1962 had not been a bad year."[15] In fact, 1962 was the first
year in which U.S. military forces were directly engaged in combat and
combat support, the bombing of villages, the gunning down of peasants
from helicopters, defoliation, etc. Only three years later, in April 1965,
did U.S. intelligence report the presence of the first North Vietnamese
battalion in the south.

It is important to recognize that these ridiculous rationalizations for American aggression in Indochina were accepted in their essentials within the American "intellectual community." Left liberal opinion, regarding itself as "opposing the war," called for a peace settlement between South and North Vietnam with American troops in place in the South, in short, a victory for American imperialism.[16] The war is described in retrospect as a "tragic error" where worthy impulse was "transmuted into bad policy," a case of "blundering efforts to do good." Such assessments are offered even by people who became committed opponents of the war in its latter phases. The plain and obvious fact that the United States was guilty of aggression in Indochina is rejected with horror and contempt; or, to be more accurate, it is simply dismissed as beyond the bounds of polite discourse by liberal commentators. These facts give an important insight into the nature of the liberal opposition to the war which later developed, largely on "pragmatic" grounds, when it became obvious that the costs of the war to us (or, for the more sensitive, to the Vietnamese as well) were too great for us to bear.[17]

The fundamental dilemma, perceived from the start, permitted only two outcomes to the American involvement in Indochina. The United States government might on the one hand choose to come to terms with the Vietnamese nationalist movement, or it might bend its efforts to the destruction of the Viet Minh and its successors. The first course was never seriously contemplated. Therefore, the United States committed itself to the destruction of the revolutionary nationalist forces in Indochina. Given the astonishing strength and resiliency of the resistance, the American intervention in Vietnam became a war of annihilation. In every part of Indochina, the pattern was repeated. As in the days of the early French conquest, "each farmer busy tying up a sheaf rice" might be "a centre of resistance." Inevitably, the United States undertook to destroy the rural society. American intellectuals dutifully supplied the rationale. We were engaged in a process of "urbanization and modernization," they explained as we drove the peasants out of their villages by bombs, artillery and search-and-destroy operations, simultaneously destroying the countryside to ensure that return would be impossible. Or, the United States was helping to control "village thugs" in violent peasant societies where terrorists can operate largely unmolested whether or not the local population supports them (Ithiel de Sola Pool).[18] More generally:

In the Congo, in Vietnam, in the Dominican Republic, it is clear that order depends on somehow compelling newly mobilized strata to return to a measure of passivity and defeatism from which they have recently been aroused by the process of modernization. At least temporarily, the maintenance of order requires a lowering of newly acquired aspirations and levels of political activity, [as] we have learned in the past thirty years of intensive empirical study of contemporary societies.

By the end, even the more cynical and sadistic were driven to silence as the horrendous record of the achievements that they had sought to justify for many years was slowly exposed to public view.

The terminology of the "behavioral sciences" was continually invoked in an effort to delude the public and the colonial administrators themselves. "Counterinsurgency theorists" explained in sober terms that "all the dilemmas are practical and as neutral in an ethical sense as the laws of physics."[19] It is simply a matter of discovering the appropriate mix of aversive conditioning (B-52 raids, burning of villages, assassination, etc.) and positive reinforcement (the detritus of the American presence) so as to overcome the unfair advantage of the revolutionaries—revolutionaries who in fact had won popular support by virtue of their constructive programs,[20] much to the dismay of the social scientists who persisted to the end with claims to the contrary based on "empirical studies" which they never produced.

In a report to President Kennedy after a 1962 study mission in Southeast Asia, Senator Mike Mansfield discussed the "widespread support of the peasants for the Vietcong" and remarked that any "reorientation" of peasant attitudes "involves an immense job of social engineering." He anticipated the unpleasant need of "going to war fully ourselves against the guerrillas—and the establishment of some form of neocolonial rule in South Vietnam," which he "emphatically" did not recommend. Others, however, took up the task of social engineering with zeal and enthusiasm. The Australian social psychologist Alex Carey, who has studied the matter in some detail, concludes that the American pacification program was "neither more nor less than a nation-sized sociological experiment in bringing about changes, desired by American policy, in the attitudes and values of a physically captive population."[21] The more sophisticated analysts went further still. They derided the concern for popular attitudes—such mysticism has no place in a scientific civilization such as ours—and urged instead that we concern ourselves solely with more objective matters, that is, with controlling behavior. This advance to the higher stages of applied science was necessitated by the miserable failure of the colonial agents in their efforts to mimic native revolutionaries.[22]

I cannot survey here the techniques that were attempted. Perhaps the mentality of the "scientists" is sufficiently indicated in one minor experiment in operant conditioning reported in Congressional hearings. An American psychiatrist working in a mental hospital in Vietnam subjected one group of patients to "unmodified electro-convulsive shock" which "produces systemic convulsions similar to a grand mal epileptic seizure and in many patients is very terrifying." Others were offered work "including tending crops for American Special Forces—Green Berets—in Viet Cong territory 'under the stress of potential or actual VC attack or ambush.'" Asked about the "research value" of this amusing study, one witness testified that "the entire field of behavior conditioning is of great interest in the treatment of mental patients as well as prisoners." This example, insignificant in context, reveals very clearly who was insane, the patients or the "scientists," just as academic studies on "control of village violence" leave no doubt as to who are the violent individuals who must be somehow controlled in a civilized society.[23]

Commenting on the "experiment" just cited, Alex Carey observes that "To be mentally ill and Asian deprives a man of most of his humanity; to be a communist and Asian deprives him of all of it." He goes on to show how this experiment exhibits in microcosm the major features of the program of social engineering devised by American descendants of [Heinrich] Himmler's SS and the Nazi physicians as they sought to design a more appropriate culture for the benighted Vietnamese once control had been gained over the population by violence and terror.

While studying the American pacification programs, Carey interviewed John Vann, field operations coordinator of the U.S. Operations Mission, who was regarded as the most important American official in Vietnam after the ambassador and the chief military commander.[24] Vann provided him with a memorandum, since privately circulated, "in response to a request for material on the concepts and theory that had guided the pacification programme."[25] In this memorandum, Vann noted that a social revolution was in process in South Vietnam, "primarily identified with the National Liberation Front" and that "a popular political base for the government of South Vietnam does not now exist." But it is "naïve" to expect that "an unsophisticated relatively illiterate, rural population [will] recognize and oppose the evils of Communism." Therefore, the United States must institute "effective political indoctrination of the population," under an American-maintained "autocratic government."

Vann was not a brutal murderer of the style of those who designed the military operations. He objected strongly to the ongoing destruction of the civilian society by American terror. His view was that of the benevolent imperialist, the bearer of the White Man's Burden, who urged that "we should make it clear [to the Vietnamese villagers] that we continue to represent that permanent revolution of mankind which the American revolution advanced; and that only the principles of that revolution can ultimately produce the results for which mankind longs." We must overcome "the pseudo-science of communism" by the techniques of the behavioral sciences, "psywar," firm in our conviction that "our system . . . is more in keeping with the fundamentals of human nature," as John F. Kennedy once explained.[26] If the Vietnamese are too stupid to comprehend these well-known facts, then we must drill them in by force—with the most benevolent of intentions. Indeed, it would be immoral to do otherwise, just as we do not permit children of retardates to injure themselves in their innocence. The United States Government and its agents in the field had to carry out two essential tasks. The first and most crucial was to destroy the society in which the resistance was rooted—the society "controlled by the Viet Cong" in the terminology of the propagandists. In South Vietnam, the primary victim of American aggression, a vast expeditionary force was let loose to accomplish this task. But by the late 1960s, Washington came to understand why earlier imperial aggressors—the French in Indochina, for example—had relied primarily on hired killers or native forces organized under colonial management to conduct a war against a resisting civilian population. To its credit the invading American army had begun to disintegrate, necessitating its withdrawal.[27] The disintegration was in part due to revulsion against its tasks, and in part to the indirect influence of the peace movement at home, which—as apologists for the state lamented—was "demoralizing American public opinion."[28] Washington's response was to assign the job of destruction to more impersonal agencies—helicopter gunships, bombers, and artillery. American technology devised fiendish devices to maximize the damage done to "enemy personnel.". . .

The task of destruction was accomplished with partial success. In South Vietnam, society was virtually demolished though the resistance was never crushed. But the aggressors faced a second and more difficult job: to construct a viable Quisling regime of the wreckage, and to rebuild the society in accordance with the imperial vision. This effort was a dismal failure. Like the French before them, the American conquerors were able to assemble "a crew of sycophants, moneygrubbers and psychopaths"[29] but rarely more. Efforts were made to integrate the mined societies into the "free world economy" by encouraging American and Japanese investment. Academic studies examined how foreign investment "must be liberated from the uncertainties and obstacles that beset it" so that it might take advantage of the cheap labor offered by a society of rootless atomized individuals driven from their villages by American urbanization, a virtually ideal labor market.[30] It was hoped that with the vast flow of arms and the expansion of the police, the merry crew of torturers and extortionists placed into power by the United States would somehow manage to control the population.

To the very end the American government was committed to victory, at least in South Vietnam. To fend off liberal criticism, Henry Kissinger and his press entourage spoke vaguely of a decent interval, but there is no evidence that they looked forward to anything short of total victory for the American client regime. Nonetheless, success was beyond their grasp. When Washington was no longer able to call forth the B-52's, the whole rotten structure collapsed from within, virtually without combat. Symbolic of the American failure in its second task—reconstruction of the society it had demolished—was the "fall of Danang" where the foreign aggression began more than a century before. Three intact ARVN divisions with more than 100,000 men and enough ammunition for a six-month siege were stationed in Danang, as of March 26. "Thirty-six hours later, without a single shot having been fired, the ARVN ceased to exist as a fighting unit." What happened is described by a French teacher who remained:

> The officers fled by air taking with them the ground crews so that the pilots that had stayed on could not get their planes started. Left without leaders the army fell apart. On March 28 widespread looting started. The rice stocks were sacked and in the hospitals the army and the local staff stole all the drugs in order to sell them on the black market. Then the army started shooting civilians at random, often to steal their motor cycles. By then half of the army was in civilian clothes, which they had stolen. For 36 hours, with Vietcong nowhere in sight but with rumors of their arrival constantly spreading, the city became a nightmare. By that time the population had but one hope: that the Vietcong would arrive as quickly as possible to restore order, any order.

Many civilians fled "because the Americans told us the communists would kill us," as they explained to reporters. America "left behind in Danang ... an empty shell and a good deal of hatred which will probably endure."[31]

The fact of the matter is that there never was any hope for the population of Indochina apart from a victory for the forces of revolutionary nationalism. . . .

The Nazi-like brutality of the American assault on Indochina is the most searing memory of these terrible years. Even though the ideologists and propagandists will labor to erase it, I cannot believe that they will succeed. Nonetheless, it must be understood that the savage programs put into operation by the Government and justified or ignored by much of the intelligentsia did not merely result from some sadistic streak in the American character. To be sure, the element of racism cannot be dismissed. One may doubt whether such maniacal "experiments in population control" would have been conducted, at least with such self-satisfaction and lack of guilt, on a white population. But in a deeper sense, the savagery of the American attack was a necessary and unavoidable consequence of the general policy that was adopted in the late 1940s—the policy of crushing a revolutionary nationalist movement that was deeply rooted in the population and that gained its support because of the appeal of its commitment to independence and social reconstruction.

This policy remained in force until the final collapse of the Saigon regime. During the 1950s, the United States hoped to regain control over all of Indochina. The National Security Council in 1956 directed all U.S. agencies in Vietnam "to work toward the weakening of the communists in North and South Vietnam in order to bring about the eventual peaceful reunification of a free and independent Vietnam under anti-communist leadership." Policy for Laos was stated in similar terms: "In order to prevent Lao neutrality from veering toward pro-Communism, encourage individuals and groups in Laos who oppose dealing with the communist [bloc]; support the expansion and reorganization of police, propaganda and army intelligence services, provided anti-Communist elements maintain effective control of these services; terminate economic and military aid if the Lao Government ceases to demonstrate a will to resist internal Communist subversion and to carry out a policy of maintaining its independence."[32] In Cambodia as well, the United States made significant efforts (in part, through the medium of its Thai, South Vietnamese, and Philippine subordinates) to reverse the commitment to neutralism.[33] A few years later, it was recognized that Viet Minh control over North Vietnam was irreversible, and the imperial managers lowered their sights. The goal was now a "non-Communist South Vietnam" instituted and guaranteed by American military force (since there was no other way), and a Western-oriented Laos and Cambodia.

Given this continuity of policy it is hardly surprising that many Vietnamese saw the Americans as the inheritors of French colonialism. The *Pentagon Papers* cites studies of peasant attitudes demonstrating that "for many, the struggle which began in 1945 against colonialism continued uninterrupted throughout [Ngo Dinh] Diem's regime in 1954, the foes of nationalists were transformed from France and Bao Dai, to Diem and the U.S., but the issues at stake never changed." By early 1964, even the U.S.-backed generals were warning of the "colonial flavor to the whole pacification effort," noting that the French in their worst and clumsiest days never tried to control the local society as the Americans were planning to do. But the American leadership saw no alternative, and rejected the objections of their clients as "an unacceptable rearward step." A Systems Analysis study concluded that unless the Viet Cong infrastructure ("the VC officials and organizers") "was destroyed, U.S.-GVN military and pacification forces soon degenerated into nothing more than an occupation army." They did not add that if this "infrastructure" was destroyed, the U.S.-GVN forces would be nothing but a gang of murderers. Both conclusions are, in fact, correct, and reflect the natural consequences of the implementation of the Indochina policy first mapped out in the late nineteen-forties.

It was only after the Tet offensive that American terror was unleashed against South Vietnam in its full fury. What was to come was indicated by the tactics employed to reconquer the urban areas that quickly fell into the hands of Vietnamese resistance forces in January–February 1968. The events in Hue were typical. Here, thousands of people "were killed by the most hysterical use of American firepower ever seen," and then designated "as the victims of a Communist massacre."[34] The "accelerated pacification program" that followed was a desperate effort to reconstruct the shattered American position. It had some success. Describing the "massive" increase in population which had been achieved by August 1970, John Paul Vann estimated that "we control two million more people than we controlled two years ago," although he added that "occupation is only the first step in pacification." As for that second step, the "willing cooperation of the people with the Government and the overt rejection of the enemy"—contrary to the pretense of ignorant social scientists, that step had not been and never would be achieved.[35]

Many people think of My Lai when recalling the post-Tet terrorism. But this is misleading. In fact, My Lai was just one of many such massacres. Some of these massacres, including My Lai, took place during "Operation Wheeler Wallawa." In this campaign over 10,000 "enemy" were reported killed, including the victims of My Lai, who were listed in the official body count. Speaking of "Wheeler Wallawa," Kevin Buckley, head of the *Newsweek* bureau in Saigon, observed that

> an examination of that whole operation would have revealed the incident at My Lai to be a particularly gruesome application of a wider policy which had the same effect in many places at many times. Of course, the blame for that could not have been dumped on a stumblebum lieutenant. Calley was an aberration, but "Wheeler Wallawa" was not.

The real issue concerning this operation was not the "indiscriminate use of firepower," as often is alleged.[36] Rather, "it is charges of quite discriminate use—as a matter of policy in populated areas."

One can gain a better understanding of American post-Tet strategy—strategy brought to its culmination under the management of Henry

Kissinger—by considering such operations as "Speedy Express." This campaign was conducted by the U.S. 9th Infantry Division in the Mekong Delta province of Kien Hoa in early 1969. Studied in detail by Alex Shimkin and Kevin Buckley, a partial description of it appeared in *Newsweek* for June 19, 1972. What follows is based on notes supplied to me by Buckley.

For many years the province had been "almost totally controlled" by the NLF:

> For a long time there was little or no military activity in the delta. The 9th Division did not even arrive until the end of 1966. Front activities went far beyond fighting. The VC ran schools, hospitals and even businesses. A pacification study revealed that an NLF sugar cane cooperative for three villages in the Mo Cay district of Kien Hoa produced revenue in 1968 which exceeded the entire Saigon government budget that year for Kien Hoa.

But the aggressive military effort carried out by the U.S. 9th Infantry Division succeeded in establishing some degree of government control. In the six months of Operation Speedy Express "a total of some 120,000 people who had been living in VC controlled areas" came under government control. To achieve this result, the Division applied "awesome firepower," including "3,381 air strikes by fighter bombers, dropping napalm, high explosives and anti-bombs," B-52's and artillery "around the clock" at a level that "it is impossible to reckon." Armed helicopters "scour[ed] the landscape from the air night and day" accounting for "many and perhaps most of the enemy kills." The 9th Division reported that "over 3,000 enemy were killed in March, 1969, which is the largest monthly total for any American division in the Vietnam War." All told, 10,899 people were killed and 748 weapons captured. From these figures alone one can make a fair judgment as to the nature of the "enemy troops" who were killed by bombing and shelling, much of it at night. In the single month of March, the Ben Tre hospital reported 343 people wounded by "friendly" fire as compared with 25 by "the enemy." And as a U.S. pacification official noted, "Many people who were wounded died on their way to the hospitals" or were treated elsewhere (at home, in VC hospitals or ARVN dispensaries). A senior pacification official estimated that "at least 5,000" of those killed "were what we refer to as noncombatants."

> The director of the nearby Canadian hospital, Dr. Alje Vennema, reports that he knew of the My Lai massacre at once but did nothing because it was not at all out of the ordinary; his patients were constantly reporting

such incidents to him.[37] In fact, the military panel investigating My Lai discovered that a similar massacre had taken place only a few miles away at the village of My Khe. Proceedings against the officer in charge were dismissed on the grounds that he had carried out a perfectly normal operation in which a village was destroyed and its population was forcibly relocated.[38] The panel's decision tells us all we need to know about "Wheeler Wallaw."

Interviews in the "pacified" areas confirm the grim picture. One VC medic reported that his hospital took care of at least 1,000 people in four villages in early 1969. "Without exception the people testified that most of the civilians had been killed by a relentless night and day barrage of rockets, shells, bombs and bullets from planes, artillery and helicopters." In one area of four villages, the population was reduced from 16,000 to 1,600. Every masonry house was in ruins. Coconut groves were destroyed by defoliants. Villagers were arrested by U.S. troops, beaten by interrogators, and sent off to prison camps. The MACV (Military Assistance Command, Vietnam) location plots for B-52's show that the target center for one raid was precisely on the village of Luong Phu. In the neighboring village of Luong Hoa, village elders estimated that there were 5,000 people in the village before 1969 and none in 1970 "because the Americans destroyed every house in the village with artillery, air strikes or by burning them down with cigarette lighters." About 100 people were killed by bombing, they report. Pounding them from the air was "relentless." Helicopters chased and killed people working in fields. Survival was possible in deep trenches and bunkers, but many small children "were killed by concussion from bombs which they could not withstand even when they were in bunkers," villagers reported. An experienced American official compared My Lai and the operations of the 9th Division as follows:

> The actions of the 9th Division in inflicting civilian casualties were worse. The sum total of what the 9th did was overwhelming. In sum, the horror was worse than My Lai. But with the 9th, the civilian casualties came in dribbles and were pieced out over a long time. And most of them were inflicted from the air and at night. Also, they were sanctioned by the command's insistence on high body counts.

He also stated that "the result was an inevitable outcome of the unit's command policy."

While the 9th Division was at work in the field, others were doing their job at home. One well-known behavioral scientist, who had long deplored the emotionalism of critics of the war and the inadequacy of their empirical data, wrote this as the campaign ground on: "the only sense in which [we have demolished the society of Vietnam] is the sense in which every modernizing country abandons reactionary traditionalism."[39]

Operation Speedy Express was regarded as a "stunning success." Lauding the commanding general—one must assume, without irony—upon his promotion, General Creighton Abrams spoke of "the great admiration I have for the performance of the 9th Division," its "unparalleled and unequaled performance," during Speedy Express. . . .

Again, it is important to bear in mind that the character of the American war cannot be attributed solely to a sadistic military leadership or to incompetent or deranged civilian advisers. It was a calculated and rational enterprise undertaken to realize goals that could be achieved in no other way: namely, the goal, stated clearly in the 1940s, of preventing Communist domination in a region where, it was always understood, the Communists had "captured" the national movement. Furthermore, the tactics employed were by no means novel. To cite only the most obvious analogy, recall the air war in Korea, and significantly, the manner in which it was later analyzed. . . .

Why feign surprise at the bombing of dikes in 1972 when 12,000 peasants (including, it seems, the remnants of My Lai) were driven from their homes in the Batangan Peninsula in January 1969, after having lived in caves and bunkers for months in an effort to survive constant bombardment, and were then shipped to a waterless camp near Quang Ngai over which floated a banner which said, "We thank you for liberating us from communist terror"?[40] Just another episode in which this "modernizing count abandons reactionary traditionalism" under the guidance of its benevolent big brother.

The same fundamental "dilemma" that made inevitable the savagery of the war always compelled the United States to evade any serious moves toward a negotiated settlement and to reject the "peaceful means" that are required by the "supreme law of the land." In the second Mansfield Report (December 1965) it is explained that:

> Negotiations at this time, as a practical matter, would leave the Viet Cong in control of the country[side] (much of which, by the way, they have controlled for many years and some of it since the time of the Japanese occupation). The Nationalists (and only with our continued massive support) would remain in control of Saigon, provincial capitals and the coastal base-cities. The status of the district seats would be in doubt.[41]

This conclusion was based on the reasonable assumption that "negotiations merely confirm the situation that exists on the ground."

Thus, despite the massacre of some 200,000 people in the preceding decade, despite the direct engagement of American military forces for four years, and despite the massive invasion and aerial bombardment of 1965, a political settlement was unthinkable, because the National Liberation Front controlled the countryside.[42]

Similar reasoning had impelled the United States to undertake overt aggression earlier in the year. Throughout 1964, the NLF made repeated efforts to arrange a negotiated settlement based on the Laos model, with a neutralist coalition government. But the United States rejected any such "premature negotiations" as incompatible with its goal of maintaining a non-communist South Vietnam under American control. The reason was quite simple. As American officials constantly reiterated, the NLF was the only significant political force and the U.S.-imposed regime had virtually no popular base. Only the politically organized Buddhists could even conceive of entering into a coalition with the NLF, and the Buddhists as General [William] Westmoreland sagely observed were not acting "in the interests of the Nation." Ambassador [Henry Cabot] Lodge later regarded them as "equivalent to card-carrying Communists" according to the Pentagon historian. Thus, the U.S. Government position was that only General Westmoreland and Ambassador [Maxwell] Taylor understood "the interests of the Nation," all political groupings in South Vietnam thereby being automatically excluded from any possible political settlement. To be sure, as William Bundy explained, we might be willing to consider the peaceful means required by law "after, *but only after* we have established a clear pattern of pressure" (i.e., military force; his emphasis). As noted earlier pacification specialist Vann took the same view, as did all other knowledgeable observers.

The United States therefore supported General [Nguyen] Khanh and the Armed Forces Council. But by January 1965, even that last hope went up in smoke. As Ambassador Taylor explained in his memoirs,[43] the United States government "had lost confidence in Khanh" by late January 1965. He lacked "character and integrity," added Taylor sadly. The clearest evidence of Khanh's lack of character was that by late January he was moving towards "a dangerous Khanh-Buddhist alliance which might eventually lead to an unfriendly government with which we could not work." Moreover, we now know from other sources, he was also close to a political agreement with the NLF.[44] Consequently, Khanh was removed. And in late January, according to the *Pentagon Papers*, Westmoreland "obtained his first authority to use U.S. forces for combat within South Vietnam." The systematic and intensive bombing of South Vietnam (accompanied by a more publicized but less severe bombing of the North) began a few weeks later, to be followed by the open American invasion.

At every other period, much the same was true. The 1954 Geneva Accords were regarded as a "disaster" by the United States. The National Security Council met at once and adopted a general program of subversion throughout the region to ensure that the political settlement envisioned in the Accords would not be achieved.[45] In October 1972, just prior to the U.S. presidential election, the DRV offered a peace proposal that virtually recapitulated the Geneva Accords and also incorporated the central positions in the founding documents of the NLF. Nixon and Kissinger could not openly reject this offer just prior to the elections, but they indicated clearly that the proposal was unacceptable while claiming deceitfully that "peace was at hand." Abetted by the subservient press, they were able to carry out this charade successfully, but when their later efforts to modify the proposals (including the Christmas bombings) failed utterly, they were compelled to accept the very same offer (with trivial changes in wording) in January 1973.

As in the case of Geneva 1954, this agreement was purely formal. Even before the Paris Agreements of January 1973 were signed, Kissinger explained to the press that the United States would reject every essential principle in the Agreements. And in fact, the United States at once committed itself to subverting these agreements by intensifying the political repression in South Vietnam and by launching military actions against PRG [Provisional Revolutionary Government (of South Vietnam)] territory through the medium of its client regime, massively supplied with arms. Again, the treachery of the mass media served to delude the public with regard to these events, helping to perpetuate the slaughter.[46]

By mid-1974, U.S. Government officials were reporting enthusiastically that their tactics were succeeding. They claimed that the [Nguyen Van] Thieu regime had conquered about 15 percent of the territory of the PRG, exploiting its vast advantage in firepower and that the prospects for further successes were great. As in the 1950s, the whole structure collapsed from within as soon as the Communists were so ungracious as to respond.

The point of this brief résumé has been to illustrate the complete refusal of the United States to consider any political settlement. The reason was always the same. It was always understood that there was no political base for the U.S. aggression so that a peaceful political settlement would constitute a defeat. This was precisely the dilemma of 1948, and it was never resolved. . . .

As I noted earlier, it was after the Tet offensive of early 1968 that the American murder machine really went into high gear in South Vietnam. The reasons were essentially two. It was feared that a political settlement of some sort would be inescapable, given the mounting pressures within the U.S. and in the international arena to limit or terminate the American war. And with the American military forces disintegrating in the field, it was evident that they would soon have to be withdrawn and replaced by native mercenaries. Given all this, it was decided to carry out the maximum amount of destruction possible in South Vietnam in the time remaining. The hope was that an imposed regime might maintain control over a sufficiently demoralized and shattered society. As noted, American officials like Vann felt that the post-Tet accelerated pacification campaigns had been partially successful in bringing the population under American "occupation," though "pacification" would, of course, still require substantial efforts.

Imperialist ideologues in the academic community generally shared this analysis. Henry Kissinger, in his last contribution to scholarship before ascending to high office, outlined "the thrust for American policy in the next phase" as follows: "the United States should concentrate on the subject of the mutual withdrawal of external forces and avoid negotiating about the internal structure of south Vietnam for as long as possible."[47] Putting aside his irrelevant rationalizations, the meaning of this prescription is obvious. If American terrorism could succeed in at last demolishing the southern resistance, an American client regime might be able to maintain itself. This would, however, only be possible if the North Vietnamese could be compelled to withdraw (the war planners had always expected that the bombing of the North and the direct American invasion of the South would draw the DRV into the southern conflict). Then, with North Vietnam out of the way, the United States could bring to bear the socio-economic programs mentioned earlier to maintain the stable, non-Communist South Vietnam it had always sought. Of course, Kissinger's prescription required that the southern resistance be smashed before the withdrawal of American troops. This is why it was under his regime that such operations as Speedy Express were launched against the South Vietnamese, while the air war was stepped up in Laos and Cambodia.

It is not surprising that Kissinger was, for a time, the great hope of American liberals. As I have already noted, left-liberal "opponents" of the war had themselves urged that the solution was a peaceful settlement between South and North Vietnam with American military forces remaining in the south. Indeed, to this day they feel that their proposals to this effect might have occasionally been questionable in "nuance," but nothing more.[48] Thus, it was perfectly natural that Kissinger should have been able to pacify much of the liberal opposition with his analysis of how an American military victory over the South Vietnamese might yet be attained.

To be sure, Kissinger was fully aware of the fundamental dilemma that had always plagued American policymakers. His way of phrasing the problem was as follows:

> The North Vietnamese and Viet Cong, fighting in their own country, needed merely to keep on being forces sufficiently strong to dominate the population after the United States tired of the war. We fought a military war; our opponents fought a political one ... our military operations had little relationship to our declared political objectives. Progress in establishing a political base was excruciatingly slow. ... In Vietnam, as in most developing countries—the problem is not to buttress but to develop a political framework. ... One ironic aspect of the war in Vietnam is that while we profess an idealist philosophy, our failures have been due to an excessive reliance on material factors. The Communists by contrast, holding to a materialistic interpretation, owe many of their successes to their ability to supply an answer to the question of the nature and foundation of political authority.[49]

Translating to simple prose: our problem is that the Vietnamese live there and we do not. This has made it difficult for us to develop a viable Vietnamese regime, whereas the Viet Minh and their successors had long ago created a functioning and successful social order in which they gained their support. There is no "irony" here. Rather, the problem is one that all imperial aggressors confront when faced with stubborn resistance, magnified in this case by the appeal of the social revolution.

Given the fundamental commitment to destroy the national movement, the United States was compelled to conduct a war of annihilation in South Vietnam and the surrounding region, and to reject any political settlement of the conflict. The question, however, remains why was it always regarded as necessary to pursue this course? As noted earlier, the fundamental "dilemma" was clearly perceived in 1948 when State Department analysts explained that the "long-term objective" of the United States was "to eliminate so far as possible Communist influence in Indochina." The rationalization offered was that we must "prevent undue Chinese penetration and subsequent influence in Indochina" because of our deep concern "that the peoples of Indochina will not be hampered in their natural developments by the pressure of an alien people and alien interests." Therefore, the United States attempted to restore French rule, in accordance with another "long-term objective": "to see installed a self-governing nationalist state which will be friendly to the U.S. and which ... will be patterned upon our conception of a democratic state" and will be associated "with the western powers, particularly with France, with whose customs, language and laws the peoples of Indochina are familiar, to the end that those peoples will prefer freely to cooperate with the western powers culturally, economically and politically" and will "work productively and thus contribute to a better balanced world economy," while enjoying a rising standard of income.

The subsequent history in Indochina (and elsewhere) reveals just how deep was the American commitment to self-government, to democracy, and to a rising standard of living for the mass of the population. We may dismiss this as the usual imperialist tommyrot.

But the concern that Indochina "contribute to a better balanced world economy" was real enough. There is compelling documentary evidence, from the *Pentagon Papers* and other sources, that this and related concerns dominated all others and impelled the United States on its course in Indochina. As the record clearly demonstrates, American planners feared that the success of revolutionary nationalism would cause "the rot to spread" to the rest of mainland Southeast Asia and beyond to Indonesia and perhaps South Asia, ultimately impelling Japan, the workshop of the Pacific, to seek an accommodation with the Communist powers. Should this all happen the United States would in effect have lost the Pacific phase of the Second World War, a phase which was fought in part to prevent Japan from constructing a "new order" closed to American penetration.

The mechanism by which the rot would spread was never clearly spelled out. But there is ample evidence that the planners understood that it would not be by military conquest. Rather, the danger was seen to lie in what they sometimes called "ideological successes," the demonstration effect of a successful revolution in Indochina (as in China). To counter this danger, pressure was put on Japan to reject "accommodation" with China. Access to Southeast Asia was promised as a reward for good behavior. And access was granted. By 1975, "Japanese commercial interests in Southeast Asia account for one-third of its US$100,000 million annual trade, more than 90% of the total 54,000 million 'yen credits' and a substantial share of the $10,000 million overseas investment balance,"[50] transactions which "have tended to enrich only a privileged few in Southeast Asia and their business and political counterparts in Japan." It is no surprise then "that Japan was the only major country which had fully supported the American war policy in Indochina, including all-out bombing of North Vietnam in [1972]."[51]

In spite of the fact that there is now substantial documentary evidence to support this analysis of American intentions,[52] it cannot be accepted by ideologists.[53] Instead, they emphasize other, peripheral factors—the need to gain French support for American programs in Europe, concern for some mystic "image," etc. To be sure, these factors were real enough. Thus, restoration of European capitalism was the primary objective of American post-war policy, and it was achieved in a manner which (not coincidentally) supported an immense expansion of overseas investment by American-based corporations. And there is no doubt that the United States was concerned to reinforce the image of a grim destroyer that would tolerate no challenge to its global order. But the primary reason why the long-term objective of destroying the communist nationalist movement could not be abandoned is precisely the one that is repeatedly and clearly stressed in the documentary record: the United States could not tolerate the spreading of the rot of independence and self-reliance over Southeast Asia, with its possible impact upon Japan, the major industrial power of the Pacific region.

The precise weight of the motives that led American planners to commit themselves to the destruction of the Vietnamese nationalist movement may be debated, but the extensive documentary record now available, and briefly surveyed here, leaves no doubt that the commitment was undertaken in full awareness of what was at stake. This fact is difficult for many American intellectuals to accept, even those who opposed the war. To cite one striking and not untypical example, Professor John K. Fairbank of Harvard argues that a "factor of ignorance" lies at the source of what he called "our Vietnam tragedy." Lacking "an historical understanding of the modern Vietnamese revolution," we did not "realize that it was a revolution inspired by the sentiment of nationalism while clothed in the ideology of communism as applied to Vietnam's needs. . . ."

The result was that in the name of being anti-Communist, vague though that term had become by 1965, we embarked on an "anti-nationalist effort." We misconceived "our role in defending the South after 1965," conceiving it as aimed at blocking aggression from North Vietnam and "forestalling a southward expansion of Chinese communism."[54] As we have seen, this analysis is refuted at every point by the historical record. The top planners knew from the start that the revolution was inspired by nationalism while clothed in the ideology of communism, and consciously embarked on an effort to destroy the national movement. They always understood that intervention from the North was a response to American aggression (which they, like Fairbank, called "fending the south"). "Chinese expansion" was fabricated to provide a propaganda cover for American aggression in Indochina. At the very moment when they were planning the 1965 escalation, William Bundy and John McNaughton noted that unless the United States expanded the war, there would probably be "a Vietnamese negotiated deal, under which an eventually unified Communist Vietnam would reassert its traditional hostility to Communist China."

As to why scholars choose to ignore the factual record, one may only speculate. We may note that it is convenient to blame the American "failure" on ignorance—a socially neutral concept—thus deflecting analysis of the systematic and institutional factors that brought about the American war.

A study group sponsored by the Woodrow Wilson Foundation and the National Planning Association once defined the primary threat of communism as the economic transformation of the Communist powers "in ways which reduce their willingness and ability to complement the industrial economies of the West";[55] American hegemony in "the West" was naturally assumed. The comment is accurate and astute. The United States, as the dominant power in the global capitalist system (the "free world"), will use what means it can muster to counter any move towards independence that will tend to "reduce" this "willingness and ability."

Three quarters of a century ago, Brooks Adams proclaimed that "Our geographical position, our wealth, and our energy pre-eminently fit us to enter upon the development of Eastern Asia and to reduce it to part of our own economic system."[56] As Oliver Wendell Holmes admiringly commented, Adams thought that the Philippine War "is the first gun in the battle for the ownership of the world."[57] American victory in the Pacific War of 1945 appeared to lay the basis for success in achieving this "long-term objective." The United States Government was not prepared to see its vision—which, in the familiar manner, was presented as utterly selfless and benign—threatened by a nationalist movement in a small and unimportant country where the peasants were too naive to understand what was in their best interests. The policy planners and intellectuals who stood by quietly while hundreds of thousands were slaughtered in Indonesia as the "Communist menace" was crushed and the country's riches again flowed towards the industrial powers or who watched with occasional clucking of tongues as countries of the Western hemisphere fell under the rule of American-backed fascist torturers, could hardly have been expected to react differently in the case of Indochina. Nor did they, until the domestic costs of the war mounted beyond tolerable levels, and a spontaneous movement of protest and resistance threatened to shatter domestic tranquility and authority.

NOTES

1. *Far Eastern Economic Review,* May 23, 1975.

2. Truong Buu Lam, *Patterns of Vietnamese Response to Foreign Intervention: 1858–1900.* Monograph Series No. 11,, Southeast Asia Studies, Yale university, 1967.

3. Helen B. Lamb, *Vietnam's Will to Live,* New York, Monthly Review Press, 1972.

4. Cited by Ngo Vinh Long, *Before the Revolution*, Cambridge, MIT Press, 1973; emphasis in original.

5. *Viet Nam: A Historical Sketch*, Foreign Languages Publishing House, Hanoi, l974.

6. Paulin Vial, cited by Lamb, *op. cit.*

7. Leopold Pallu, cited by Lamb, *op. cit.*

8. French resident minister Muselier, 1897, cited in *Vietnam: Fundamental Problems*, Vietnamese Studies no. 12, Foreign Languages Publishing House, Hanoi, 1966.

9. Lamb, *op. cit.*

10. Cited in *Viet Nam: A Historical Sketch.*

11. Major F. M. Small, Memorandum of Strategic Services Unit, War Department, 25 October 1945, cited in Frank M. White, *Causes, Origins, and Lessons of the Vietnam War*, Hearings before the Committee on Foreign Relations, U.S. Senate, 92nd Congress, 2nd session, May 1972, U.S. Government Printing Office, l973. The Intelligence reports cited below are from the same source.

12. Congressional Testimony, May 11, 1972. In *Causes.*

13. Cited from the Government edition of the *Pentagon Papers* in my *For Reasons of State,* New York, Pantheon 1973, p.28. Unless otherwise indicated, citations from the *Pentagon Papers* are given with precise sources here.

14. For a review of the intelligence record as presented in the *Pentagon Papers*. See *For Reasons of State*, pp. 5lf.

15. Arthur M. Schlesinger, Jr., *A Thousand Days*, New York, Fawcett Crest Books, 1965, p. 695.

16. See note 48 below.

17. For some discussion, see my article in *Ramparts*, July 1975.

18. Ithiel de Sola Pool, formerly chairman of the Council on Vietnamese Studies of SEADAG and chairman of the Political Science department at MIT, cited, with some discussion, in my *American Power and the New Mandarins*, New York, Pantheon, 1969, p. 36. For further discussion of his contributions and those of his colleague, Samuel Huntington, also past chairman of the Council on Vietnamese Studies and chairman of the Department of Government at Harvard, see my *At War with Asia*, New York, Pantheon, 1970, pp. 54–63, and *For Reasons of State*. It was Huntington who first explained how "In an absent-minded way the United States in Vietnam may well have stumbled upon the answer to 'wars of national liberation,'" namely, "forced-draft urbanization and modernization" by application of military power "on such a massive scale as to produce a massive migration from countryside to city."

19. George K. Tanham and Dennis J. Duncanson, "Some Dilemmas of Counterinsurgency," *Foreign Affairs*, vol. 48, no. 1, 1969.

20. For evidence on this matter, cf. Jeffrey Race, *War Comes to Long An*, Berkeley, University of California Press, 1971; Robert L. Sansom, *The Economics of Insurgency in the Mekong Delta*, Cambridge, MIT Press, 1970; Georges Chaffard, *Les Deux Guerres du Vietnam, La Table Ronde*, Paris, 1969; David Hunt, *Organizing for Revo-*

lution in Vietnam, Radical America, vol. 8, nos. 1 & 2, 1974. Race and Sansom were associated with the U.S. military; Hunt's study is based on material released from the RAND Corporation's "Viet Cong Motivation and Morale" project; Chaffard was a French journalist with many years experience in Vietnam. There are many other sources. For the "Mansfield Reports," cited below, see *Two Reports on Vietnam and Southeast Asia,* Dec. 18, 1962 and Dec. 17, 1965. U.S. Government Printing Office, April 1973. For a despairing assessment of the success of the guerrillas and the popularity of the Hanoi government, see Konrad Kellen, "1971 and Beyond: The View from Hanoi," June 1971, paper delivered at SEADAG meeting, May 8, 1971. Kellen is a RAND analyst.

21. Alex Carey, "Clockwork Vietnam: Psychology of Pacification (i)," mimeographed, 1972. See *Meanjin Quarterly,* Australia, 1973, for parts of this and subsequent sections of his "Clockwork Vietnam." Carey is lecturer in Psychology of International Relations at the University of New South Wales. His investigations are based in part on several months research in South Vietnam in 1970.

22. See, for example, Charles Wolf, *United States Policy and the Third World*, Boston, Little Brown, 1967. For discussion of this and other similar contributions, see *American Power and the New Mandarins*, chapter 1, my *Problems of Knowledge and Freedom*, New York, Pantheon, 1972, chapter 2, and *For Reasons of State*, pp. 98f.

23. Hearings before the Subcommittee on Health of the Committee on Labor and Public Welfare, U.S. Senate, 93rd Congress. First Session. February 21 and 22, 1973, Part 1, U.S. Government Printing Office, 1973, p. 268. For the original study, see Dr. Lloyd Cotter, *American Journal of Psychiatry*, July 1967.

24. See the obituary in *Newsweek*, June 19, 1972.

25. Carey, "Clockwork Vietnam: The Social Engineers Take Over (2)," *Meanjin Quarterly,* Australia, 1973.

26. Quotes in Carey, "Clockwork Vietnam: Psychology of Pacification (i)." From Colonel Reuben Nathan, "Psychological Warfare: Key to Success in Vietnam," *Orbis*, Spring 1967. Nathan was director of U.S. psychological warfare in Vietnam.

27. On the collapse of the military forces, see David Cortright, *Soldiers in Revolt,* New York, Doubleday, 1975.

28. Ithiel de Sola Pool, Introduction to his privately printed "Reprints of Publications on Vietnam, 1966–1970," May 1971.

29. David G. Marr, "The Rise and Fall of Counterinsurgency," in Noam Chomsky and Howard Zinn, eds. *The Cold War and the University, Toward and Intellectual History of the Post-War Years*, New York, The New Press, 1998, p. 208. Marr was a U.S. Marine Corps Intelligence officer, the only Vietnamese-speaking American in the first marine helicopter squadron sent to Vietnam by President Kennedy.

30. For a review of such programs, see *For Reasons of State*, chapter 4.

31. "Max Austerlitz," pseudonym of a journalist who remained in Danang after its "fall." "After the Fall of Danang," *New Republic*, May 17, 1973.

32. NSC Memorandum 5612/1, 5 September 1956. Volume 10 of *United States–Vietnam Relations, 1945–67*, U.S. Government Printing Office, 1971, in the government edition of the *Pentagon Papers*.

33. On this period in Cambodia, see D. R. SarDesai, *Indian Foreign Policy in Cambodia, Laos, and Vietnam, 1947–1964*, Berkeley, University of California Press, 1968. Also Malcolm Caldwell and Lek Tan, *Cambodia in the Southeast Asian War*, New York, Monthly Review Press, 1973. See also references cited in *For Reasons of State,* chapter 2.

34. Philip Jones Griffiths, *Vietnam Inc.*, New York, Macmillan, 1971, p. 137. Griffiths is a British journalist-photographer who was in Hue at the time. For more on the massacres at Hue, both the actual and fabricated ones, see *For Reasons of State*, pp. 230 ff; N. Chomsky and E. S. Herman, *Counterrevolutionary Violence*, Warner Modular Inc., 1973; and references cited in these sources. For a recent summary, see B. S. Herman and D. G. Porter, "The Myth of the Hue Massacre," *Ramparts*, May-June 1975.

35. Interview with Vann in Carey, "Clockwork Vietnam: Psychology of Pacification (i)." On the great progress allegedly being made on all fronts by the Saigon government, as revealed by "applied social science," cf. Pool, *op. cit.* His final conclusion: "Not that South Viet Nam will fall after American combat troops are withdrawn: it seems too strong for that."

36. Cable from Buckley and Shimkin to *Newsweek* U.S. offices, January 18, 1972.

37. Cf. his interview in the *Ottawa Citizen*, January 12, 1970; cited in *For Reasons of State*, p. 222.

38. See references in *For Reasons of State*, p. xx; also the two studies by Seymour Hersh: *My Lai Four*, New York, Random House, 1970; *Cover-up*, New York, Random House, 1972.

39. Ithiel de Sola Pool, letter, *New York Review of Books,* February 13, 1969. For news reports on the exploits of the 9th Division in early 1969, cf. *At War with Asia*, pp. 99 f.

40. For references and further details, see *At War with Asia*, p. 104; *For Reasons of State*, p. 225. For additional comment on this military operation ("Bold Mariner," reportedly the largest American amphibious operation since World War II), which coincided with "Speedy Express," see the statement by Martin Teitel of the American Friends Service Committee, Hearing before the Subcommittee to Investigate Problems Connected with Refugees and Escapees (Kennedy Subcommittee) of the Committee on the Judiciary, U.S. Senate, 92nd Congress, Second Session, May 8, 1972, U.S. Government Printing Office, 1972. Teitel also describes the U.S.-GVN atrocities of April 1972 in the same area subsequent to the bloodless liberation by the NLF-NVA.

41. Cf. note 20.

42. On the relative U.S.-DRV troop levels, as revealed by the *Pentagon Papers*, see my article "The Pentagon Papers as Propaganda and as History," in Chomsky and Zinn, eds., *op. cit.;* also *For Reasons of State*, pp. 82 (and note 147), p. 239 f.

43. General Maxwell D. Taylor, *Swords and Plowshares*, New York, Norton, 1972.

44. Speaking in Paris, January 26, 1965, Khanh released correspondence with Huynh Tan Phat, then Vice-President of the Central Committee of the NLF, from late January 1965, indicating that agreement was close. Cf. my article in *Ramparts*, July 1975, for further details. There is, incidentally, also evidence that the Diem regime may have been approaching a negotiated settlement just prior to the U.S.-backed coup in which Diem was murdered. Cf. Chaffard, *op. cit.*, chapter 8; and Mieczyslaw Maneli, *War of the Vanquished*, New York, Harper and Row, 1971. John P. Roche, an unreconstructed hawk, claims that he had furnished evidence to the Pentagon historians, which they ignored, that the Kennedy Administration had decided not to permit a deal between Diem and Ho Chi Minh. Cf. his "Pentagon Papers," *Political Science Quarterly*, vol. 87, no. 2, 1972.

45. For details on this important document misrepresented beyond recognition in the *Pentagon Papers* history, see *For Reasons of State*, pp. 100 f.

46. For details on these matters see my "Endgame: The Tactics of Peace in Vietnam," *Ramparts*, April 1973; and "Reporting Indochina: The News Media and the Legitimization of Lies," *Social Policy*, September/October 1973.

47. On United States intervention in Laos, see the articles by Haney and Chomsky in Chomsky and Zinn, eds., *op. cit.;* also *At War with Asia*, chapter 4, and *For Reasons of State*, chapter 2, and the references cited there.

48. See the comment by the editors in *Dissent*, Spring 1975, in response to a letter of mine correcting a wholly fabricated version of my criticisms of their earlier editorial position. As indicated in their response, they prefer to restrict attention to the fabrication rather than attending to the entirely different original, which suggests that they perhaps do have some reservations about their long-held position. For further details, see the interchange in the *New Republic* referred to in this exchange.

49. *Op. cit.*, pp. 104–6.

50. Koji Nakamura, "Japan: A New Face for Asia," *Far Eastern Economic Review*, May 23, 1975.

51. Correspondent, "Putting Washington before ASEAN," *ibid*. The text gives the date 1968 instead of 1972, presumably an error.

52. Cf. *At War with Asia*, chapter 1; *For Reasons of State*, chapter 1, section V; the articles by John W. Dower, Richard B. Du Boff and Gabriel Kolko in Chomsky and Zinn, eds., *op. cit.*

53. For discussion of some misunderstandings of this critique by Richard Tucker, Charles Kindelberger and others, cf. *For Reasons of State*, pp. 42–46, 56–58.

54. John K. Fairbank, "Our Vietnam Tragedy," *Newsletter*, Harvard Graduate Society for Advanced Study and Research, June 1975. Fairbank also remarks that our "greatly accelerating the urbanization of Vietnam" after 1965 was "not necessarily to our credit or to the benefit of South Vietnam." Scholarly caution, perhaps appropriate in an issue of the *Newsletter* that announced a new professorship of Vietnamese Studies named for Kenneth T. Young, formerly Chairman of SEADAG and Director of Southeast Asian Affairs in the State Department in 1954–58, when the United States took over

direct responsibility for repression and massacre in South Vietnam. Young was one of those to urge publicly that the United States and its local subordinates "should deliberately increase urbanized markets and the town groupings coupled with fewer remote villages and fewer dispersed hamlets outside the modernizing environment to outmatch and outclass the Viet Cong where they are weak" (cf. note 18), thus making "a virtue out of necessity." *Asian Survey*, August 1967. At that time, no rational person could be deceived as to how "urban realignment," as Young called it, was being and must be effected by the American Expeditionary Force.

Perhaps some day the University of Berlin will institute an Eichman chair of Jewish Studies.

55. William Y. Elliott, ed., *The Political Economy of American Foreign Policy*, New York, Holt, 1955, p. 42.

56. Quoted in Akire Iriye, *Across the Pacific*, New York, Harcourt, Brace and World, 1967, p. 77.

57. Cited by Frank Freidel, in *Dissent in Three American Wars*, Cambridge, Harvard University Press, 1970.

24

A Vietnam Reappraisal

CLARK M. CLIFFORD*

Clark M. Clifford succeeded Robert McNamara as U.S. Secretary of Defense on March 1, 1968. It was generally expected that Clifford would be more of a hawk on Vietnam than McNamara and that there would be an escalation in the military effort in that theater of war. When a journalist asked him whether he was a hawk or a dove, he responded, "I am not conscious of falling under any of those ornithological divisions."

Clifford served only eleven months as secretary of defense. The war was going badly. By the end of Clifford's first month in office, President Johnson announced that his administration would place an absolute limit on the number of U.S. troops in Vietnam (549,500), that the South Vietnamese troops would need to take on a greater share of the fighting, and that he himself would not seek re-election for the office of the president. Very soon, in mid-May 1968, negotiations with North Vietnam would begin in Paris. Clifford had moved closer to McNamara's position, which favored gradual disengagement, as opposed to that of Secretary of State Dean Rusk, who declared that the war in Vietnam would be won "if America had the will to win it." Clifford resigned on January 20, 1969. He explained his position succinctly in the article he wrote for *Foreign Affairs*, which is reproduced below.

∼

I took office on March 1, 1968. The enemy's Tet offensive of late January and early February had been beaten back at great cost. The confidence of

---

*Clark M. Clifford, "A Vietnam Reappraisal," *Foreign Affairs* 47, no. 4 (July 1969): 609–622.

the American people had been badly shaken. The ability of the South Vietnamese Government to restore order and morale in the populace, and discipline and esprit in the armed forces, was being questioned. At the President's direction, General Earle G. Wheeler, Chairman of the Joint Chiefs of Staff, had flown to Viet Nam in late February for an on-the-spot conference with General Westmoreland. He had returned and presented the military's request that over 200,000 troops be prepared for deployment to Viet Nam. These troops would be in addition to the 525,000 previously authorized. I was directed, as my first assignment, to chair a task force named by the President to determine how this requirement could be met. We were not instructed to assess the need for substantial increases in men and materiel; we were to devise the means by which they could be provided.

My work was cut out. The task force included Secretary (of State) Rusk, Secretary Henry Fowler, Under Secretary of State Nicholas Katzenbach, Deputy Secretary of Defense Paul Nitze, General Wheeler, CIA Director Richard Helms, the President's Special Assistant, Walt Rostow, General Maxwell Taylor and other skilled and highly capable officials. All of them had long and direct experience with Vietnamese problems. I had not. I attended various meetings in the past several years and I had been to Viet Nam three times, but it was quickly apparent to me how little one knows if he has been on the periphery of a problem and not truly in it. Until the day-long sessions of early March, I had never had the opportunity of intensive analysis and fact-finding. Now I was thrust into a vigorous, ruthlessly frank assessment of our situation by the men who knew the most about it. Try though we would to stay with the assignment of devising means to meet the military's requests, fundamental questions began to recur over and over.

It is, of course, not possible to recall all the questions that were asked nor all the answers that were given. . . . All that is pertinent to this essay is an impression that I formed, and the conclusions I ultimately reached in those days of exhausting scrutiny. In the colloquial style of those meetings, here are some of the principal issues raised and some of the answers as I understood them:

"Will 200,000 more men do the job?" I found no assurance that they would.

"If not, how many more might be needed—and when?" There was no way of knowing.

"What would be involved in committing 200,000 more men to Viet Nam?" A reserve call-up of approximately 280,000, an increased draft call and an extension of tours of duty of most men then in service.

"Can the enemy respond with a build-up of his own?" He could and probably would.

"What are the estimated costs of the latest requests?" First calculations were on the order of $2 billion for the remaining four months of that fiscal year and an increase of $10 to $12 billion for the year beginning July 1, 1968.

"What will be the impact on the economy?" So great that we would face the possibility of credit restrictions, a tax increase and even wage and price controls. The balance of payments would be worsened by at least half a billion dollars a year.

"Can bombing stop the war?" Never by itself. It was inflicting heavy personnel and materiel losses, but bombing by itself would not stop the war.

"Will stepping up the bombing decrease American casualties?" Very little, if at all. Our casualties were due to the intensity of the ground fighting in the South. We had already dropped a heavier tonnage of bombs than in all the theaters of World War II. During 1967, an estimated 90,000 North Vietnamese infiltrated into South Viet Nam. In the opening weeks of 1968, infiltrators were coming in at three to four times the rate of a year earlier, despite the ferocity and intensity of our campaign of aerial interdiction.

"How long must we keep on sending our men and carrying the main burden of the combat?" The South Vietnamese were doing better, but they were not ready yet to replace our troops and we did not know when they would be.

When I asked for a presentation of the military plan for attaining victory in Viet Nam, I was told that there was no plan for victory in the historic American sense. Why not? Because our forces were operating under three major political restrictions: the President had forbidden the invasion of North Viet Nam because this could trigger the mutual assistance pact between North Viet Nam and China; the President had forbidden the mining of the harbor at Haiphong, the principal port through which the North received military supplies, because a Soviet vessel might be sunk; the President had forbidden our forces to pursue the enemy into Laos and Cambodia, for to do so would spread the war, politically and geographically, with no discernible advantage. These and other restrictions which precluded an all-out, no-holds-barred military effort were wisely designed to prevent our being drawn into a larger war. We had no inclination to recommend to the President their cancellation.

"Given these circumstances, how can we win?" We would, I was told, continue to evidence our superiority over the enemy; we would continue to attack in the belief that he would reach the stage where he would find it inadvisable to go on with the war. He could not afford the attrition we were inflicting on him. And we were improving our posture all the time.

I then asked, "What is the best estimate as to how long this course of action will take? Six months? One year? Two years?" There was no agreement on an answer. Not only was there no agreement, I could find no one willing to express any confidence in his guesses. Certainly, none of us was willing to assert that he could see "light at the end of the tunnel" or that American troops would be coming home by the end of the year.

After days of this type of analysis, my concern had greatly deepened. I could not find out when the war was going to end; I could not find out the manner in which it was going to end; I could not find out whether the new requests for men and equipment were going to be enough, or whether it would take more and, if more, when and how much; I could not find out how soon the South Vietnamese forces would be ready to take over. All I had was the statement, given with too little self-assurance to be comforting, that if we persisted for an indeterminate length of time, the enemy would choose not to go on.

And so I asked, "Does anyone see any diminution in the will of the enemy after four years of our having been there, after enormous casualties and after massive destruction from our bombing?"

The answer was that there appeared to be no diminution in the will of the enemy. This reply was doubly impressive, because I was more conscious each day of domestic unrest in our own country. Draft card burnings, marches in the streets, problems on school campuses, bitterness and divisiveness were rampant. Just as disturbing to me were the economic implications of a struggle to be indefinitely continued at ever-increasing cost. The dollar was already in trouble, prices were escalating far too fast, and emergency controls on foreign investment imposed on New Year's Day would be only a prelude to more stringent controls, if we were to add another $12 billion to Viet Nam spending—with perhaps still more to follow.

I was also conscious of our obligations and involvements elsewhere in the world. . . . Even accepting the validity of our objective in Viet Nam, that objective had to be viewed in the context of our overall national interest, and could not sensibly be pursued at a price so high as to impair our ability to achieve other, and perhaps even more important, foreign policy objectives.

Also, I could not free myself from the continuing nagging doubt . . . that if the nations living in the shadow of Viet Nam were not persuaded by the domino theory, perhaps it was time for us to take another look. . . . I could see no reason at this time for us to continue to add to our commitment. Finally, there was no assurance that a 40 percent increase in American troops would place us within the next few weeks, months, or even years in any substantially better military position than we were in then. All that could be predicted accurately was that more troops would raise the level of combat and automatically raise the level of casualties on both sides.

And so, after these exhausting days, I was convinced that the military course we were pursuing was not only endless, but hopeless. A further substantial increase in American forces could only increase the devastation and the Americanization of the war, and thus leave us even further from our goal of a peace that would permit the people of South Viet Nam to fashion their own political and economic institutions. Henceforth, I was also convinced, our primary goal should be to level off our involvement, and to work toward gradual disengagement.

To reach a conclusion and to implement it are not the same, especially when one does not have the ultimate power of decision. It now became my purpose to emphasize to my colleagues and to the President, that the United States had entered Viet Nam with a limited aim—to prevent its subjugation by the North and to enable the people of South Viet Nam to determine their own future. I also argued that we had largely accomplished that objective. Nothing required us to remain until the North had been ejected from the South, and the Saigon government had been established in complete military control of all South Vietnam. An increase of over 200,000 in troop strength would mean that American forces would be twice the size of the regular South Vietnamese Army at that time. Our goal of building a stronger South Vietnamese Government, and an effective military force capable of ultimately taking over from us, would be frustrated rather than furthered. The more we continued to do in South Viet Nam, the less likely the South Vietnamese were to shoulder their own burden.

The debate continued at the White House for days. President Johnson encouraged me to report my findings and my views with total candor, but he was equally insistent on hearing the views of others. Finally, the President, in the closing hours of March, made his decisions and reported them to the people on the evening of the 31st. Three [of them] related directly to the month's review of the war. First, the President announced he was establishing a ceiling of 549,500 [troops] in the American commitment to Viet Nam; the only new troops going out would be support troops previously promised. Second, we would speed up our aid to the South Vietnamese armed forces. We would equip and train them to take over major combat responsibilities from us on a much accelerated schedule. Third, speaking to Hanoi, the President stated he was greatly restricting American bombing of the North as an invitation and an inducement to begin peace talks. We would no longer bomb north of the Twentieth Parallel. By this act of unilateral restraint, nearly 80 percent of the territory of North Viet Nam would no longer be subjected to our bombing. . . .

It seems clear that the necessity to devote more of our minds and our means to our pressing domestic problems requires that we set a chronological limit on our Vietnamese involvement. A year ago, we placed a numerical limit on this involvement, and did so without lessening the effectiveness of the total military effort. There will, undeniably, be many problems inherent in the replacement of American combat forces with South Vietnamese forces. But whatever these problems, they must be faced. There is no way to achieve our goal of creating the conditions that will allow the South Vietnamese to determine their own future unless we begin, and begin promptly, to turn over to them the major responsibility for their own defense. This ability to defend themselves can never be developed so long as we continue to bear the brunt of the battle. Sooner or later, the test must be whether the South Vietnamese will serve their own country sufficiently well to guarantee its national survival. In my view, this test must be made sooner, rather than later. . . .

This, then, is the case history of the evolution of one individual's thinking regarding Viet Nam. Throughout this entire period it has been difficult to cling closely to reality because of the constant recurrence of optimistic predictions that our task was nearly over, and that better times were just around the corner, or just over the top of the next hill.

We cannot afford to lose sight of the fact that this is a limited war, for limited aims and employing limited power. The forces we now have deployed and the human and material costs we are now incurring have become, in my opinion, out of all proportion to our purpose. The present scale of military effort can bring us no closer to meaningful victory. It can only continue to devastate the countryside and to prolong the suffering of the Vietnamese people of every political persuasion.

Unless we have the imagination and the courage to adopt a different course, I am convinced that we will be in no better, and no different, a position a year from now than we are today.

At current casualty rates, 10,000 more American boys will have lost their lives.

We should reduce American casualties by reducing American combat forces. We should do so in accordance with a definite schedule and with a specified end point.

Let us start to bring our men home—and let us start *now*.

25

Pol Pot's

Rise to Power

BEN KIERNAN*

Benedict F. Kiernan, educated in Australia and currently teaching at Yale University, is the world's leading authority on the genocide that took place when the Khmer Rouge under Pol Pot ruled Cambodia from 1975 through 1978. Under Pol Pot, Cambodia "went to Pot," as Karl Jackson titled one of his articles. Cambodian cities, notably the capital, Phnom Penh, whose population had swollen from a mere 300,000 to 3 million (60 percent of the country's population) from 1969 to 1974, was ordered to be emptied. The regime de-monetized the currency, shut down all major establishments, and closed the country to the rest of the world. Pol Pot's pogroms killed more than 1 million people. With the Vietnamese invasion of Cambodia in December 1978 and subsequent decade-long occupation of the country, the Pol Pot regime collapsed; he and his cohort fled to western Cambodia.

News of the horrors of the Pol Pot regime trickled to the outside world in 1978. To most observers, however, the rise of Pol Pot and the Khmer Rouge and the reasons for their excesses were a mystery. Ben Kiernan's account of the unraveling of Cambodia under the Khmer Rouge is among the most authoritative, based on extensive interviews and meticulous research. He has written several books on modern Cambodia in the two decades since he received his Ph.D. in 1983. *The Pol Pot Regime: Race, Power, and Genocide in Cambodia, 1975–1979* was published in 1996. The

---

*Ben Kiernan, *The Pol Pot Regime: Race, Power, and Genocide in Cambodia, 1975–1979*, 2nd ed. (New Haven, CT: Yale University Press, 2002).

extract below on the rise of Pol Pot to power is drawn from a revised edition published in 2002.

~

The shadowy leaders of this closed country gave few clues to their personal lives. The first journalists to enter Democratic Kampuchea came from Yugoslavia in 1978. They had to ask the prime minister, "Who are you, comrade Pol Pot?" He was evasive. . . .

On May 19, 1928, Pol Pot was born Saloth Sar, the youngest of seven children. His parents owned nine hectares of rice land, three of garden land, and six buffalo. Pol Pot's father Saloth, with two sons and adopted nephews, harvested enough rice for about twenty people. In later years the family would have been "class enemies." But few villagers thought so then. Rich or poor, everyone tilled the fields, fished the river, cooked tasty soups, raised children, propitiated local spirits and French colonial officials, or thronged Buddhist festivities in Kompong Thom's pagoda. In 1929, a French official described Kompong Thom people as "the most deeply Cambodian and the least susceptible to our influence."

But the Saloth family were Khmer peasants with a difference. They had royal connections. Pol Pot's cousin had grown up a palace dancer, becoming one of King Monivong's principal wives. At fifteen, his eldest sister, Saroeung, was chosen as a consort. In 1928, the eldest brother, Loth Suong, began a career in palace protocol. Pol Pot joined him in 1934, at the age of six.

The country boy Saloth Sar never worked a rice field or knew much of village life. A year in the royal monastery was followed by six in an elite Catholic school. His upbringing was strict. . . . The palace compound was closeted and conservative, the old king a French puppet. Outside, Phnom Penh's 100,000 inhabitants were mostly Chinese shopkeepers and Vietnamese workers. Few Cambodian childhoods were so removed from their vernacular culture.

At fourteen, Pol Pot went off to high school in the bustling Khmer market town of Kompong Cham. . . . In 1948, he received a scholarship to study radio-electricity in Paris. He set out with another youth, Mey Mann. The first stop was Saigon, the largest town they had ever seen. In the heart of commercial Vietnam, the two young Cambodians felt "like dark monkeys from the mountains." They were relieved to board ship for Marseilles, arriving in September 1949.

Two other young Cambodians with palace connections, Thiounn Thioeunn and Thiounn Chum, had been sent to study in Hanoi from 1942 to

1945; according to their 1979 account, they found that "Vietnamese intellectuals spoke of Angkor as their own!" After the war the two men went on
to Paris; Thioeunn completed a degree in medicine and Chum a doctorate
in law. Their brother Mumm gained a doctorate in science, and the fourth
brother, Prasith, was also sent to study in France, where he lived for over
twenty years. The Thiounns all developed left-wing contacts, but their nationalism was so fierce that they refused to meet the Vietnamese communist
leader, Ho Chi Minh.

Saloth Sar wrote his brother Suong occasionally, asking for money. But
one day a letter arrived asking for the official biography of King Sihanouk.
Suong sent back advice: Don't get involved in politics. But Pol Pot was already a member of the Cambodian section of the French Communist Party,
then in its Stalinist heyday. Those who knew him then insist that "he would
not have killed a chicken"; he was self-effacing, charming. He kept company with Khieu Ponnary, eight years his senior, the first Khmer woman to
get the *baccalaureat*. The couple chose Bastille Day for their wedding back
home in 1956.

Most of Pol Pot's Paris friends, like the Thiounn brothers, Khieu Sam-
phan, and two Khmer Krom students, Ieng Sary and Son Sen, remained in
his circle for over forty years. Sary married Khieu Ponnary's sister, Shake-
speare studies major Khieu Thirith. Pol Pot had disagreements in Paris with
Hou Yuon, later a popular Marxist intellectual who would be one of the
first victims after Pol Pot's seizure of power in 1975 ... Pol Pot's scholarship ended after he failed his course three years in a row. His ship arrived
home in January 1953.

The previous day, King Sihanouk had declared martial law in order to
suppress Cambodia's independence movement which was becoming radi-
calized by French colonial force. Pol Pot's closest brother, Saloth Chhay,
joined the Cambodian and Vietnamese communists and took him along. In
this first contact, Vietnamese communists began teaching him, as one of
them later put it, how to "work with the masses at the base, to build up the
independence committees at the village level, member by member." It
seemed a patronizing slight; he did not quickly rise to leadership, despite
overseas training. A former Cambodian comrade claims that Pol Pot "said
that everything should be done on the basis of self-reliance, independence
and mastery. The Khmers should do everything on their own.". . .

By 1954, when the French abandoned their Indochinese colonial war and
withdrew from Cambodia and Vietnam, Son Ngoc Minh and Tou Samouth
had built up a formidable Issarak, or "independence" movement. It had an
army of five thousand Cambodian fighters (and numerous village militias)
backed by an alliance with the Vietnamese victors of Dien Bien Phu. The

movement, called the Khmer Issarak Association was spearheaded by its communist organizational backbone, the Khmer People's Revolutionary Party. Minh and Samouth had established the KPRP in 1951 under the supervision of Vietnamese communists. In three years it recruited over one thousand members, mainly from the two largest sectors of Cambodian life: the peasantry and the monkhood. Out of this nationalist struggle for independence, the first precondition for Pol Pot's Democratic Kampuchea had been realized; a viable communist party had emerged on the Cambodian political scene.

The KPRP's influence among sections of the peasantry was one reason Prince Sihanouk, after the Geneva Conference of 1954, adopted a new policy of neutrality in foreign affairs. Party leaders Tou Samouth and Son Ngoc Minh, like their Vietnamese mentors, welcomed this departure from the previous pro-colonial policies of the prince. After all, their own conversion to communism had been provoked by their nationalist awakening. But this left the party open to criticism by younger militants, such as Saloth Sar, who had been students in France during the anti-colonial war. Whatever the prince's stand on independence or neutrality these younger communists aimed to confront his feudalist autocracy. Indeed, Sihanouk's initial repression of democrats and leftists only fueled their case. It drove Son Ngoc Minh, a third of the KPRP's members, and hundreds of Issarak supporters into exile in Hanoi. Sihanouk's government rigged the 1955 general election, denying any seats to either the winner of all previous elections, the Democratic Party, or the KPRP's new legal organ, the Pracheachon Party. Ominously, the middle ground, along with the left, was now unrepresented on the open political stage.

Later Sihanouk relaxed the pressure on some dissidents. But his erratic repression of the left played into the hands of the younger party group. Sihanouk's secret police suppressed the orthodox grassroots KPRP veterans, partly because of their historical affinity with Hanoi, while sparing younger, educated militants with more privileged backgrounds. The former Paris students grew in importance with police harassment and silencing of their party elders. Their own greater familiarity with the urban political scene, and their apparent murder of Tou Samouth in 1962, eventually enabled the Pol Pot group to take over leadership of the communist party in early 1963.

The new leaders quickly went underground, forestalling any serious party debate while preparing a rebellion against Sihanouk. This meant a party break not only with Hanoi, but also with the Khmer Issarak such as Son Ngoc Minh and half the party's membership who remained in Vietnam, and with their policy of accommodation to the prince's neutralism. But propaganda from Pol Pot's rebels in the bush carefully encouraged Sihanouk's erroneous presumption that the pro-Vietnamese left, the old KPRP leadership, was behind the unrest. This provoked him to crack down on the remaining above-ground Khmer Leftists, who in accord with Hanoi's strategy had been trying to work within the framework of the prince's regime. His repression drove them to rebellion and into Pol Pot's emerging guerrilla movement in the countryside. This strengthened these orthodox communist veterans' acceptance of party discipline, even though their position was now subordinate. Stage Two of Pol Pot's rise to power had been accomplished. From 1967, he found himself at the head of an authentic communist insurgency.

In 1954 the Cambodian communist party had been largely rural, Buddhist, moderate, and pro-Vietnamese. By 1970 its leadership was urban, French-educated, radical, and anti-Vietnamese. A major factor in this "changing of the vanguard" was the rivalry between Chinese and Vietnamese communists for influence in this part of Southeast Asia. While China supported Sihanouk, it also encouraged a formerly pro-Vietnamese communist movement whose new leaders were preparing to distance themselves from Hanoi. Thus Beijing's sponsorship provided Pol Pot's faction with maneuverability that it would not otherwise have enjoyed.

But the party's membership, unlike its Center, or national leadership, had not abandoned the tradition of solidarity with the Vietnamese communists. And the party's regional committees, or zones, were mostly strongholds of these Issarak veterans. The most orthodox and effective was the Eastern Zone, led by So Phim, who had worked closely with the Vietnamese since the 1946–1954 war. He was more reluctant than Pol Pot to force a violent confrontation with Sihanouk's forces or a political break with Hanoi. By January 1970, So Phim's eastern branch of the Cambodian communist insurgency was described by U.S. intelligence as being "in close liaison with the Viet Cong," who sheltered them on Vietnamese soil when they were attacked by government forces. They were considered "the most ideologically communist-oriented of all the Khmers Rouges," but they were also "much better educated," "the best organized," and "the most immediate insurgent threat." So Phim's Eastern Zone insurgency had a potential "far and away greater than that of a combination of the others." The other Khmer Rouge groups, the American intelligence report went on, "have more of a bandit flavor than an ideological one."

The rebellion's political success was also limited by its confrontation with Sihanouk's nationalism. Meanwhile, however, Sihanouk began to face a challenge from the right. By 1969 Pol Pot had to abandon his claim that Sihanouk was "a secret agent of the United States." As the party later put it, "when the storm came [he] had to come and take shelter in our refuge." In March 1970, the Vietnam War engulfed the country. The prince was overthrown by General Lon Nol, who enjoyed American support. From exile in Beijing, Sihanouk now aligned himself with the continuing insurgency. And from their own exile in Hanoi, about one thousand veteran Issaraks returned home after a sixteen-year absence. Working with them and with Sihanouk's supporters, Vietnamese communists successfully mobilized Khmer peasant support for the second time since World War II.

With regional autonomy persisting in the Cambodian party, all this necessitated a long series of secret purges and executions if the party Center was to secure organizational control and pursue its extremist domestic and foreign policies. These purges were begun in 1971, but most of the country, although in the hands of the insurgents, remained untouched by the Center for several years. (Meanwhile, former party leader Son Ngoc Minh died of illness in 1972, after eighteen years in exile.)

The Center eclipsed and nearly destroyed its Sihanoukist and moderate communist rivals, including the one thousand Issarak returnees from Hanoi, in most regions between 1973 and 1975. Even in the East, where the intact zone party branch remained dedicated to more moderate goals, So Phim was required by 1974 to abandon his long-standing cooperation with the Vietnamese communists. The next year the party triumphed over Lon Nol's U.S.-backed regime, two weeks before the Vietnamese communists won in their own country.

U.S. Intervention

Although it was indigenous, Pol Pot's revolution would not have won power without U.S. economic and military destabilization of Cambodia, which began in 1966 after the American escalation in next-door Vietnam and peaked in 1969–73 with the carpet bombing of Cambodia's countryside by American B-52's. This was probably the most important single factor in Pol Pot's rise. . . .

. . . [T]he Vietnamese communists were resorting increasingly to the use of Cambodian territory for sanctuary from American attack. By the end of 1965, according to the U.S. intelligence report, they had established "clandestine and probably temporary facilities" there, but that year had already seen "eight instances of fire fights between Cambodian border forces and the Viet Cong." And U.S. aircraft in hot pursuit bombed and strafed Cambodia's border areas. Sihanouk's government claimed in 1966 that "hundreds of our people" had already died in American attacks.

The U.S. intervention in Vietnam also produced a wave of Khmer refugees. From the early 1960s, Khmer Krom began fleeing to Cambodia to escape the Saigon government's repression in the countryside. . . .

Since the early 1960s, U.S. Special Forces teams, too, had been making secret reconnaissance and mine-laying incursions into Cambodian territory. In 1967 and 1968, in Operation Salem House, about eight hundred such missions were mounted, usually by several American personnel and up to ten local mercenaries, in most cases dressed as Viet Cong . . . . [F]rom early 1969, the number of these secret missions doubled. By the time of the 18 March 1970 coup against Sihanouk, over a thousand more had been mounted. . . .

Starting exactly a year before the coup (on 18 March 1969), over thirty-six hundred secret B-52 raids were also conducted over Cambodian territory. These were code-named Menu; the various target areas were labeled Breakfast, Snack, Lunch, Dinner, Dessert, and Supper. About 100,000 tons of bombs were dropped; the civilian toll is unknown. The U.S. aim was to destroy Vietnamese communist forces in Cambodia or drive them back into Vietnam. But in September 1969, Lon Nol reported an increase in the number of communist troops in the sanctuaries, an increase that he said was partly motivated by "the cleaning-up operation" of the U.S.-Saigon forces. He added ominously, "In this period, nothing suggests that these foreign units will soon leave our territory." Like the failing economy, this was one of the major factors in Sihanouk's downfall at Lon Nol's hands. Both factors were exacerbated by the U.S. escalation of the Vietnam War.

By 1970 Cambodia's frontier with Vietnam was breaking down. It was unable to withstand the pressure exerted by the two mighty contending forces that had been expanding and straining against one another in the limited space of southern Vietnam since the escalation of 1965. The pressure was economic, demographic, political, and military. Cambodia's rice crop drained into devastated Vietnam, while both Khmers and Vietnamese fled into Cambodia, with the U.S. military and air force in pursuit.

Richard Nixon's May 1970 invasion of Cambodia (undertaken without informing Lon Nol's new government) followed simultaneous invasions by Saigon and Vietnamese communist forces. It created 130,000 new Khmer refugees, according to the Pentagon. By 1971, 60 percent of refugees surveyed in Cambodia's towns gave U.S. bombing as the main cause of their displacement. The U.S. bombardment of the Cambodian countryside continued until 1973, when Congress imposed a halt. Nearly half of the 540,000 tons of bombs were dropped in the last six months.

From the ashes of rural Cambodia arose Pol Pot's Communist Party of Kampuchea (CPK). It used the bombing's devastation and massacre of civilians as recruitment propaganda and as an excuse for its brutal, radical policies and its purge of moderate communists and Sihanoukists. . . .

In the early years of the Cambodian war, Sihanoukists, moderates, and pro-Vietnamese communists predominated in a factionalized insurgency. The CPK Center admitted it still needed to "get a tight grasp, filter into every corner." Before defeating Lon Nol, it needed to eclipse its revolutionary rivals and allies.

In 1973 the United States withdrew its troops from Vietnam and trained its air force on Cambodia. . . .

The early bombing had been disastrous enough. In 1970 a combined U.S. aerial and tank attack in Kompong Cham province had taken the lives of two hundred people. When another raid killed seven people nearby, a local peasant recalls, "some people ran away . . . others joined the revolution." In 1971, the town of Angkor Borei in southwest Cambodia was heavily bombed by American B-52's and Lon Nol's U.S.-supplied T-28's. It was burnt and leveled. Whole families were trapped in trenches they had dug for protection underneath their homes. Over one hundred people were killed and two hundred houses destroyed, leaving only two or three standing, local residents say. In the same year Sihanouk's former advisor, Charles Meyer, accused the U.S. air force of "systematic pillage" of "peaceful and captivating villages, which are disappearing one after another under bombs or napalm" and ended with a prescient observation: "According to direct testimonies, peasants are taking refuge in forest encampments and are maintaining their smiles and their humor, but one might add that it is difficult to imagine the intensity of their hatred towards those who are destroying their villages and their property. Perhaps we should remember that the Cambodians have the deserved reputation for being the most spiteful and vindictive people in all Southeast Asia and this should in any case hold the attention of President Nixon."

U.S. intelligence soon discovered that many training camps against which Lon Nol had requested air strikes "were in fact merely political indoctrination sessions held in village halls and pagodas." Lon Nol intelligence noted that "aerial bombardments against the villagers have caused civilian loss on a large scale" and that the peasant survivors of the U.S. bombing were turning to the CPK for support.

One young Khmer joined the communists a few days after an aerial attack took the lives of fifty people in his village. Not far away, bombs fell on O Reang Au market for the first time in 1972, killing twenty people, and twice more in 1973, killing another twenty-five people, including two Buddhist monks. When bombs hit Boeng village, it was burnt to the ground, and according to peasants, many people were caught in their houses and burnt to death. Nearby Chalong village counted over twenty dead. An inhabitant told me: "Many monasteries were destroyed by bombs. People in our village were furious with the Americans; they did not know why the Americans had bombed them. Seventy people from Chalong joined the fight against Lon Nol after the bombing."

The B-52's scored a direct hit on Trapeang Krapeu village. Twenty people died. Anlong Trea was napalmed and bombed, killing three and driving over sixty people to join the Khmer communist army "out of anger at the bombing," locals recall.

In March 1973, the bombardment spread west to envelop the whole country. Around Phnom Penh, three thousand civilians were killed in three weeks. At the time UPI reported: "Refugees swarming into the capital from target areas report dozens of villages . . . have been destroyed and as much as half their population killed or maimed in the current bombing raids."

Days later, the U.S. bombardment intensified reaching a level of thirty-six hundred tons per day. . . . As . . . the chief of the Political section in the U.S. embassy, William Harben, one night . . . said: "a mass of peasants" went out on a funeral procession and "walked straight into" a bombing raid. "Hundreds were slaughtered." And Donald Dawson, a young air force captain, flew twenty-five B-52 missions but refused to fly again when he heard that a Cambodian wedding party had been razed by B-52's.

One Cambodian villager lamented in April 1973: "The bombers may kill some Communists but they kill everyone else, too!" The next month the *New York Times* reported that "extensive" destruction had wiped out "a whole series of villages" along the main highway, including seven villages in the eastern part of the country with many people killed. "Nothing was left standing for miles.". . .

But in July and August 1973 the Southwest Zone of Cambodia was carpet bombed. It was the most intensive B-52 campaign yet. Its impact in the Southwest was not simply to destroy many more civilian lives. Politically, it tipped what had been a delicate CPK factional balance there in favor of Pol Pot's "Center."

The political effect reached the highest level of the CPK in the Southwest Zone, its ruling party committee. In 1973—74, four of the eight leaders of this zone committee were purged. Two of these CPK moderates were murdered by Pol Pot allies Mok and Vorn Vet. The other two were killed after 1975, when the Southwest became the stronghold of the Pol Pot regime and Mok went on to purge all other zones in the country.

During the 1973 bombardment, a similar process occurred at the local level. . . . The CPK was now able to recruit many peasants by highlighting the damage done by air strikes. The CIA's Directorate of Operations, after investigations in the Southwest Zone, reported on 2 May 1973 that the CPK had launched a new recruiting drive:

> They are using damage caused by B-52 strikes as the main theme of their propaganda. The cadre tell the people that the Government of Lon Nol has requested the air strikes and is responsible for the damage and the "suffering of innocent villagers" . . . The only way to stop "the massive destruction of the country" is to . . . defeat Lon Nol and stop the bombing. This approach has resulted in the successful recruitment of a number of young men. Residents . . . say that the propaganda campaign has been effective with refugees and in areas . . . which have been subject to B-52 strikes.

Communist Party cadres told young peasant victims of the bombing that "the killing birds" had come "from Phnom Penh" (not Guam), and that Phnom Penh must pay for its assault on rural Cambodia. On the day the bombing ended, CPK's propaganda leaflets found in bomb craters attacked the "Phnom Penh warriors" who were, they vowed, soon to be defeated. The popular outrage over the U.S. bombing, predictably manipulated by the CPK, was as fatal for the two million inhabitants of Phnom Penh as it was for moderate Khmer Rouge and for Lon Nol's regime.

In April 1975, when CPK troops took the country's second largest city, Battambang, they headed straight for the airport. Finding two T-28s, they tore the planes apart with their bare hands, according to a witness. "They would have eaten them if they could," he added. Refugees reported "the lynching of hated bomber pilots." When they forcibly evacuated Battambang and Phnom Penh, CPK forces told the urban populations that the exodus was necessary because "American B-52s" were about to bomb the city. . . .

The Key Issues

Interpretations of the Pol Pot regime vary. Democratic Kampuchea claimed to be "the Number 1 Communist state." In the early 1970s, the CPK had ranked Albania first, followed by China, and then itself, whereas Vietnam was described then as "Comrade Number 7." In 1976, DK proclaimed itself "four to ten years ahead" of the other Asian communist states, having "leaped" from feudalism "to a socialist society straight away." Interestingly, from a conventional anticommunist perspective, historian David Chandler concurs, asserting that the CPK was "the purest and most thoroughgoing Marxist-Leninist movement" and that "what happened in Cambodia, although more intense, was standard operating procedure" in China and the USSR, a case of "socialist practice." By contrast, another historian, Michael

Vickery characterizes DK as an anti-Marxist "peasant revolution," whereas Hanoi's publicists and their Cambodia protégés saw it as a Maoist deviation from orthodox Marxism.

The two most important themes in the history of the Pol Pot regime are the race question and the struggle for central control. . . . The Khmer Rouge conceptions of race overshadowed those of class. The leaders of the CPK Center—from elite backgrounds and without experience of peasant life— privileged themselves and each other to the detriment of alternative leaders from grassroots backgrounds, whether of Khmer or ethnic minority origin. Over time the membership of the top CPK circle became increasingly restricted to the French-educated Pol Pot group. Race also overshadowed organizational imperatives. Non-Khmer Cambodians with extensive revolutionary experience and CPK seniority were removed from the leadership and usually murdered.

At the other extreme—the bottom of the social ladder—non-Khmers, who comprised a significant part of the supposedly favored segment of the peasantry, were singled out for persecution because of their race. This was neither a communist proletarian revolution that privileged the working class nor a peasant revolution that favored all farmers. Favors in DK, such as they were, were reserved for approved Khmers. . . .

The power accumulated by the CPK Center was unprecedented in history. Yet its revolution failed. Much of the horror of DK resulted from the goals of true reactionaries: their attempts to turn back the clock. The regime was confronted with the human and material forces of history in an endeavor to destroy existing social groups (for instance, those of foreign origin, education, or employment). In terms of population as well as of territory, history was to be undone. Here Maoism proved a useful ideological tool, for it stresses the capacity of human willpower to triumph over material conditions and so reverse historical trends. Orthodox Marxism, with its faith in history as inevitable progression, was doubly inappropriate for DK's goals. The CPK Center saw Cambodian history up to 1975 neither as progress nor as inevitable. The Cambodian people and their neighbors paid the price of the attempt to reverse it.

26

Freedom from Fear

AUNG SAN SUU KYI*

Aung San Suu Kyi has arguably become the most well-known "prisoner of conscience" since she was placed under house arrest by the military rulers of Myanmar in 1989. Daughter of the foremost Burmese anti-colonial and nationalist leader, Aung San (assassinated in 1947), she spent several years of her early life in India, where her mother served as her country's ambassador. She was educated mainly in India and Great Britain. Later, Aung San Suu Kyi lived in England with her husband, Michael Aris, an expert on Tibet. In 1988, when she was visiting Myanmar to see her ailing mother, she was struck and distressed by the political repression and lack of human rights under the rule of the generals who had seized power in 1962. Her subsequent involvement in the public life of her country is detailed in the presentation speech of the Chairman of the Nobel Committee reprinted below. Aung San Suu Kyi's husband and sons accepted on her behalf the Nobel Prize for Peace awarded to her in October 1991.

Among the most notable qualities of this physically slight but courageous leader are "Freedom from Fear" (the subject of one of her speeches and the title of one of her articles) and her adherence to nonviolence, following the example of Mahatma Gandhi. She acknowledges him as one of the two main influences in her life, the other being her father, Aung San. Aung San Suu Kyi's "Freedom from Fear" is reprinted here in addition to the presentation speech at the Nobel Prize award ceremony.

The article "Freedom from Fear" was first published to commemorate the European Parliament's award to Aung San Suu Kyi of the 1990 Sakharov Prize for Freedom of Thought. The award ceremony took place

---

*Aung San Suu Kyi, *Freedom from Fear* (New York: Penguin Books USA, 1991), pp. 180–185.

in her absence in Strasbourg on July 10, 1991. During that week, the article appeared in full or in part in the London *Times Literary Supplement,* the *New York Times,* the *Far Eastern Economic Review,* the *Bangkok Post,* the *Times of India,* and numerous newspapers in Europe.

~

It is not power that corrupts but fear. Fear of losing power corrupts those who wield it, and fear of the scourge of power corrupts those who are subject to it. Most Burmese are familiar with the four *a-gati,* the four kinds of corruption. *Chanda-gati,* corruption induced by desire, is deviation from the right path in pursuit of bribes or for the sake of those one loves. *Dosa-gati* is taking the wrong path to spite those against whom one bears ill will, and *moga-gati* is aberration due to ignorance. But perhaps the worst of the four is *bhaya-gati,* for not only does *bhaya,* fear, stifle and slowly destroy all sense of right and wrong, it so often lies at the root of the other three kinds of corruption.

Just as *chanda-gati,* when not the result of sheer avarice, can be caused by fear of want or fear of losing the goodwill of those one loves, so fear of being surpassed, humiliated or injured in some way can provide the impetus for ill will. And it would be difficult to dispel ignorance unless there is freedom to pursue the truth unfettered by fear. With so close a relationship between fear and corruption it is little wonder that in any society where fear is rife corruption in all forms becomes deeply entrenched.

Public dissatisfaction with economic hardships has been seen as the chief cause of the movement for democracy in Burma, sparked off by the student demonstrations in 1988. It is true that years of incoherent policies, inept official measures, burgeoning inflation and falling real income had turned the country into an economic shambles. But it was more than the difficulties of eking out a barely acceptable standard of living that had eroded the patience of a traditionally good-natured, quiescent people—it was also the humiliation of a way of life disfigured by corruption and fear. The students were protesting not just against the death of their comrades but against the denial of their right to life by a totalitarian regime which deprived the present of meaningfulness and held out no hope for the future. And because the students' protests articulated the frustrations of the people at large, the demonstrations quickly grew into a nationwide movement. Some of its keenest supporters were businessmen who had developed the skills and the contacts necessary not only to survive but to prosper within the system. But their affluence offered them no genuine sense of security or fulfillment, and they could not but see that if they and their fellow citizens, regardless of economic status, were to achieve a worthwhile existence, an accountable administration was at least a necessary if not a sufficient condition. The people of Burma had wearied of a precarious state of passive apprehension where they were 'as water in the cupped hands' of the powers that be.

Emerald cool we may be
As water in cupped hands
But oh that we might be
As splinters of glass
In cupped hands.

Glass splinters, the smallest with its sharp, glinting power to defend it-self against hands that try to crush, could only be seen as a vivid symbol of the spark of courage that is an essential attribute of those who would free themselves from the grip of oppression. Bogyoke Aung San [Myanmar's esteemed leader and Suu Kyi's father] regarded himself as a revolutionary and searched tirelessly for answers to the problems that beset Burma dur-ing her times of trial. He exhorted the people to develop courage: 'Don't just depend on the courage and intrepidity of others. Each and every one of you must make sacrifices to become a hero possessed of courage and in-trepidity. Then only shall we all be able to enjoy true freedom.'

The effort necessary to remain uncorrupted in an environment where fear is an integral part of everyday existence is not immediately apparent to those fortunate enough to live in states governed by the rule of law. Just laws do not merely prevent corruption by meting out impartial punish-ment to offenders. They also help to create a society in which people can fulfill the basic requirements necessary for the preservation of human dig-nity without recourse to corrupt practices. Where there are no such laws, the burden of upholding the principles of justice and common decency falls on the ordinary people. It is the cumulative effect on their sustained effort and steady endurance which will change a nation where reason and conscience are warped by fear into one where legal rules exist to promote man's desire for harmony and justice while restraining the less desirable destructive traits in his nature.

In an age when immense technological advances have created lethal weapons which could be, and are, used by the powerful and the unprinci-pled to dominate the weak and the helpless, there is a compelling need for a closer relationship between politics and ethics at both the national and in-ternational levels. The Universal Declaration of Human Rights of the United Nations proclaims that 'every individual and every organ of soci-ety' should strive to promote the basic rights and freedoms to which all human beings regardless of race, nationality or religion are entitled. But as long as there are governments whose authority is founded on coercion rather than on the mandate of the people, and interest groups which place short-term profits above long-term peace and prosperity, concerted international action to protect and promote human rights will remain at best a partially realized struggle. There will continue to be arenas of struggle where victims of oppression have to draw on their own inner resources to defend their inalienable rights as members of the human family.

The quintessential revolution is that of the spirit, born of an intellectual conviction of the need for change in those mental attitudes and values which shape the course of a nation's development. A revolution which aims merely at changing official policies and institutions with a view to an improvement in material conditions has little chance of genuine success. Without a revolution of the spirit, the forces which produced the iniquities of the old order would continue to be operative, posing a constant threat to the process of reform and regeneration. It is not enough merely to call for freedom, democracy and human rights. There has to be a united determination to persevere in the struggle, to make sacrifices in the name of enduring truths, to resist the corrupting influences of desire, ill will, ignorance and fear.

Saints, it has been said, are the sinners who go on trying. So free men are the oppressed who go on trying and who in the process make themselves fit to bear the responsibility and to uphold the disciplines which will maintain a free society. Among the basic freedoms to which men aspire that their lives might be full and uncramped, freedom from fear stands out as both a means and an end. A people who would build a nation in which strong, democratic institutions are firmly established as a guarantee against state-induced power must first learn to liberate their own minds from apathy and fear.

Always one to practice what he preached, Aung San himself constantly demonstrated courage—not just the physical sort but the kind that enabled him to speak the truth, to stand by his word, to accept criticism, to admit his faults, to correct his mistakes, to respect the opposition, to parley with the enemy and to let people be the judge of his worthiness as a leader. It is for such moral courage that he will always be loved and respected in Burma—not merely as a warrior hero but as the inspiration and conscience of the nation. The words used by Jawaharlal Nehru to describe Mahatma Gandhi could well be applied to Aung San: 'The essence of his teaching was fearlessness and truth, and action allied to these, always keeping the welfare of the masses in view.'

Gandhi, the great apostle of non-violence, and Aung San, the founder of a national army, were very different personalities, but as there is an inevitable sameness about the challenges of authoritarian rule anywhere at any time, so there is a similarity in the intrinsic qualities of those who rise up to meet the challenge. Nehru, who considered the instillation of courage in the people of India one of Gandhi's greatest achievements, was a political modernist, but as he assessed the needs for a twentieth-century movement for independence, he found himself looking back to the philosophy of ancient India: 'The greatest gift for an individual nation . . . was *abhaya*, fearlessness, not merely bodily courage but absence of fear from the mind.'

Fearlessness may be a gift but perhaps more precious is the courage acquired through endeavor, courage that comes from cultivating the habit of refusing to let fear dictate one's actions, courage that could be described as 'grace under pressure'—grace which is renewed repeatedly in the face of harsh, unremitting pressure.

Within a system which denies the existence of basic human rights, fear tends to be the order of the day. Fear of imprisonment, fear of torture, fear of death, fear of losing friends, family, property or means of livelihood, fear of poverty, fear of isolation, fear of failure. A most insidious form of fear is that which masquerades as common sense or even wisdom, condemning as foolish, reckless, insignificant or futile the small, daily acts of courage which help to preserve man's self-respect and inherent human dignity. It is not easy for people conditioned by fear under the iron rule of the principle that might is right to free themselves from the enervating miasma of fear. Yet even under the most crushing state machinery courage rises up again and again, for fear is not the natural state of civilized man.

The wellspring of courage and endurance in the face of unbridled power is generally a firm belief in the sanctity of ethical principles combined with a historical sense that despite all set-backs the condition of man is set on an ultimate course for both spiritual and material advancement. It is his capacity for self-improvement and self-redemption which most distinguishes man from mere brute. At the root of human responsibility is the concept of perfection, the urge to achieve it, the intelligence to find a path towards it, and the will to follow that path if not to the end at least the distance needed to rise above individual limitations and environmental impediments. It is man's vision of a world fit for rational, civilized humanity which leads him to dare and to suffer to build societies free from want and fear. Concepts such as truth, justice, and compassion cannot be dismissed as trite when these are often the only bulwarks which stand against ruthless power.

~

THE NOBEL PEACE PRIZE, 1991

Presentation Speech by Francis Sejersted,
*Chairman of the Norwegian Nobel Committee**

Your Majesties, Your Excellencies, Ladies and Gentlemen,

We are assembled here today to honor Aung San Suu Kyi for her outstanding work for democracy and human rights, and to present to her the Nobel Peace Prize for 1991. The occasion gives rise to many and partly conflicting emotions. The Peace Prize Laureate is unable to be here herself. The great work we are acknowledging has yet to be concluded. She is still fighting the good fight. Her courage and commitment find her a prisoner of conscience in her own country, Burma. Her absence fills us with fear and anxiety, which can nevertheless only be a faint shadow of the fear and anxiety felt by her family. We welcome this opportunity of expressing our deepest sympathy with them, with her husband, Michael Aris, and with her sons, Alexander and Kim. We feel with you, and we are very grateful to you for coming to Oslo to receive the Nobel Prize on behalf of your wife and mother.

Our fear and anxiety are mixed with a sense of confidence and hope. In the good fight for peace and reconciliation, we are dependent on persons who set examples, persons who can symbolize what we are seeking and mobilize the best in us. Aung San Suu Kyi is just such a person. She unites deep commitment and tenacity with a vision in which the end and the means form a single unit. Its most important elements are: democracy, respect for human rights, reconciliation between groups, non-violence, and personal and collective discipline.

She has herself clearly indicated the sources of her inspiration: principally Mahatma Gandhi and her father, Aung San, the leader in Burma's struggle for liberation. The philosopher of non-violence and the General differ in many respects, but also show fundamental similarities. In both, one can see genuine independence, true modesty, and "a profound simplicity," to use Aung San Suu Kyi's own words about her father. To Aung San, leadership was a duty, and could only be carried out on the basis of humility in face of the task before him and the confidence and respect of the people to be led.

While no doubt deriving a great deal of inspiration from Gandhi and her father, Aung San Suu Kyi has also added her own independent reflections to what has become her political platform. The keynote is the same profound

---

*"The Nobel Peace Prize 1991 Press Release Presentation Speech: Aung San Suu Kyi," in *Nobel Lectures, Peace: 1991–1995*, ed. Irwin Abrams (Singapore: World Scientific Publishing, 1999).

simplicity as she sees in her father. The central position given to human rights in her thinking appears to reflect a real sense of the need to protect human dignity. Man is not only entitled to live in a free society; he also has a right to respect. On this platform, she has built a policy marked by an extraordinary combination of sober realism and visionary idealism. And in her case this is more than just a theory: she has gone a long way towards showing how such a doctrine can be translated into practical politics.

For a doctrine of peace and reconciliation to be translated into practice, one absolute condition is fearlessness. Aung San Suu Kyi knows this. One of her essays opens with the statement that it is not power that corrupts, but fear.[1] The comment was aimed at the totalitarian regime in her own country. They have allowed themselves to be corrupted because they fear the people they are supposed to lead. This has led them into a vicious circle. In her thinking, however, the demand for fearlessness is first and foremost a general demand, a demand on all of us. She has herself shown fearlessness in practice. She opposed herself alone to the rifle barrels. Can anything withstand such courage? What was in that Major's mind when at the last moment he gave the order not to fire? Perhaps he was impressed by her bravery, perhaps he realized that nothing can be achieved by brute force.[2]

Violence is its own worst enemy, and fearlessness is the sharpest weapon against it. It is not least Aung San Suu Kyi's impressive courage which makes her such a potent symbol, like Gandhi and her father Aung San. Aung San was shot in the midst of his struggle. But if those who arranged the assassination thought it would remove him from Burmese politics, they were wrong. He became the unifying symbol of a free Burma and an inspiration to those who are now fighting for a free society. In addition to his example and inspiration, his position among his people, over forty years after his death, gave Aung San Suu Kyi the political point of departure she needed. She has indeed taken up her inheritance, and is now in her own right the symbol of the revolt against violence and the struggle for a free society, not only in Burma, but also in the rest of Asia and in many other parts of the world.

We ordinary people, I believe, feel that with her courage and her high ideals, Aung San Suu Kyi brings out something of the best in us. We feel we need precisely her sort of person in order to retain our faith in the future. That is what gives her such power as a symbol, and that is why any ill treatment of her feels like a violation of what we have most at heart. The little woman under house arrest stands for a positive hope. Knowing she is there gives us confidence and faith in the power of good.

Aung San Suu Kyi was born in 1945. Her father was killed when she was two. She has no personal memories of him. Her mother was a diplomat, and Aung San Suu Kyi was to spend many of her early years and much of her later life abroad. In 1967, she took a degree in Politics, Philosophy and Economics at St. Hugh's College, Oxford. From 1969 on, she worked for two years for the United Nations in New York. In 1972 she married Michael Aris, a British specialist on Tibet. For a time the family lived in Bhutan, but in the mid-seventies they moved back to Oxford. In addition to being a housewife with two small children, Aung San Suu Kyi kept up her academic work, gradually concentrating on modern Burmese history and literature. She was a visiting scholar at Kyoto University in Japan and at the Indian Institute of Advanced Studies in New Delhi. On her return to Burma in 1988, she broke off her studies at the London School of Oriental and African Studies. There is little in these outward events to suggest the role she was to embark on in 1988. But she was well prepared.

There is a great deal of evidence that the fate of her own people had constantly weighed on her mind. Her husband has told us how she often reminded him that one day she would have to return to Burma, and that she would count on his support.[3] Her studies, too, as we have seen, became increasingly concentrated on Burma's modern history. The study of her father and the part he played in Burmese history no doubt increased her political commitment and sense that his mantle had fallen on her.[4]

In moving to Japan, she was virtually following in her father's footsteps. During the Second World War, it was from a base in Japan that Aung San built up Burma's independent national army. When Japan invaded Burma, Aung San and his men went too. Before long, they switched from fighting the British colonial power to resisting the occupying Japanese and supporting the retaking of Burma by the Allies. After the war, he led the negotiations with the British which were to lead to final independence. Aung San Suu Kyi appears to have felt an urgent need to study the process which led to Burma's independent statehood, and to understand the ideals governing the politics. In a beautiful essay comparing the Indian and Burmese experience of colonization, she also brings out the special features of Burma's cultural heritage.[5] History is important. You choose who you are by choosing which tradition you belong to. Aung San Suu Kyi seeks to call attention to what she sees as the best aspects of the national and cultural heritage and to identify herself with them. Such profound knowledge and such a deep sense of identity are an irresistible force in the political struggle.

The occasion of Aung San Suu Kyi's return to Burma in 1988 was, characteristically enough, not the political situation but her old mother's illness. The political turbulence had just begun, however. There had been demonstrations and confrontations with the police with some two hundred killed. The unrest continued while she was nursing her dying mother. That was the situation in which she resolved to take an active part in what she herself called "the second struggle for national independence."

The military regime had seized power in Burma in 1962. The disturbances which broke out in 1988 were a reaction to growing repression. In
the summer of that year, at a time when the situation was very uncertain,
Aung San Suu Kyi intervened with an open letter to the government,
proposing the appointment of a consultative committee of respected independent persons to lead the country into multi-party elections. In the letter,
she emphasized the need for discipline and for refraining from the use of
force on either side, and demanded the release of political prisoners.[6]

A couple of days later, she addressed several hundred thousand people in
front of the large Shwedagon Pagoda in Rangoon, presenting a political
program based on human rights, democracy and non-violence. On the 18th
of September, after hesitating for a few weeks, the armed forces reacted by
tightening the restrictions. The so-called "State Law and Order Restoration
Council" (SLORC) was established, and martial law was introduced under
which meetings were banned and persons could be sentenced without trial.

Political parties were not prohibited (perhaps with meetings banned it
was thought unnecessary). A week after the establishment of SLORC,
Aung San Suu Kyi and a few other members of the opposition founded the
National League for Democracy, the NLD. She went on to engage in vigorous political activity, defying the ban on meetings and military provoca-
tions, and holding heavily attended political meetings all over the country.
One remarkable feature of her political campaign was the appeal she had for
the country's various ethnic groups, traditionally at odds with each other.

It must have been her personal prestige which caused the regime to hesitate so long, but in July 1989 she was placed under house arrest. In May
1990, elections were held, in which the NLD won an overwhelming victory
and over 80 per cent of the seats in the national assembly. There is general
agreement that this was principally a triumph for Aung San Suu Kyi.

Why did the SLORC allow free elections? Probably because they expected a very different result, a result which would somehow have provided
the legitimacy they needed to retain power. The dilemma of such regimes
was demonstrated—trapped in their own lies. At any rate, they refused to
accept the election result. The election was in effect annulled. The SLORC
continued, but with reduced legitimacy. Lack of legitimacy is often made up
for by increased brutality. Amnesty International has reported continuing
serious violations of human rights.[7] Today, the Burmese regime appears to
have developed into one of the most repressive in the world.

In recent decades, the Norwegian Nobel Committee has awarded a number
of Prizes for Peace in recognition of work for human rights.[8] It has done so in
the conviction that a fundamental prerequisite for peace is the recognition of
the right of all people to life and to respect. Another motivation lies in the

knowledge that in its most basic form, the concept of human rights is not just a Western idea, but common to all major cultures. Permit me in this connection to quote a paragraph of Aung San Suu Kyi's essay in "Quest of Democracy":

> Where there is no justice there can be no secure peace.
> . . . That just laws which uphold human rights are the necessary foundations of peace and security would be denied only by closed minds which interpret peace as the silence of all opposition and security as the assurance of their own power. The Burmese associate peace and security with coolness and shade:
> The shade of a tree is cool indeed
> The shade of parents is cooler
> The shade of teachers is cooler still
> The shade of the ruler is yet more cool
> But coolest of all is the shade of the Buddha's teachings.
> Thus to provide the people with the protective coolness of peace and security, rulers must observe the teachings of the Buddha. Central to these teachings are the concepts of truth, righteousness and loving kindness. It is government based on these very qualities that the people of Burma are seeking in their struggle for democracy.[9]

This is not the first time that political persecution at home has prevented a Peace Prize Laureate from receiving the prize in person. It happened to Carl von Ossietzky in 1936, ill in one of Hitler's concentration camps.[10] It happened to Andrei Sakharov and to Lech Walesa. Ossietzky died before the regime fell, but Sakharov and Walesa saw their struggles succeed. It is our hope that Aung San Suu Kyi will see her struggle crowned with success.

However, we must also face up to the likelihood that this will not be the last occasion on which a Peace Prize Laureate is unable to attend. Let that remind us that in a world such as ours, peace and reconciliation cannot be achieved once and for all. We will never be able to lower our standards. On the contrary, a better world demands even greater vigilance of us, still greater fearlessness, and the ability to develop in ourselves the "profound simplicity" of which this year's Laureate has spoken. This applies to all of us as individuals, but must apply especially to those in positions of power and authority. Show humility and show fearlessness—like Aung San Suu Kyi. The result may be a better world to live in.

NOTES

1. "Freedom from Fear" in *Freedom*, pp. 180–185. The reference is to the oft-quoted dictum of Lord Acton, "Power tends to corrupt, and absolute power corrupts absolutely."

2. In 1988, despite opposition by the government, Aung San Suu Kyi made a speech-making tour throughout the country. She was walking with her associates along a street in a town, when soldiers lined up in front of the group, threatening to shoot if they did not halt. Suu Kyi asked her supporters to step aside, and she walked on. At the last moment the major in command ordered the soldiers not to fire. She explained later, "It seemed so much simpler to provide them with a single target than to bring everyone else in."

3. *Freedom*, Introduction, p. xvii.

4. "My Father," *in Freedom*, pp. 3–38. First published by Queensland Press in 1984 in the Leaders of Asia series under the title of Aung San. Reprinted in 1991 by Kiscadale, Edinburgh, as *Aung San of Burma: A Biographical Portrait by His Daughter*.

5. "Intellectual Life in Burma and India under Colonialism," in *Freedom*, pp. 82–139.

6. "The Formation of a People's Consultative Committee," 15 August 1988, translated by Suu Kyi, in *Freedom*, pp. 192–197. Her first political initiative.

7. Amnesty International received the Nobel Peace Prize in 1977. See Irwin Abrams, ed., *Nobel Lectures, Peace: 1971–1980* (Singapore: World Scientific, 1997): 161–177. Amnesty International campaigned for Suu Kyi's release from detention as a "prisoner of conscience."

8. The 1935 award to the concentration camp prisoner Carl von Ossietzky may be considered the earliest human rights prize. Later such recipients were Albert Lutuli (1960), Martin Luther King, Jr. (1964), René Cassin (1968), Séan MacBride (1974), Amnesty International (1977), Adolfo Pérez Esquivel (1980), Lech Walesa (1983), Desmond Tutu (1984), Elie Wiesel (1986), and the 14th Dalai Lama (1989). After 1991 such grantees were Rigoberta Menchú Tum (1992), and the 1996 laureates from East Timor, José Ramos-Horta and Bishop Belo. See Abrams, *The Nobel Peace Prize and the Laureates* (Boston: G. K. Hall, 3rd printing, 1990): 175–176 and entries on these laureates. Also the lectures of the most recent human rights laureates in Abrams, ed., *Nobel Lectures, Peace: 1971–1980*, cited in the previous endnote, and the companion volume for 1981–1990.

9. "Quest for Democracy," in *Freedom*, pp. 167–179, esp. pp. 177–178.

10. The international campaign for the prize for Carl von Ossietzky had already brought about his removal from the camp to a hospital in Berlin before the Norwegian Nobel Committee announced in 1936 that he would be awarded the postponed prize of 1935. The Nazi government refused permission for him to go to Oslo for the award ceremony. See Irwin Abrams, *The Nobel Peace Prizes*, pp. 125–129; Abrams, "Carl von Ossietzky Retrospective," *The Nobel Prize Annual, 1989* (Boston: G. K. Hall, 1990): 12–23.

27

Islam in

Southeast Asia

GREG FEALY*

Indonesia's Muslim population estimated at 185 million (87 percent of the total population) makes Indonesia the largest Muslim country in the world. Two other states in Southeast Asia—Malaysia and Brunei—are Muslim-majority states. There are sizeable Muslim minorities in other countries, notably in the southern Philippines, where the Moros have been demanding autonomy, if not independence. Greg Fealy rightly notes that historically, Southeast Asian Islam has been known as "the world's most moderate and tolerant expressions of the faith." The fundamentalist wave of Islam in the Middle East, notably in Iran and Saudi Arabia, and earlier in Afghanistan under the Taliban, and the terrorist attacks sponsored by al-Qaida have influenced the mood and methods of some Moslems in Southeast Asia. This is evidenced not only in the growing popularity of the Islamic party in the northern Malaysian states but also in the growing number of terrorist incidents, including kidnappings and violence by the Abu Sayyaf group in the southern Philippines, bombings in Bali, armed conflict against Christians in Sulawesi, and attacks against the Rohingyas in Myanmar.

Despite such changes in Southeast Asian Islam, there is a paucity of literature on the subject. Greg Fealy, whose doctoral dissertation focused on Indonesia's traditionalist party, Nahdatul Islam, has for the past several years conducted research on the Islamic Brotherhood and terrorism. In the article

---

*Greg Fealy, "Islam in Southeast Asia: Domestic Pietism, Diplomacy, and Security," in *Contemporary Southeast Asia: Regional Dynamics, National Differences,* ed. Mark Beeson (London: Palgrave Macmillan, 2004), pp. 136–155.

reprinted here, Fealy describes the key aspects of contemporary Islam in Southeast Asia.

~

Southeast Asian Islam has until recently been a neglected subject for scholars and policy-makers. Strategic analysts saw Islam as a relatively minor element in the region's politics and diplomacy despite the fact that Southeast Asia is home to nearly one-fifth of the world's Muslims. Meanwhile, students of Islam tended to see the region as geographically, intellectually and politically peripheral to the 'real center' of the Muslim world, the Middle East. Hence, there are remarkably few books dealing with Islam in a specifically Southeast Asian context, and many works dealing with Southeast Asian affairs or world Islamic politics pay only scant attention to the role of [the] region's Muslims.

This discounting of Southeast Asian Islam began to change in the 1970s as a result of growing Islamization. Islam grew in popularity in Indonesia and Malaysia, the region's two significant majority Muslim nations, particularly among urban Muslims, and gradually increased its political influence in domestic politics. At the same time, Muslim insurgencies in the southern Philippines, Aceh in Indonesia and to a lesser extent, southern Thailand created major security problems in the region and also attracted the attention of Muslim groups and nations elsewhere in the Islamic world.

But it has been the emergence of the terrorism issue in the wake of the 11 September 2001 (commonly referred to as '9/11') attacks on the World Trade Center and Pentagon which has concentrated international attention in Southeast Asia's Islamic community. Soon after the attacks, investigators disclosed that al-Qaida operatives had been based in the region and that a number of Southeast Asians were involved in assisting the perpetrators. In mid-2001, Malaysian officials began arresting members of suspected terrorist groups, and in December of that year a terrorist cell connected to the Jemaah Islamiyah (JI) network was discovered in Singapore, setting off a string of arrests across the region. On 12 October 2002, the worst terrorist attack since 9/11 took place in Bali, Indonesia. Bomb blasts in two nightclubs killed 202 people, the majority of them Western tourists, and injured more than 350 others. Police investigations have adduced extensive *prima facie* evidence that JI members carried out the attack, quite probably with the knowledge and possible assistance of al-Qaida. Not surprisingly, the international media began to refer to Southeast Asia as the 'second front in the war against terrorism' and the 'new frontier of Islamic extremism.'[1] As a result governments and scholars began devoting considerable resources to

TABLE 27.1   Southeast Asian Muslims

Country	Total Population	% Muslims	Muslim Population	% Total SE Asian Muslims
Brunei	343,653	67	230,248	0.1
Burma	41,994,678	3.8	1,679,787	0.81
Cambodia	12,491,501	2.4	299,796	0.14
Indonesia	212,195,000	87	184,609,605	89.5
Laos	5,635,967	1.0	57,000	0.1
Malaysia	22,229,040	55	12,225,972	5.93
Philippines	82,841,518	4.6	4,142,076	2.0
Singapore	4,300,419	14	602,059	0.29
Thailand	61,797,751	3.8	2,348,315	1.14
Vietnam	79,939,014	0.7	531,000	0.25
Southeast Asia	468,011,411	44.2	206,725,858	

SOURCES: These figures are drawn from a variety of sources, including John L. Esposito, ed., *Islam in Asia* (New York: Oxford University Press, 1987), pp. 262–263; K. F. Bin Mohd. Noor, "Muslim Statistics for Year 2000," cited at http://www.adherents.com/; Central Intelligence Agency, *The World Fact Book 2002*, available at http://www/cia.gov//publications/factbook/geos/us/html; and World Bank, "Country Profiles," available at http://devdata.Worldbank.org/external/CPProfile.

analyzing the region's Islamic groups. Much of this recent research and analysis has tended to view Islam through the prism of terrorism, rather than seeing extremism as but one of many manifestations of Islamic life.

This chapter will consider recent trends in Southeast Asian Islam and examine the role which Islam plays in the region's affairs. It will look at four specific issues: (1) the character of Islam in the region and the nature of the resurgence; (2) the impact of Islam upon domestic politics and social cohesion; (3) the influence of 'Islamic issues' on diplomatic and economic relations; and (4) the importance of Islam for regional security. It will argue that, with the exception of matters of security, Islam has had a less significant role in regional affairs than the size of the Muslim community would suggest.

Southeast Asia's Muslim Community

Muslims make up almost half of Southeast Asia's population, and the available data indicate a total Muslim population of about 206 million, approximately 18 per cent of the world's estimated 1.2 billion Muslims. Muslims can be found in all of the region's nations but most are concentrated in two countries: Indonesia which has 90 per cent of the total, and Malaysia 6 per cent. (see Table 27.1) Along with Brunei, these are the only nations with majority Muslim communities.

Most Indonesian Muslims are found on the islands of Java, Sumatra, Kalimantan and Sulawesi, whereas Malaysia's Muslims predominate on the Malayan Peninsula and are overwhelmingly Malay. The Philippines, Thailand and Burma have significant localized minority Muslim communities. Filipino Muslims, commonly known as 'Moros,' are found on the southern island of Mindanao and in the Sulu archipelago. Thailand's Islamic community is divided into two main groups: 'Thai Muslims,' a heterogeneous community of diverse ethnic origins residing mainly in the central and northern regions and 'Malay Muslims' who are concentrated in the four southern provinces near the Malaysian border. The main Muslim population of Burma (Myanmar) is in the western state of Arakan and is known as the Rohingyas, a sizeable number of whom live as refugees across the border in Bangladesh. There are also pockets of Chinese and West and South Asian Muslims. In Indochina there is a Muslim community of almost 900,000 comprising mainly Chams who are concentrated in the south of Vietnam and east Cambodia.

Southeast Asian Islam is usually described as one of the world's most moderate and tolerant expressions of the faith. Most of the region's Muslims are Sunni, and in many areas religious life has been syncretic, blending Islamic devotions with pre-existing Hindu, Buddhist and folk practices. This reflects the manner in which Islam has spread through the region since the twelfth century. For the most part, the bearers of Islam were prepared to adapt to local conditions and seek conversion through persuasion rather than through conquest or coercion. Pluralism has been another feature. Muslims have generally lived peacefully in religiously mixed communities even in areas where they constituted a large majority. While moderation has been an essential characteristic of Southeast Asian Islam, it is also true that historically a very small minority of Muslims have been drawn to the more puritanical or extremist variants of the faith. Such groups have typically opposed any accretions to the 'pure' prescription of Islam set out in the Qur'an and the Sunnah (example of the Prophet Muhammad). As a result, they were critical of many of their co-religionists and were also more exclusivist in their attitudes towards non-Muslim communities. Despite their strict or unyielding stance on matters of doctrine or ritual practice, very few Muslims in this category were disposed to violence to achieve their objectives.

Southeast Asian Islam has been undergoing a resurgence in recent decades, particularly in Indonesia and Malaysia. This resurgence is not a numerical one; the available data suggest that the percentage of Muslims to non-Muslims in the region is relatively stable. What is rising is the percentage of Muslims who are more self-conscious and devout in the practice of their faith. The extent of this growing pietism is difficult to quantify but it is manifest in such trends as the growing popularity of 'Islamic dress' (headdresses and flowing gowns for women; white skull caps and collarless long white shirts for men), increasing mosque construction and attendance, burgeoning sales of books and magazines on Islam, a proliferation of Islamic symbols (including Islamic-style geometric patterns and Arabic terms and script), and growing numbers of Southeast Asian Muslims taking the pilgrimage (hajj) to Mecca. There has also been greater interaction with other areas of the Islamic world. This has come through enhanced mass communications and access to cyber-technology as well as through increased numbers of Southeast Asian Muslims studying in the Middle East. These phenomena have led to a cultural efflorescence of Islam as Muslims not only seek to deepen their understanding of the faith but also find new ways of interpreting and applying it in a rapidly modernizing world. As will be seen below, this rise in Islamic observance and culture has flowed through to the region's politics and diplomacy.

Islam in Domestic Affairs

Islam's influence within the national life of Southeast Asian states has been limited. Even in the three majority Muslim states, divisions within the Islamic community and the perceived desirability of accommodating minority aspirations have, for the most part, ensured a pluralist orientation and prevented the more exclusivist Islamist proposals from being adopted. Nonetheless, in Indonesia and Malaysia, demands that there be special recognition of Islamic law as well as state support for Islamic activities have been a constant source of tension and have occasionally led to physical conflict.

Indonesia provides a striking example of a polity where Islam, the declared faith of more than four out of five citizens, has been a major rather than a determining factor in shaping the state and social relations. The defeats for political Islam have been manifold and Islamic parties have repeatedly failed to win constitutional acknowledgement of Islamic law. In 1945 when the founding constitution was finalized, Islamic leaders reluctantly agreed to omit a clause that would have obliged Muslims to implement the Shariah. They did so after warnings that predominantly Christian provinces in the east of the country might secede. Unsuccessful bids to reinsert the clause (commonly known as the Jakarta Charter) were made in 1959, 1967, 2001 and 2002. Despite a seeming sharp decline in support for the Charter, the Islamic law question remains one of the more divisive issues in Indonesian politics. Electorally, Islamic parties have also failed to attract the votes of many Muslims. In the country's two free and fair elections—1955 and 1999—Islamic parties (defined here as those parties which are either ideologically based on Islam or rely largely upon an Islamic identity and leadership to attract support) got a total of 44 per cent and 38 per cent respectively of the total vote.[2] At the 1999 election Islamist parties that supported the Jakarta Charter gained less than 17 per cent. Furthermore, for much of Indonesia's history, political Islam has been oppressed and marginalized. Beginning with Sukarno's Guided Democracy regime (1959–66) and Suharto's New Order (1966–98), Islamic parties were subject to a growing range of restrictions and interference from the state. Suharto, in particular, viewed Islam as a discordant element in national affairs as well as the most serious potential threat to his own dominance. During the first two decades of his presidency, he systematically set about containing and controlling political Islam. In 1973, all Islamic parties were pushed into an unstable merger and then progressively stripped of much of their Islamic identity. The culmination of this process came in 1985 when the regime obliged all Islamic organizations to have the religiously neutral state philosophy of *Pancasila* as their ideological basis rather than Islam. Devout Muslims were also viewed with suspicion by the regime and few were entrusted with positions at senior levels of government.

The fortunes of political Islam began to turn in the late 1980's, when there was a rapprochement with the regime. Suharto sought to offset declining support from within the military for his rule by cultivating Muslim constituencies. As part of this process, he offered a range of concessions to Muslims including expanded powers for the Islamic courts, the introduction of Islamic banking and insurance, easing restrictions on Islamic dress for students, and accelerated recruitment and promotion of Muslims to upper levels of the military and bureaucracy. The regime's embracing of Islam created resentment and suspicion among secular nationalists and non-Muslims and caused splits within the military, political elite and civil society. It has been seen as a factor contributing to a rise in religious conflict in areas such us Maluku and Central Sulawesi from the late 1990s. Following Suharto's downfall in May 1998, political Islam has experienced mixed fortunes. The emergence of a genuine multiparty system since the 1999 elections has meant that many of the larger Islamic parties have a share of power in coalition governments at both the national and local levels, though Islam remains a secondary rather than primary issue in most areas of policy.

Compared to Indonesia, Islam has had a greater impact on Malaysian life, even though the Muslim community is about 30 per cent less of the total population. One key difference between the two is that the identity of the majority Malay community is inextricably linked to Islam. Put simply, to be Malay is to be Muslim. In Indonesia, the Islamic community is ethnically, geographically, socio-economically and ideologically diverse, with the result that Islamic politics has been more often than not deeply divided. While the Malaysian Islamic community is not monolithic, it does enjoy a much higher level of cohesion than is the case with Indonesia. The central purpose of the dominant party UMNO (United Malays National Organization) is to promote Malay interests and Islam. UMNO leads the governing National Front (BN) coalition, in which its main partners are Chinese and Indian parties. Although it has usually possessed a parliamentary majority in its own right, the party has a strong commitment to maintaining an inter-communal alliance in government. In the seven elections between 1974 and 1999, the BN vote ranged from 53 per cent to 65 per cent. The main 'Islamic' rival to UMNO is PAS (Parti Islam Se-Malaysia), which has a more Islamist outlook. Its highest vote at a general election is just 15 per cent but it controls the two northern peninsular states of Kelantan and Trengganu and continues to attack UMNO's Islamic credentials. UMNO has pursued a policy of 'affirmative action' for the Malays following the 1969 race riots. This programme includes preferential treatment for Malays in education and business, as well as state-sponsored Islamization. This has particularly been the case since Dr. Mahathir Mohammad became Prime Minister in 1981; the state has made religious education in schools and tertiary institutions mandatory, has sponsored proselytization and mosque-building programmes, sought to inculcate Islamic values into the public service, established an Islamic bank and International Islamic University and promoted Islamic broadcasting in the media. Mahathir's most controversial decision came in 2001 when he declared Malaysia to be an Islamic state; previously Islam had been the official religion. These policies reflect several factors: Islamic sentiment is becoming more pronounced within Malay society, especially among the urban middle classes, and Mahathir and UMNO have wanted to appear responsive to this. The government is also determined to avoid being outflanked on Islamic issues by PAS. Islamization has caused irritation and disquiet among non-Muslims, but in general Mahathir has been careful not to alienate his Chinese and Indian coalition partners or alarm foreign investors.[3]

Islam also figures prominently in Brunei's internal affairs. Brunei is a sultanate and the only ruling monarchy in Southeast Asia. Islam is its official religion and the sultan combines both religious and political roles. Thailand is the only other Southeast Asian state in which Muslims have played a significant role. Several southern Thai Muslims have held positions in government including Surin Pitsuwan, who served as Foreign Minister from 1997 to 2001 and the current Interior Minister Wan Muhammad Nor Matha, whose 'Wadah' faction joined Prime Minister Thaksin Shinawatra's Thai Rak Thai party. In addition to this, southern Muslims hold eight seats in the Senate, allowing them a direct role in legislative processes and the monitoring of state agencies.[4]

Islam in Diplomacy and Trade

Given Southeast Asia's religious diversity, it is not surprising that Islam has not been a dominant factor either in relations among ASEAN states or in relations between ASEAN countries and the broader world. But Islam has helped to shape the region's outlook on a range of issues which have aroused strong feeling within the Muslim community. This is particularly so for Indonesia and Malaysia, and a good deal of this section will be devoted to discussing how Islam has influenced their international relations. For the other ASEAN nations (excepting Brunei), Islam has occasionally intruded into their foreign policies but has generally been a peripheral concern.

A number of common elements can he observed in the impact of Islam on Indonesia's and Malaysia's external relations. First, domestic political imperatives have been a major determinant of foreign policy. Successive governments in both countries have used foreign affairs as a means of enhancing their domestic legitimacy and have also modified policy settings on particular issues in response to pressure from their Islamic communities. Second, the 'Islamic' component of foreign policy has tended to emphasize form over substance. Thus, many initiatives, such an involvement in international Islamic institutions, have a higher symbolic value than they do a practical value. This has been especially true of Indonesia. Third, regional considerations have usually taken precedence over wider international Islamic concerns. Repeatedly, the Malaysian and Indonesian governments have sought to downplay Islamic issues that might have harmed intra-ASEAN relations. Fourth, the Islamic revival since the late 1970s and 1980s has led governments to give greater attention to Islamic issues in international affairs. Fifth, Malaysia and Indonesia have only limited economic integration with the broader Islamic world.

Since independence, Indonesian and Malaysian governments have always acknowledged Islamic issues in their foreign policies. Both nations had long expressed concern about the plight of the Palestinian people and had taken a critical stance towards Israeli government actions. They were also participants in the founding meeting of the Organization of the Islamic Conference (OIC) in 1969, which was intended to strengthen solidarity and cooperation among Islamic nations following the 1967 Arab-Israeli War and burning of the al-Aqsa mosque in Jerusalem two years later. A closer examination, however, suggests that neither Indonesia nor Malaysia gave high priority to such issues. For example, the Suharto government, despite its expression of support for the Palestinian cause, refused a 1974 request by the Palestine Liberation Organization (PLO) to open an office in Jakarta; the PLO was only given formal recognition and permission for official representation in Indonesia in 1989. Similarly, Indonesia refused to sign the OIC charter in 1972 apparently for fear of being seen by its Western donors as an Islamic state. Suharto did not attend his first OIC summit until 1991.[5] The Malaysian government gave greater attention to the OIC but it was not till Mahathir became Prime Minister in 1981 that the organization figured prominently in the nation's diplomacy. Pre-Mahathir governments did, however, condemn Israeli occupation of Arab territories but did so on the grounds of international law and human rights rather than religion. . . .[6]

In contrast to their equivocation on Islamic issues Indonesia and Malaysia were emphatic in their commitment to ASEAN. Malaysia's Deputy Prime Minister, Datuk Musa Hitam, spelt this out in 1983 when he said that his nation's commitment to ASEAN is 'paramount' and its commitment to the OIC secondary (he went on to rank the Non Aligned Movement and the Commonwealth, third and fourth respectively). A practical example of this could be seen in the early 1970s when Malaysia and Indonesia helped to block Libyan attempts to place the Muslim uprising in the Philippines on the OIC agenda. Both argued that this was an internal matter for the Philippines government and that other nations should not interfere. Undoubtedly though, they were motivated by a desire to maintain good relations within ASEAN.[7]

The influence of Islam in both Malaysian and Indonesian foreign policy did rise significantly from the 1980s. Especially in Malaysia, Mahathir made clear from the early years of his prime ministership that his government would devote greater attention to the 'Islamic bloc' and he soon began supporting a range of causes elsewhere in the Islamic world. These included the *mujahiddin* war against Soviet forces in Afghanistan, the Chechen independence struggle in Russia and the plight of the Bosnians and Kosovars in the former Yugoslavia. Bosnia-Herzegovina was a particular preoccupation of Mahathir's. He dispatched 1,500 Malaysian peacekeepers there and sold arms to Bosnian Muslims, despite the strong protests of many Western nations. In addition to this, he took a far harder line against Israeli treatment of the Palestinians than his predecessors had done, and attacked the West for supporting Zionism. He also made regular use of international Islamic fora such as the OIC and the Regional Islamic Dakwah Council for Southeast Asia and the Pacific (RISEAP) in conveying Malaysian attitudes.

Mahathir even took a firmer stance on ASEAN Islamic issues. In 1992, he resisted Indonesian efforts to include Burma in ASEAN because of its mal-treatment of the Rohingyas, and he took a more active role in seeking a set-tlement to the Moro unrest in the southern Philippines.[8]

Suharto did not embrace a more overtly Islamic foreign policy until the late 1980s. The 1989 decision to allow a PLO mission in Jakarta was fol-lowed by an increase in aid to the PLO and the feting of Yassar Arafat during his 1992 visit to Indonesia for the Non-aligned Movement Summit. From this time the frequency of high-level diplomatic exchanges with the Islamic world increased markedly. Diplomatic relations were established with Libya in 1991, and Indonesia was elected chair of the OIC two years later. Suharto and his senior ministers began making regular visits to the Middle East. In 1993, Indonesia, partly by virtue of its position as OIC leader, played a pivotal role in negotiating a peace deal between the Moro National Liberation Front (MNLF) and Manila. In 1997, Suharto attended the first summit of the Developing Eight (D8) nations, comprising eight Muslim and Islamic states (the other members were Bangladesh, Turkey, Iran, Malaysia, Egypt, Pakistan and Nigeria). The D8 aimed primarily to increase economic ties within member nations.[9]

This greater orientation to the Islamic world was due in no small part to the growing influence of Islam in the domestic politics of both Malaysia and Indonesia. As noted above, Mahathir and Suharto were both seeking to harness the growing political clout of the Muslim middle classes in their countries and were thus keen to respond to pressure from this constituency. To take the Indonesian case, many of the issues on which Suharto took 'Is-lamic initiatives,' such as the Palestinian and Moro questions, were matters on which local Muslim leaders had been most outspoken. Significantly, Suharto refrained from actions which would antagonize Indonesia's West-ern donors, and many of his foreign-policy gestures did not dramatically al-ter the substance of Indonesia's external affairs. The Islamization of Malaysian foreign policy was more substantive in nature and reflected not only Mahathir's personal commitment to Islamic causes but also the greater appeal of Islamic issues within the Malay electorate. . . .

Extremism and Security Issues

As mentioned earlier, Islamic extremism has been confined to a very small minority of Southeast Asia's Muslim community. It is also the case, how-ever, that extremists have had a far larger impact upon regional security and politics than their small numbers might suggest. Repeatedly, militant action has created security crises, prompted harsh crackdowns by governments and tarnished the image of Islamic politics and social movements, often giving rise to hostility towards Muslims among non-Muslim and secular nationalist groups. This has been true of the numerous armed insurgencies, rebellions and terrorist acts which have been carried out in the name of Islam (though in many cases, Islam has arguably not been the primary motivating factor).

Muslim insurgency and terrorism have led to significant security problems in the Philippines and Indonesia, but Thailand, Burma, Malaysia and Singapore have also had either sporadic violent extremism or a high risk of such actions. Most Southeast Asian extremist groups are based within a single country or locality and their members are usually citizens of that country. A number of these groups have links to each other and have cooperated on training and operational matters. Only one extremist movement, the Jemaah Islamiyah (JI), has a genuine transnational network across Southeast Asia. Although most of JI's leadership and the majority of its membership is Indonesian, it has active cells in Singapore, Malaysia, the Philippines, Thailand and possibly Cambodia. Its leaders have moved extensively throughout the region, and key planning meetings for terrorist attacks have taken place in several countries and have involved people of various nationalities.

In the Philippines, there are three prominent groups: the MNLF and its two offshoots, the Moro Islamic Liberation Front (MILF) and Abu Sayyaf (Bearer of the Sword). All have engaged in armed struggle with the aim of creating a separate Muslim state, though the degree of Islamic commitment of each group varies widely. The MNLF was formed by Nur Misuari in 1969 and began its armed rebellion in 1972. The organization split in 1978 due to tribal tensions and personal and policy differences among the leadership. Misuari's main rival, Salamat Hashim, established the MILF which quickly emerged as the more religiously and politically militant of the two organizations. Whereas Misuari was prepared to negotiate with Manila over political autonomy for the Muslim south, the MILF emphasized its determination to found an Islamic state, and it continues to mount insurgent attacks against government forces. Abu Sayyaf was formed in 1991 by the Libyan trained Abubakar Janjalani, a former middle-ranking MNLF leader. Though strongly anti-Christian and steadfast in its opposition to any accommodation with the Philippines government, Abu Sayyaf has gained notoriety in recent years for its violent brigandage and its kidnappings of Westerners and Filipinos.[10]

Indonesia has been the main base for JI since 1999, though the movement was originally founded in Malaysia in the early 1990s by two expatriate Arab-Indonesian preachers, Abdullah Sungkar and Abubakar Ba'asyir. JI's avowed aim is to establish a caliphate across Southeast Asia and northern Australia, and its rhetoric is suffused with strident anti-Christian and anti-Western sentiment. JI members have been charged with carrying out the Bali bombings and are also held responsible for the Christmas Eve bombings in 2000 in which 19 died in a series of church bombings across the country. They have also been accused of attempting to assassinate the then Vice-President . . . Megawati Sukarnoputri, and of planning attacks on Western embassies across the region. Some writers have described JI as the Southeast Asian arm of al-Qaida, but the publicly available evidence for this is inconclusive. While is it clear that JI has had on-going high-level contact with al-Qaida leaders, it has yet to be established that JI was subordinate to or an organizational component of al-Qaida. Indeed, recent research suggests that JI enjoys considerable autonomy in operational matters and is driven as much by domestic concerns as it is by pan-Islamist sentiment.[11]

Indonesia also has a number of paramilitary extremist groups such as the Laskar Jihad, Laskar Jundullah and Laskar Mujahidin. The largest of these, Laskar Jihad, was formed by Ja'far Umar Thalib, a fiery preacher of Yemeni extraction, in 2000 and had up to 10,000 fighters at its peak. It engaged in armed conflict with Christians in Maluku and Central Sulawesi. Laskar Jundullah and Laskar Mujahidin are much smaller groups but of high militancy: both were also involved in the Maluku conflict. The separatist movement in Acheh is often portrayed as Islamically inspired, but socio-economic grievances and the trauma of large-scale human rights abuses by the Indonesian security forces have been more fundamental factors in the campaign to secede.

In Malaysia. the government asserts that the Kumpulan Mujahidin Malaysia (KMM) is engaged in both domestic and international terrorist activities. Reportedly, the KMM was formed in 1995 by Zainon Ismail with the aim of creating a pan-Islamic state in Southeast Asia. The government accuses KMM of committing bank robberies, murders and bombings and also alleges that the organization has links to or is part of JI and the main Islamic opposition party, PAS.[12] Too little evidence has been adduced to substantiate either of these claims, and some analysts suspect that at least some of the government's case against KMM has been driven by political considerations rather than by serious security concerns.[13] But there is little doubt that JI operatives have been active in Malaysia and that Malaysians have been involved in al-Qaida activities.

Thailand's Islamic extremism problems have occurred mainly in the south, most of which have been linked to the Pattani United Liberation Organization (PULO). Established in 1968 by Kabir Abdul Rahman, PULO has been involved in occasional acts of violence over the past two decades but is regarded as posing only a minor threat to security. Although home-grown extremism is isolated, Thailand has been an important link in regional terrorism.[14] Several high-level JI meetings were reportedly held in Thailand, and Bangkok has been frequently used to obtain forged documents and weapons as well as to channel funds to terrorist cells elsewhere in the region. In early 2003, Thai authorities claimed to have uncovered active JI cells in the south, and in August of that year the JI operations head, Hambali, was captured near Bangkok, seemingly while preparing for new terrorist attacks.

The Cambodian government also declared in mid-2003 that it had arrested JI members in Islamic schools in predominantly Cham communities, though few details have been released. The Rohingyas of western Burma and Bangladesh have a number of militant organizations, the most prominent of which are the Rohingya Solidarity Organization (RSO) and the Arakan Rohingya National Organization (ARNO). The RSO was formed in 1982 by Mohammad Yunus and Nurul Islam and conducted guerrilla operations in Burma from camps inside the Bangladeshi border. In 1999 Nurul Islam set up ARNO with the aim of establishing an independent Islamic state for the Rohingyas. Both organizations are numerically small, with an active membership of several thousand at most. While an irritant to the Burmese regime, neither pose a significant threat. Recently, it has been claimed that Rohingyas were recruited into various international extremist groups, including al-Qaida.[15]

Domestic Factors

A complex interplay of domestic and external forces has driven Islamic extremism in Southeast Asia. Domestically, an important factor in radicalization has been the economic and political sidelining of Islamic communities, often accompanied by brutal state oppression of Muslim dissent. The Philippines provides a good example of this. The Christian-dominated national political elite has systematically marginalized Muslims in the south, and in the 1940s and 1950s the central government encouraged large-scale resettlement of Christians into traditional Muslim areas in the south. Over time, Moros were displaced from their land and from positions of significance in local politics and the economy. Muslim anger was heightened by a number of violent attacks on the community by Christian groups and Philippines security forces in the late 1960s and early 1970s and also by perceived growing official discrimination against Muslims. These grievances triggered the MNLF's resort to armed rebellion in 1972 and have also been a key driver of MILF and Abu Sayyaf violence.[16]

From 1976 there have been various attempts to bring peace to the southern Philippines but a significant breakthrough did not occur till 1996 when Manila and the MNLF agreed to the establishment of an Autonomous Region of Muslim Mindanao (ARMM). Nur Misuari became Governor of the new region but was defeated in elections held in late 2001. The MILF and Abu Sayyaf refused to endorse ARMM's formation, though the former has been involved in as yet inconclusive peace negotiations with the central government.

In Burma, the Rohingyas and other Muslim minorities have been among the poorest and least enfranchised of minorities. The Buddhist majority has traditionally mistrusted and often denigrated Muslims, and the Rohingyas in particular have been subject to state persecution. During the late 1970s and 1980s several hundred thousand Rohingyas were forced into Bangladesh by a discriminatory new citizenship policy. Tens of thousands remain in refugee camps and have provided fertile ground for recruitment by radical groups such as RSO and ARNO.

The failure of political Islam to play a central role in Indonesia has long rankled with Indonesian Islamists who have tended to see this historical marginalization as the product of a conspiracy by both non-Muslims, particularly Christians, and nominal Muslims to deny Islam its proper place in national affairs. Many Islamists are also convinced that the USA and international capital are complicit in this plot to subordinate Islam. Furthermore, Chinese and Christian domination of key sectors of the economy is much resented by many Muslims. Also, a large number of Muslims continue to be aggrieved by what they see as past state brutality towards them. Events such as the Tanjung Priok and Lampung incidents (1984 and 1988 respectively), in which several hundred Muslims were killed by the Armed Forces have created a sense of persecution. Even in the post-Suharto era, many Muslims are mistrustful of the Armed Forces and the police. Indonesia's intelligence agencies and military have contributed to the radicalization of militant groups through consistent and duplicitous manipulation. For example, former Darul Islam (DI) activists were recruited by intelligence services from the late 1960s supposedly to help the government in its fight against communism. Many of these recruits were subsequently arrested on trumped-up subversion charges and jailed for long periods. The two founders of DI—Abdullah Sungkar and Abubakar Ba'asyir—were among those to suffer this fate.[17]

Malaysia has had less severe problems with extremist groups due in part to the fact that Islamic constituencies dominate the UMNO party and BN governing coalition. Government policies ensure a significant flow of economic and career opportunities to Muslims, and as a result Malaysian Muslims harbour little of the politico-economic resentment found in most other Muslim communities in Southeast Asia. Despite this, pockets of extreme militancy exist, as is apparent by occasional violent actions perpetrated usually by small sects. Such groups were involved in armed clashes with police on several occasions in the 1980s, and in 2000 the shadowy al-Ma'unah group seized government weapons and was involved in a shoot-out with the security forces.[18]

Thailand provides a very instructive example of the impact of state policies on Muslim attitudes. In the late 1930s and early 1940s, the central government pursued a heavy-handed policy of culturally assimilating Muslims into the majority Buddhist community. This, and the lack of economic opportunities, alienated Muslims and led to large refugee flows into northern Malaya and a short-lived rebellion against Bangkok in 1948. The rise of PULO and sporadic insurgency in the late 1960s reflected the continuing frustration of southern Muslims. The democratic reforms of 1976 brought about changes that allowed Muslims to be better integrated into the national political and economic system than most of Southeast Asia's other minority Islamic communities. Muslims now regularly hold positions in government and the legislature and also experience less discrimination in business and the bureaucracy than their co-religionists in the Philippines and Burma.[19]

Another regional factor, which has had a powerful catalytic effect on extremist groups, has been the upsurge in violent Muslim-Christian conflict, particularly in the Indonesian provinces of Maluku and Central Sulawesi. The Maluku conflict broke out in January 1999 and is estimated to have claimed at least 5,000 lives, and clashes between Muslims and Christians in the Poso region of Central Sulawesi have raged sporadically over the last three years and have cost several thousand lives. In both cases, the involvement in the conflict of Muslim paramilitary forces from other parts of Indonesia with the apparent support of sections of the Armed Forces has given many thousands of young Muslims 'battlefield' experience and a heightened sense of jihadist struggle against 'hostile anti-Islamic forces.' Anti-Christian animus has become particularly intense. Not only Indonesian Muslims fought in Maluku and Poso; small numbers of Malaysians, Moros, Thais and some Middle-Eastern and central Asian fighters have also been involved. These conflicts have made Southeast Asian radicals more receptive to terrorist appeals and have helped to create a perception that Islam was locked in a mortal struggle with its enemies. It was, they felt, incumbent upon all Muslims of good faith to take up this fight. Whereas once they had read about the dire threats to Islam in distant countries, Maluku and Poso brought the struggle to their own region.

International Factors

Prior to the 1980s, external influences had little effect upon the dynamics of Southeast Asian Islamic extremism. Darul Islam, for example, was almost entirely an Indonesia-based movement with negligible support from other countries in the region, let alone from the broader Islamic world. The *mujahiddin* war against the Soviet occupation of Afghanistan from the late 1970s was critical to the rise of extremism and especially terrorism in Southeast Asia. Many hundreds, possibly thousands, of Muslims from Indonesia, Malaysia, the Philippines, Thailand and Burma went to Afghanistan to fight as *mujahiddin*. This was to have a deep impact on most of those who joined the anti-Russian forces. Southeast Asian *mujahiddin* gained experience as soldiers in arduous battlefield conditions, learned terrorist-related skills such as bomb-making and running clandestine operations, absorbed pan-Islamic and virulently anti-Western ideologies and developed a heightened sense of global Islamic solidarity. Importantly, these fighters were able to establish relations with Muslim radicals from across the Islamic world which would later prove invaluable in gaining financial assistance, access to technical know-how and connections into global terrorist networks. Fighting in Afghanistan was also regarded as a badge of honour in the home communities of the *mujahiddin*, and many were accorded great respect when they returned to Southeast Asia. Not all former *mujahiddin* became involved in militant activity, but most of the major radical groups have Afghanistan veterans within their leadership ranks. Much of JI's leadership are 'alumni' of the Afghanistan war. The practical effect of the '*mujahiddization*' of Southeast Asian extremist groups is that their capacity to wreak havoc and destruction—critical elements in terror campaigns—has been greatly enhanced. Money, explosives, technical expertise and covert operational methods were available to experienced and resourceful Afghanistan veterans and associates. Without this direct personal experience of the war and networks which it fostered, Southeast Asian terrorist acts such as the Bali bombing would have been more difficult to mount.

In addition to the *mujahiddin* factor, the increasing numbers of Southeast Asian Muslims receiving their education in the Middle East has meant greater exposure to more puritanical and radical expressions of the faith, such as Salafi-Wahhabism from Saudi Arabia and Yemen. Students have brought back the powerful rhetorical language and concepts of these ideologies as well as lucrative sources of funding. Numerous Middle Eastern and South Asian Islamist groups have grown rapidly in Southeast Asia in recent years including the Hizbut Tahrir which supports the reestablishment of the caliphate, the Muslim Brotherhood, and Jemaah Tabligh.

Globalization, particularly as it relates to the transmission of information, has also had a significant effect. Cyber-technology and satellite television stations such as al-Jazeera and al-Arabiah have greatly increased the speed and volume of information flows to radical groups in Southeast Asia from other parts of the Island world. Extremist groups have become adept at harnessing new technologies to communicate their views and recruiting others to join their struggle. Paramilitary groups such as Laskar Jihad have run attractive and sophisticated websites, with Indonesian, English and Arabic services and a wide range of contact information for other radical groups.

Conclusion

Given that nearly half of Southeast Asia's population is Muslim, Islamic influence on the region's affairs has been disproportionately small. In matters of diplomacy, Islamic issues have usually been of secondary importance to regional considerations, particularly maintaining harmonious intra-ASEAN relations. Economically, there has been only minimal integration with the broader Islamic world, though trade between OIC countries and Southeast Asia is rising. Only in matters of security has Islam consistently been a significant factor. The frequency and persistence of Muslim insurgency and separatism across the region coupled with the rise of terrorism since 2000, has made Islam a critical element in regional order.

The reasons for the limited impact of Islam are not hard to find. The overwhelming majority of the region's Muslims live in Indonesia, a country in which the Islamic community is fissured along multifarious ethnic, political, geographical and doctrinal lines. In this regard the oft-repeated phrase that Indonesia is the world's largest Islamic community is somewhat misleading; only on the most essential of religious issues are Indonesian Muslims united, and they often behave as if they were divided into numerous rival Islamic communities. In addition to this, from the late 1950s to the 1980s, Islam-wary authoritarian regimes emphatically suppressed Islamist sentiment. While restrictions on Islam have largely been lifted since Suharto's downfall, the Islamic aspects of foreign policy are circumscribed and driven largely by domestic political concerns rather than a deep philosophical or emotional commitment to international Muslim solidarity. Islam does exert a greater influence on Malaysian foreign policy due not only to a higher level of overtly Islamic consciousness among the Malay majority but also to the dynamics of domestic politics. As the dominant UMNO party has Islam as part of its raison d'être, it must continually demonstrate its Islamic credentials, particularly in response to pressure from the Islamist PAS.

For ASEAN as a whole, Islam remains an issue of great sensitivity. The seven non-Muslim majority states are mindful of the capacity of Islamic groups to destabilize the region and are also wary of actions that may provoke Muslim sentiment in the three majority Muslim states. In the current environment of heightened terrorist threat and the risk of economic downturn, careful management of Islamic issues has rarely been of greater importance.

NOTES

1. *Time Asia,* 4 March 2002.
2. Fealy, 2002.
3. Crouch, 1996; Ung-Flo Chin, 2002.
4. Funston, 2003.
5. Sukma, 1999: 16, 34.
6. Nair, 1997: 59-61; Milne and Mauzy, 1999: 135.
7. Piscatori, 1987: 236–237.
8. Piscatori, 1987: 235–236: Milne and Mauzy, 1999: 127, 135–136.
9. Sukma, 1999: 33; see also the D8 website: http://www.d8net.org.
10. Noble, 1987; Morada and Collier, 1998.
11. International Crisis Group, 2003.
12. *Straits Times,* 2 September 2001.
13. Abuza, 2002: 445; Funston, 2002.
14. Funston, 2002b.
15. Lintner, 2002a, b.
16. Noble, 1987; McKenna, 1998.
17. International Crisis Group, 2002.
18. Funston, 2002a.
19. Leifer, 1996: 199–200.

Bibliography

This is a select bibliography. It is divided into five parts. The general section includes reference works and those works covering more than one time period. The other four sections correspond to the four parts of the book (see the Table of Contents).

GENERAL

Armstrong, C. Jocelyn, R. Warwick Armstrong, and Kent Mulliner, eds., *Chinese Population in Contemporary Southeast Asian Societies: Identities, Interdependence and International Influence*, Curzon, Richmond, Surrey, U.K., 2001.

Beeson, Mark, ed., *Contemporary Southeast Asia: Regional Dynamics, National Differences*, Palgrave Macmillan, New York, 2004.

Brown, Michael E., and Sumit Ganguly, eds., *Government Policies and Ethnic Relations in Asia and the Pacific*, MIT Press, Cambridge, Mass., 1997.

Bunnel, Tim, Lisa B. W. Drummond, and K. C. Ho, eds., *Critical Reflections on Cities in Southeast Asia*, Times Academic Press, Singapore, 2002.

Cady, John F., *Southeast Asia, Its Historical Development*, McGraw-Hill, New York, 1964.

Chan, Raymond K. H., Kwan Kwok Leung, and Raymond M. H. Ngan, eds., *Development in Southeast Asia: Review and Prospect*, Ashgate, Aldershot, Hampshire, U.K., 2002.

Cowan, C. D., and O. W. Wolters, eds., *Southeast Asian History and Historiography*, Cornell University Press, Ithaca, N.Y., 1976.

Dewitt, David B., and Carolina G. Hernandez, eds., *Development and Security in Southeast Asia*, Ashgate, Burlington, Vt., 2003.

Duncan, Christopher, *Civilizing the Margins: Southeast Asian Government Policies for the Development of Minorities*, Cornell University Press, Ithaca, N.Y., 2004.

Engelbert, Thomas, and Hans Dieter Kubitscheck, eds., *Ethnic Minorities and Politics in Southeast Asia*, Peter Lang, New York, 2004.

Ganguly, Rajat, and Ian Macduff, eds., *Ethnic Conflict and Secessionism in South and Southeast Asia: Causes, Dynamics, and Solutions*, Sage Publications, Thousand Oaks, Calif., 2003.

Hall, D. G. E., *A History of South-East Asia*, Fourth Edition, Macmillan, London, 1981.

———, *Historians of South-East Asia*, Oxford University Press, London, 1961.

———, ed., *Atlas of South-East Asia*, St. Martin's Press, New York, 1964.

Heryanto, Ariel, and Sumit K. Mandal, eds., *Challenging Authoritarianism in Southeast Asia: Comparing Indonesia and Malaysia*, Routledge Curzon, New York, 2003.

Institute of Southeast Asian Studies, *Developing ASEAN-China Relations: Realities and Prospects: A Brief Report on the ASEAN-China Forum,* ISEAS, Singapore, 2004.

Lee, Hok Guan, ed., *Civil Society in Southeast Asia*, Institute of Southeast Asian Studies, Singapore, and NIAS Press, Copenhagen, 2004.

Purcell, Victor, *The Chinese in Southeast Asia*, Oxford University Press, London, 1965.

Ramakrishna, Kumar, and See Sang Tan, eds., *After Bali: The Threat of Terrorism in Southeast Asia*, Institute of Defence and Strategic Studies and World Scientific, Singapore, 2003.

SarDesai, D. R., *Southeast Asia, Past and Present*, Fifth Edition, Westview Press, Boulder, Colo., 2003.

Suryadinata, Leo, ed., *Ethnic Relations and Nation-building in Southeast Asia: The Case of the Ethnic Chinese*, Institute of Southeast Asian Studies, Singapore, 2004.

Than, Mya, ed., *ASEAN Beyond the Regional Crisis: Challenges and Initiatives*, Institute of Southeast Asian Studies, Singapore, 2001.

Yamashita, Shinji, and J. S. Eades, eds., *Globalization in Southeast Asia: Local, National, and Transnational Perspectives*, Bergahn Books, New York, 2003.

PART I

Ahmad, Ibrahim, Sharon Siddique, and Yasmin Hussain, eds. *Readings on Islam in Southeast Asia,* Institute of Southeast Asian Studies, Singapore, 1985.

Briggs, Lawrence P., *The Ancient Khmer Empire,* American Philosophical Society, Philadelphia, 1951.

Coedes, Georges, *The Indianized States of Southeast Asia*, East-West Center Press, Honolulu, 1968.

Gomez, Louis, and Hiram Woodward Jr., eds., *Barabudur: History and Significance of a Buddhist Monument,* University of California Press, Berkeley, 1981.

Hall, Kenneth R., *Maritime Trade and State Development in Early Southeast Asia,* University of Hawaii Press, Honolulu, 1985.

Hall, Kenneth R., and John K. Whitmore, eds., *Explorations in Early Southeast Asian History: The Origins of Southeast Asian Statecraft,* University of Michigan, Center for South and Southeast Asian Studies, Ann Arbor, 1976.

Heine-Geldern, Robert, "Conceptions of State and Kingship in Southeast Asia," *Far Eastern Quarterly* 2 (1942), pp. 15–30.

Higham, Charles, *The Archaeology of Mainland Southeast Asia from 10,000 BC to the Fall of Angkor*, Cambridge University Press, Cambridge, 1989.

Hill, A. H., "Hikayat Raja Pasai," *Journal Malayan Branch Royal Asiatic Society* 33, Part 2 (1960), pp. 1–215.

Janse, J. M., *Archaeological Research in Indo-China: The Ancient Dwelling Site of Dong-S'on*, Harvard University Press, Cambridge, Mass., 1958.

Kasetsiri, Charnvit, *The Rise of Ayuthaya*, Oxford University Press, Kuala Lumpur, 1976.

Lieberman, Victor B., *Burmese Administrative Cycles: Anarchy and Conquest, c. 1580–1760*, Princeton University Press, Princeton, N.J., 1984.

Mabbett, I. W., "The 'Indianisation' of Southeast Asia: Reflections on the Historical Sources," *Journal of Southeast Asian Studies* 8, 2 (September 1977), pp. 143–161.

_____, "The 'Indianisation' of Southeast Asia: Reflections on Prehistoric Sources," *Journal of Southeast Asian Studies*, 8, 1 (March 1977), pp. 1–14.

Marr, David G., and A. C. Milner, eds., *Southeast Asia in the Ninth to Fourteenth Centuries*, Institute of Southeast Asian Studies, Singapore, 1986.

Marrison, G. E., "The Coming of Islam to the East Indies," *Journal Malaya Branch Royal Asiatic Society* 24, Part 1 (1951), pp. 28–37.

Meilink-Roelofsz, M. A. P., *Asian Trade and European Influence in the Indonesian Archipelago Between About 1500 and 1630*, Martinus Nijhoff, The Hague, 1962.

Pe Maung Tin, U., and G. H. Luce (trans.), *The Glass Palace Chronicle of the Kings of Burma*, Oxford University Press, London, 1923.

Phelan, J. L., *The Hispanisation of the Philippines: Spanish Aims and Filipino Responses, 1565–1700*, University of Wisconsin Press, Madison, 1959.

Pires, Tome, *Suma Oriental*, Hakluyt Society, London, 1944.

Quaritch-Wales, H. G., *The Making of Greater India*, Second Edition, Bernard Quaritch, London, 1961.

Reid, Anthony, and Lance Castles, eds., *Pre-Colonial State Systems in Southeast Asia*, JMBRAS Monograph Series, Kuala Lumpur, 1975.

Shrieke, B., *Indonesian Sociological Studies*, 2 vols., W. van Hoeve, The Hague, 1955–1957.

Smith, R. B., and W. Watson, eds., *Early Southeast Asia: Essays in Archaeology, History and Historical Geography*, Oxford University Press, London, 1979.

Taufik, Abdullah, and Sharon Siddique, eds., *Islam and Society in Southeast Asia*, Institute of Southeast Asian Studies, Singapore, 1985.

Taylor, Keith W., *The Birth of Vietnam*, University of California Press, Berkeley, 1983.

Taylor, Keith W., and John K. Whitmore, eds., *Essays into Vietnamese Pasts*, Cornell University Southeast Asia Program, 1995.

van Leur, J. C., *Indonesian Trade and Society*, W. van Hoeve, The Hague, 1955.

Wheatley, Paul, *The Golden Khersonese: Studies in the Historical Geography of the Malay Peninsula Before AD 1500*, University of Malaya Press, Kuala Lumpur, 1966.

Wolters, O. W., *Early Indonesian Commerce: A Study of the Origins of Srivijaya*, Cornell University Press, Ithaca, N.Y., 1967.

Woodside, Alexander B., *Vietnam and the Chinese Model*, Harvard University Press, Cambridge, Mass., 1970.

PART II

Aung, Htin, *The Stricken Peacock: Anglo-Burmese Relations, 1752–1948*, Nijhoff, The Hague, 1965.

Bastin, John, *The Native Policies of Sir Stamford Raffles in Java and Sumatra: An Economic Interpretation*, Clarendon Press, Oxford, 1957.

Booth, A., W. J. O'Malley, and A. Weidemann, *Indonesian Economic History in the Dutch Colonial Era*, Yale University Press, New Haven, Conn., 1990.

Bowring, John, *The Kingdom and People of Siam*, 2 vols., Parker, London, 1857.

Cady, John F., *A History of Modern Burma*, Cornell University Press, Ithaca, N.Y., 1958.

_____, *The Roots of French Imperialism in Eastern Asia*, Cornell University Press, Ithaca, N.Y., 1954.

Cowan, C. D., *Nineteenth Century Malaya*, Oxford University Press, London, 1961.

Cribb, R., ed., *The Late Colonial State in Indonesia: Political and Economic Foundations of the Netherlands Indies, 1800–1942*, Royal Institute, Leiden, 1994.

Day, Clive, *Policy and Administration of the Dutch in Java*, Macmillan, New York, 1904; reprint, Oxford University Press, Kuala Lumpur, 1966.

Fasseur, C., *The Politics of Colonial Exploitation: Java, the Dutch and the Cultivation System*, Cornell University Press, Ithaca, N.Y., 1992.

Furnivall, John S., *Colonial Policy and Practice: A Comparative Study of Burma and Netherlands India*, New York University Press, New York, 1956.

Laubach, Frank C., *Rizal: Man and Martyr*, Community Publishers, Manila, 1936.

Mullatuli [E. D. Dekker], *Max Havelaar*, House and Maxwell, New York, 1967.

Murray, Martin J., *The Development of Capitalism in Colonial Indochina, 1870—1940*, University of California Press, Berkeley, 1980.

Osborne, Milton E., *The French Presence in Cochin China and Cambodia: Rule and Response, 1859–1905*, Cornell University Press, Ithaca, N.Y., 1969.

SarDesai, D. R., *British Trade and Expansion in Southeast Asia, 1830–1914*, Allied Publishers, New Delhi, 1977.

Skinner, G. William, and A. Thomas Kirsh, eds., *Change and Persistence in Thai Society*, Cornell University Press, Ithaca, N.Y., 1975.

PART III

Agoncillo, Teodoro A., *Filipino Nationalism, 1872–1970*, R. P. Garcia Publishing, Quezon City, 1974.

_____, *The Revolt of the Masses: The Story of Bonifacio and the Katipunan*, University of the Philippines, Manila, 1965.

Anderson, B. R. O'G., *Java in a Time of Revolution: Occupation and Resistance, 1944–1946*, Cornell University Press, Ithaca, N.Y., 1972.

Ariffin, Omar, *Bangsa Melayu: Malay Concepts of Democracy and Community, 1945–1950,* Oxford University Press, Oxford, 1993.

Benda, Harry J., *The Crescent and the Rising Sun: Indonesian Islam Under the Japanese Occupation,* W. van Hoeve, The Hague, 1958.

Bradley, Mark Phillip, *Imagining Vietnam and America: The Making of Postcolonial Vietnam, 1919–1950,* University of North Carolina Press, Chapel Hill, 2000.

Brocheux, Pierre, *The Mekong Delta: Ecology, Economy, and Revolution, 1860–1960,* University of Wisconsin Press, Madison, 1995.

Buttinger, Joseph, *A Dragon Embattled: A History of Colonial and Post-Colonial Vietnam,* 2 vols., Praeger, New York, 1967.

Coates, John, *Suppressing Insurgency: An Analysis of the Malayan Emergency, 1948–1954,* Westview Press, Boulder, Colo., 1992.

Craig, Austin, *Lineage, Life and Labors of Jose Rizal, Philippine Patriot,* Philippine Education Co., Manila, 1913.

Duiker, William J., *The Rise of Nationalism in Vietnam, 1900–1941,* Cornell University Press, Ithaca, N.Y., 1976.

Elsbree, Willard H., *Japan's Role in Southeast Asian Nationalist Movements, 1940–45,* Harvard University Press, Cambridge, Mass., 1953.

Englehart, Neil A., *Culture and Power in Traditional Siamese Government,* Cornell University Press, Ithaca, N.Y., 2001.

Fenn, Charles, *Ho Chi Minh: A Biographical Introduction,* Charles Scribner's, New York, 1973.

Friend, Theodore, *Between Two Empires: The Ordeal of the Philippines, 1929—1946,* Yale University Press, New Haven, Conn., 1965.

Goscha, Christopher E., *Vietnam or Indochina? Contesting Concepts of Space in Vietnamese Nationalism, 1887–1954,* NIAS Reports No. 28. Nordic Institute of Asian Studies, Copenhagen, 1995 (reprinted 1999).

Halberstam, David, *Ho,* Vintage Books, New York, 1971.

Hindley, Donald, *The Communist Party of Indonesia,* University of California Press, Berkeley, 1964.

Jackson, Robert, *The Malayan Emergency: The Commonwealth's Wars, 1948–1966,* Routledge, New York, 1991.

Kiernan, Ben, *The Pol Pot Regime: Race, Power, and Genocide in Cambodia, 1975–1979,* Yale University Press, New Haven, Conn., 1996, 2002.

Lacouture, Jean, *Ho Chi Minh: A Political Biography,* Random House, Vintage Books, New York, 1968.

Lam, Truong Buu, *Patterns of Vietnamese Response to Foreign Intervention, 1858–1900,* Yale University, Southeast Asia Studies, New Haven, Conn., 1967.

_____, ed., *Colonialism Experienced: Vietnamese Writings on Colonialism, 1900–1931,* University of Michigan Press, Ann Arbor, 2000.

Landon, Margaret, *Anna and the King of Siam,* Hamilton, London, 1956.

Leonowens, Anna, *An English Governess at the Court of Siam*, Osgood and Co., Boston, 1870.

Linther, Bertil, *Burma in Revolt: Opium and Insurgency Since 1948*, Westview Press, Boulder, Colo., 1994.

Marr, David G., *Vietnam 1945: The Quest for Power*, University of California Press, Berkeley, 1995.

_____, *Vietnamese Tradition on Trial, 1920–1945*, University of California Press, Berkeley, 1981.

_____, *Vietnamese Anti-Colonialism, 1885–1925*, University of California Press, Berkeley, 1971.

McAlister, John T., Jr., and Paul Mus, *The Vietnamese and Their Revolution*, Harper and Row, New York, 1970.

Milner, Anthony Crothers, *The Invention of Politics in Colonial Malaya: Contesting Nationalism and the Expansion of Public Sphere*, Cambridge University Press, New York, 1995.

Moffat, A. L., *Mongkut, the King of Siam*, Cornell University Press, Ithaca, N.Y., 1961.

Neumann-Hoditz, Reinhold, *Portrait of Ho Chi Minh*, Herder and Herder, Berlin, 1972.

Palma, Rafael, *Pride of the Malay Race: A Biography of José Rizal*, Prentice-Hall, New York, 1949.

Phan Boi Chau, *Overturned Chariot: The Autobiography of Phan Boi Chau*, trans. by Vinh Sinh and Nicholas Wickendam, University of Hawaii Press, Honolulu, 1999.

Pike, Douglas, *History of Vietnamese Communism, 1925–76*, Hoover Institution Press, Stanford, Calif., 1978.

Pomeroy, William, *The Philippines: Colonialism, Collaboration, and Resistance*, International Publishers, New York, 1992.

Rajchagool, Chaiyan, *The Rise and Fall of the Thai Absolute Monarchy*, White Lotus, Bangkok, 1994.

Rizal, José, *Noli Me Tangere (The Lost Eden)*, trans. Leon Ma Guervero, Indiana University Press, Bloomington, 1961. (Originally published in 1887.)

Roff, William R., *The Origins of Malay Nationalism*, Yale University Press, New Haven, Conn., 1967.

Sainteny, Jean, *Ho Chi Minh and His Vietnam: A Personal Memoir*, Cowles Book Co., Chicago, 1970.

Shipway, Martin, *The Road to War: France and Vietnam, 1944–1947*, Berghahn Books, Oxford, 1996.

Singh, Balwant, *Independence and Democracy in Burma, 1945–1952: The Turbulent Years*, Michigan University Press, Ann Arbor, 1993.

Tai, Hue-Tam, *Radicalism and the Origins of the Vietnamese Revolution*, Harvard University Press, Cambridge, Mass., 1992.

Tips, Walter E. J., *Siam's Struggle for Survival: The Gunboat Incident at Paknam and the Franco-Siamese Treaty of October 1893*, White Lotus, Bangkok, 1996.

Tuck, Patrick, *The French Wolf and the Siamese Lamb: The French Threat to Siamese Independence, 1858–1907*, White Lotus, Bangkok, 1995.

Van Niel, Robert, *The Emergence of the Modern Indonesian Elite*, W. van Hoeve, The Hague, 1960.

Van Praagh, David, *Thailand's Struggle for Democracy: The Life and Times of M. R. Seni Pramoj*, Holmes and Meier, New York, 1996.

Vella, Walter F., *The Impact of the West on Government in Thailand*, University of California Press, Berkeley, 1955.

Von der Mehden, Fred, *Religion and Nationalism in Southeast Asia*, University of Wisconsin Press, Madison, 1963.

Warbey, William, *Ho Chi Minh and the Struggle for a Free Vietnam*, Merlin Press, London, 1972.

Williams, Lorraine, *American Education in the Philippines: The Early Years*, University of California Press, Berkeley, 1991.

Worthing, Peter, *Occupation and Revolution: China and the Vietnamese August Revolution*, University of California Institute of East Asian Studies, Berkeley, 2001.

Wyatt, David K., *Politics and Reform in Thailand: Education in the Reign of King Chulalongkorn*, Yale University Press, New Haven, Conn., 1969.

PART IV

Abdillah, Masykuri, *Responses of Indonesian Muslim Intellectuals to the Concept of Democracy, 1966–1993*, Abera Verlag, Hamburg, 1997.

Aditjondro, George J., *Is Oil Thicker than Blood? A Study of Oil Companies' Interests and Western Complicity in Indonesia's Annexation of East Timor*, Nova Science Publishers, Commack, N.Y., 1999.

Albin, David A., and Marlowe Hood, eds., *The Cambodian Agony*, M. E. Sharpe, Armonk, N.Y., 1987.

Anderson, Benedict R. O'G., ed., *Violence and the State in Suharto's Indonesia*, Southeast Asia Program, Cornell University, Ithaca, N.Y., 2001.

Artaud, Denise, and Lawrence Kaplan, eds., *Dienbienphu: The Atlantic Alliance and the Defense of Southeast Asia*, Scholarly Resources, Wilmington, Del., 1989.

Aung Myoe, Maung, *The Tatmadaw in Myanmar Since 1988: An Interim Assessment*, Australian National University Strategic Defense Studies Center, Canberra, 1999.

Aung San, Suu Kyi, *Freedom from Fear and Other Writings*, Penguin Books, New York, 1991.

Barlow, Colin, ed., *Modern Malaysia in the Global Economy: Political and Social Change into the 21st Century*, Edward Elgar, Cheltenham, U.K., 2001.

Barr, Michael D., *Lee Kuan Yew: The Beliefs Behind the Man*, Georgetown University Press, Washington, D.C., 2000.

Barron, John, and Anthony Paul, *Murder of a Gentle Land: The Untold Story of Communist Genocide in Cambodia*, Reader's Digest Press, New York, 1977.

Barry, Kathleen, ed., *Vietnam's Women in Transition*, Macmillan, Hampshire, U.K., 1996.

Becker, Elizabeth, *When the War Was Over: The Voices of Cambodia's Revolution and Its People*, Simon and Schuster, New York, 1986.

Berman, Larry, *No Peace, No Honor: Nixon, Kissinger, and Betrayal in Vietnam*, Free Press, New York, 2001.

_____, *Lyndon Johnson's War*, Norton, New York, 1989.

_____, *Planning a Tragedy: The Americanization of the War in Vietnam,* Norton, New York, 1982.

Bernstein, Irving, *Guns or Butter: The Presidency of Lyndon Johnson*, Oxford University Press, New York, 1996.

Binh, Tran-Nam, and Do Pham Chi, eds., *The Vietnamese Economy: Awakening the Dormant Dragon*, Routledge Curzon, London, 2003.

Borer, Douglas A., *Superpowers Defeated: Vietnam and Afghanistan Compared*, Frank Cass, London, 1999.

Brands, H. W., *Bound to Empire: The U.S. and the Philippines*, Oxford University Press, New York, 1992.

Bresnan, John, ed., *Crisis in the Philippines: The Marcos Era and Beyond,* Princeton University Press, Princeton, 1986.

Bui, Diem, *In the Jaws of History*, Houghton Mifflin, Boston, 1987.

Buttinger, Joseph, *A Dragon Embattled: A History of Colonial and Post-Colonial Vietnam*, 2 vols., Praeger, New York, 1967.

Buzzanco, Robert, *Masters of War: Military Dissent and Politics in the Vietnam Era,* Harvard University Press, Cambridge, Mass., 1996.

Campagna, Anthony, *The Economic Consequences of the Vietnam War*, Praeger, New York, 1991.

Carey, Peter, *From Burma to Myanmar: Military Rule and the Struggle for Democracy,* Research Institute for the Study of Conflict and Terrorism, London, 1997.

Challis, Roland, *Shadow of a Revolution: Indonesia and the Generals,* Sutton, Shroud, 2001.

Chandler, David P., *The Tragedy of Cambodian History: Politics, War, and Revolution Since 1945*, Yale University Press, New Haven, Conn., 1991.

Chandler, David P., and Ben Kiernan, eds., *Revolution and Its Aftermath in Kampuchea*, Yale University Southeast Asia Council, New Haven, Conn., 1983.

Clammer, John, *Race and State in Independent Singapore, 1965–1990: The Cultural Politics of Pluralism in a Multiethnic Society*, Ashgate, Aldershot, U.K., 1998.

Clements, Alan, *Burma's Revolution of the Spirit: The Struggle for Democratic Freedom and Dignity*, Aperture, New York, 1994.

Clifford, Clark, "A Vietnam Reappraisal," *Foreign Affairs* 47 (July 1969), pp. 601–622.

Corfield, Justin J., *Khmers Stand Up! A History of the Cambodian Government, 1970–1975*, Monash University, Clayton, Australia, 1994.

Cristalis, Irena, *Bitter Dawn: East Timor, A People's Story*, Zed Books, London, 2002.

Croce, Larry W., *Vietnamese Economic Reform: How Important to U.S.-Vietnam Relations*, Worldfact Book, Washington, D.C., 2000.

Dhiravegin, Likhit, *Demi Democracy: The Evolution of the Thai Political System*, Times Academic Press, Singapore, 1992.

Dommen, Arthur J., *The Indochinese Experience of the French and the Americans: Nationalism and Communism in Cambodia, Laos, and Vietnam*, Indiana University Press, Bloomington, 2001.

Donaldson, Gary A., *America at War Since 1945: Politics and Diplomacy in Korea, Vietnam, and the Gulf War*, Greenwood Press, Westport, Conn., 1996.

Duiker, William J., *Sacred War: Nationalism and Revolution in a Divided Vietnam*, McGraw Hill, New York, 1995.

_____, *Vietnam: Nation in Revolution*, Westview Press, Boulder, Colo., 1983.

_____, *The Communist Road to Power in Vietnam*, Westview Press, Boulder, Colo., 1981.

Ebihara, May M., *Cambodian Culture Since 1975*, Cornell University Press, Ithaca, N.Y., 1994.

Edmonds, Anthony O., *The War in Vietnam*, Greenwood Press, Westport, Conn., 1998.

Eklof, Stefan, *Indonesian Politics in Crisis: The Long Fall of Suharto, 1996–1998*, NIAS, Copenhagen, 1999.

Elliott, David W. P., *The Vietnamese War: Revolution and Social Change in the Mekong Delta*, M. E. Sharpe, Armonk, N.Y., 2002.

Elman, Benjamin A., John B. Duncan, and Herman Ooms, eds., *Rethinking Confucianism; Past and Present in China, Japan, Korea, and Vietnam*, UCLA Asian-Pacific Monograph Series, Los Angeles, 2002.

Emmerson, Donald K., ed., *Indonesia Beyond Suharto: Polity, Economy, Society, Transition*, M. E. Sharpe, Armonk, N.Y., 1999.

Fall, Bernard B., *The Two Viet-Nams: A Political and Military Analysis*, Revised Edition, Praeger, New York, 1964.

Fischer, Tim, *Seven days in East Timor: Ballot and Bullets*, Allen & Unwin, St. Leonard's, NSW, Australia, 2000.

Fitzgerald, Frances, *Fire in the Lake*, Vintage Books, New York, 1972.

Forrester, Geoff, ed., *Post-Soeharto Indonesia: Renewal or Chaos?* St. Martin's Press, New York, 1999.

Fox, James J., ed., *Out of the Ashes: Destruction and Reconstruction of East Timor*, Crawford House, Adelaide, 2000.

Freedman, Lawrence, *Kennedy's Wars: Berlin, Cuba, Laos, and Vietnam*, Oxford University Press, New York, 2000.

Frost, Frank, *Vietnam's Foreign Relations: Dynamics of Change*, Institute of Southeast Asian Studies, Singapore, 1993.

Gardner, Lloyd C., *Approaching Vietnam: From World War II Through Dienbienphu, 1941–1954*, Norton, New York, 1988.

Ghazalie, Shafie, *Malaysia, ASEAN, and the New World Order*, Penerbit Universiti Kebangsaan, Bangi, Malaysia, 2000.

Gilbert, Marc Jason, ed., *Why the North Won the Vietnam War*, Palgrave, New York, 2002.

Gomez, Edmund Terence, and K. S. Jomo, *Malaysia's Political Economy: Politics, Patronage and Profits*, Second Edition, Cambridge University Press, Cambridge, U.K., 1999.

Haas, Michael, *Cambodia, Pol Pot, and the U.S.,* Praeger, New York, 1991.

_____, ed., *The Singapore Puzzle*, Praeger, Westport, Conn., 1999.

Hainsworth, Paul, and Stephen McCloskey, eds., *The East Timor Question: The Struggle for Independence from Indonesia,* St. Martin's Press, New York, 2000.

Halberstam, David, *The Making of a Quagmire*, Random House, New York, 1965.

Harrison, James P., *The Endless War: Fifty Years of Struggle in Vietnam,* Free Press, New York, 1982.

Hayslip, Le Ly, *When Heaven and Earth Change Places: A Vietnamese Woman's Journey from War to Peace*, Doubleday, New York, 1989.

Heder, Stephen R., *Kampuchean Occupation and Resistance,* Institute of Asian Studies, Chulalongkorn University, Bangkok, 1980.

Hefner, Robert W., *Civil Islam: Muslims and Democratization in Indonesia,* Princeton University press, Princeton, N.J., 2000.

Herring, George C., *America's Longest War: The United States and Vietnam, 1950—1973,* Temple University Press, Philadelphia, 1986.

Hess, Gary R., *Vietnam and the United States: Origins and Legacy of War,* Twayne, Boston, 1990.

Hewinon, Kevin, ed., *Political Change in Thailand: Democracy and Participation*, Routledge, London, 1997.

Hickey, Gerald C., *Village in Vietnam,* Yale University Press, New Haven, Conn., 1964.

Hildebrand, George, and Gareth Porter, *Cambodia: Starvation and Revolution,* Monthly Review Press, New York, 1976.

Hill, Hal, ed., *Indonesia's New Order: The Dynamics of Socio-Economic Transformation*, University of Hawaii Press, Honolulu, 1994.

Hill, Hal, and Joao M. Saldanha, eds., *East Timor: Development Challenges for the World's Newest Nation,* Institute of Southeast Asian Studies, Singapore, 2001.

Hood, Steven, *Dragons Embattled: Indochina and the China-Vietnam War*, Praeger, Westport, Conn., 1993.

Hunt, Michael H., *Lyndon Johnson's War: America's Cold War Crusade in Vietnam, 1945–1965,* Hill & Wang, New York, 1996.

Huyen, N. Khac, *Vision Accomplished? The Enigma of Ho Chi Minh,* Macmillan, New York, 1971.

Isaacson, Jason F., and Colin Rubenstein, eds., *Islam in Asia: Changing Political Realities,* Transaction Publishers, New Brunswick, N.J., 2002.

Jackson, Karl D., ed., *Cambodia, 1975–1978: Rendezvous with Death,* Princeton University Press, Princeton, N.J., 1989.

Jardine, Matthew, *East Timor: Genocide in Paradise,* Odonian Press, Monroe, Maine, 1999.

Kahin, George M., ed., *Intervention: How America Became Involved in Vietnam,* Knopf, New York, 1986.

Kahn, Joel S., ed., *Southeast Asian Identities: Culture and the Politics of Representation in Indonesia, Malaysia, Singapore, and Thailand,* St. Martin's Press, New York, 1998.

Kaiser, David, *American Tragedy: Kennedy, Johnson, and the Origins of the Vietnam War,* Harvard University Press, Cambridge, Mass., 2000.

Karnow, Stanley, *Vietnam, a History: The First Complete Account of Vietnam at War,* Viking Press, New York, 1983.

Kenny, Henry J., *Shadow of the Dragon: Vietnam's Continuing Struggle with China and the Implications for U.S. Foreign Policy,* Brassey's, Washington, D.C., 2002.

Kingsbury, Daniel, ed., *Guns and Ballot Boxes: East Timor's Vote for Independence,* Monash Asia Institute, Clayton, Australia, 2000.

Kipp, Rita Smith, *Disassociated Identities: Ethnicity, Religion, and Class in an Indonesian Society,* University of Michigan Press, Ann Arbor, 1993.

Kohen, Arnold S., *From the Place of the Dead: The Epic Struggles of Bishop Below of East Timor,* St. Martin's Press, New York, 1999.

Kutler, Stanley I., ed., *Encyclopedia of the Vietnam War,* Macmillan, New York, 1996.

Langguth, A. J., *Our Vietnam/Nuoc Viet Ta: The War, 1954–1975,* Simon & Schuster, New York, 2000.

Lewallen, John, *Ecology of Devastation: Indochina,* Penguin Books, Baltimore, 1971.

Lind, Michael, *Vietnam, the Necessary War: A Reinterpretation of America's Most Disastrous Military Conflict,* Free Press, New York, 1999.

Lloyd, Grayson, and Shannon Smith, eds., *Indonesia Today: Challenges of History,* Rowman and Littlefield, Lanham, Md., 2001.

Logevall, Fredrik, *The Origins of the Vietnam War,* Longman, New York, 2001.

———, *Choosing War: The Lost Chance for Peace and the Escalation of War in Vietnam,* University of California Press, Berkeley, 1999.

Lomperis, Timothy J., *From People's War to People's Rule: Insurgency, Intervention, and the Lessons of Vietnam,* University of North Carolina Press, Chapel Hill, 1996.

Loveard, Keith, *Suharto, Indonesia's Last Sultan,* Horizon Books, Singapore, 1999.

Low, Linda, ed., *Singapore: Towards a Developed Status,* Oxford University Press, Oxford, 1999.

Luong, Hy V., ed., *Post-war Vietnam: Dynamics of a Transforming Society,* Rowman and Littlefield, Lanham, Md., 2003.

Mangold, Tom, *The Tunnels of Cu Chi,* Hodder and Stoughton, London, 1985.

Mann, Robert, *A Grand Delusion: America's Descent into Vietnam,* Basic Books, New York, 2001.

Martin, Marie Alexandrine, *Cambodia: A Shattered Society*, University of California Press, Berkeley, 1994.

Maung Maung Than, Tin, *Myanmar: The Dilemma of Stalled Reforms,* Institute of Southeast Asian Studies, Singapore, 2000.

McMaster, Herbert R., *Dereliction of Duty: Lyndon Johnson, Robert McNamara, the Joint Chiefs of Staff, and the Lies That led to Vietnam,* HarperCollins, New York, 1997.

Means, Gordon P., *Malaysian Politics: The Second Generation,* Oxford University Press, Singapore, 1991.

Military History Institute of Vietnam, *Victory in Vietnam: The Official History of the People's Army of Vietnam, 1954–1975,* trans. by Merle I. Pribbenow. University Press of Kansas, Lawrence, 2002.

Milne, R. S., and Diane K. Mauzy, *Malaysian Politics Under Mahathir,* Routledge, London, 1999.

Moise, Edwin E., *Historical Dictionary of the Vietnam War,* Scarecrow Press, Lanham, Md., 2001.

Mus, Paul, "The Role of the Village in Vietnamese Politics," *Pacific Affairs* 23 (September 1949), pp. 365–372.

Neese, Harvey, and John O'Donnell, eds., *Prelude to Tragedy: Vietnam, 1960–1965,* Naval Institute Press, Annapolis, Md., 2001.

Ngor, Haing S., *Surviving the Killing Fields: The Cambodian Odyssey,* Chatto and Windus, London, 1988.

Nguyen, Cao Ky, *How We Lost the Vietnam War,* Stein and Day, New York, 1984.

Nguyen-Vo, Tho-Huong, *Khmer-Viet Relations and the Third Indochina Conflict,* Mc-Farland, Jefferson, N.C., 1992.

Pentagon Papers, Bantam Books, New York, 1971.

Philpott, Simon, *Rethinking Indonesia: Postcolonial Theory, Authoritarianism, and Identity*, St. Martin's Press, New York, 2000.

Picq, Laurence, *Beyond the Horizon: Five Years with the Khmer Rouge,* St. Martin's Press, New York, 1989.

Ponchaud, Francois, *Cambodia Year Zero,* Holt, Rinehart, New York, 1977.

Rabasa, Angel, and Peter Chalk, *Indonesia's Transformation and the Stability of Southeast Asia,* Rand, Santa Monica, Calif., 2001.

Ramage, Douglas E., *Politics in Indonesia: Democracy, Islam, and the Ideology of Tolerance,* Routledge, New York, 1995.

Record, Jeffrey, *The Wrong War: Why We lost in Vietnam,* Naval Institute Press, Annapolis, Md., 1998.

Rosser, Andrew, *The Politics of Economic Liberalization in Indonesia, State Market and Power,* Curzon, Richmond, Surrey, U.K., 2001.

SarDesai, D. R., *Indian Foreign Policy in Cambodia, Laos, and Vietnam, 1947–1964,* University of California Press, Berkeley, 1968.

Schanberg, Sydney Hillel, *Death and Life of Dith Pran,* Penguin, New York, 1985.

Schulzinger, Robert D., *A Time for War: The United States and Vietnam, 1941–1975,* Oxford University Press, New York, 1997.

Schwab, Orrin, *Defending the Free World: John F. Kennedy, Lyndon Johnson, and the Vietnam War, 1961–1965,* Praeger, Westport, Conn., 1998.

Schwarz, Adam, and Jonathan Paris, eds., *The Politics of Post-Suharto Indonesia,* Council on Foreign Relations, New York, 1999.

Scwarz, Adam, *A Nation in Waiting: Indonesia's Search for Stability,* Westview Press, Boulder, Colo., 2000.

Shawcross, William, *Sideshow: Kissinger, Nixon, and the Destruction of Cambodia,* Simon and Schuster, New York, 1979.

_____, *The Quality of Mercy: Cambodia, Holocaust, and Modern Conscience,* Simon and Schuster, New York, 1984.

Sihanouk, Norodom, *My War with the CIA,* Penguin Books, Harmondsworth, U.K., 1973.

_____, "Cambodia Neutral: The Dictate of Necessity," *Foreign Affairs* 36 (July 1958), pp. 582–586.

Singh, Bilveer, *Succession Politics in Indonesia: The 1998 Presidential Elections and the Fall of Suharto,* St. Martin's Press, New York, 2000.

Sison, Jose Maria, *The Implosion of the Communist Party of the Philippines,* Monash University, Clayton, Australia, 1995.

Steinberg, David I., *Burma, the State of Myanmar,* Georgetown University Press, Washington, D.C., 2001.

Stuart-Fox, Martin, *The Murderous Revolution: Life and Death in Pol Pot's Kampuchea,* Alternate Publishing, Denver, Colo., 1986.

Subritzky, John, *Confronting Sukarno: British, American, Australian, and New Zealand Diplomacy in the Malaysia-Indonesian Confrontation, 1961–1965,* St. Martin's Press, New York, 2000.

Summers, Jr., Harry G., *Historical Atlas of the Vietnam War,* Houghton Mifflin, Boston, 1995.

Taylor, Robert et al., eds., *Burma: Political Economy Under Military Rule,* Palgrave, New York, 2001.

Tetreault, Mary Ann, *Women and Revolution in Vietnam,* Michigan State University, East Lansing, 1992.

Truong, Nhu Tang, *Journal of a Vietcong,* Cape, London, 1986.

Tucker, Spencer C., ed., *Encyclopedia of the Vietnam War: A Political, Social, and Military History,* 3 vols., ABC-CLIO, Santa Barbara, Calif., 1998; Oxford University Press, New York, 2000.

Vandiver, Frank E., *Shadows of Vietnam: Lyndon Johnson's Wars,* Texas A & M University Press, College Station, 1997.

Vasil, R. K., *Governing Singapore: Democracy and National Development,* Allen & Unwin, St. Leonards, NSW, Australia, 2000.

Vatikiotis, Michael, *Indonesian Politics Under Suharto*, Routledge, New York, 1993, Third Edition, 1998.

Vickery, Michael, *Cambodia, 1975–1982*, South End Press, Boston, 1984.

Westmoreland, William C., *A Soldier Reports*, Doubleday, New York, 1976.

Woodside, Alexander B., *Community and Revolution in Modern Vietnam*, Houghton Mifflin, Boston, 1976.

Young, Kenneth B., *Vietnam's Rice Economy: Developments and Prospects*, Agricultural Experiment Station, Fayetteville, Ark., 2002.

Young, Marilyn B., and Robert Buzzano, eds., *A Companion to the Vietnam War*, Blackwell, Malden, Md., 2002.

Index